D1042396

Bound Upon a Wheel of Fire

bound upon a wheel of fire

Why So Many German Jews Made
the Tragic Decision to Remain
in Nazi Germany

JOHN V. H. DIPPEL

BasicBooks
A Division of HarperCollins*Publishers*

Excerpts from letters to Albert Einstein are reprinted with permission from the Albert Einstein Archives, The Hebrew University of Jerusalem, Israel.

Passages from the Martin Buber Archive are quoted with permission from the Jewish National and University Library, The Hebrew University of Jerusalem, Israel.

Selected quotations from the Berlin Collection and the Morris Waldman Files are reprinted with permission from the YIVO Institute for Jewish Research.

Quotations reprinted from the American Jewish Joint Distribution Committee, Inc.

Copyright © 1996 by John V. H. Dippel.
Published by BasicBooks, A Division of HarperCollins Publishers, Inc.

All rights reserved. Printed in the United States of America. No part of this book may be reproduced in any manner whatsoever without written permission except in the case of brief quotations embodied in critical articles and reviews. For information, address BasicBooks, 10 East 53rd Street, New York, NY 10022-5299.

Designed by Elliott Beard

Library of Congress Cataloging-in-Publication Data
Dippel, John Van Houten, 1946–
    Bound upon a wheel of fire : why so many German Jews made the tragic decision to remain in Nazi Germany / John V. H. Dippel.
      p. cm.
    Includes index.
    ISBN 0-465-09103-2
    I. Jews—Germany—History—1933–1945. 2. Jewish leadership–
Germany.   3. Germany—Ethnic relations.   I. Title
DS135.G3315D57   1996
943'.004924'0019—dc20   95-45212
                                           CIP

96 97 98 99 ❖/HC 9 8 7 6 5 4 3 2 1

To Cecilia, Stephen, and David
With all my love

Thou art a soul in bliss; but I am bound
Upon a wheel of fire, that mine own tears
Do scald like molten lead.

—*King Lear*

Contents

Acknowledgments

Like the German Jewish community itself, the documents that record the opinions, thoughts, and feelings of its members during the Nazi era suffered a grievous fate. In hastily fleeing abroad or out of fearful self-censorship, many Jews destroyed or abandoned letters, diaries, and other written evidence of their lives. Others, even more circumspect, kept no such records or wrote only in a camouflaged language that was designed to defy Nazi scrutiny but that has also veiled the underlying truth from subsequent historians. Those documents that did manage to survive the Holocaust were scattered widely around the world, in a kind of archival diaspora.

For all these reasons, anyone who attempts to re-create the lives of German Jews under the Third Reich starts at a decided disadvantage. Fortunately, however, one institution has taken on the task of preserving the existence of this remarkable Jewish community—if not, sadly, in fact, at least in historical memory. This is the Leo Baeck Institute, in New York. The Irish writer James Joyce once boasted that if the city of Dublin were ever to be wiped off the face of the earth, it could be reconstructed, street by street, pub by pub, from the pages of his fiction. No one at the Leo Baeck Institute would ever be so immodest as to make an analogous claim for the array of manuscripts gathered under its unassuming roof, but the simple fact is that here lie most of the important historical remnants of German Jewry, and without them much of the research for this book would have been impossible. For two years, I was a habitué of the institute's reading room, the grateful recipient of box after box of letters, newspapers, organizational minutes, and microfilms redeemed from its mysterious recesses. For their unfailing assistance during this time, I would like to extend my deep gratitude to Robert A. Jacobs and his staff members Frank Mecklenburg, Evelyn Ehrlich, Diane Spielmann, and the late Yitzhak Kertesz.

Other archivists, both in this country and abroad, were equally courteous and accommodating in response to my relentless inquiries about documents in their possession. In particular, I would like to thank the following: Kevin Proffitt, at the American Jewish Archives in Cincinnati; Adina Eshel, at the Central Zionist Archives in Jerusalem; Timothy D. Murray, at the University of Delaware Library; Dr. Ralf Breslau and Dr. Jutta Weber, at the Staatsbibliothek preussischer Kulturbesitz in Berlin; Margot Cohn, at the Jewish National and University Library in Jerusalem; Dr. Shlomo Mayer, at the Leo Baeck Institute in Jerusalem; Dr. Marion Kazemi, at the Bibliothek und Archiv zur Geschichte der Max-Planck-Gesellschaft in Berlin; Kenneth P. Scheffel, at the Bentley Historical Library in Ann Arbor, Michigan; David Massel and his staff at the Board of Deputies of British Jews in London; Hadassah Modlinger, at the Yad Vashem Archives in Jerusalem; Nehama Chalom, at the Weizmann Archives in Rehovot, Israel; the late Nathan M. Kaganoff and his staff at the American Jewish Historical Society in Waltham, Massachusetts; Howard B. Gotlieb and his staff at the Mugar Memorial Library of Boston University; Saundra Taylor and Faye E. Mark, at the Indiana University libraries in Bloomington; Darwin H. Stapleton and his staff at the Rockefeller Archive Center in North Tarrytown, New York; Hadassah Assouline, at the Central Archives for the History of the Jewish People in Jerusalem; Julian Kay, at the Jewish Colonization Association in London; Dr. David Marwell, at the Berlin Document Center; Cyma M. Horowitz and her staff at the Blaustein Library of the American Jewish Committee in New York; Albert Limmer at the Deutsches Museum in Munich; Harold L. Miller, at the State Historical Society of Wisconsin in Madison; Dr. Ben Primer, at the Seeley G. Mudd Manuscript Library in Princeton, New Jersey; and Dr. Beat Glaus, at the ETH-Bibliothek in Zurich.

In addition to these librarians and archivists, I would also like to express my appreciation to Mrs. Marianne Schäffer Breslauer, Mrs. Alice Haurowitz Sievert, and Prof. Dr. Julius H. Schoeps for granting permission to publish excerpts from documents for which they hold the copyrights. Dr. Werner A. Stoll kindly shared with me information about his father's association with Richard Willstätter. Willstätter's nephew, bearer of the same name, sent me important correspondence concerning his uncle. In Berlin, Fritz Tangermann graciously tracked down materials for me.

During the course of researching this book, I was given advice and encouragement by several scholars in modern German history, most notably Fritz Stern at Columbia University and Richard Breitman at American University. Gary Lease, professor of the history of consciousness at the University of California, Santa Cruz, and biographer-to-be of Hans-Joachim Schoeps, generously shared many nuggets from his own indefatigable research. All along, Brooks Peters, correspondent for the *New York Times* in Berlin during the late 1930s, Holocaust lecturer, and lunchtime confrere, has stimulated my thinking with his recollections of the dilemma faced by Germany's Jews, and to him goes a final tip of my hat.

Introduction

Wir sind entweder Deutsche, oder heimatlos.

[We are either Germans, or without a country.]

—*Gabriel Riesser*

Vertreibt man mich von meinem deutschen Boden, so bleibe ich deutsch und es ändert sich nichts.

[Even if they drive me off German soil, I will remain German and nothing will have changed.]

—*Walther Rathenau*

They came for the chief rabbi in the cold darkness. When they rang the bell, a tall, gaunt, bearded Leo Baeck let them into his apartment. Even though it was before dawn, he was already dressed, as if he had been waiting for them, as if they were simply keeping an appointment. Bluntly one of the Gestapo agents told him: "We have orders to take you to Theresienstadt." The chief rabbi nodded, without showing any emotion. Then he asked for a few minutes, so he could settle his affairs. The request was granted.[1]

It was a raw January morning in Berlin. The year was 1943. Over the past twelve months, the Holocaust had taken its most murderous toll: More Jews—some 2.7 million—had died at the hands of the Nazis during this period than in all the previous years of the Third Reich combined.[2] On that morning the chief rabbi was not wholly ignorant of the nature and scope of the Final Solution, of what lay in store for him. He had known for some time what happened to Jews who were shipped to the east. In the few minutes granted to him, Baeck sat down at his desk and wrote a farewell letter to his daughter and her husband, who were safe in London. As his final act before leaving his apartment to be taken off to a concentration camp from which he might never emerge alive, he made out a postal money order, in the full amount, to pay his gas and electric bills.[3]

Richard Willstätter, the Nobel laureate, who had for so long stubbornly refused to abandon his country, tried in his despair after Kristallnacht to flee to Switzerland. He had no passport or visa. It was an act of sheer madness. On the shores of Lake Constance, in a fierce rainstorm, frantic and exhausted, he searched in vain for a boat to row him across. At last the Gestapo picked him up and questioned the internationally renowned chemist for hours. Then they let him go back to Munich.[4] Twelve days later, in March 1939, Willstätter received his passport. He crossed the frontier of the Third Reich near Basel. At last safe on Swiss soil, still an unwilling refugee, he felt more like crying than rejoicing at his newfound freedom.

Tired of waiting for her papers in 1938, Bella Fromm, the Berlin society columnist, went to see a fortune-teller, who predicted that she would leave Germany by September.[5] He was right. When the time came, Fromm had a van brought around to transport her belongings to America. While many other Jews were lucky to escape with the clothes on their backs, Fromm filled the fifteen-foot-long container with chairs, vases, tables, bookshelves, lamps, a mirror, pictures, armoires, wastebaskets, a broom, and a complete tea and coffee service. Her friends in the Finance Ministry had assured her there would be no problem shipping her furniture.[6] After she paid a bribe of 200 marks, her trunks were sealed and sent directly to the ship. On September 5 she boarded the Warsaw–Paris express with eight suitcases in tow, along with her family jewelry.

En route, alone and removed from her well-placed protectors, Fromm was cornered by loutish customs officials, who called her crude names and made her hand over her rings, brooches, and other treasures. To them, she was just another dirty Jew on the run. As a consequence, the former darling of Berlin's diplomatic corps exited Germany with scarcely four dollars on her person.[7]

Hans-Joachim Schoeps, the right-wing Jewish youth leader, stayed on as long as he could, until the Gestapo became exceedingly "unpleasant" toward him in the summer of 1938.[8] By then, no university, no country, would take him in. Visas were impossible to come by. Kristallnacht sent a shudder of panic through him, and Schoeps appealed to an official in the Foreign Ministry, who arranged to have him entrusted with a "secret mission" to Sweden.[9] The airplane bore him away swiftly on Christmas Eve, leaving behind his parents and many other equally patriotic German Jews whom he had urged with such persistence to seek an accommodation with Hitler's "new Germany."

At the beginning of 1938, Max Warburg, Germany's leading Jewish banker, was informed that he could no longer expect to do business with the Nazi government. Hjalmar Schacht, the wily president of the Reichsbank, could no longer fend off the party radicals, who wanted all Jews purged from the economy.[10] The fabled family firm, bulwark of Hamburg, would have to be liquidated or else Aryanized. Warburg chose the lesser of the two evils. He was allowed to do so. In a farewell speech to his employees that spring, he spoke of the bank's guiding principles and praised their loyalty, which had brought "the ship through all storms and past all rocks."[11] Then he wished them all well, shook their hands solemnly, and set sail for America.

Robert Weltsch, the Zionist editor, realized earlier the same year that it was "senseless" to remain in Berlin.[12] His love for the *Jüdische Rundschau* (Jewish Observer), the newspaper that had helped sustain him and much of German Jewry throughout these five dark and difficult years, had ceased to buoy his spirits. Now he simply felt "depressed"and trapped.[13] How much longer would the Nazis allow him to go on publishing? And what difference would it make now? Palestine beckoned, even though Weltsch sagaciously predicted no nirvana for Jews there— only more hatred, confrontation, and bloodshed.[14]

In the end, the Zionist dream proved more compelling than the bleak German reality. Weltsch reached the warm Mediterranean climes as the nations of the world were declaring their abhorrence of German anti-Semitic outrages but still adamantly refusing to let the Jews in. The feisty, idealistic journalist, who, in April 1933, had implored assimilated Jews to drop their pretense of being like other Germans and symbolically affix with pride the yellow badge proclaiming their racial identity, now felt a touch of remorse. Instead of warning them daily about what the Nazis might do to them, he had filled their heads with thoughts of Palestine. During these five years, the Jews of Germany had not fought back, had not protested, fearing that to do so would only make matters worse. Weltsch had not objected. Now the soothing mantra "It cannot happen here" had lulled the Jews too long. Now, Weltsch believed, they were about to face a war of annihilation.[15] He wondered if they would arrive at this conclusion in time.

These six German Jews—all prominent figures in a proud and prosperous community virtually obliterated by the Holocaust—chose to stay in their homeland when the unthinkable happened: Adolf Hitler became the ruler of Germany in 1933. All declined chances to leave as the Nazis solidified their grip on power, molding German society in their image and transforming those they decreed could not belong—the Jews—from loyal, "good Germans" into subhuman pariahs. All six remained in the Third Reich while less fortunate Jews were boycotted, beaten, and dragged off to prison. In the end, they all escaped, and all but one eluded the horrors of the camps (and he, too, miraculously survived).

All were survivors or, rather, victims of survival. They were from widely disparate walks of life—a rabbi, a chemist, a society columnist, a youth leader, a banker, and a newspaper editor—with ideologies that ranged from Zionist to monarchist and with personalities so dissimilar that it took the hate-laced chant "Jewish pig" to bring them together, to face the same fate. However, they all shared one passion—a deep and abiding love for their country. Perhaps even more than their Judaism, their "Germanness" defined them, as it had their forebears, and then, as a torrent of anti-Semitic hatred swirled around them, it held them transfixed, blinding and immobilizing them. By the time they awoke from the trance, it was nearly too late.

Sadly, they were not alone. When Hitler came to power on January 30, 1933, some 525,000 Jews were living within the borders of Germany[16]—over 160,000 of them congregated in the capital city of Berlin.[17] Of this community, between 250,000 and 300,000 either chose or were forced to emigrate by 1939.[18] But nearly the majority—

some 250,000—remained behind. Many of them escaped in the final
months before the start of World War II, but nearly one in four German Jews (or over 120,000) did not make it out. Indeed, as late as the
spring of 1942, at a time when the coldly efficient machinery of the
Final Solution was running at high gear, as many as 40,000 Jews were
still carrying on their daily lives as best they could in the capital of a
regime that was bent on annihilating them.[19] Most of this remnant
were ultimately deported to concentration camps, where all but a few
perished.[20]

Thus, these six leading figures in the German Jewish community were
atypical not in their choice to stay on under the Nazis, but in their
escape of death afterward. Clearly, as leaders of that community they
were "special cases"—holders of trust and responsibility, better
informed about what was going on, both in the government and in the
concentration camps. As such, they were more deeply enmeshed in the
approaching German Jewish tragedy and better able to discern its coming and sound the alarm. Yet, they chose to listen to their hearts and
instincts, rather than to their heads, and to endure the deepening Nazi
nightmare, even though doors abroad were open to them. This choice
makes them, and other Jews who made the same decision, controversial.

Why did they stay? As leaders of the Jewish community, they can be
accused, after the fact, of myopia. In the 1930s other Jews turned to
them for guidance, whether spiritual, moral, political, or practical, as
they assayed the fluctuating policies and deeds of a virulently hostile
regime and sought to estimate their prospects for survival. "Patience
and perseverance" were what, in essence, these leaders advised. And
many thousands of German Jews, like-minded or so persuaded, adopted
this cautious credo, too. For them, the bond to Germany was too complex, too emotionally and psychologically compelling, to be neatly rent
asunder. It was, in fact, a relationship akin to an abusive marriage. When
the Jews were first attacked, their reaction was to deny the accusations
of infidelity, profess continuing love and devotion, and endure in
silence, with stoic forbearance. Verbal threats and even outbursts of violence, they believed, were momentary excesses that, in a more sober
mood, would pass. They were not part of Germany's true nature; they
could not annul a centuries-old affection. Rumors of worse treatment
to come were dismissed as panic-inspired exaggerations from faint-
hearts, none of which would come to pass. It was this mentality that

prevailed among Germany's Jews and that was reflected in so many of their leaders' words and deeds.

It would be misleading, however, to overstate the influence that figures like Leo Baeck, Richard Willstätter, Hans-Joachim Schoeps, Bella Fromm, Max Warburg, and Robert Weltsch may have exercised over German Jewry, for two reasons. First, "German Jewry" did not really exist as an entity until the Nazis created it with their calumny. Second, perhaps no other Jewish community in Europe was so decentralized and diffuse in its views and allegiance. Huddled masses of tattered *Ostjuden* from Poland and Russia lived on the other side of Berlin from assimilated, highly cultivated professors, lawyers, and physicians whose Jewishness, they felt, was only an embarrassing (and best-concealed) anachronism—like some hopelessly old-fashioned suit still hanging in the bedroom wardrobe. There was, in short, no Jewish establishment, no Jewish value system, no Jewish Führer to rally around.

Yet the interesting fact remains that in all the sectors of German Jewry represented by these six persons—from wholly assimilated to Zionist—the message conveyed during the first Nazi years was essentially the same: Except for the young and the rootless, emigration was not the answer; for better or worse, their destiny still lay in Germany, where the Jews had lived and endured for centuries.

To qualify this generalization, one must keep in mind that this is an examination of German Jewry during the period 1933 to 1938, in other words, of those Jews who were able to continue their lives under Hitler or who resisted the impulse to pack their bags and flee the moment the Nazis took over their country. It does not include the Jews who got out right away. Among those who left in the early months of 1933 were many of the most illustrious and influential German Jews— persons of the caliber of Albert Einstein, Alfred Döblin, Max Reinhardt, and Herbert Marcuse, who were driven out not because of their Jewishness (that would come later), but because of their politics. Ideology, not race, was the foe the Nazis assailed first. When they fled Germany, these Jews left behind a more conservative, less vulnerable Jewish community, for whose members the idea of a modus vivendi with Hitler could not be dismissed out of hand, if only for practical reasons: Where could they go? How would they make a living? The leadership that remained for this politically more quiescent (and patriotic) German Jewry reflected and articulated their ambivalent feelings. If only by default, these were the individuals to whom other Jews, increasingly despairing and frightened as the 1930s unfolded, looked for guidance and support. For this reason alone, the words and actions of these six prominent leaders take on a larger historical significance.

As individuals, Baeck, Willstätter, Schoeps, Fromm, Weltsch, and Warburg have a representative importance as well. Atypical in that they held positions of authority, respect, and attendant influence, they were much more typical of German Jewry in how they surveyed the situation they faced under the Nazi regime and the options they believed were open to them. Their personal reasons for staying in Hitler's Germany, despite humiliation, ostracism, the loss of livelihoods, and threats of violence, correspond to what many other Jews thought, felt, and did. Thus, they offer a window into the souls and minds of thousands of Jews whose anguish and inner debate have gone unrecorded.

Why didn't they just leave? The question echoes through time with reproach. How could the Jews of Germany—the trip wire for Jews throughout Europe, the first to face the Nazis' wrath—have been so blind, naive, and foolish? How could they believe that they could coexist in a racially defined *Volksgemeinschaft* (national community) ruled by the most rabidly and aggressively anti-Semitic leader of modern times, a Führer who did not conceal his eagerness to get rid of them, one way or the other?

The tone of incredulity and scorn in such questions leveled at the ghosts of German Jews is both inevitable and regrettable: We cannot help but picture and judge these unfortunate Jews not as they actually were during the 1930s—individual human beings racked by doubts and conflicted emotions, trying merely to get by from one day to the next—but only in light of what happened to them later in the fires of the crematoria. The horrors of the Holocaust have been seared into our consciousness so deeply that they have destroyed our ability to make logical sense not only of the slaughter itself, but of the events and conditions that preceded it. Half a century after the concentration camps were liberated, the Holocaust refuses to be consigned to history. It still haunts and imprisons us, blinding our vision.

The period of German history that led up to Auschwitz is a primary casualty of this distortion. We can view it today only as one would squint toward a horizon suffused by a brilliant, setting sun. The lives of Jewish men, women, and children during the years 1933 to 1938 are as remote and incomprehensible to most people with no personal link to them as the daily existence of Japanese who happened to be living in Hiroshima in August 1945. What divides our world from theirs is the knowledge of horror. It is a yawning, chilling chasm. As the Israeli historian Leni Yahil aptly observed: "The gap between what the Jewish leaders knew then and what we know now is as abysmal as the hell into which the Jews were cast during the Hitlerite era."[21]

Into that great gulf, in lieu of understanding, critics have injected accusation, and accusation has been met with defensive retort: Who could have foreseen what was coming? How can one expect the Jews to have been any more prescient than their fellow Germans or, for that matter, anyone else? What real options did the Jews have? To the charge of passivity under the Nazi fist, defenders of German Jewry have recounted the Jews' powerlessness. To the charge of myopia, they have traced the vagaries of Nazi Jewish policy during the 1930s—certainly no clear, well-marked road leading unmistakably toward Auschwitz. To the charge of letting opportunities to escape slip through their fingers, they have offered many justifications—family ties; a well-paying job; a sense of immunity ("They wouldn't dare touch me"); inadequacy (Who had the money and the prospects to start a new life abroad?); historical perspective ("We Jews have been through all this before"); old age (German Jewry was an aging and slowly shrinking community); and, most of all, love of country. And to the charge of sheer inertia, they have pointed to the immigration barriers that were hastily erected all over the world to keep unwanted refugees out. Jews who desperately wanted to leave had no place to go, no welcoming haven.

Although there is some truth in all these responses, they are more properly ex post facto rationalizations than explanations. Yes, there *were* tight restrictions on entry into the United States and other countries, but were Germany's Jews really blocked by them before 1938? Most evidence, as you will see, suggests that the Jews could have circumvented these obstacles in greater numbers if they had wanted to escape Germany badly enough, if they had grasped the desperateness of their plight earlier on. But they had not. Despite everything, Germany was still their home. And, despite almost everything, they were prepared to stay there.

Jews had lived in Germany for over sixteen centuries and had been emancipated during the Enlightenment. Henceforth they had moved to the front rank of many professions; had intermarried with Gentiles; had become enamored of Goethe as well as Heine, Wagner as well as Mozart; and had become assimilated into bourgeois society to the point of losing their attachment to Jewish tradition, practices, and identity. More than anywhere else in the world, Jews were *zu Hause* in Germany— attune to its culture, part of its history, and beneficiaries of its prosperity, riding the crest of its modernity. The anti-Semitism they had periodically faced seemed a thing of the distant past. How can one expect these Jews to have lightly countenanced voluntary banishment?

In brief, Jewish ties to Germany were deep and emotionally strong. *More German than the Germans,* the saying goes. Unlike Jews in many other countries—particularly in eastern Europe and the Soviet Union—they experienced no unsettling ambivalence about either their identity or their loyalty to the state in which they resided and no closeted passion for Theodor Herzl's dream of a Jewish homeland in the barren and remote sands of Palestine. So it is not surprising that the first rumblings of Nazism, swelling to a roar of hate in the 1930s, did not send them scurrying for the nearest frontier. There was too much to overcome first— rootedness, complacency, incredulity, smugness, naïveté, wishful thinking, even opportunism. (Some Jews, especially those in the armaments business, would fare embarrassingly well under a resurgent Nazi Germany.) All these factors played a part. But so did history, language, art, music, and patriotism. How else can one explain Richard Willstätter's curt response to Chaim Weizmann's entreaty that the scientist flee his Munich home: "One does not leave one's mother, even when she behaves badly"?[22] Indeed, when one steps back through time and attempts to weigh the choices presented to German Jews during the 1930s from their limited and not particularly farsighted standpoint, the more apt question easily becomes, "Why leave?" Why abandon friends and family, a comfortable home, a well-paying job, a cherished culture—in short, a rare feeling of truly belonging—for unknown shores, an alien tongue, unemployment, isolation, hardship, and despair? Seen in this light, the dilemma of the German Jews assumes perplexing complications. One becomes less quick to judge.

Yet it is between the more unequivocal, post-Holocaust positions that the debate rages on—the attacks on German Jewry (and its leaders) emanating invariably from Jews themselves, seeking to condemn the German Jews' perceived indecisiveness, accommodation, and inaction as

being at least partially to blame for the mass murder that later decimated Jews all over Europe. As Bruno Bettelheim summed up in *The
Informed Heart:* "One wonders if the notion that millions of Jews . . .
would submit to extermination did not also result from seeing how
much degradation they would accept without fighting back. The persecution of the Jews worsened, step by slow step, when no violent resistance occurred."[23]

On the other side are arrayed those—mainly Jews, too—who refuse
to shoulder this charge, who argue that the Jews of Germany had few
options and made the best of what was an increasingly hopeless
dilemma, and who, in essence, bridle at blaming the victim.

There is a largely unstated subtext to this debate: What is the proper
role of Jews in the world? More than nearly any other country, pre-
Hitler Germany offered the Jews a sanctuary in the Diaspora. It represented the triumph of assimilation. From their lofty perch, German
Jews cast an eye down at the plight of less fortunate Jews elsewhere,
viewing them with pity but certainly not with envy or guilt. *They*—the
good burghers—were the ones to be admired and emulated. Zionism
and its call for a return to Jewish roots would thus make few converts
on German soil—until the Nazis emblazoned the word *Jew* on their
psyches. For the foes of assimilation, the German Jewish experience
under Hitler was the lesson learned the hard way: The big lie of emancipation, of equality, of racial tolerance was brutally exposed. Afterward
Jews could never again feel securely at home among non-Jews. In this
sense, the argument is as much about the Jewish future as it is about the
Jewish past. In fact, the *reality* of the Jewish past in Germany has been
largely ignored amid the swirl of attack and counterattack. Instead, both
sides have fashioned a caricature of Germany's Jews that suits their own
rhetorical purposes in laying out a case for how Jews should conduct
themselves henceforth. The real choices that the German Jews had during the 1930s are overlooked in this obsessive preoccupation with how
they faced the unavoidable finality of the death camps. As the Israeli
historian Otto Dov Kulka put it:

> The description of Jewish society and leadership through the entire
> period of Nazi domination is limited exclusively to judging the posi-
> tions assumed in situations in which decisions were categorically irre-
> versible and final, those during the phase of the mass deportations

and exterminations. The only categories are "collaboration" versus "resistance" or "participation in the extermination process" versus "attempts at rebellion and rescue."[24]

At the heart of all this turmoil, German Jewry has few surviving voices to speak on its behalf. From a vibrant community of over half a million, its numbers have been reduced to some 60,000 today.[25] Many of these Jews have origins abroad and few ancestral memories of Germany. The debate over what German Jewry should have done more than half a century ago rages over a fallen and broken gravestone. Those Jewish testimonies that did outlive the Holocaust are, understandably, layered with pat apologias ("No one could have imagined this would happen") or warped, self-protective memories. The written records from the 1930s are sparse. Jews lived in fear for their lives and took few chances committing their innermost thoughts to paper. Those who left did not, as a rule, court disaster by bringing a diary or bundle of letters along with them. And those who remained behind too often perished without a trace.

So, overshadowed by the death camps, immortalized by the grim facts of their extermination, the Jews of Nazi Germany have become merely objects of scorn or glorification (for enduring bravely what they had to face) but rarely of dispassionate understanding. In his admirable study, *The Holocaust in History,* Michael R. Marrus made this point in speaking of the "bystanders" in Europe and the United States who allowed the Holocaust to happen, but his observation can be equally applied to this scrutiny of German Jewry itself:

> There is a great danger that the historian will apply to subjects the standards, value systems, and vantage point of the present, rather than those of the period being discussed. We believe that people should have acted otherwise, and we set out to show how they did not.
>
> Put more simply, there is a strong tendency in historical writing on bystanders to the Holocaust to condemn, rather than to explain. And while opinions differ on the degree to which historians should exercise some form of judgment, I suggest that we shall go much further in the attempt to comprehend the behavior and activity (or inactivity) of bystanders by making a painstaking effort to enter into their minds and sensibilities.[26]

It is with this advice in mind that this book was researched and written. The vehicle I chose to reenter and explore this now-vanished world of German Jewry, without any conscious intent to condemn or defend, is the surviving record of the words, beliefs, and deeds of these six disparate, but collectively representative figures. It is in their concrete particulars that I hoped to find a skein of unfolding Jewish reality and reaction under Nazi rule during the years 1933 to 1938. Unavoidably, I extrapolated the patterns of thought and behavior that emerged in each of these individuals to apply to the community as a whole. If there is a great deal to be found in common, then one can perhaps fairly conclude that their actions and reactions speak with validity for a great many other German Jews and can postulate some tentative generalizations about *their* lives under Hitler. If, however, these six individuals exhibited a wide variety of responses to Nazi oppression before Kristallnacht, then one ought more fairly to conclude that it is fallacious to think of the German Jews after January 1933 as a single entity; their different lives, sense of place in German society, and destinies do not lend themselves to categorical analysis.

Why, then, these six? In addition to their prominence, professional diversity, and wide range of personal attitudes toward both Judaism and Jewishness (I omitted from my selection only Orthodox Jews—a tiny minority—and eastern Jews, although the Czech-born Weltsch was technically one of them, because their ties to Germany were largely ephemeral), these Jewish figures share several traits that made them appropriate subjects for this study. First, as I noted earlier, all voluntarily chose to stay in the Third Reich even though they had the means and the opportunities to escape. Thus, they cannot be easily classified as helpless victims of circumstance. Second, none died in the camps. It is therefore easier to avoid the trap of seeing them only as victims of the Nazis, to be mourned rather than scrutinized. They were survivors, but survivors from within. Third, each of these six German Jews left behind at least a partial record of what they thought and did during those fateful years, 1933–38. In that, they are truly exceptional. Even if their written legacies are regrettably incomplete (limited by self-censorship, hasty departure, Nazi confiscation, or continuing familial reticence), they stand out as some of the few extant, relatively voluminous, records of individual German Jews that were compiled during the prewar Nazi era. These personal papers have—except for those of Bella Fromm and

Richard Willstätter—been augmented by documents describing these individuals' organizational activities in Germany: Leo Baeck's for the Reichsvertretung der deutschen Juden (National Representation of German Jews); Robert Weltsch's for the Zionist newspaper the *Jüdische Rundschau;* Max Warburg's for the Jewish welfare agency the Hilfsverein der deutschen Juden; and Hans-Joachim Schoeps for the right-wing student group he founded, the Deutscher Vortrupp (the German Vanguard). Because of their wider distribution, documents of German Jewish organizations such as these survived when most personal papers did not.

Running through this survey of primary, contemporary sources is a deliberate, self-imposed limitation: The materials I consulted were, in the main, written documents produced prior to 1939. In other words, I focused my research on materials that are innocent of the Holocaust. Written during this era, these records of German Jewry are not colored by any feelings of guilt, self-serving memories, or regret. Their limitations as historical documents are the limits of the persons who recorded them, at that particular moment in time. In this sense, they are more akin to jottings in a notebook or diary than to a distanced historical analysis. But it is my hope that they will serve as the appropriate foundation for this kind of analysis.

There are other limitations in these sources that should be made clear at the outset. First, the letters and public statements were written and uttered in a totalitarian state, under the ever-watchful eye of a regime that was ruthlessly bent on crushing any opposition to its policies. Therefore, these statements could be candid and forthright only to the extent that their authors thought it was safe to be so. Second, most of the contemporary German Jewish documents available to researchers are public ones, expressing views that may or may not have coincided with what the writers or speakers actually felt or believed. In Nazi Germany, private opinions were generally better kept to oneself, especially if one was a Jew or a less than fervent Nazi. Thus, what the reader will find here are records of public personalities, not profound psychological insights into their motives or their deepest hopes and fears.

I should also add that one of the most complete and valuable records of Jewish life during the 1930s is an improbable one—the Jewish press. Ironically, until 1939 Jewish newspapers actually flourished under Nazi rule. On the surface this situation seems patently bizarre: The violently repressive, virulently anti-Semitic regime did not harass or ban the written voice of its sworn enemy, the Jews. Indeed, it actually allowed Jewish newspapers and magazines, as well as Jewish book publishers, to disseminate a flood of materials on Jewish values, hopes, concerns, plight, thought, and community activities to a widening circle of Jews (and even non-Jews) whose only other sanctioned outlets for information were the organs of Nazi propaganda. But, on reflection, this seeming incongruity fits into a niche in the Nazis' twisted logic: As non-Aryans, incapable of being absorbed into the *Volksgemeinschaft,* the Jews were not supposed to be coerced into the Nazi value system or way of life. Racial ostracism and separation were the order of the day (at least until late 1938), and within their own sphere, Jews were entitled to indulge in their own culture, sports, religious observances, and written expression. Naturally, in Nazi Germany such freedom of expression came with many strings attached, and writers and editors alike exercised a great deal of self-restraint; they had to select "news that would be fit to print" or risk being silenced.[27] Still, the testimony of fact and opinion that was tolerated by Nazi censors is extraordinary—an invaluable source of material for any historian of Jewish leaders and Jewish community life.

In the half century since the full dimensions of the Holocaust were revealed to a stunned world, German Jewry, along with the rest of European Jewry, has undergone a kind of statistical apotheosis. The number of people who were gassed in the camps is so appallingly large that it dwarfs to triviality the fate of any one person. Furthermore, the collective efforts of Jews and non-Jews to enshrine the Holocaust in our cultural memory have entailed a commemoration of its victims—and their victimizers—to the point where all we know, or are perhaps capable of knowing, about Europe's Jews is how, and in what number, they perished. The Jews' existence prior to their deaths is rendered curiously irrelevant. To counter this numerical depersonalization and morbid preoccupation, I have sought to resurrect the day-to-day reality of a handful of German Jews.

It is necessarily jolting to do so. Our sympathies with the German Jews as victims do not easily yield to an understanding of them as persons like ourselves, caught up in the ebb and flow of an imperfect existence, trying to extract some measure of happiness and success from the world around them. Our finding these Jews nonplussed, hopeful, baffled, indecisive, and even coolly calculating in the face of a descending Nazi noose does not easily deepen our appreciation of human frailty. Yet it was these very fluctuating moods, captured so poignantly in the novels of the Israeli writer Aharon Appelfeld, that held sway over German Jewry as the 1930s took shape.

A few years before he committed suicide, the Italian Jew Primo Levi turned his attention to some of the nagging questions so frequently directed at European Jewry in an essay entitled "Beyond Judgment," which appeared in the *New York Review of Books*. He, too, took incomprehension as his starting point—the inability of those who circumvented the Holocaust to fathom the acts (or nonacts) of those who endured it. Although Levi was writing mainly about his own experience in the camps and the difficulty of escaping from them, he also touched on the disbelief of German Jewry before the Holocaust that kept them from leaving. Basically bourgeois in outlook, German Jews looked at events around them in a rational, logical manner. Their failure to escape was, in Levi's view, primarily a failure to realize that the world had been turned upside down—a failure of imagination. It was as if the laws of physics had suddenly been reversed, and objects that one let go of rose toward the heavens instead of falling to the earth. To make his point, Levi quoted from a poem written, in 1910, by an obscure, non-Jewish Bavarian, Christian Morgenstern. It is the mentality so succinctly captured by these verses that we must seek to fathom as we go back over the cold and (to us) lifeless ground of the 1930s. Here is Morgenstern's poem, "Die unmögliche Tatsache" (The Impossible Fact), in its entirety:

> Palmström, old, an aimless rover,
> walking in the wrong direction
> at a busy intersection
> is run over.
>
> "How," he says, his life restoring
> and with pluck his death ignoring,
> "can an accident like this
> ever happen? What's amiss?
>
> "Did the state administration
> fail in motor transportation?

Did police ignore the need
for reducing driving speed?

"Isn't there a prohibition,
barring motorized transmission
of the living to the dead?
Was the driver right who sped . . . ?"

Tightly swathed in dampened tissues
he explores the legal issues,
and soon is clear as air:
Cars were not permitted there!

And he comes to the conclusion:
His mishap was an illusion,
for, he reasons pointedly,
that which *must* not be, *cannot* be.[28]

Ultimately, this endeavor to reconstruct the lives of six German Jews during the period 1933–38 should accomplish more than make their actions assume a certain circumstantial normalcy and contribute to an understanding of their words and behavior, as well as those of their confederates. More importantly, I hope that this book will fill a large gap in our historical preoccupation with the Holocaust. As Lucy Dawidowicz stated in her seminal work, *The War Against the Jews, 1933–1945,* the Nazi murder of the Jews raises three fundamental categories of questions—questions about the Nazis, their motives and policies; questions about the reactions of the world community to the Nazis' persecution and systematic slaughter of the Jews; and questions about the Jews themselves, their role as both participants in, and victims of, Hitler's Germany.[29] Much has been written about the first two sets of questions. Much has yet to be written, however, about the third, for the agonizing dilemma encountered by Germany's Jews is at once too close to home and too distant. It is now time to rescue the German Jews from our own predilections and inadequacies and to give them their due.

1

Antecedents

They were all children of an enlightened, imperial Germany, born at a time of Jewish emancipation and social mobility. In the forty-two years separating the births of the oldest—Max Warburg, in 1867—and the youngest—Hans-Joachim Schoeps, in 1909—the Jews of Germany would rise from being second-class citizens, denied the right to practice their religion freely, barred from many professions, and treated as pariahs, to a degree of equality and acceptance unknown to many Jews in other parts of the world. They grew up in an era when the complicated, symbiotic German-Jewish bond became as close as it ever would, as the aspirations and outlooks of the Jews and their fellow Germans merged, as the kaiser's Germany itself entered the modern world. They were offspring of a Jewish "golden age," marred only by sporadic, isolated anti-Semitism that seemed more the residue of an older, dying Germany than the harbinger of a holocaust.

The same year that Max Warburg, the second son of an eminent Hamburg banker, was born, Otto von Bismarck took a giant step toward his goal of forging a second German Reich by unifying the states of northern Germany in the Norddeutsche Bund (North German Federation). When young Max began toddling around his family's frugal new home on the Ferdinandstrasse two years later, Kaiser Wilhelm signed a proclamation granting equal civil and voting rights to Germans of all religious faiths. This proclamation opened doors for Jews to enter political office and civil service posts that had previously been denied them.

By the time Richard Willstätter and Leo Baeck were born, in 1872 and 1873, respectively, these rights had been formally embedded in the constitution of the fledgling Second German Empire. Dominated by Prussia, this union of Protestant north German states had won a crushing victory over the French in 1871, crowned Wilhelm emperor in the palace at Versailles, and now basked in the dazzling sun of a late-emerging nationalism.

Grateful for their elevated status in this new Reich, the Jews embraced the liberal-democratic values that seemingly upheld it and threw their political support largely behind the one organization, the National Liberal Party, that had fought the hardest for these rights. One study found that as many as 90 percent of Jewish voters backed liberal or progressive parties after 1870.[1] As the pace of the assimilation in German society accelerated, the Jews' appreciation for the franchise and attendant economic opportunities mingled easily with a more conservative patriotism. Like their non-Jewish friends and neighbors, the Jews of the Second Empire overwhelmingly endorsed the policies and social norms of an expansive, imperial state.

Growing up in Karlsruhe, the capital of the Grand Duchy of Baden, Willstätter would look forward fondly to the prospect of encountering the liberal-minded grand duke during his nightly stroll with his mother through the Schloss garden.[2] Enamored of royal pomp and circumstance as a boy, he would remain a monarchist all his life.

Emancipation had come late to Germany's Jews. For hundreds of years they had been confined to urban ghettos, shunned, and scorned, and they now welcomed their equality with some nervousness, out of a habitual suspicion and fearfulness. This was a gift horse they would have to watch closely. As a consequence of this unrelieved insecurity, the Jews of Bismarck's Germany were more wont to consolidate and defend the rights they had already won (or, rather, that had been won for them by non-Jews) than to press vigorously for more. The barriers that remained intact, preventing the Jews from holding many governmental posts or from receiving invitations to socially elite Berlin homes, *were* disturbing and fed misgivings about whether the Germans really loved the Jews as much as the Jews loved Germany.

Still, these remaining obstacles were generally ignored because most German Jews were busy enjoying their newly acquired freedom to become physicians and lawyers, teach in universities, and own department stores and factories. If, as the poet Heinrich Heine had realized earlier in the century, abandoning the Jewish religion was the price of the admission ticket to German social and economic life (he converted to Protestantism to land a governmental post), then the Jews of the imperial era were even more willing to cast aside their religious beliefs and practices in a period when such rites and convictions were deemed atavistic and detrimental to further assimilation.

If Judaism was no longer a legal disqualification for equal rights, it was no longer a compensating bond either. Being a practicing Jew now brought only largely spiritual rewards, and to the extent that their faith marked Jews as alien, it held them back—on the outside looking in—and denied them more attractive material ones. So, it is not surprising that many Jews lapsed in their observance. They viewed their overt Jewishness, their Judaism, as belonging to a rapidly vanishing era. It was in this spirit of the times that Willstätter, product of a "liberal" but unbaptized merchant family, chose to explore, in an essay on religion during his final year at his Nuremberg Realgymnasium, "What does Judaism teach about the immortality of the soul?"[3] His conclusion: "Not very much." And it was this outlook that prompted the Nobel Prize–winning chemist, in his memoirs, to insist that "Judaism was for me history, acknowledgment of my ancestors. It was not the obeying of thousand-year-old laws, that is, obedience to Jewish law, not genuine, strict Judaism, let alone any sort of search for belief."[4]

And in this secular outlook Willstätter was clearly speaking for many. Reaching his majority in an age of entrepreneurs and deal makers, Warburg shrewdly assessed his Jewishness as being a liability and lapsed in his observance of the kosher practices that his father and grandfather had followed.[5] Indeed, of these six future leaders in the Jewish community, only Leo Baeck was raised in an observant Jewish home, in which the beliefs of previous generations were proudly kept alive.

The German Jews expected that assimilation would work. Having paid the price of admission to German society, they assumed they would pass through the turnstiles like everyone else. They would cease to be seen as different in any negative way and enjoy the fruits of German prosperity along with their fellow citizens. The "Jewish question" that had dogged Jews for so long, making their very presence "problematic," would no longer exist now that the Jews had become outwardly invisible, adopting the mores of non-Jews.[6] Such was the great faith that the Jews put in the doctrine of the Enlightenment, only to discover that, for anti-Semites, a Jew by any other religion was still a Jew. What assimilated ways and secular manner could mask, Jewish racial stereotyping could strip away.

When Germany's political and military successes in the Franco-Prussian War (1870–71) were followed by a crash on the Berlin stock market and a period of economic uncertainty and decline, the Jews were once again blamed for everything.[7] Pro-monarchy and other right-wing forces began using anti-Semitism to rally voters and to attack their more progressive rivals.[8] For a time a loose coalition was formed between Christian conservatives and racial anti-Semites.[9]

But the thrust of German anti-Semitism was changing. Whereas the Jews were once hated for being too *different* in their beliefs and way of life, anti-Semites now preyed on the growing fears of the lower middle class by accusing the Jews of trying to be *too much like* other Germans and of insinuating themselves into positions of power and wealth at the expense of non-Jews. Race was the distinguishing feature that could not be gainsaid, and it was on these grounds that the Jews were henceforth to be labeled and vilified. German nationalism, on the rise, readily adopted this line of attack. What was the German nation, after all, but an expression of the German volk, superior in its culture and accomplishments to the peoples (read "races") of other lands?

According to this way of thinking, the Jews could be marginalized—or demonized—depending on the depth of one's political convictions, in an appeal to common blood lines (and racial pride). Thus, German Jews in the 1880s found they could hide, but not escape, as an ugly anti-Semitic mood swept the country. Instead of fighting back, most Jews endured this hostile mood stoically as a "temporary aberration,"[10] as a natural reaction to recent Jewish advances that would soon fade away. Some, like the young, devout Leo Baeck, growing up as the son and grandson of rabbis in the small city of Lissa in eastern Prussia, encountered little of this hatred of Jews,[11] while others, like Willstätter, were not so fortunate.

At age six, in 1878, Richard Willstätter was taunted as a "Jew boy" by his classmates and dodged stones hurled down a Karlsruhe street.[12] Max Warburg, too, found that money and social class did not shield Jews from hatred, as his father, prominent in relief work for Russian Jews, had discovered before him.[13] Because of his financial power and visibility, the elder Warburg had attracted the wrath of followers of Adolf Stoecker, the political court chaplain of Wilhelm I who founded the Christian Socialist Workers Party on the rock of anti-Jewish economic resentment.[14]

Unwilling to admit it to themselves, Germany's Jews were caught in a no-man's-land. Having left the ghetto and much of their Jewish identity behind for the promise of equal rights via assimilation and having now come under right-wing fire for being too zealous in this ambition, the Jews had no handy refuge. As Heine had predicted, they had become double outsiders—from their ethnic (and religious) past and from the secular German world around them. In time, most would come to accept this precarious position in Germany as their inevitable lot. They would do so with misgivings, with ambivalence, with lurking fear, but still with the belief that Germany *was* moving forward. History, they thought, was ultimately, on their side. Therefore, they could endure occasional setbacks with some equanimity.

In the early 1880s, coincident with one of the many pogroms in Russia, anti-Semitism was formally institutionalized in German political life with the formation of such parties as the Deutschkonservative Partei (German Conservative Party) and the League of Anti-Semites. These groups were dedicated to restricting Jewish rights, influence, and power. In light of these parties and mounting charges of ritual murder, some German Jews gradually realized that they would have to fight back, in an equally well-organized and disciplined manner. In February 1893 some two hundred Jews gathered to lay the groundwork for a body that was to be given the awkward but appropriate name, Centralverein deutscher Staatsbürger jüdischer Glaubens (Central Organization of German Citizens of the Jewish Faith).

As its name implied, this organization sought to confront the ambiguities of German-Jewish identity head on: Jews in Germany were primarily loyal German citizens, entitled to the same rights enjoyed by their fellow countrymen. Their Jewish faith was only of secondary importance. Through its pronouncements and activities, the Centralverein emphasized the Germanness of Jews. Any behavior that tended to bring out Jewish differences would only incite anti-Semitism and was thus to be condemned.[15] Presenting themselves as German to the core, its supporters aggressively assumed the task of defending individual Jews in the courts, against discrimination, false accusations, and denial of rights, without making an issue of their Jewishness per se. Their goal was to make Jews inseparable from other Germans, under the protection of existing laws.

The legalistic thinking of the Centralverein reflected the moderate, assimilated attitude of the great majority of Germany's Jews[16] that they were bona fide children of the Enlightenment, beneficiaries of an evolutionary human advance toward justice for all. Above all else, they were deeply rooted in their fatherland.

Jews had lived on German soil as far back as Roman days. They had been in Cologne since 321, in Augsburg since 800, in Magdeburg and Merseburg since 950, and in Meissen since 1009. The family of Max Warburg could trace its German roots back to the thirteenth century; his ancestors had first settled in the vicinity of Hamburg in 1645. One of Leo Baeck's forebears had fallen victim to a pogrom in southern Germany during the time of the Crusades.[17] (Unlike many German Jews of that era, the Baeck family, then spelled "Bäck," had later decided against emigrating.) Richard Willstätter could proudly point to his family's presence in the southern German city of Karlsruhe for over 250 years before his birth—to within a few years of the city's founding.[18] Seven generations of Bella Fromm's family had produced wines on the same Bavarian estate in the Main Valley, having come to Germany from Spain early in the seventeenth century.[19] The Prussian bonds of Hans-Joachim Schoeps extended back over 150 years.[20] The sole exception among this group was Robert Weltsch, born to a German Jewish family in Prague, then part of the Hapsburg Empire, in 1891.

What such pedigrees gave these German Jews was a pride and a legitimacy in claiming Germany as their country, in affirming their patriotism. As their Jewishness receded, the strength of this attachment to the land of their ancestors would grow.

In the 1880s, despite the emergence of organized anti-Semitic forces, German Jews could still take a good deal of comfort in being German, especially in light of the terrible pogroms that befell Russian Jews from 1881 to 1884—the worst massacre in that country since the Cossack revolution of the seventeenth century.[21] In Germany, hostility toward Jews appeared to be concentrated in certain reactionary quarters that were opposed to democracy as well as capitalism. It was not a widespread problem.[22] Whatever opposition the German Jews faced could be confidently countered with organizations like the Centralverein (one of some twenty-four Jewish groups created between 1890 and 1910 for sports, science, literature, politics, youths, and women). The German Jews could also count on their Christian friends, particularly in the Social Democratic Party and the League for Defense Against Anti-Semitism (Verein zur Abwehr des Anti-Semitismus), founded in 1891.

For some Jews, the organizational response went beyond a vigorous defense of their rights. For them, rejection and antipathy toward Jews awakened deeper doubts: Did they really belong in an essentially non-Jewish milieu? These Jews began to wonder if the basic premise of their existence was wrong and if the anti-Semites were right: that Jews and Gentiles were *not* compatible, that their aspirations for identity, well-being, security, group cohesiveness, and even nationhood could not be reconciled under the banner of the Enlightenment. They came to believe that, in the Diaspora, alienation was an inexorable fact of Jewish life and a perennial cause of anti-Semitism. For the fulfillment of their hopes as a people, the Jews would have to look elsewhere.

To many of these disquieted Jews, "elsewhere" meant Palestine. In 1896 these vague longings were given a firm and forceful airing by the publication of the landmark book, *Der Judenstaat* (The Jewish State), by Theodor Herzl, a Viennese journalist. This book sparked the birth of modern Zionism—a movement that established a foothold in Germany the following year when a group of Jewish academics formed the Zionistische Vereinigung für Deutschland (Zionist Organization for Germany), with the aim of creating a legally guaranteed homeland in Palestine.

But, for the time being, it was little more than a foothold. In the main, German Jews found that Zionist appeals made them feel embarrassingly self-conscious, just when they were beginning to enjoy the peace of mind that came from not being thought of as Jews. Worse, they saw Zionism as confirming all the anti-Semites' propaganda—that these Jews actually celebrated their otherliness—and thus threatening to undo all that they, their assimilated brethren, had achieved in Germany with their new freedoms. Many sided with the industrialist Walther Rathenau, who mockingly chided Jews who sought a separate (Zionist) destiny, in his 1897 essay, "Höre, Israel!" ("Listen, Israel!") and urged his coreligionists to make their behavior and attitudes as Germanic as possible.[23]

Zionism struck more of a responsive chord among the Ostjuden—the Jews of Russia and eastern Europe—for whom existence in the Diaspora was associated with more immediate conflicts and perils, as well as fewer rewards. Set apart by their traditional dress, their kosher observances, their poverty, their ghettolike clannishness, and their less "cultivated" manners, most Ostjuden had little chance of being assimilated and scant desire to be so. For a great many of the eastern Jews who did not choose to migrate to a more secular West, Zionism and a Jewish homeland in Palestine seemed to offer the logical fulfillment of their steadfast attachment to Judaism and an escape from their barely tenable existence among hostile non-Jews.

For Robert Weltsch, a young German-speaking Jew growing up in fin de siècle Prague, the Zionist credo offered a clarity of purpose that transcended the confusion of competing nationalisms. As was the case with his older contemporary Franz Kafka (born in 1883), Weltsch (born in 1891) discovered that he did not feel at home with either the Czech-speaking Catholic majority (which defined him as a German) or the economically and culturally dominant German population (which considered him, ethnically, a Jew).[24] (Out of a population of some 400,000, only about 25,000 were Jews.) As a university student in Prague, Weltsch heard many völkisch-minded classmates from the Sudetenland argue that Jews could not be Germans, and he came to believe they were right.[25] He also met many young Zionists, also from the Sudetenland, who had learned this same truth from bitter experience.

By the time he was seventeen, in 1908, Weltsch had gravitated toward the student Zionist organization Bar Kochba (literally "Son of the Star"), named after an early Jewish rebel against the Romans. Greatly influenced by the views of Martin Buber (who, in turn, had been inspired by the "spiritual Zionism" of Ahad Ha'aim, also known as Asher Ginzberg), this branch of the Zionist movement stressed the importance of reviving the true ideals and spirit of Judaism and of developing a homeland in Palestine to achieve this end.

Buber, a native of Vienna who was steeped in the culture of central Europe, gave a tremendous boost to the nascent Zionist movement in Prague. In 1903 he spoke to a Bar Kochba gathering there and served as its representative to the international Zionist Congress.[26] In January 1909, Buber delivered the first of three lectures on the "meaning of Zionism" that had a galvanizing impact on the young Jews who attended them, including Weltsch.[27] Suddenly, to be a Jew was a source of pride and commitment. Buber's talk of a deeper bond of "blood" uniting Jews all over the world deeply moved the idealistic Weltsch and his intellectual circle of friends.

Throughout the pre–World War I years, Weltsch's fascination with Buber's philosophy of Zionism gave new focus to his life, sidetracking his plan to take over his father's law practice. Instead, Weltsch wrote articles for Bar Kochba's journal *Bericht* and sought to cement ties with like-minded young Zionists in Berlin and Vienna. Bar Kochba promoted greater Jewish consciousness by sponsoring lectures on Jewish culture and youth education and courses in the Hebrew language.

The second major milestone in the evolution of Weltsch's thinking occurred when he heard the German Zionist Kurt Blumenfeld address members of the Prague branch of Bar Kochba in 1912. Here was an established, western Jew from Berlin telling his audience that they needed a "radical reorientation" of their lives toward Judaism to lift them out of the emptiness of their present existence.[28] Blumenfeld's "postassimilationist Zionism" astonished Weltsch for its parallels with his own thinking. Blumenfeld spoke knowledgeably of Nietzsche and Friedrich Hölderlin, not of the Talmud, and made Zionism sound relevant to the Jews of western Europe, among whom Weltsch felt he belonged. It was his realization of a plausible link between Zionism and German Jewry that would later induce Weltsch to leave Prague for Berlin, to assume the editorship of Germany's major Zionist newspaper, the *Jüdische Rundschau* (Jewish Observer).

If Weltsch's early years in Prague were marked by ethnic clashes, confused identity, and his discovery of a liberating Judaism, this period was much more tranquil for Germany's Jews. Anti-Semitic sentiments, articulated by right-wing political parties, conservative Christians, and economically threatened groups like the Agrarian League, abated during the final years of the century, as the nation's attention shifted to imperialist expansion in Africa and Asia, guided by Wilhelm II's vague notions of *Weltpolitik*, and to a new enemy, Marxism. In their desire for a greater place in the sun for the German empire and in opposing Marxists, Germany's Jews displayed great fervor, eager to show they could be reliable "good" Germans. Their children matured with a sense that this was an attainable goal.

In Hamburg Max Warburg passed a carefree and somewhat desultory childhood, free of both lofty ambitions and base fears. He stood out from his four brothers by his boldness of action, keenness of mind, and personal charm—all essential qualities for a future banker.[29] When Aby, his senior by a year, was thirteen, he made an Esau-like pact with Max, abdicating his right as the eldest to go into the family banking business in lieu of pursuing his real passion, science. (To keep his end of the bargain, Max agreed to buy Aby all the books he would ever need—a collection that eventually swelled to some sixty thousand volumes and became the famed Warburg Library, now housed in London.)[30] This pact charted Max's fate, but he embarked on his banking career with little relish. (His motto may have been "En avant"—"Forward!"—but Max was in no great hurry to succeed.)

In 1898, bored and unhappy with his first post in Frankfurt, Max Warburg gladly swapped his formal banker's attire for the infinitely more fashionable uniform of the Third Royal Bavarian Light Cavalry Regiment, to perform his obligatory one year of military service. Indeed, he found the dashing life of a cavalry officer so captivating that he toyed with the idea of making soldiering a career, despite the stigma of being a Jew.[31] It fell to his father, Moritz, a former army trumpeter, to remind young Max of his family obligations.[32]

Like any other dutiful, well-born German son of his generation, Warburg completed his professional apprenticeship as expected; then, in 1893, his father made him a full partner in the two-hundred-year-old family-owned bank. Warburg's assumption of greater responsibility, both in the bank and in the city of Hamburg, happened to coincide with the rise of his family's fortunes (chiefly through the marriages of his brothers Felix and Paul to wealthy American Jewesses) and with the equally impressive rise of "self-made" German Jews, such as the shipping tycoon (and Warburg's friend), Albert Ballin, head of the Hamburg-America Line. What had been, just a few years before, a small, discreet, little-known concern specializing in money changing and trade bills, operating out of sparsely furnished and overcrowded offices, now mushroomed into a bank of international stature, largely through its currency transactions. It did so under Max Warburg's ever more capable hand.

By now married and settled in Hamburg, Warburg had grown confident in his own abilities and station in life, free of any gnawing self-doubts—certainly not in regard to his Jewishness. ("Only one thing gives life satisfaction," Warburg wrote to his three-month-old son Eric in 1900. "Struggle with yourself until you achieve self-knowledge—and live life through your own personality.")[33] Ten years later, following his father's death, Warburg took over the running of M. M. Warburg and Co., and it flourished, extending profitable, money-lending ties to banks in London, Paris, New York, Copenhagen, and Stockholm.[34]

As his wealth and influence grew (symbolized by the purchase, for 200,000 marks, of a sprawling country estate, Kösterberg, on the banks of the Elbe), Warburg did not turn his back on his Jewish ties, even if their religious content meant little to him. (Once he took his son Eric past a synagogue, remarking:"Here is where the Jews worship." This was to be the full extent of Eric's religious indoctrination.)[35] Like his father, who had founded the Hilfsverein der deutschen Juden (the Welfare Society of the German Jews), Max Warburg committed himself to advancing the lot of less fortunate Jews elsewhere in the world. Together with his friend Albert Ballin, he helped to ease the exodus of persecuted and downtrodden Ostjuden to the United States by improving conditions for would-be émigrés and having the cost of the transatlantic passage lowered to twenty dollars.[36] As a consequence of these efforts, over 1.25 million Jews were able to start new lives overseas between 1904 and 1914, thereby greatly expanding and strengthening the American Jewish community.[37]

In his noblesse oblige concern for his fellow Jews, Warburg was more broadly involved in social issues than were most of his coreligionists, who were, for the most part, focused on building better lives for themselves. For example, at the tender age of twelve, Richard Willstätter set his sights on becoming a chemist. Neither the departure of his father for America (where he was to remain, alone, for seventeen years, seeking his fortune in textiles) nor the family's subsequent move from idyllic Karlsruhe to the "narrow and gray" confines of medieval Nuremberg ("like a flight from Paradise," Willstätter later lamented)[38] nor poor grades in school (except in arithmetic and geology) nor a near-fatal bout of diphtheria as a teenager could deter him from fulfilling that aspiration.

Even the more widespread anti-Semitism that Willstätter faced in Bavaria posed no insurmountable barrier to his ambition and intellect. Recommended by his Realgymnasium teachers for the Royal Maximil-ianeum, a school for the gifted, Willstätter was rejected because he was a Jew but persevered with his dream to become a scientist (over parental objections) by enrolling first, in October 1890, in Munich's Technische Hochschule and then in the city's university.[39]

Zealously protected by his "Victorian" mother, who kept the novels of Zola, Tolstoy, and Dostoyevski far from his reach,[40] Willstätter sought solace at the laboratory bench, carrying out experiments on the mysteries of life that had fascinated him since boyhood. In an organic chemistry course, he fell under the spell of the eminent researcher Adolf von Baeyer, a pioneer in the field of synthetic dyestuffs and a future Nobel laureate. In Baeyer, the nineteen-year-old Willstätter found both a professional mentor, who taught him the strict rigor of the scientific method ("not to try to direct Nature, but to heed her,")[41] and a career counselor. Half Jewish, Baeyer was well acquainted with the obstacles confronting a Jewish scientist, particularly in conservative Bavaria, and twice tactfully urged his talented student to convert to Christianity.[42] But Willstätter would have none of this. To him, Judaism was history— *his* history and that of his family for centuries—and he was not about to repudiate it for the sake of certain "bourgeois" advantages. The aspiring young chemist who praised the New Testament as the "great-est progress of humanity"[43] and dismissed traditional Jewish beliefs as "dangerous" to his people's advance would remain proudly, steadfastly, a Jew, come what may.

What came, at first, was scientific success and rewards. Studying for his doctorate under Alfred Einhorn, the discoverer of novocaine, Will-stätter sufficiently impressed Baeyer to be invited, as a rare exception, to work as his assistant, analyzing the structure of cocaine-related com-pounds. This seminal research led to similar studies of morphine deriv-atives and a lifelong preoccupation with chemical ways of alleviating pain. Willstätter's studies of natural pharmaceuticals would pave the way for a major breakthrough in the development of anesthetics— Avertin.

Despite his laboratory triumphs and his inclusion in Baeyer's inner circle as a docent and lecturer in 1896, Willstätter could not shake the liabilities of his Jewish blood. Baeyer's personal assistant intimated that

Willstätter's race would bar him from ever succeeding to Baeyer's pres-tigious academic post.[44] But Willstätter did not seem to care. Like an explorer of continents, he loved the thrill of the scientific quest so much that its practical, material rewards held little attraction for him. Later in his career, he remarked: "To delve into Nature's secrets is something beautiful beyond description . . . to penetrate far enough to lift Nature's veil a little more and more from her treasures."[45] That was his passion.

In his devotion to chemistry, Willstätter was almost monastically single-minded, always the first to arrive at Baeyer's laboratory and the last to leave.[46] This dedication did not dissipate when, during Easter vacation in 1903, he met an elegant young woman, Sophie Leser, the daughter of a Jewish historian in Heidelberg, and fell in love with her. Characteristically, Willstätter made a quick decision: Here was the woman he was going to marry. Equally characteristically, he told his bride-to-be, after their engagement a few weeks later, that he was not prepared to devote as much time to her as to his work.[47] Two years later, Willstätter accepted a teaching and research appointment at the Eid-genössische Technische Hochschule (Swiss Polytechnic Institute) in Zurich, to conduct the experiments that would make him famous—and earn him the Nobel Prize—for elucidating the chemical makeup of chlorophyll and thereby laying the foundation for modern biochemistry. But the next seven years of satisfying scientific achievement (paralleling Warburg's financial rise in Hamburg) would be marred by personal tragedy. In the fall of 1908, his wife Sophie died of a ruptured appen-dix, leaving him to care for their two young children, Ludwig, aged four, and Margarete, aged two. It was the second time in his life that he had been abruptly abandoned by someone he loved dearly, and Willstätter responded this time by burrowing deeper into his laboratory work, denying himself a vacation for the next ten years and seeking few other compensating pleasures in life. On balance, he proved a good and car-ing father, who even applied his scientific training on his children's behalf; for example, told by a pediatrician to feed his son and daughter spinach and oranges, Willstätter conducted chemical analyses to deter-mine why these particular foods were so good for them.[48]

Although he grew attached to Zurich for the peace it afforded him to pursue his research, free of anti-Semitic undercurrents and political con-flict,[49] Willstätter was drawn back to Germany at the urging of his fellow chemist (and Jew) Fritz Haber, who helped arrange a professorship for him, free of administrative duties, at the brand-new Kaiser Wilhelm Institute for Chemistry in Berlin. At the opening ceremonies, held in October, Willstätter managed to coax the German emperor into peering at chlorophyll crystals under the microscope.[50] As a loyal German, Willstätter felt deeply honored and glad to be home again.

Home was equally, if not more, important to the German Jewess Bella Fromm, who could not bring herself to stray from it. From her early years spent among the lakes and woods surrounding her family's vineyards, she developed an elemental bond to this ancestral estate, which, she recalled years afterward, "answered an old need of my deeper self, the self that had become part of the land. . . . I was rooted deeply in its [Germany's] soil and in its history and in its language."[51] An only child, orphaned while still a young woman, Fromm would be sustained by this bond throughout her life and find it nearly impossible to break.

Less compelling were her ties to Judaism. The Fromm family (ironically, the name means "pious" in German) had prospered in the Bavarian countryside by subordinating their Jewishness to their Germanness: They ardently sought to be good patriots. Bella's grandfather had lost a leg fighting the French for Wilhelm I in 1870, and her mother tended to the poor and ill in the nearby villages and farms.[52] Frequently, the family played host to the princes of Bavaria, and it was through their vineyards that "mad" Ludwig—his head full of Wagnerian lore—had wandered without bodyguards.[53] Although Fromm attended public schools in Kitzingen, outside Würzburg, her parents also had her take French and needlework classes at a local convent. From the nuns she acquired a fascination with the mysteries of the Catholic faith that had more emotional resonance for her than the creed of her forebears.[54] Not that being a Jew was a liability for young Bella. Like her parents, she made no secret of her heritage, and there was no reason to do so. Anti-Semitism was not part of her childhood world; it seemed to have disappeared at some point in the Middle Ages, as had knights in armor galloping forth to slay the infidels.[55]

Hans-Joachim Schoeps was too young to experience much of the glory years of the *Kaiserzeit* and what it meant to be a Jew during them. He was only five when World War I erupted in 1914. Yet his family had also followed the pattern of growing prosperity and social acceptance in the "liberal" German empire. On his father's side, the family ran a flourishing brickyard. The family had eventually settled in Berlin, and

Schoeps's father, Julius, became a physician. Schoeps's mother's family, the Franks, owned a chemical factory outside Brandenburg and subsequently purchased two other plants. Her father traveled around Germany selling his wares, settling with his family in Berlin, in 1886, near the Stettiner railroad station. Käthe Frank, or "Kätchen," as she was called—a petite, pretty girl with a love of gymnastics and painting—met Julius Schoeps through a school connection and married him in 1908.

It was a heady time to be living in the imperial capital, at the heart of a militarily and economically mighty Germany, the strongest industrial nation on the continent. On the international scene, Germany was openly challenging the supremacy of the British Empire, laying claim to land and influence in such faraway places as South Africa, China, Morocco, and equatorial Africa and building up its fleet of dreadnoughts to back up these expanded claims. Jews, too, were benefiting from this surge of power and wealth, and more came pouring into the Reich from the east. (Between 1871 and 1900, the Jewish population of Germany rose from 383,000 to 497,000.) Increasingly, they were drawn to the large cities of Prussia (especially Berlin), where the opportunities for economic advancement and integration were the greatest; by 1910, 54.5 percent of Prussian Jews lived in cities, up from 32.7 percent in 1885.[56] Berlin was the mecca for Jews of all nationalities—Russian, Polish, Czech, Hungarian, Austrian, and German—walks of life, and ambitions, their number growing steadily toward a peak of 173,000 (or 4.3 percent of all Berliners) by 1925.[57]

In Berlin, the Jews were excelling in many professions, guiding Germany to new heights of national attainment. In the world of industry, business, and finance, there was Emil Rathenau, founder of the Allgemeine Elektricitäts-Gesellschaft (the German General Electric Company); the department store magnate Adolf Jandorf; the financier and physicist Leo Arons; and the banker Franz von Mendelssohn. In politics, Berlin-based Jews like Eduard Bernstein, Hugo Preuss, Rosa Luxembourg, Paul Hirsch, and Hugo Haase played pivotal roles. In science, technology, and medicine, there were such luminaries as Hermann Senator, Hermann Munk, Fritz Haber, Magnus Hirschfeld, and Emil Berliner. In the arts Berlin Jews dominated: Ludwig Barnay, Oscar Blumenthal, Max Reinhardt, Otto Brahm, Alfred Döblin, Kurt Tucholsky, and Max Liebermann, to name just a few. In short, the influence of

Berlin's Jews on German culture and society was extraordinary, far out of proportion to their actual number in the imperial capital. This was the Berlin that Schoeps, descendant of a patriotic Prussian family, encountered during his boyhood.

It was also the Berlin that attracted Leo Baeck, just shy of his forti-eth birthday, in 1912, although for slightly different reasons. Baeck had attended Berlin's liberal Lehranstalt für die Wissenschaft des Judentums (Institute for the Scientific Study of Judaism) over his parents' objec-tions as a young rabbinical student and had promptly fallen under the spell of its swirling intellectual currents, including the writings of Immanuel Kant, Hermann Cohen, Wilhelm Dilthey, and Baruch Spin-oza, on whom he wrote his dissertation in 1895. The confluence of contrasts—the unadorned piety of eastern European Judaism colliding with the ultra-sophisticated, assimilated ways of western Jews—fasci-nated him and taught him the virtue of tolerance. (In 1898 Baeck would be one of only two rabbis—out of ninety-four—on the rab-binical executive board to vote against condemning the newly formed Zionist Congress.)[58] So did the complicated interaction between Jews and Gentiles and the need to increase understanding between these two groups. This was the subject on which the twenty-two-year-old rabbi published his first article, in 1895.[59] Promoting dialogue to achieve rec-onciliation and harmony suited his restrained temperament, and with this prospect in mind, Baeck, along with his wife Natalie and their young daughter Ruth, gladly left the provincial Rhineland city of Düs-seldorf for a teaching position at the large, Moorish-style synagogue—towering symbol of Jewish emancipation and material prosperity—located in the center of Berlin on Fasanenstrasse. Here Baeck would remain, aside from a brief wartime interlude, until the Gestapo came to pick him up thirty years later.

In August 1914 the fate of all Germans was dramatically altered by the outbreak of World War I. For German Jews, the declaration of war against Russia and the sending of troops into Belgium and Luxembourg was not merely an occasion for patriotic rejoicing. It also gave them the perfect opportunity to dispel any lingering hostility and resentment about their place in German society. When Kaiser Wilhelm proclaimed, in an effort to draw all Germany's bickering political factions together, "I recognize only Germans," German Jews felt he was speaking directly to them,[60] and they responded with the enthusiasm of a once-scorned suitor. Laying one's body literally on the line for one's country was the ultimate retort to the salon whispers that Jews were not really as German as everyone else, and the young sons of German Jewish families with centuries-old ties to the Fatherland swarmed to the front—Zionist and assimilated Jew marching elbow to elbow with soldiers named Schultz and von Schulenburg. The 3,500 Jews serving in the imperial army before the war rose dramatically to 100,000 (or nearly 18 percent of the entire German Jewish population) during the course of the conflict. Four-fifths of these volunteers served on the front lines.

Baeck was one of the first German rabbis to volunteer for military duty. He reached troops entrenched in France by September. The following fall he traveled on horseback all the way to Russia,[61] where he consoled Jewish enlisted men and officers during a Rosh Hashanah service, held in a Catholic church, by reminding them of the continuity of history—of the better times that lay ahead after this terrible ordeal.[62] It was a theme and a view of Jewish history that he would return to during a much darker hour for Germany's Jews.

In Prague, twenty-four-year-old Robert Weltsch less willingly donned the uniform of an Austrian army officer and trudged eastward into Poland in the spring of 1915. In the trenches, cold, dirty, and exhausted, he found time to read the Bible and Hölderlin's lyrical, epistolary novel *Hyperion* and to dream that the war would lead to the reawakening of a Jewish consciousness, freed from the materially corrupting liberalism that had cut off western Jews from their heritage.[63] For the first time in his life, Weltsch found himself in the midst of a predominantly Jewish population, and although he could not mingle with these strange Russian peasants, they vividly testified to a living Jewish identity and common bond, awakening deep feelings of pride. To celebrate Hannukah in 1915, Weltsch was moved to sing religious songs out loud in his trench, while his Christian comrades-in-arms looked on in amazement.[64] (He had to make do without a menorah. Ironically, the Russians—his enemies—had collected all of them.)[65]

Weltsch's coming face-to-face on the eastern front with a thriving, deeply spiritual Judaism was an experience repeated by the thousands of German Jews who ended up in neighboring outposts of the kaiser's army. German patriotic fervor ran headlong into an opposing, ancestral kinship. When these soldiers returned home—to Frankfurt, Berlin, and Hamburg—they would never again so easily deny their Jewishness. On the home front, German civilians saw matters less ambivalently. Almost without exception they rallied to the colors. Those who were too old to fight helped out in other ways. By now internationally famous for his banking acumen, Max Warburg had at first opposed going to war against his beloved Great Britain. An unprepared Germany would lose, he knew, and this defeat would greatly harm the family bank. But when the guns roared in August, he dutifully made himself available to the war provisions office, helping to provide relief to Dutch and Belgian populations under German occupation.[66]

Richard Willstätter, ever the monarchist at heart, was less troubled by any such economic fears. Together with his good friend Fritz Haber, the forty-two-year-old head of Germany's most eminent chemistry research center sought out the head of the Kaiser Wilhelm Society the day war was declared and offered his services to help defend the Fatherland.[67] There was no crying need for middle-aged scientists in the army's ranks, so for a time, Willstätter lingered in his laboratory, watching it empty out as his younger assistants disappeared one by one for the front, and taking care of his two children. His resolve to serve the nation—and his close ties to the recently deceased Adolph von Baeyer—prompted him to accept an offer of Baeyer's chair at the University of Munich, the most distinguished academic post in his field—the one he had been told could never be his. Signing the appointment in September 1915, an irritated King Ludwig III, Bavaria's last monarch, remarked sotto voce: "This is the last time I appoint a Jew."[68]

Earlier in 1915 personal tragedy had again befallen Willstätter, dimming the luster of his professional achievement, reminding him of the frailty of human love. After complaining of weakness and thirst, his ten-year-old son Ludwig slipped into a diabetic coma and died. At almost the same time, Willstätter learned from the Swedish Academy of Science that he had been awarded the Nobel Prize in chemistry for his work with chlorophyll. It was undoubtedly a great relief to him that the conflict raging across Europe would prevent him from publicly claiming this honor. Instead, he could bury his sorrow, as before, under a mound of all-consuming research—this time devoted to the kaiser and his war.

First involved with finding ways to expand Germany's wartime food supply, Willstätter soon shifted his energies to a pressing battlefield need—gas masks. Since Germany's initial use of chlorine gas in 1915, soldiers on both sides had found themselves ill equipped to deal with this new horror of modern warfare. Having developed poison gas, Haber now enlisted his friend's assistance in finding a defense against it. In short order Germany's newest Nobel laureate devised a three-layer, absorbent filter that worked. By 1917, some 30 million gas masks containing Willstätter's life-protecting device were in use.[69] For this success, the noncombatant chemist was awarded the Iron Cross, second class. He could not have asked for more.

Other German Jews, too old or too young for combat, served as best they could. Like all other proud Prussian lads, Hans-Joachim Schoeps responded exuberantly. Scarcely five years old, little "Hase" (or "Rabbit," as his parents affectionately called him),[70] helped drive nails into Berlin's famed "iron Hindenburg"—a statue made of scrap metal donated for the war.[71] Along with his classmates, he celebrated German victories in far-off battlefields by placing tiny flags on a classroom map or by staying home for the day.[72] His father, Julius, a man with a keen sense of patriotic obligation, signed up as an army staff physician. Eventually he headed a rehabilitation center near the Polish border and became the only civilian—and Jew—named an honorary member of his regiment.[73] After the war he would continue to wear his uniform, his badge of honor, for several years.

Bella Fromm, still a teenager, cast aside her carefree life as the "princess of Kitzingen" to join the Red Cross and tend wounded soldiers who trickled back from the front to a nearby Bavarian hospital. Without any hesitation, she assumed this duty to the Fatherland over her domestic obligations. (Married earlier in 1914 to a German army officer, she had been left to bear and raise a daughter, Grete-Ellen, "Gonny," on her own after he departed with his unit.) Fromm was later honored for her service to the kaiser, receiving the King Ludwig cross (given to Red Cross volunteers). But this was a small consolation for the personal losses Fromm suffered. Both her parents died, leaving her an orphan. Her marriage was not a happy one, and in 1919 she obtained a divorce. On top of these tribulations, Fromm grimly perceived a disaster looming for Germany's Jews—a return to a "medieval era of darkness" as her battered and defeated country began looking around for scapegoats to blame.[74]

Her fear was well grounded. The "baptism by fire" that German Jews had welcomed in 1914 backfired on them. Many who had marched off ready to lay down their lives to prove they were good Germans ran into sobering realities on the front lines other than gas and the stench of the dead.[75] Although some two thousand Jews became officers for the first time since the Napoleonic wars, breaking down this humiliating barrier, others were crudely discriminated against and denied promotions. Worse, the entire German Jewish community became the target of a right-wing, anti-Semitic charge, propagated early in the conflict, that its members were shirking military service, saving their own skins while "real" Germans were quietly bleeding to death. This accusation led to a so-called *Judenzählung*—or head count of Jews—conducted by the Prussian War Ministry at the end of 1916. Unfortunately, the results of this survey were not published, fueling suspicions about the Jewish commitment to fighting the war. The actual facts told a much different story: Of the 100,000 Jews who served in the German military, 35,000 were decorated, and 12,000—or 12 percent—died (only slightly less than the 16 percent of casualties suffered by the 11-million-strong imperial forces during the entire war).

The hopes of German Jews that dying for their country would prove their loyalty beyond question and gain them full equality were doubly dashed. First, instead of fading away, anti-Semitism was revived by the war: Jews were branded war profiteers, members of an international conspiracy feeding off Germany's misfortune. Second, their sacrifice in blood was gainsaid. Just when they thought they had made the final payment for entrance into German society, the Jews found more doors being rudely slammed in their faces. And this ill treatment during World War I only augured worse ordeals to come once the guns fell silent and the boys came home.

2

Setting the Trap

Defeat in World War I, compounded by the humiliating peace terms dictated by the victorious Allies at Versailles, stunned the German people. No living German had ever known defeat: No German army had lost a war since Napoleon's legions had stormed across and ignominiously subdued Prussia over a century before. Traumatic defeat demands scapegoats, and this powerful psychological need drove many embittered, conservative Germans to blame not the generals who had lost the battles and frittered away lives so extravagantly, but the Social Democratic malcontents back home who had "stabbed" the kaiser's army in the back, by objecting to its imperialistic ambitions, stirring up trouble, and clamoring for a democratic revolution. Jews were easy to tar with the same brush, for they were widely viewed as leftists, if not outright revolutionaries—with the Berlin communist leaders Rosa Luxembourg and Karl Liebknecht, as well as key figures in the short-lived Soviet Republic of Bavaria, the most visible. And Jews—rich Jews—were despised for having profited from the war. This irrational chain of association between mayhem in the cities, left-wing politics, and wealthy industrialists caused many German Jews first embarrassment and then alarm.[1] *They* were certainly not keen about fomenting street brawls or radical social upheavals. *They* had not benefited from the war. *They* had nothing to do with these other, notorious Jews.

Max Warburg was one who was dumbfounded to find himself the focus of such hatred. As Germany had slid toward the defeat he had long predicted, Warburg had been asked by the new chancellor, Count Georg von Hertling, to go to Holland to make peace overtures to the invincible Americans.[2] The banker was curtly rebuffed in this diplomatic mission, and when he returned home to Hamburg, he was accused by General Erich Ludendorff, the army's commander in chief, of consorting with the enemy. (Ludendorff would be forced to swallow the bitter pill and sue for peace six months hence.) For a while Warburg wisely evaded the limelight, working quietly in his native city to bring peace among the warring workers, Social Democrats, and ex-soldiers, but not for long. Once again he was hurled unwillingly onto the international stage. Following the suicide (by an overdose of sleeping pills) of his good friend, the shipping magnate Albert Ballin, Warburg was asked to join the German delegation at Versailles. He did not want to go—it was a doomed mission, he could see that—but his sense of duty prevailed over his cautious banker's judgment, and he went.

Almost immediately Warburg grasped the ruin that lay in store for Germany if it acceded to the exorbitant Allied demands for reparations. He put his foot down. "We have to fight for our rights to the very last moment," he wrote, with a dramatic flourish, to his wife.[3] When the representatives of England, France, and Italy set the amount Germany would have to pay at an astronomical $33 billion, Warburg resigned from the delegation rather than put his name to the treaty. On the way to his train Warburg's limousine was hit by stones hurled by angry Frenchmen, who found all Germans despicable. This was but a foreshadowing of the wrath of his countrymen, who, convinced he had sold out the fatherland, impugned Warburg's loyalty, penned him threatening letters, and even plotted to kill him.[4]

In the years after the war Max Warburg was too immense a Jewish target to escape mounting anti-Semitic harassment and intimidation. The success and stature of his bank had made his name a household word, albeit not a beloved one. Indeed, he was the archetypal "Jew financier," a ready-made locus of hate. Instead of hiding from his attackers, Warburg at first chose to fight back, true to the spirit and practice of the legalistic Centralverein deutscher Staatsbürger jüdischer Glaubens (Central Organization of German Citizens of the Jewish Faith). During the 1920s, he and his bank gamely parried thrusts from the Left and the Right. When the anti-Semitic, Hamburg-based publication *Hammer* alleged that the Warburg bank had secretly bankrolled the Bolshevik revolution in Russia by funneling some 50 million rubles through Sweden,[5] Warburg defended himself—ultimately with success—against this charge in court.[6] By other fanatics he was branded the "chief of the general staff of world Jewry."[7]

The occupation of the Ruhr by French and Belgian troops in 1923 and the crushing burden of reparations, worsened by a dizzying spiral of inflation, stoked the anger of right-wing German nationalists, who kept up a steady stream of invective against Warburg. When the Jewish foreign minister Walther Rathenau perished in a hail of bullets in a Berlin motorcar in June 1922, Warburg accepted a police guard, moved to a different address, and traveled abroad for a brief spell. Six months later the firm of M. M. Warburg and Company quietly celebrated its 125th anniversary, glad to have survived both the war and the ensuing enmity at home. But just a few weeks afterward, matters took a turn for the worse. The Nazi mouthpiece, the *Völkischer Beobachter,* urged that Warburg and his brothers Paul and Felix be physically assaulted. Right-wing instigators denounced the banker in speeches delivered on the streets of Hamburg. Realizing he was bucking a rising tide of anti-Semitic nationalism, Warburg decided to maintain a low profile and resigned abruptly from several public offices—a step that he later regretted.[8] He also turned down offers of high posts in the Reich government, including that of finance minister, to spare himself the Jew baiting. But, characteristically, Warburg did not let fear get the best of him. He surveyed the bad times that German Jews like himself were enduring from a detached philosophical standpoint with a wry sense of humor—this, too, would pass. His lifelong "sunny optimism" and forward-looking mentality were not so easily undermined, even as the situation in Germany further deteriorated.[9] It was a trait that would see him through much adversity, but would also blind him to its full dimensions—then and later.

Warburg was by no means the only prominent German Jew to face a rekindled anti-Semitism after World War I. In Bavaria, where Richard Willstätter had resettled, along with his surviving daughter Margarete, to conduct research in organic chemistry and be of greater use to the nation in its hour of need, hostility toward the Jews was rampant. This widespread anti-Semitism came as a shock to the new Nobel laureate after his ten-year absence in Zurich and Berlin. Still a firm believer in the monarchy, Willstätter had watched with dismay as the Jewish writer Kurt Eisner and a band of socialists had taken over the splendid baroque capital of the Wittelbachs, proclaimed a "people's state," and forced King Ludwig to abdicate. Indignant, he denounced those who lumped all Jews together with the handful of radicals who had seized power, but few were prepared to listen.[10] In a few short months the political tide in Munich swung the other way. Inside his laboratory at the Ludwig-Maximilians University, Willstätter was distracted by the rat-a-tat-tat of machine-gun bursts as regular army troops and Bavarian Freikorps volunteers entered the city and overthrew Eisner's republic. The chemist's sympathies may have lain with the Right, but the nationalist movement that was coalescing in Munich had little room for him, or for any other Jew, for that matter.

Certainly, this was true of the fledgling German Workers' Party, formed in Munich in 1919 and joined shortly thereafter by a disaffected ex-corporal by the name of Adolf Hitler. Soon renamed the National Socialist German Workers' Party, it embraced anti-Semitism as one of its credos and declared that Jews should be barred from public office and stripped of their citizenship. The Nazis quickly found common cause with other right-wing fringe groups. These resurgent nationalists appealed particularly to conservative students in Munich, who turned the university into an ideological battleground. Foreign Jews were to be kept out, they demanded, and a cap—or *numerus clausus*—put on the number of German Jews who could be enrolled. The students' animosity reflected a broader, popular anti-Semitism. In April 1920 a second, newly installed right-wing regime ordered the expulsion of some 1,500 Ostjuden on the grounds of "hostility to the state." (They were Russian Jews.) The following Passover two Munich synagogues were smeared with swastikas. In September 1922 the downtown streets were choked with Nazi flags, and cries of "Death to the Jews!" resounded below the city hall. It was in this tense atmosphere that Richard Willstätter, fifty years old and at the height of his scientific career, was elected to the faculty senate and named dean.

This appointment threw the retiring and intensely private chemist into the political maelstrom. Willstätter was doubly appalled at what he saw happening around him—first, the ranting students who broke into faculty meetings and trampled on the right of free speech that he cherished, and second, his colleagues, who meekly allowed themselves to be intimidated by this student riffraff. Some professors were even openly backing the antidemocratic, ultra-right forces gaining momentum in Munich and elsewhere in a Weimar Republic battered by inflation and political instability. (Fellow faculty members who signed membership cards in the Nazi Party confided to Willstätter that its anti-Semitism was of minor consequence, certainly not an impediment to their remaining friends.)[11] But the "peaceful island"[12] that his research laboratory had once been was soon overrun by chauvinistic demagogues. This was a disruption of Willstätter's life as fundamentally threatening as the policies the Nazis proposed.

By 1924, in the wake of more attacks on Jews, Willstätter was forced to conclude that his career could no longer remain uncontaminated by politics. Emblematic of this realization was the medal he was awarded in January—replacing one smashed by a Spartacus band that had stormed the Berlin Schloss a few years before.[13] In Munich Willstätter came upon posters prophesying "In the future no German youth will sit at the feet of a Jewish leader."[14] Willstätter's passionate, almost religious dedication to advancing scientific knowledge could not take place in a vacuum the way it had in the past. His very being was in jeopardy. On a trip to Baden-Baden over spring vacation, he brooded to the surgeon Ferdinand Sauerbruch: "My chair no longer stands secure; it will tip over."[15]

To the gentle, blue-eyed scholar with the white Vandyke beard and courtly manners, it all came down to a matter of principle—and personal survival. The issue at stake was academic freedom—keeping politics out of the university and its sacred work—and Willstätter vowed to meet the challenge head-on. The occasion presented itself later that spring. Willstätter's old teacher, the mineralogist Paul von Groth, announced his intention to retire. For years Groth had argued that only one person was qualified to succeed him—the pioneering, internationally renowned, geochemist Viktor M. Goldschmidt, then a member of the faculty at the University of Göttingen. This was, coincidentally, the third Goldschmidt—and the third Jew—to be proposed for a Munich post that year. The other two, a biologist and an organic chemist, had been informally rejected because of their ethnicity. This time Willstätter was not prepared to acquiesce. When Viktor Goldschmidt's name was brought before the philosophical faculty, the physicist Willy Wien, the dean, spoke privately to his colleagues and let his opposition be known. By the time a preliminary vote was to be taken, a majority had already lined up against Goldschmidt—not, they said, because he was a Jew or a "non-Aryan," but simply because he was a foreigner. Xenophobia was officially permissible, even if anti-Semitism was not. (Goldschmidt had been born in Zurich.) So, when a final list of candidates was submitted, on June 24, Goldschmidt's name was not on it. As swiftly and as surely as he had asked Sophie Leser to be his wife, Willstätter now made the second most fateful decision of his life. He sat down that evening and wrote a letter of resignation to Wien, saying he could no longer serve when he found himself "so little in agreement with the attitude of the faculty majority in hiring questions."[16] His decision was final. Willstätter also declared that he was stepping down from his post as head of the Bavarian state chemistry laboratory.

Willstätter's associates and students were stunned. Here was one of the scientific giants of his day, a Nobel Prize winner comparable in his genius to Albert Einstein, walking away from the most prestigious post in his field—on a matter of principle, in a fit of pique. To dissuade Willstätter, a large group of his students, colleagues, and assistants gathered in the chemistry lecture hall on the evening of Friday, June 27. The dapper, diminutive chemist was led into the hall by his friend Ferdinand Sauerbruch and Friedrich von Mueller from the medical faculty. He was handed a petition signed by 337 students and faculty, urging him to stay on, to provide German youths with the kind of leadership they so sorely needed during this turbulent time. A student then spoke, praising Willstätter as a human being and a teacher, begging him to remain on the Munich faculty. Professor Mueller made the same plea. Moved by these appeals, Willstätter nonetheless stood firm. In a measured, calm voice he told his hushed audience that it would be better for him to set "an example of how a decent man behaves" under these circumstances than to bow to their wishes. ("Of genius there is no dearth, but character is a rare article," the Nobel laureate would later remark.)[17] He could not be part of a faculty that chose its members because of their race, not on the basis of merit.[18] Willstätter then rose from his seat and left the hall without saying another word, his eyes straight ahead. Everyone else stood and watched him go in silence. It was, as his fellow researcher Felix Haurowitz recalled decades later, "like a funeral."[19]

In the weeks and months that followed, Willstätter's friends and admirers, as well as Bavarian officials, labored to change his mind. The successor he had chosen, Heinrich Wieland, wrote that Willstätter had exaggerated the prejudice against Jews: "In Germany there is absolutely no anti-Semitism of any importance," he claimed.[20] University officials likewise expressed surprise at Willstätter's charge of anti-Jewish bias. On the other hand, the industrialist Carl Duisberg told him his resignation had caused great pleasure and satisfaction in certain circles. The nationalist press expressed its hearty approval, saying that the university had lost only a "Paradenjuden" ("show Jew"), not a true German.[21] Somewhat embarrassed by all this fuss, Willstätter still did not budge. He was as unshakable in his decision to resign his professorship as he had been in his commitment to his research.

But Willstätter did not want to leave Munich, his cherished "second home" (where his mother still lived) either.[22] He rejected attractive offers from Berlin, Heidelberg, and ten other universities, not wishing to capitalize on his resignation, preferring to retreat to his Munich home, isolated and more alone than ever. Out of a sense of professional obligation, he agreed to stay on at the university for two semesters, to oversee his doctoral students and to smooth Wieland's assumption of his position. Immediately after he resigned, Willstätter cleaned out his university office but continued his preliminary investigations into the nature and function of enzymes, working initially with the Czech-born Felix Haurowitz, who was also Jewish. Instead of packing his bags, he had a stately villa built at Möhlstrasse 29, along the banks of the slowly meandering Isar River. Not far away stood a monument to the German Jewish poet Heinrich Heine, which gave Willstätter some comfort.[23] The new dwelling, into which he moved late in 1925, housed his tasteful, eclectic collection of paintings, an art library, and an antechamber with "monastic pews" imported from Italy.[24] It had a rose garden—his great delight—boasting a species bearing his name. It was a perfect retreat, and when Willstätter walked out of his laboratory on the Arcisstrasse for the last time in September 1925, he did so with a sense of satisfaction that his life—that is, his professional life, which was what really mattered to him—could go on from this new, closeted base.

Willstätter had worked out a curious, but singularly appropriate arrangement. Removed from his university colleagues and his scientific facilities, he had made plans to carry on his research on enzymes for the Munich Academy of Sciences by means of telephone conversations with his laboratory assistant, Margarete Rohdewald. Every evening she would call and report on the day's progress, and he would offer comments and suggestions on how to proceed the next day. Support for his work was forthcoming from the Rockefeller Foundation, which paid for his assistant's salary and for the necessary chemicals and equipment.[25] This form of scientific collaboration suited Willstätter's purposes; in fact, it gave him back the tranquility and freedom from political interference he craved. He had made a virtue out of moral necessity, and he was pleased. Sequestered in the new house on the Möhlstrasse, with only a faithful housekeeper and his daughter Margarete, now a student of physics at the university, for company, the world-famous chemist was hardly a downcast or broken man. Not long after Willstätter's retirement, his friend, the surgeon Sauerbruch, found him "full of beans," as busy and enthusiastic as ever.[26] He was to remain that way, shielded from the brutal, unsavory mess of German politics, producing a steady stream of scholarly papers and expanding his investigations into the regulatory process of life, for the next fourteen years. During that time, he would achieve a true form of "internal exile," becoming a towering citadel of independent scientific inquiry amid the gathering Nazi revolution that was out to smash both Jews and their science.

Richard Willstätter thus made a dramatic, early exit from the chaotic Weimar stage. His lack of visibility, his reputation, and his disengagement from public affairs would continue to protect him from worsening anti-Semitic persecution. Unlike Max Warburg, Willstätter had no reason to fear personal attack. His outlook and his decision to remain in Munich were not influenced by the fact that he happened to be a Jew or that he might one day be persecuted as such. Nor could he imagine that, in the end, his Jewishness alone would be what would define him in the minds of those numerous Germans who were becoming enthralled by the fiery speeches of Adolf Hitler. Having made his personal protest against the anti-Semites, Willstätter was now content to go on with his life undisturbed, devoting himself to a higher calling. This was his destiny—and his undoing.

If the notion of Jewishness aroused hatred and abuse toward a public figure such as Max Warburg during the fractious 1920s, it had the opposite impact on thousands of German Jews who, until then, had not thought of themselves, in any positive sense, as Jews. They had gone off to fight in World War I vowing to prove they were Germans like every-body else but discovered instead they were, at heart, Jews. This shift in self-perception grew out of two important experiences—their failure to be accepted as equals despite the "blood sacrifice" in the trenches and their encounter with "authentic Jews" in the East, who reminded them that a devout, traditional way of life could still be possible and admirable in this modern, secular age. Many German Jews—though still a distinct minority within their community—pondered these two pivotal lessons of the war and drew the same conclusions: Jewish values and identity were their lot in life and were nothing to be ashamed of. Indeed, Jewishness was a deep source of strength, pride, and purpose, counterbalancing the disappointment and frustration they felt living in an ungrateful and hostile homeland.

For many Europeans, the war had discredited the old order of courts, emperors, and kings and blind devotion to the nation. It had stirred up dreams of new kinds of human affiliation and new values to shape them. Lines were drawn in Germany and elsewhere between the older generation of leaders and restless, idealistic youths; between the capital-ist bourgeoisie and the downtrodden proletariat; between those inspired by spiritual hunger for a better world and those consumed by a material appetite for the world as they found it; between those who believed in social progress and those who feared it; between those who reaffirmed their allegiance to their country and those who fell under the sway of other attachments—to Marx, "blood," race, or the volk. German Jews were divided by these polarities, too. They struggled inwardly as well as outwardly to discover who they were and how they should live. They were part of a larger, evolving Zeitgeist, trying to get its bearings.

Before the war Robert Weltsch had taken nineteenth-century liberal-ism to task for corrupting Jews and for debasing and destroying their community.[27] To overcome their inner lack of security, Jews needed to restore themselves, he said, by shedding the "sick" rationalism of the Enlightenment and asserting their solidarity with one another as Jews. They needed their own brand of nationalism. Jewish nationalism was different from French or German nationalism in that it was rooted in a common history, values, and community rather than a common geogra-phy. It rested on the notion of the Jews as a "volk."[28] As soon as he was out of uniform, early in 1918, Weltsch threw himself into the task of making this idea a reality. In Vienna, forsaking a career as a lawyer, he took over the editorship of the radical Zionist newspaper the *Jüdische Zeitung* (Jewish Newspaper) to lead the fight against the prevailing "ghetto mentality" among the Jewish bourgeoisie in Austria and for recognition of a Jewish nationality. Weltsch also became general secretary of the Jüdisches Nationalrat (Jewish National Council), the political wing of the Zionist movement in Austria, and representative of the Ha-Po'el ha Za'ir ("The Young Worker") labor party in the international Zionist executive. The *Jüdische Zeitung* was instrumental in convening the largest gathering of Austrian Jews ever assembled, in a Viennese concert hall in October 1918—an event that left an indelible mark on Weltsch's consciousness and bolstered his hopes for a Jewish renewal in western Europe.

The devastating pogrom in Russia later that year and the ensuing flight of tens of thousands of Ostjuden into Germany and Austria caused Weltsch to reconsider. Seeing firsthand the abuse and suffering inflicted by anti-Semites on these refugees in internment camps in Pomerania made him feel pessimistic about the future of European Jewry in the Diaspora.

Zionism provided a catalyst for Jews seeking a fundamental change and reorientation in their lives. Its most concrete desire, first espoused by Theodor Herzl and his followers, was for Jews to return to the ancient Jewish homeland, where they would create a modern Jewish state. That desire had received a tremendous boost in November 1917 with the issuance of the Balfour Declaration, which affirmed the British government's backing for a "national home for the Jewish people" in Palestine and its willingness to use its "best endeavours to facilitate the achievement of this objective." British support for Herzl's dream, coming at a time of the Ottoman Empire's collapse, suddenly made a Jewish homeland seem a palpable, attainable reality. The gates to a new world were opening to Jews, just as the old, European world was crumbling in a Wagnerian Götterdämmerung. In a postwar letter written in Vienna to his mentor Martin Buber, Weltsch expressed his feeling that, for Jews, the most important facts were that the war was over and "Palestine lies before us."[29]

In 1919 Weltsch received an offer to further the Zionist cause that he could not resist. He was asked to become editor of the German Zionist newspaper, the *Jüdische Rundschau,* the oldest and most influential publication of its kind, founded two years before Herzl's Zionist organ,

Die Welt (The World). Published in Berlin, the *Jüdische Rundschau* spoke directly to a small but important audience of German Zionists (its circulation was roughly 7,000 during the 1920s,[30] and the number of Zionists about 20,000[31]), who were in the forefront of what was becoming a worldwide movement. It was a podium Weltsch could exploit to its fullest, to articulate his hopes for a "creative renewal" of the Jewish people, in light of the Balfour Declaration and greater contact with eastern Jews,[32] and to win converts to Jewish nationalism and the notion of a Jewish state in Palestine.

In the artistically dynamic, politically unstable Weimar Republic, Berlin was a haven for Jews, drawn there in growing numbers because of its modern, cosmopolitan lifestyle and economic opportunities. Berlin also appealed to Germany's Jews for its open-mindedness and liberal bent. There they could expect to encounter fewer barriers against their advance. Anti-Semitism was rarely experienced. Berlin offered racial anonymity and the promise of further assimilation. By 1925 the Jewish population in the city had reached its all-time high of 173,000 (4.3 percent of the total)—up from 92,000 at the turn of the century—or nearly a third of all German Jews. Of these Berlin Jews, a substantial number—almost 44,000—were Ostjuden who had migrated to Germany seeking a better life or fleeing persecution in their native countries.[33] These immigrants brought their own distinctive dress, customs, language, and manner and tended to congregate in certain run-down neighborhoods, kept at arm's length by their fellow Berliners, Jews and Gentiles alike. Native German Jews were ill at ease with this throng of odd-looking "ethnic" Jews who—they thought—undermined their assiduous efforts to blend quietly into Berlin's business and professional circles to the point of invisibility. "Strange sight!" declared the paragon of Jewish self-hating assimilation, Walther Rathenau:

There in the midst of German life is an alien and isolated race of men. Loud and self-conscious in their dress, hot-blooded and restless in their manner. An Asiatic horde on the sandy plains of Prussia . . . forming among themselves a closed corporation, rigorously shut off from the rest of the world.[34]

To most middle-class Berlin Jews, these outlandish newcomers seemed to incite anti-Semitism by behaving in a crass and ostentatious way[35] and by reviving the very stereotypes of the wandering "internationalist" Jew they had tried to lay to rest.[36]

Germany—and Berlin in particular—thus posed a formidable challenge to Robert Weltsch and the coterie of Jews who belonged to the Zionistische Vereinigung für Deutschland (Zionist Organization for Germany), or ZVfD. After 1924, the ZVfD was headed by Kurt Blumenfeld, a longtime Zionist activist, who had joined the movement in 1904, soon after Herzl's death. Son of a member of the Prussian judiciary and grandson of a Polish immigrant, Blumenfeld readily admitted that the German anti-Semites were right: Jews *were* ethnically different and would always remain rootless and unwanted on German soil.[37] The only solution that would satisfy both the Jews and their adversaries was to separate the Jews from other Germans by intensifying the Jews' "ethnic consciousness" and national identity, rather than their religiosity.[38] Blumenfeld and most other German Zionists did not favor emigration to Palestine. They were generally happy in Weimar Germany and wanted to stay there, but only as proud, affirming Jews. Rather than dwell on the evils of anti-Semitism, the ZVfD and its mouthpiece, the *Jüdische Rundschau*, emphasized the positive: the lofty if somewhat vague ideals and goals of the international Zionist movement and its work to create a Jewish national home in Palestine.

Jewish identity preoccupied other Jews throughout the 1920s as faith in emancipation and assimilation suffered blow after blow delivered by the hate mongers on the far Right. When Leo Baeck returned from the war to his wife and daughter in Berlin in July 1918, he was eager to take up the questions that German Jews would confront once the war ended: How were Jews to respond, spiritually and intellectually, to this changing political climate? and How were Jews to live in postwar Germany, where full equality and acceptance had yet to be gained? Baeck explored these questions in a small circle of Jewish intellectuals, which included the Zionist Martin Buber.[39] He was worried about the waning commitment to Judaism. In this century, thanks to greater social acceptance, more and more Jews were intermarrying. During the 1920s alone, at least 100,000 of Germany's 620,000 Jews left the community by marrying non-Jews.[40] Others, like the chemist Fritz Haber, were converting to Christianity or simply jettisoning Judaism for career or "patriotic" reasons—a marked change from a generation or so earlier.[41] It was estimated that only one in five still observed Jewish religious customs and rituals.[42] These desertions were depleting the German Jewish community at a time when its birthrate was also falling. By the end of the 1920s, 40 percent of Germany's Jews would be forty-five years or older—a sure sign of a dying-out minority. And while this downswing was occurring, the number of Ostjuden in Germany was rising, up to more than a fifth of all Jews.

Clearly the fundamental nature of the German Jewish community was undergoing change, and not—at least from Baeck's perspective—for the better. Intermarriage, secularization, and alienation from their Gentile countrymen all ran counter to his deepest convictions, both as a devout rabbi and as a patriotic German. Since his days as a young scholar of Judaism, Baeck had been as committed to reviving Jewish pride and faith as he had been to attaining an amiable modus vivendi with non-Jews. His first and most important book, *The Essence of Judaism* (1905), laid out his duality of thought. Although the book argued for a strong, modern Judaism, based on acts more than faith, its tone, language, and logic revealed a thoroughly Germanic mind. In his way of reasoning as much as in his appearance, manner, and style, Baeck was a living bridge between Jews and Gentiles—an ideal figure to promote their reconciliation without Jews having to forego their heritage and identity. As his prominence as a teacher and scholar grew, Baeck assumed greater leadership responsibilities in the Berlin community, becoming head of the Central Welfare Office of German Jews, of the fraternal order B'nai B'rith, and of the General Association of German Rabbis, as well as a member of the executive committee of the Centralverein, still the chief voice of liberal German Jewry. In 1929 he extended his scope of involvement to Keren Hayesod, the Zionist fund-raising organization for Palestine.

With his nearly six-foot build, keen intellectual ability, talent as a teacher and conciliator, and dignified, formal *bürgerlich* manner, Baeck engendered a degree of respect among Jews (and some non-Jews) unmatched by any other Jewish leader. Soon he was spoken of as the "chief rabbi" of Berlin—the spiritual and moral head of that community and, by virtue of Berlin's size and stature, the leader of all Germany's Jews. In this capacity Baeck sought to reach out to the various branches of the community—liberals and Zionists, war veterans and orthodox—to revive their common Jewish heritage. Unwittingly he was preparing himself for a test of leadership far greater than he could ever have imagined.

The internal "Jewish concerns" that weighed so heavily on Leo

Baeck's mind during the Weimar era did not trouble many of his core-religionists. Anti-Semitism—and the specter of violence that hovered around it—*did* worry them, but most looked for peace of mind and protection under Germany's legal system or by becoming more "invisible"—less obvious as Jews. To many assimilated Jews, Jewishness was akin to being left-handed or bald—a regrettable but inescapable deviation from the norm, a nuisance, a social handicap, something mildly embarrassing and undesirable that one had to cope with as best as one could.

Other, more stark realities preoccupied the citizens of Germany in the wake of Versailles. Chief among them was economic hardship. Bella Fromm watched with consternation and regret as a "warm-hearted and kind" King Ludwig was bundled off into exile,[43] and German political life deteriorated into gun battles in the streets. She also winced at "radical" outbursts against Jews in her childhood home of Kitzingen and lashed back, in the privacy of her diary, at the right-wing parties sowing hatred of the Jews among their growing ranks.[44] ("It is sickening," she wrote of one Nazi rally. "My people have lived here for centuries. They have always been good Germans and have proved their loyalty and their patriotism over and over again.")[45] But Fromm had her own future to worry about first. When her parents had died during the war, they had left her their vineyards and old homestead. But runaway inflation soon devoured this inheritance, and Fromm was forced to find work to support herself and her young daughter, Gonny. Vivacious, charming, and attractive, she gravitated to Weimar's more exclusive social circles, particularly to the aristocratic and worldly diplomatic corps. When her financial situation turned bleak in the fall of 1928, she decided to fashion a career by building on these top-drawer connections, as well as her upbringing as "something of a bluestocking."[46] In short order she was hired to be a society columnist for the Ullstein papers in Berlin, with the assignment of writing lively, entertaining pieces "in the American manner."[47] Accustomed to speaking and writing forthrightly, Fromm soon ran afoul of the norms of this form of journalism. After reading her first piece, her editor, Dr. Carl Misch, realized he had better spell them out for her:

A social reporter does not write realistically. Just remember this: Every ambassadress is a beauty. Every minister is an excellent politician—the best in the world, in fact. Every newcomer in the diplomatic corps is always the shining star of the homeland's Foreign Office. If you remember these things you can never go far wrong.[48]

It was advice more suited to a hostess of tea parties than to a professional reporter, but Fromm heeded it, and it worked. She quickly learned how to put on, like an evening gown, a glib and agreeable public persona that allowed her to enter into and report on the lighthearted and superficial world of diplomatic receptions, saving her penetrating and trenchant thoughts about politics and public figures for her close friends and the pages of her diary. This double life suited her. Fromm happily immersed herself in the gathering of material for interviews of governmental officials, as well as for articles on ladies' fashions, the latest culinary triumphs, sports, and Berlin's social happenings, writing for the provincial press under the Jewish-aristocratic pseudonym "Isa von Franken." (The Ullstein house jealously held the exclusive right to her byline.)[49] She was a perceptive journalist, with a good ear for the revealing after-dinner remark, a knack for winning friends among Berlin's starched diplomatic set, and a resourceful way of getting a story under difficult circumstances. (When reporters were not invited to a formal reception hosted by President Paul von Hindenburg in 1931, Fromm slipped into a man's suit and loitered inconspicuously on a street corner, mentally noting the license-plate numbers of the arriving limousines so she could reconstruct the comings and goings for her column.)[50]

Most of all, Fromm honed a talent for gaining the confidence of high-level officials, who whispered to her their insights into Weimar politics, notably the startling rise of Adolf Hitler's National Socialist Party. They also offered her a measure of safety from these advancing forces. In 1920, for example, Dr. Max Glaser, a director of the Krupp works, tried to dispel her fears of growing anti-Semitism by murmuring, "Don't worry, Bella. I'll protect you if we have any pogroms."[51] Over the next decade Fromm would hear this reassurance repeated again and again by persons of great power and influence. It would be as if she were some little girl frightened of the dark, and they were well-meaning old gentlemen patiently trying to get her to go to sleep. Their guarantees of protection formed a cocoon around her. When thousands of nameless and ordinary Jews all over the country fell victim to taunts, abuse, and violence, Fromm was able to remain where she was, at the heart of Nazi Germany, a modern-day Hofjude on the lookout.

For Hans-Joachim Schoeps, still a teenager during the 1920s, such social issues as fighting anti-Semitism took a backseat to private, coming-of-age concerns. He was a bit of a rebel (expelled from one school, he nearly ran away from home once), who chafed against the values and ways of his comfortable, middle-class Berlin family and eagerly sought a new orientation and world for himself. Too young to have served in World War I, Schoeps and many of his contemporaries grew up envious of the generational camaraderie of the veterans, hungry to discovery a common cause and purpose to substitute for it.[52] This desire to belong to a movement larger than himself, separate from the wholly assimilated bourgeois world of his parents, sharpened Schoeps's curiosity about history (he devoured all of Shakespeare's historical dramas[53]), particularly religious history.

Schoeps's quest for a new kind of identity also involved him with the various youth groups that were springing up across Germany, picking up the banners of the romantic, middle-class Wandervögel movement. This had flourished briefly before World War I; had fallen in love with the glory of battle; and then been decimated by it, losing a quarter of its members in the blood-soaked trenches.[54] Arm in arm with other like-minded youth groups, the Wandervögel had declared a revolt against the materialistic, blindly self-absorbed mores of their elders and consecrated themselves to a liberating life of service to each other; to inner exploration; and to a higher, purer existence that put ideas ahead of deeds and steered clear of politics. Those of its members who survived the war came home convinced of the folly of petty nationalism and of the need for deeper human ties based on a kind of brotherly love.

This resurgent youth movement first captured Schoeps's attention during his final years in high school.[55] It appealed to him immediately because of its rejection of bourgeois values and its inner "passion" and spiritual aura, auguring a rebirth.[56] But the youth movement enticed his body as well as his mind: His nascent, fifteen-year-old homoerotic feelings were aroused and given a "healthy" outlet in the weekend hikes, earnest mountainside discussions, campfire chants, and nudist sun worshipping that made up the core of the movement's activities. (In this, Schoeps was hardly an anomaly; many young men attracted to the youth movement had homosexual inclinations.)[57]

In the 1920s the youth movement split into numerous factions, mimicking the ideological fault lines of Weimar's political life. Disappointed by this loss of unity and original purpose, Schoeps drifted from group to group, looking for just the right blend of friendship and philosophy.[58] By the mid-1920s, articles of his started appearing in youth-movement publications, lamenting the in-fighting that had torn the movement apart and calling for a return to the spirit of true brotherhood as exemplified by Jesus.[59] Schoeps had not only important philosophical reasons for urging unity but important personal reasons as well. As a Jew his position in the youth movement was precarious at best. The mainly Protestant Wandervögel had started out with a conservative bias against Jews, and although this bias had been tempered somewhat since, its enthusiasm for German regeneration steered it ever more toward a race-based, antimodern völkisch philosophy that was also anti-Semitic. Schoeps, incidentally, was by no means opposed to the rightist tilt of such groups as the Jungdeutsche Bund; the Deutscher Freischar; the Bündische Jugend; and, to a lesser extent, the Freideutsche movement. (He gravitated from the romantic Freideutsche group to the more pragmatic and organized Bundische Jugend in 1924.) Like many young Germans, he welcomed this steadfast Germanic chauvinism, this yearning for a uniquely Teutonic response to the challenges (and evils) of the modern era, this commitment to the group over the individual, this inwardness, this belief in an authoritarian structure of power and need for a strong charismatic leader to dominate it.

Deeply attached to traditional Prussian values, including a firm grounding in the law and tolerance, Schoeps felt at home in the mainstream of the youth movement, which in many ways presaged the Hitler Youth of the 1930s. Indeed, the Bündische Jugend, which he joined at age fifteen, early on debated the merits of National Socialist ideas, such as the clarion call for a new "staatliche Ordnung" (political order). Schoeps kept his distance from youth organizations that advanced any cause that could be construed as alien or detrimental to a mythically defined "Germanness," whether it was the *Blau-Weiss* movement of young Zionists or communist- or socialist-inspired groups.

In his admiration for bedrock conservative views, Schoeps was closely aligned with a sizable contingent of Germany's Jews during the Weimar era. As these Jews had defended the pillars of Germany's cultural heritage—Goethe, Kant, Schiller—against modernist trends in the arts, so did many of them cling to their nineteenth-century political allegiances when confronted by radical, left-wing movements. To some degree, they were motivated by the same old desire for acceptance—to become part of the crowd, to be "more German than the Germans." But, more to the point, they were also genuinely proud of their fatherland for what it had achieved—economically, politically, and socially—over the past half a century. In spite of the anti-Semitic resentment they had encountered as soldiers of the kaiser, their war service had strengthened their feelings of patriotism.

And if some right-wing "racial" elements were unwilling to admit "un-German" Jews into their ranks, then these same Jews were more than prepared to go off by themselves and form their own parallel organizations, espousing virtually the same positions—minus the anti-Semitism, of course. For example, World War I veterans, excluding Jews, banded together in November 1918 to form the Stahlhelm (Steel Helmet) to maintain their wartime solidarity, restore order, and resurrect the monarchy or anoint a "strong hand" in its stead to battle the "plague of parliamentarianism," the Social Democrats, and their frightening vision of a German republic. Many Jewish ex-soldiers reacted by rallying around Leo Löwenstein, a onetime rocket pioneer and army reserve captain (who was also the inventor of sonar), in an organization called the Reichsbund jüdischer Frontsoldaten (RjF) (Reich Association of Jewish War Veterans). The RjF attempted to counter the anti-Semites by calling attention to the war service of tens of thousands of Jews. Like the Stahlhelm, it sought to perpetuate the transcendent feeling of solidarity experienced on the front lines as an antidote to Weimar's fractious squabbling and violence.[60] From an initial membership of fifteen thousand, the RjF grew during the 1930s to twice that size—a number equivalent to a third of all the Jewish soldiers who had come back from the war. Even though it subscribed to a conservative agenda, in many ways compatible with that of the Nazis,[61] the RjF attracted Jewish veterans from across the political spectrum. The former *Feldrabbiner* Leo Baeck, for one, found time in the midst of all his other official duties to speak frequently at Reichsbund fund-raising affairs.[62]

Another conservative Jewish group that went to great lengths to stress its loyalty was the Verband nationaldeutscher Juden (VndJ) (Organization of Nationalistic German Jews). The VndJ came into being in March 1921, in Berlin, under the leadership of Max Naumann, a forty-six-year-old assimilated, middle-class Jew. Formerly a reserve officer in the Bavarian army, Naumann believed the roots of anti-Semitism lay in the perception that Jews were different from other Germans. Therefore, any Jewish activities that brought out a distinctive identity or values only confirmed this view and inflamed racial hatred. So Naumann and his followers vehemently rejected the Zionists and their notion of Jewish nationalism. The VndJ also turned its wrath on the Ostjuden who were pouring into German cities, giving good German Jews a bad name. Naumann scornfully labeled them a weakening "bacillus"[63] (ironically, Hitler and his henchmen would apply the same term to all Jews) and argued for their expulsion from German soil. In their wish to forge an "indissoluble bond" between German Gentiles and Jews,[64] members of the small (never more than 30,000)[65] organization disparaged even the moderate Centralverein for not shedding all semblance of Jewish identity and for defending their rights *as Jews.* In its wholesale embrace of all things Germanic and non-Jewish, the VndJ even endorsed the idea of a "German God" and observed such Christian holidays as Christmas.[66] (It was high time, Naumann wrote in an essay entitled "Ganz-Deutsche oder Halb-Deutsche" ["Hundred-Percent German or Half-German"], for all German Jews to close ranks behind the slogan "Deutschland über alles."[67] At first, Naumann regarded Hitler as a positive force on the political stage. He pooh-poohed the Nazi leader's anti-Semitism and vowed that he would have joined the Nazi party if only it had been possible.[68])

The impulse to affirm a quasi-spiritual Germanness grew stronger in Hans-Joachim Schoeps in the years leading to Hitler's assumption of power. In 1928 he enrolled at the over five-hundred-year-old University of Heidelberg and promptly joined a militaristic fraternity, Burschen von Bund, whose initiation rite involved the quaffing of red wine from a steel helmet.[69] By dint of his strong intellect and forceful personality (if not by his physical attractiveness as well) the twenty-year-old Schoeps attracted like-minded young men to him, who accepted his leadership. After a year at Heidelberg he brought together a few friends—all self-proclaimed "outsiders" from bourgeois society—to ponder the Nietzschean dictum of "subverting all values."[70] In 1930 Schoeps helped establish a new *Freideutsche Kameradschaft* (Free German Comradeship), deep in a forest in Thuringia,[71] while he continued to churn out articles rejecting materialistic, political concerns for a "turning inward" in search of existential truth. In this quest for an authentically German response to the dangers of a "surging" bolshevism, he reasoned, National Socialism would be "of little consequence": The power of the unfettered mind would easily triumph over the jackboot.[72]

As the interbellum period of the Weimar Republic branched out in many directions, groping tentatively for some new, galvanizing principle to guide Germany, German Jews joined in this wide-ranging exploration. In fact, their own eclectic search for a collective identity, for a secure and comfortable place in a strange and alien modern world, mirrored, in reverse, what Germany as a whole was undergoing. The left-wing German desire to be subsumed by larger social ideologies found its counterpart in the *conservative* Jewish longing to be part of *Deutschtum.* The striving of the radically nationalistic German Right for a social contract based on race and blood—*Gemeinschaft* over *Gesellschaft*—was paralleled by the Zionist longing for an ethnic Jewish nationalism and return to an ancestral Palestine. Dominant in the loosely defined middle ground between these two extremes, a faith in democratic values, the rule of law, and social justice sustained many Jews and non-Jews alike. Of the two groups, Jews were more attached to this relatively untilled liberal territory. It had been the seedbed of their emancipation and of their economic and social rise out of the ghetto and was the guarantor of their new freedoms. Of Germany's 525,000 Jews, between 300,000 and 400,000 looked to the shaky institutions of Weimar to safeguard their status and to a group like the Centralverein to plead their case, rationally, legitimately, and successfully.

Yet the overriding fact about "Jewish life" during the Weimar era was that there was no such thing. Rather, there were half a million individual Jews who were busily building their own lives and pursuing points of view along many different and independent lines. This, after all, was the import of assimilation—not to be defined and restricted by Jewishness, but to be as free as other Germans to find their own values, political affiliations, careers, and stations in life.

Thus the Czech-born journalist and editor Robert Weltsch could be drawn to Berlin to proselytize about a Jewish spiritual renewal under Zionism; a few blocks from his *Jüdische Rundschau* offices, the rabbi Leo Baeck could be simultaneously pleading the cause of Jewish World War I veterans *and* raising funds for Palestine. With little interest in any such strictly Jewish affairs, the recently arrived society columnist Bella Fromm could be off hobnobbing with high-ranking German generals and diplomats. To the northwest, in the Hanseatic port city of Hamburg, the banker Max Warburg could be assiduously shoring up his inflation-ravaged family firm, fighting back at anti-Semites with a quiet confidence that they could never really touch him. In Munich, in the eye of the gathering Nazi storm, the scientific giant Richard Willstätter could seek a refuge from anti-Jewish tirades on the city's streets, and from their reverberations in the university's lecture hall, by simply withdrawing into his sacred realm of scientific inquiry. In the depth of a Teutonic forest, a bright-eyed and inspired Hans-Joachim Schoeps could acclaim the power of idealistic Germanic youth to free the nation from its discredited past.

What all these individuals had in common was not their Jewishness, but their German predicament. The chauvinistic unity that Kaiser Wilhelm had exhorted by declaring all Germans equal in his eyes had given way to a bewildering proliferation of "isms," each ardently laying claim to the German soul. Jews moved and led within each of these competing circles, with their Jewishness being merely an appendage to a greater purpose. It was not yet clear that this proliferation of Jewish thought and political involvement would ultimately come to naught, that Jews in Germany would one day be defined not by what they said or did, how they voted, or what they wore, but by who they were. Out of the unity that had ushered in Weimar would arise another, darker kind, which would precipitate the republic's demise. With an ironic twist on the kaiser's words, it would take Adolf Hitler to bring the Jews together and consign them to a common fate by declaring, in essence, "From now on I recognize only Jews."

3

The Gathering Storm

As the strife-torn, self-doubting 1920s drew to a close, the flux of German political life suddenly and dramatically shifted. The Weimar Republic's effete and ineffectual parliamentary democracy ran aground on the shoals of its own endless squabbling (there were twelve chancellors in twelve years, compared to only five in the half century leading up to World War I), and popular disgust with it. The economy, already racked by runaway inflation and massive war reparations, was dealt a body blow by the worldwide depression that was triggered by the Wall Street stock market crash in October 1929. The Nazi Party rode this mounting discontent to national prominence. Merely a regional fringe party in 1928, it had attracted only 2.6 percent of the votes cast during that year's Reichstag elections. A scant two years later, in September 1930, nearly 6.5 half million Germans—or 18.3 percent of the total—cast their ballots for the Nazis. As a result, the Nazi Party emerged overnight as the second strongest party (after the Social Democrats) in the country. The Nazis had a clear program: get rid of the "bourgeois" parties, restore strong leadership, and steer Germany through a process of "national renewal" to restore its pride and greatness. They also had, in Adolf Hitler, a mesmerizing, fanatical leader with unrivaled oratorical powers. And the Nazis had a scapegoat to rally their anxious, volk-conscious countrymen against—the Jews. The Jews were to blame for all Germany's current woes. Therefore, the Jews had to be driven out of their positions of power and influence. To this end, the 1920 Nazi platform called for denying citizenship and public office to Jews, removing them from the press and other mass media, and dismissing them from their jobs so that unemployed "Aryan" Germans could find work.

"The Jew" was a Nazi caricature, fashioned out of blind hatred. It was a caricature drawn with all kinds of contradictions—the Jew as blood-sucking capitalist, the Jew as defiler of German blood and race, the Jew as international Bolshevik, the Jew as traitor to his or her country. In the Nazis' perverted language the word *Jew* became a lightning rod for all the seething rage and frustration that countless Germans felt as they watched their country being destroyed. In this twisted logic the Jews embodied all evil. They were antithetical to Germany's volk not because of anything they believed, but because of their innate biological nature. Jewishness was in their blood, so there was no way that a Jew could erase this identity. It did not matter how much a Jew ridiculed his fellow Jews or how often he prayed in a Christian church or how long he had forgotten to think of himself as a Jew. He was a Jew, nonetheless, and would remain one until the day he died.

The anti-Semitic far Right made this point crystal-clear when Walther Rathenau, the foreign minister and the most assimilated of German Jews, was gunned down on a Berlin street in June 1922. The Nazis had made the same point in their early public pronouncements, but hardly anyone had paid any attention. The Jews themselves did not fathom who they were up against. They did not realize this was a new kind of hatred—one they could not dodge by behaving like good Germans; by looking to the courts for redress; by quietly going about their daily business; or by simply ignoring the animosity and concentrating, instead, on building their common Jewish bond and a national homeland. And so, Germany's Jews individually adopted each and all these responses, each confident that his or her strategy was right and would succeed. Anyone who read the telltale signs of the times too darkly was disparaged as an "alarmist."[1] As Weimar came to a close, the Jews were not really frightened about their future or their safety.

In Munich, Richard Willstätter had little sense of what was happening because he lived in almost total isolation inside his new villa on the Möhlstrasse—physically and psychologically too far from the torchlit parades and the anti-Jewish curses to take note. Aside from his daily telephone conversations with his assistant, who was now running his laboratory on her own, Willstätter had almost no regular contact with the outside world. His daughter, Margarete, was immersed in her own scientific studies, equally content in this apolitical realm. "I live completely withdrawn," the Nobel laureate affirmed with some satisfaction in September 1929 to a colleague who had invited him to attend an international conference, "and I don't want to change this at all."[2] The death of his beloved mother two years before had only deepened his feeling of aloneness.

Wholly devoted to organic chemistry, Willstätter had no interest in other causes. He had dealt in his own way with the anti-Semites, and now he was done with them. The plight of the Jews did not move him because, at heart, he defined himself as a German scientist, not as a Jew. When the German Zionist leader Kurt Blumenfeld traveled to Munich to seek his support for Palestine (at the request of Chaim Weizmann, a fellow chemist and an admirer of Willstätter), the Nobel Prize winner was not responsive. At the mention of Weizmann's name, he bristled. "I'll have nothing to do with Weizmann. He's partially responsible for the death of German soldiers."[3] (He was referring to Weizmann's courting of British backing for a Jewish state during the World War I.) The adroit Blumenfeld then mentioned another supporter of Palestine whom Willstätter thought highly of—Albert Einstein. But this gambit, too, led nowhere. Willstätter simply expressed his envy of Einstein's ability to raise money for his own research. Exasperated, Blumenfeld ventured to suggest that Willstätter, after all, could not just ignore his ties to other Jews. To this remark, his irritated host retorted: "When it affects me, you can be sure that I will react."[4]

The shield of his splendid isolation protected Willstätter against other external demands as well. His industrialist friend and financial backer Carl Duisberg wrote saying it was Willstätter's duty to place his talents once again at the service of his country and to accept a senior research post at the Kaiser Wilhelm Institute for Chemistry in Berlin,[5] but Willstätter demurred. He wrote that he preferred to go on living as he was and proposed, in his stead, Otto Hahn, Lise Meitner, or Fritz Haber.[6] Fortunately, Willstätter could well afford to turn down an attractive offer like this; the newly formed chemical conglomerate IG Farben paid him well for synthesizing new chemicals, and the Rockefeller Foundation annually renewed its stipend for more basic enzyme-related studies.[7] This work sprang from a lifelong interest in narcotics, which led to the discovery of Avertin and other painkillers. Willstätter was not immune from suffering. In a letter to Haber a few years later, he would liken himself to Job, visited by trials to test his soul,[8] but he would vow to fight back not with rash words or deeds, but by raising the wall around him that much higher. The entreaties he received from abroad to teach and do research thus held no appeal for him. Germany, his country, and Munich, his home, were his deepest attachments— what he would cling to all at all costs.

If Willstätter's retreat inward represented an extreme form of escape from growing anti-Semitic tensions, he was certainly not alone in devoting his attention to other matters and leaving German politics for someone else to sort out. (Many Jews emulated Thomas Mann in disdaining the political arena.) The Zionists, for example, were busy exhorting Jews to return to a revived Judaism. Throughout the 1920s, many of them tried to turn the onus of anti-Semitism to their advantage, first, by tacitly conceding that their enemies were right—Jews *were* different, a distinct volk—and then by urging their fellow Jews to take greater pride in this racial identity. Jewish solidarity, grounded in such feelings, could also serve as the best bulwark against the hatred of groups like the Nazis.[9] But beyond that, the German Zionists under Blumenfeld did not take any steps to confront anti-Semitism head-on, believing their task was to accentuate the positive by promoting the virtues of the Jewish community. This strategy was maintained until the September 1930 election, when the Nazis showed they were a national force to be reckoned with.

As the editor of the major Zionist newspaper in the country, Robert Weltsch put out issue after issue of the *Jüdische Rundschau* (Jewish Observer) from his inconspicuous Meineckestrasse office, lauding the achievements of Jewish settlers in Palestine and of Jewish artists, philosophers, and athletes in Germany and all over the world. He scrupulously avoided any discussion of Weimar political affairs. By taking any position on these matters, Weltsch thought that the *Jüdische Rundschau* would only play into the hands of the anti-Semites, who would rail: *Here are the Jews meddling where they have no business.*[10] So, when the incidence of anti-Jewish harassment, charges of ritual murder, and violence started to creep upward in the late 1920s, readers of the *Jüdische Rundschau* would not hear of these problems in its pages or sense that they should feel outraged. Privately, Weltsch was not critical of all the nationalistic ideals the Nazis were advancing, some of which corresponded to what he thought Germany's Jews needed for *their* renewal.[11]

Finally, in 1930, the Zionistische Vereinigung für Deutschland (ZVfD) (Zionist Organization for Germany) woke up to the fact that as long as all German Jews could not emigrate to Palestine overnight (a prospect made more remote by recent Arab violence there), they would have to come to grips with the ever-more- imminent dangers they faced at home in Germany. The struggle with other Jews for control over the Jewish soul would have to defer to the fight for Jewish survival. In September 1930 the ZVfD agreed, for the first time, to join forces with its arch ideological enemy, the assimilationist Centralverein deutscher Staatsbürger jüdischer Glaubens (Central Organization of German Citizens of the Jewish Faith), as well as with the conservative Reichsbund jüdischer Frontsoldaten (RjF) (Reich Association of Jewish War Veterans), to oppose anti-Semitic candidates in the upcoming national elections that month. However, the various Jewish organizations could not agree on which party they should throw their support behind. The old philosophical rifts remained too deep to span, so they ended up not endorsing any of Hitler's adversaries. When the votes were counted on the evening of September 14, Jews of all political persuasions were shocked to discover that no single party had stood up successfully for them. The moderate parties were in disarray, and the dreaded nationalist Right was clearly in ascendancy.

Oddly enough, once the election was over, the *Jüdische Rundschau* again devoted most of its editorial space to telling its readers about what was going on in faraway Palestine, not in the streets of Berlin. It was as if the setback at the polls had only confirmed the Zionists' misgivings about getting involved in German politics.

Like most German Jews, Bella Fromm could not so easily overlook the implications of this Nazi success. In many of the posh social circles she frequented, she noted a "touch of panic," even though she did not feel any danger herself. Some Jews were beginning to murmur about getting out of Germany before it was too late. These fears came closer to home on September 19, when Fromm observed a parade of Nazi "roughnecks" swaggering toward the Reichstag, which was about to hold its opening session, smashing the windows of Jewish shops along the Leipziger Strasse and chanting "Germany awake! Jew perish!"[12] (Robert Weltsch was too distracted by personal tragedy to notice these warning signals. On October 18 his wife and fellow Zionist, Martha, died suddenly of a heart attack; she was only thirty-seven years old.)

Still, it was possible to see matters in a larger, more reassuring perspective. Yes, anti-Semitic elements were gaining ground inside Germany, but so was a healthy awareness of Jewishness—what so many Jews had, up to now, been so reluctant or ashamed to acknowledge. Leo Baeck, ever eager to subsume conflict within a greater moral framework, looked beyond the Nazi threat to the promise of Palestine, like a man in a rat-infested tenement greeting the distant dawn. He, too, hailed the birth of the "new man, the new Jew" in the far-away desert settlements—both as a noble and uplifting process and as a future that Germany's Jews might have to prepare themselves to accept.

To the north, in Hamburg, Max Warburg found consolation not so much in thoughts of another homeland as in the security of his own position. Although he pronounced the Nazis' September jump in popularity "serious," the sixty-three-year-old banker retained his fundamentally optimistic outlook.[13] He was, after all, a pillar of the German economy, a true patriot who had refused to sign the Versailles treaty, a friend of the powerful—in short, an untouchable. The best way to cope with Nazi threats was to maintain a low profile, avoiding any provocation. Warned in 1932 about a plot to kill him, Warburg declined to speak up. ("Personally," wrote a somewhat frustrated Stephen Wise, head of the American Jewish Congress, "I have no confidence in the capacity of Warburg to act with vigor on Jewish questions.")[14] Warburg, too, saw a bright spot on the horizon for German Jews in Palestine, even though most Germans tended to think of him as uninterested in strictly Jewish concerns, if not as an outright anti-Zionist.[15] In fact, Warburg's first visit to Palestine in 1929, accompanying his brother Felix, had sparked his desire to see a Jewish homeland created there. Echoing

Robert Weltsch, he foresaw the possibility that some kind of peaceful coexistence could be worked out between Jews and Arabs.

Most of Warburg's energies were invested in sustaining the fortunes of his bank. Under his growth-oriented management, M. M. Warburg and Company had expanded exponentially during the 1920s, borrowing heavily to do so. In 1928 the bank occupied 192 seats on 87 different boards of directors, and its partners held 86 directorships, in Germany, Austria, the Netherlands, Czechoslovakia, and the United States.[16] M. M. Warburg was now the largest and most prominent private bank in the country. In large part, its branching out abroad was designed to circumvent Germany's postwar financial vagaries and give the bank safe foreign footholds in case anti-Semitic forces ever came to power at home. But the outcome of the September 1930 election and the financial fallout—with panicked foreign banks pulling their funds out and the German stock market losing 10 percent of its value—took Warburg by surprise and brought the bank to the brink of collapse. To save it, Warburg had to turn to his brother Paul, then a partner in the New York banking firm of Kuhn, Loeb and Co. (and a founder of the Federal Reserve Board)—who had accurately predicted the coming economic crisis.[17] Paul poured half his personal fortune and all his financial acumen into rescuing the Hamburg firm, but even this effort, coupled with an influx of cash from a third brother, Felix, did not reverse the downward spiral. Paul's unexpected death in January 1932—brought on, some family members groused, by his brother's financial mistakes[18]—deprived Max of a trusted adviser and undercut the bank's chance of long-term recovery. So as the Weimar Republic was unraveling, it was the prospect of bankruptcy, far more than the possibility that the Nazis might come to power, that weighed on Warburg's mind. In New York to attend his brother's funeral, Warburg conveyed the impression to American Jewish leaders that he "discounted the effects of the coming into power of the Hitlerites . . . the resulting responsibilities would act as a sobering influence and they would not carry out many of the planks of their platform, which were made part of it largely in the nature of bait to win adherents."[19] The Nazis, in other words, would be brought to their senses by the harsh realities of ruling Germany—if it ever came to that. In voicing this sanguine thought, Max Warburg joined a growing chorus of German business and financial leaders.

From her chats with friends in the government in Berlin, Bella Fromm could sense that a sea change was in the offing. German parliamentarianism was definitely on the way out.[20] Astonishingly, few of the old guard of Junkers and generals expressed alarm at the thought of Hitler stepping forward to take its place. In silent dismay Fromm listened as one high-ranking intimate after the other confided to her his admiration for the Nazi "gang"—this "plebeian movement," as she disdainfully jotted in her diary.[21] Before her very eyes, the *feine Leute* (well-bred people) she felt so much at ease among at cocktail parties and on the tennis court were showing their true "brown" colors, their aversion for her people. Her friends were all sitting down to have tea with Adolf Hitler, the man of the moment.[22] Depressed by this situation and in ill health, Fromm took the cure at Bad Reichenhall, literally in the shadow of Hitler's Alpine retreat in Bavaria, only to find the narrow streets clogged with Brown Shirts, stomping their way to the Führer's doorstep.[23] Back in Berlin, on the day before Hitler asked President Paul von Hindenburg to name him chancellor, Fromm's boss Louis Ullstein laughed off the vision of marching hordes that she had brought back with her. "You're beginning to hear voices, Bella," he said. "You ought to do something about those nerves of yours."[24]

While the movement that preached hatred of the Jews was gaining momentum, many Jews, especially those in Berlin, were preoccupied by fights with each other. At stake was influence and control over Germany's largest Jewish community, or *Gemeinde.* This was, in essence, a struggle for the hearts and minds of German Jewry. The Nazis may have presented a grave challenge to Jewish survival, but instead of closing ranks to face this shared threat, the Jews were squabbling over whose response to this threat was correct and who could best lead the community through the crisis. The brief, ad hoc united Jewish front against the common foe could not hold. The Zionists, for their part, saw their message as being vindicated: The Nazi rise meant that the "Jewish problem" could not be solved within the Diaspora; Jews could find peace only within the borders of their own nation. Palestine was the only real solution. To the Zionists, the popularity of Nazism unmasked the lie of Jewish equality and acceptance in Western society. Only by abandoning this illusion and adopting the Zionist creed could the Jews of Germany be saved. Both Jews and non-Jews had to be convinced of this truth. It had been clear for some time that the ZVfD held certain philosophical views about Jewish identity that closely matched those of the rabidly

anti-Semitic Right. Now there was good reason to make this congru-
ence of outlook better known to a larger audience, to show that at least
some German Jews accepted the premises of the coming "German
renewal," specifically that nations should be defined along racial lines. If
this was right for "Aryan" Germans, shouldn't it be right for the Jews as
well? Shouldn't the Jews have their own state?

It was with this goal in mind that Robert Weltsch began to publish
the *Jüdische Rundschau* on a more frequent, monthly, basis starting in January 1932, "to acquaint the non-Jewish public in Germany with the
aims and activities of the Zionist movement."[25] In a letter written about
a month later, he revealed his underlying premise: Jews cannot deal
effectively with the Nazis' brand of anti-Semitism, for it exists mainly
as a political tool to stir up the masses. Rather than oppose it, Jews must
stand firmly by their Judaism, and then most of the "abnormalities" of
the German-Jewish relationship will disappear.[26] (Privately, in a February
23, 1932, letter to Chaim Weizmann, Weltsch did worry about "dangerous events" ahead for Germany's Jews, but none of these fears was articulated in the pages of his newspaper.)[27]

Meanwhile, the task of defending Jews against Nazi calumny was left
largely to the Centralverein. With a staff of sixty operating out of its
Berlin headquarters, the mainstream organization began directing its
propaganda attacks more specifically at the Nazi Party after 1928, realizing that this party was its most dangerous enemy.[28] It had to do so
cautiously, working closely but quietly with the Social Democrats, cam-
ouflaging its sponsorship of brochures and flyers to ward off any anti-
Jewish backlash.[29] The Centralverein and other liberal-minded Jews were
fighting a two-front war, battling both the Nazis and the Zionists, who
were only making matters worse by boasting about how different and
un-German the Jews were. So, in the fall of 1930, as Jewish cemeteries
were being desecrated with swastikas, members of the Berlin Gemeinde
were locked in a bitter leadership feud. Some older liberal Jews labeled
the Zionists "Jewish Nazis"[30] and inveighed against a "return to the
ghetto,"[31] while a Zionist splinter group, the Jüdische Volkspartei (Jewish People's Party), called for unity among Jews worldwide and the
building of a Jewish state in Palestine. In the midst of all this verbal
sniping, Max Naumann's tiny band of "nationalistic German Jews" ran
its own "German list" of candidates. Leo Baeck, as usual, tried to build
bridges between the warring factions and to end the infighting, but to

no avail. The liberals refused to bury the hatchet with the despised Zionists for a second time.[32]

When the votes were tallied on November 30, the liberals had retained their hold on power (with the backing of 41,704 Berlin Jews, gaining twenty-four seats on the Gemeinde's governing body). Still, the Jüdische Volkspartei had made impressive gains—its 25,526 votes (and fourteen seats) represented a 52 percent increase over 1926.[33] After this election, the battle over strategy continued, as the Centralverein kept drumming its tried-and-true message that "the German Jew is a German, and he remains so even when countless millions of Nazis dispute it."[34] The Zionists countered this message by insisting that Jews were flailing against windmills by trying to stop the greatest wave of anti-Semitism in 150 years. The simple fact of their existence in Germany was the reason for this hostility.[35] Jews had to wake up to this fact. At the same time, editorials in the *Jüdische Rundschau* assailed the Centralverein for seeking to "monopolize" the Jewish response to the Nazis.[36] Meanwhile, the increasing incidence of violence aimed at Jews could no longer be ignored, and both liberal and Zionist newspapers began to carry more reports of such acts.[37]

Exerting his influence on the conscience of German Jewry, Leo Baeck peered beyond the economic hardship and abuse of the day, characterizing them as potentially a "blessing in disguise" if they induced Jews to create a "new life, a new Mensch, a return to true life, true humanity."[38] The same month a mob of roughly one thousand Nazis attacked Jews as they were leaving the synagogue off the Kurfürstendamm on the first day of Rosh Hashanah, sending a clear signal to Baeck and the entire community: The Nazis meant business. The new man *they* were creating was a mortal enemy of the Jews.

Back in June 1927 Max Warburg had been lavishly feted by Hamburg's business and civic elites, as well as by his fellow Jews, on the occasion of his sixtieth birthday. He was lauded for his role in founding the city's university, for bolstering its economy, and for increasing "the honor of the Jewish race."[39] He was hailed as one of Hamburg's leading citizens. In many ways his life had reached its pinnacle; thereafter, his outlook was colored by these triumphs. Hence, when events turned ugly for Germany's Jews in the years that followed, Warburg was slow to appreciate their seriousness. He viewed these developments with concern, but not alarm;[40] his optimistic nature would not be so easily altered. What Germany's Jews needed, Warburg reasoned, was simply more money to defend themselves. Emigration, he thought, did not offer a realistic alternative for most Jews, now that so many countries, especially the United States, were closing their doors to emigrants in light of the worldwide economic depression (By 1933, for example, the total number of German Jews admitted into the United States would be only 535,[41] out of a scant 23,000 aliens admitted during that entire year.[42]) In early 1929 Warburg reported on these shrinking immigration quotas to officers of the Hilfsverein der deutschen Juden (the German Jewish Welfare Association), which he headed.[43]

If there was one place where Jews could still look for spiritual and material sustenance, it was Palestine. After his initial visit there in 1929, Warburg had become enthusiastic about that country's long-term potential for economic development and settlement.[44] As he busied himself promoting schemes to finance the development of Palestine and to relieve the economic plight of Jews elsewhere in Europe, Warburg would continue to discount the likelihood of Hitler's coming to power, let alone carrying out any of his shrill threats against Germany's Jews.

As a self-proclaimed "German conscious" Jew,[45] with a "völkisch rootedness,"[46] Hans-Joachim Schoeps eyed the groundswell of fervor for the Nazi movement differently, with far more ambivalence. His worldview was essentially and proudly Germanic,[47] as much in rebellion against "bourgeois society" and its "betrayal" of Germany's ideals as was Hitler's. Both the Nazi Party and the post–World War I youth movement, in which Schoeps played a prominent part, stressed that the bonds of blood and soil were more meaningful for Germany's identity and renewal than was parliamentary democracy. In the small circle of like-minded, youthful intellectuals who were attracted to his newly formed Deutsche Freischar (German Volunteer Corps) in 1930, there was a desire for self-sacrifice and "spiritual regeneration" that echoed the rhetoric of the right-wing nationalists. Where Schoeps and his followers broke ranks with groups like the Nazi Party was, first, on the defining question of race and, second, over the method of achieving these idealized ends. Like the Zionist thinker Martin Buber, whom he admired greatly, Schoeps believed in an inner process of spiritual reawakening—a revolution within the mind. This belief was reflected in his attempts, in various essays written during these years, to define a systematic Jewish theology, The Nazis preferred to start their revolution on the sidewalks. For this reason alone, Schoeps dismissed them as unworthy for falling into the same political-action trap that had undone the earlier youth movement. (Still, he conceded that Nazi philosophy was "ethically of high stature.")[48] A bare-knuckled political brawl over power, Schoeps believed, was not the way to realign the German soul. In his arch-conservatism, in his love of the monarchy and Prussian order-liness, Schoeps considered the Nazis too much enraptured by violent upheaval, too eager to sweep away the traditions and principles that had infused the pre-Weimar Germany he adored and wanted to restore. To deter their rise, he considered it necessary for truly conservative groups to join forces and assert a countervailing authority.

On the position of Jews in a Germany dominated by the Nazis, Schoeps assumed a conciliatory position. He rejected outright the notion that *all* Jews were, by definition, anathema to a Nazi-run state. Instead, certain Jews—and here he clearly excluded the Zionists and the eastern Jews, whose hearts lay elsewhere—were so steeped in German culture and values as to be inseparable from their fatherland. These ties were equivalent to blood or race and could survive even in the face of unceasing hatred and ostracism, if it came to that. In his patriotic sen-timents Schoeps reaffirmed what a leading proponent of Jewish eman-cipation, Gabriel Riesser, had vowed a hundred years before: "It is ter-rible to be treated with hatred in one's fatherland; but it would be a thousand times more terrible to hate one's fatherland."[49] That this say-ing might someday need to be repudiated did not strike Schoeps as even remotely possible.

The problem for Schoeps, as it was for all Germany's Jews, was to sort out what the Nazis *said* they were going to do from what they might actually *do* if they ever came to power. Politics was a shouting match in Weimar's waning days, and the words hurled about by back-alley orators wearing swastika armbands carried the same incendiary charge as sticks of dynamite. The Nazis were stirring up the masses with their campaign rhetoric of getting back at the Jews—eliminating them from Germany's cultural and political life, denying them their rights, and throwing the Ostjuden out of the country. But most Jews—like Max Warburg—con-cluded that if the Nazis ever took over the government, with Hitler at the helm, they would tone down this outrageous talk and "behave," or "sober down" as Warburg's brother Felix put it.[50] Power would tame the wild street brawlers.

In late 1931 the optimists received a rude jolt. The Frankfurt police made public some documents belonging to the Hessian Nazi Party that revealed Hitler's intent to carry out his threats. These documents, known as the Boxheim papers (after the estate near Worms where National Socialist leaders had gathered to draft them), contained a blueprint for a Nazi coup in case the communists tried to seize power. They also described the "ruthless measures"[51] that Nazi Party would take against political opponents and the planned repression of the Jews, including barring them from economic activities and slowly starving them to death.[52] The Boxheim papers were signed by Werner Best, a local Nazi leader in Hesse, but they bore the imprimatur of the top echelon of the party. They provoked a public uproar. When the Zionists Robert Weltsch and Kurt Blumenfeld read the published documents, they were shaken to the core by what they saw as a scheme to destroy German Jewry. Weltsch's earlier hope—that Jews and Nazis might reach some kind of modus vivendi—was shattered.[53] In an article in the assimilationist *Centralverein Zeitung*, Ludwig Holländer condemned the Boxheim documents, saying they exposed a Nazi agenda that had not changed since the days of the Munich putsch: "Boxheim is the systematic summary of all that the Nazis have said, dozens of times, all that they are emphatically and deliberately striving toward."[54] A week later another essay in the same newspaper blasted the alleged Nazi plan for "revealing an attitude that will not stop at any atrocity."[55] At the same time, the *Centralverein Zeitung* urged its readers not to panic: Calm and faith in Germany's system of laws remained the Jews' best defense. These words of advice were then followed by a sunny assessment of the political climate. The high point of Hitler's popularity had passed, the newspaper said, and "it appears that even in a worsening of the economic situation Hitler and the NSDAP [National Socialist German Workers' Party, or Nazis] will never have the opportunity to win over the majority of the German people by democratic means."[56]

Many German foes of the Nazis—both Jews and Gentiles—inclined toward this belief. Even if worse came to worse, the Nazis would not do what they had threatened. Even though Max Warburg now admitted it was possible that Hitler would either assume power himself or install Nazis in the cabinet,[57] he did not lose any sleep pondering the consequences that this arrangement might bode for the Jews.

At the editorial offices of the *Jüdische Rundschau*, Robert Weltsch was still reluctant to harp on anti-Semitic harangues by the radical Right. This was not the purpose of his newspaper. He had a more important, positive message to convey. His job was to win over more Germans to the notion of a distinctive Jewish identity and a Jewish homeland, for herein lay the true solution to Europe's "Jewish problem." Hence, aside from a report on an interview that Hitler had with foreign journalists, in which the Nazi Führer refused to answer questions about the Box-heim papers,[58] the *Jüdische Rundschau* skirted this inflammatory story, leaving it to other newspapers to cover. Even when the Nazis divulged, in February 1932, that they *would* take away the citizenship of Jews who had entered Germany after 1914 and force them out of the country and prohibit all remaining Jews from participating in German life,[59] the Zionist organ did not give any space to this unsettling confirmation of the Boxheim papers.

In her diary Bella Fromm soberly observed that the National Socialists were "causing trouble everywhere."[60] She found the "brown plague" increasingly visible at the social affairs she attended, but this revelation of their plans for the Jews did not cause her to think about leaving the country. She was, after all, an acquaintance of Franz von Papen, who was shortly to be Germany's next chancellor, and a close friend of General Kurt von Schleicher, whose door stood open to her at any time.[61] What did she have to fear? What preoccupied Fromm was the utter stupidity and shortsightedness of conservative friends who were flocking like sheep to Hitler's camp, thinking they could use him as a "tool" to further their own ends. Little did they know who the real master was, she dourly noted.[62]

Throughout 1932 it was hard to tell who was going to be the new master of Germany. That year was seen by many, including the Jewish community, as a decisive one. The Nazis would either gain more strength and take over the government or be beaten back, once and for all. It was a roller-coaster year, kicked off by Hitler wooing top German industrialists during a January speech in Düsseldorf and by the ominous closing of the University of Berlin because of anti-Semitic protests. Jews responded to these danger signs by meeting, at the end of the month, to discuss forming a unified organization to protect their economic well-being.[63] (In a letter written around this time, Robert Weltsch privately criticized Jewish efforts to combat anti-Semitism, saying his people ought to affirm their Judaism and Jewish identity instead;

then the "abnormalities" of the current situation would disappear.[64] It was the Jews' attempt to assimilate themselves, trying to pass as real Germans, that was infuriating the völkisch Right. In the *Jüdische Rundschau* he was nearly as blunt, pointing out that the Zionists found a "tragic confirmation" of their views in Hitler's growing popularity.[65])

The presidential election in March gave Jews a chance to voice their opposition to Hitler, if only by casting their ballots for the conservative old soldier Paul von Hindenburg. The first round of voting was inconclusive. Hitler failed to gain the 15 million votes he had boasted of (he got only 11.5 million) but still came in a formidable second. The runoff elections the following month saw the Nazi leader pick up 2 million votes but again fail to defeat the venerated, eighty-two-year-old Hindenburg. Then the moderate Brüning government resigned, with the dubious and unpredictable Papen becoming the new chancellor. Meanwhile, the drumbeat of threatened anti-Semitic measures grew louder: The Prussian parliament passed a law barring Jewish ritual slaughter and dismissing Jewish actors from German theaters.[66] Hindenburg's earlier ban of the SA (Sturmabteilung, the quasi-military Brownshirts) and SS (Schutzstaffel, Hitler's elite guard) was lifted. Nazi placards in Berlin told Jews to "prepare yourself for Palestine."[67] An Italian newspaper carried a report on Hermann Goering's plan for Germany's Jews, calling for an end to marriage between them and "Aryans," the expulsion of the Ostjuden, and the firing of any other Jews who were deemed to be antinationalist or "internationalist."[68] At about the same time, the Nazi leader in Prussia, Wilhelm Kube, mused aloud about "cleansing" the bureaucracy of Jews.[69] In the late July elections for the Reichstag, the Nazis did not increase their numerical support, but they did edge closer to parliamentary power by adding 123 seats, for a total of 230. This election made them the largest faction in the Reichstag, although still not a majority. Nearly two out of three Germans had voted *against* Hitler's party.

Robert Weltsch reacted to this election by running an editorial stating that, although the *Jüdische Rundschau* had previously condemned the Nazis' policies and plans for the Jews, it understood their "psychological and intellectual basis" and respected their goal of national renewal. This was, after all, the same as what the Zionists wanted for the Jews. "We believe," the unsigned essay went on, "that a nationally conscious Jewry could find its way to a modus vivendi with an inwardly strengthened German nationalism, freed from the dross of a crude anti-Semitism."[70]

Weltsch was giving voice to a new assertiveness within the German Zionist movement. Sensing that the liberal, assimilationist position was crumbling, the ZVfD was smugly saying *I told you so*, appealing to Jews to switch their allegiance to a revitalized Judaism—one that, in many ways, paralleled Nazism. Jews have to fight "life with life," Kurt Blumenfeld told a Berlin audience in May: A creative, dynamic Judaism was the best way to counter an equally vital German nationalism.[71] (Not bothering to conceal its Schadenfreude, the *Jüdische Rundschau* declared that a victory for Hitler would mean "a collapse of the Jewish assimilationist way of thinking.")[72]

The Zionist appeal for wider support translated into more intensified internecine fighting, especially among Berlin's Jews. Control of the Gemeinde was again at stake. Once again, Leo Baeck worked to defuse the conflict, joining with other leaders of the Berlin lodge of B'nai B'rith in calling for tolerance and cochairing a meeting of regional Jewish organizations to orchestrate a united Jewish response to the Nazis.[73] Baeck was spending more and more of his time as a peacemaker in the Jewish community, arguing for reason and calm in a time of uncertainty, resisting the impulse to fear the worst. Unity was an admirable aspiration for the Jews but increasingly elusive. If anything, the Nazi surge was widening the gaps within the community, with each faction insisting vociferously that its strategy was the right one. At one extreme the Jewish nationalist leader Max Naumann went as far as to propose that Jews should join the Nazi Party.[74]

As tensions and anxieties grew—Joseph Goebbels issued what amounted to a call for a pogrom in an article published in August— Richard Willstätter quietly celebrated his sixtieth birthday by taking a vacation by himself on Lake Poschiavo, near the Italian-Swiss border.[75] Far from his scientific labors and the turmoil of a Nazi-ridden Munich, he somberly pondered the course that his life and career had taken. His energy, his curiosity, his creativity all now seemed spent. The years of working doggedly in isolation, pretending he could carry on as before, had exacted their toll. Willstätter realized now—perhaps for the first time—that resigning his cherished university post over a matter of principle had broken him. Abandoned by his only surviving child—Margarete had married Ernst Bruch, a physician, in May—he would have to face his approaching old age all alone. On the lake's lapping shore he thought back upon his life and saw its losses and failures loom larger

than any successes.[76] This depressed state lingered. When Chaim Weizmann visited Willstätter toward the end of the year, he found his fellow
chemist mired in the same gloomy mood that had descended upon other
Munich Jews.[77]

Hans-Joachim Schoeps was similarly preoccupied with personal matters that summer. Completing his doctoral studies in Leipzig, he had
abandoned a dissertation on Kafka in lieu of one that would lay out the
"basis for a systematic Judaism"—a theme that he had been mulling
over for some time.[78] His ruminations led to a series of essays, which he
succeeded in having published under the title *Jüdische Glaube in dieser Zeit*
(Contemporary Jewish Faith). These essays were an iconoclastic assault
on established Jewish thinking in all camps, orthodox as well as liberal,
taking them to task for confusing morality and religion and for neglect-
ing the historical dimension of Judaism.[79] Only a new definition of
their faith, clearly opposed to secularism, could give Jews the inner
strength they needed to survive the present period of grave danger. Neither the liberal hope for tolerance—through denial of their Jewishness—nor the Zionist credo of racial solidarity (within a Jewish volk)
had any real validity, he declared. Neither could save the Jews. Zionism
Schoeps found the most despicable for its bogus claim to represent a
return to a "true" Jewish identity. In a letter to Max Brod, with whom
he was then editing a posthumous collection of Kafka's writings, he
denounced the Zionist movement as a latter-day version of "Western
imperialism."[80] (Shortly thereafter he and Brod would break off their
correspondence, realizing that their views diverged too widely.)

By now Schoeps had set his sights on an academic career. But he soon
found his way in that direction blocked by anti-Semitism. In Marburg,
where he had studied briefly, Schoeps had been told he had no hope of
earning a doctorate since he was Jewish. Then, ironically, after receiving
his degree in the Saxon city of Leipzig, he learned he would be prevented from doing his student teaching there because he was Prussian.[81]
(Later, in Berlin, Schoeps found out that teaching posts were not open
to Jews.)[82] As the year drew to a close, his long-term prospects were
cloudy, to say the least. Schoeps hoped his horoscope for 1933 would
offer some better predictions.

The November 1932 Reichstag election campaign galvanized the
German public as perhaps never before. The nation now clearly stood at
a crossroads. Papen's leadership was weak and uncertain. Angered by

Hindenburg's persistent refusal to name him chancellor, Hitler was becoming increasingly petulant, ranting against the Jews. In mid-October he called for a boycott of Jewish businesses.[83] Fear was spreading among the Jewish community: Their rights—even their lives—might not be protected much longer.

Then a strange thing happened. The Nazis, short on cash, their energies drained, suffered a setback at the polls. Two million German voters switched their allegiance, mostly to the conservative German National Party, and the Nazi Party lost thirty-four seats in the Reichstag. Overnight the myth of Nazi inevitability evaporated. Jews and other opponents of Hitler's forces rejoiced. The most important result of this election, Robert Weltsch proclaimed in an editorial two days afterward, was to rule out "once and for all" the possibility of the Nazis gaining power by means of the ballot box.[84] (He did not bother to consider any alternative routes.) Then, at General Schleicher's urging, with thoughts of striking a deal with Hitler to end the parliamentary impasse, Papen abruptly resigned. The Nazi leader spurned a power-sharing offer: He wanted the chancellorship for himself, without any strings attached. So the aged and nearly senile Hindenburg turned to another old soldier, Schleicher, to form a new government.

Meanwhile, the Nazis suffered another defeat, this time in Thuringia. The *Centralverein Zeitung* crowed: Hitler's boast that 1932 would be a "year of decision" for him and his party had not come true.[85] In a speech delivered in Halle, the once intimidating Nazi Führer was seen by one observer to have grown "small and pitiable."[86] In this uncertain moment, the political signals were still mixed, hard to act on. At a reception hosted by her friend, the American consul George Messersmith, three days before Christmas, Bella Fromm listened to his cryptic prediction—"There are going to be fireworks pretty soon, unless I'm mistaken"[87]—and found it convincing. Scarcely a week later, she learned of intrigues being concocted against Schleicher and passed this news to him at a party. Looking pale and tired, her powerful protector, now head of the German government, tried to reassure her: "You journalists are all alike," he laughed. "You make a living out of professional pessimism."[88] His dear Bella should not lose any sleep worrying about him; he could hold off the Nazis.

The dawning of 1933 seemed to prove Schleicher right. In his New Year's address Hitler sounded deflated; for a change, he made no claims of imminent victory.[89] His party stood on the verge of bankruptcy, in debt to the tune of 2 million marks, it was reported.[90] As the backstage jockeying for power intensified, Bella Fromm grew more restless, more distressed at this "mass blindness" of playing games with Adolf Hitler.[91] One day in mid-January she dropped in on her friend Schleicher, bearing a bouquet of flowers, to share the latest "palace gossip" she had picked up: Hitler was getting ready to take over the government at any moment, waiting impatiently in the wings.[92] She regretted having to be so "coldly realistic," but Schleicher seemed already to know this news, even as he chided her for being so pessimistic. Fromm wondered if there was really any way left to stop Hitler now. Perhaps it was better to let him have his day in the sun and fail—"run himself into the ground," as she put it.[93]

As the final moments of the Weimar era ticked away, Germany's Jews were still trying to go about their business as usual. Hans-Joachim Schoeps wrote to his collaborator Max Brod that the publishing firm of Kiepenheuer had agreed to bring out their second volume of Kafka's papers.[94] Presiding over the general meeting of the Hilfsverein in Berlin's elegant Hotel Kaiserhof, symbolically sealed off from the suite in the same building where Hitler and Papen were negotiating a Nazi takeover, Max Warburg delivered a speech that asked for inner calm and steadiness. The Jews were being blamed for Germany's ills—ills that grew out of a war he had urged his fellow countrymen not to fight. The same old lies were now being told about the Jews as had been laid at their doorstep in medieval days—Jews were always the handiest scapegoat when times grew tough. Their fate now, as in the past, was pegged to Germany's well-being. As the economy improved, as Warburg believed it would, the hatred would subside, and the Nazis would fade away.[95] In the meantime, Germany's Jews would have to speak up, affirm their loyalty, and remind their fellow Germans of the sacrifices they had made at Verdun and the Somme.[96]

Bella Fromm could stand the suspense no longer. She drove from her office at the Ullstein publishing house directly to Schleicher's office in the chancellery, barging in to tell him point-blank that Papen and Joachim von Ribbentrop were plotting with Hitler against him: His friends were deserting him. The suave, ever-charming ex-general offered her soothing words one last time: "Don't worry so hard, Bella, dear. I'll see you tonight at the Press Ball."[97]

That was Saturday morning, January 28. By the afternoon, Schleicher had resigned after only fifty-seven days in office, outfoxed by Hitler, thwarted in his bid to rule Germany with dictatorial powers. At the Press Ball, Fromm endured an evening of anguished waiting for the next shoe to drop, trying to keep her mind on her journalistic obligations to record who came with whom, what they wore, who flirted with whom, with a wisp of a smile playing on her lips.[98]

The smile did not last long. The word passed on to the steering committee of the Centralverein, meeting on Sunday in Berlin, that Hitler had failed in his bid for power, turned out to be erroneous. At 11 A.M. on Monday, January 30, Adolf Hitler was appointed German chancellor by the same President Hindenburg who, just a week before, had scoffed at ever naming "this Austrian corporal" to such a lofty post. Returning to greet his followers in the Kaiserhof with the news, Hitler was seen to have tears in his eyes. Germany was finally his, his alone. That night the pavement below the Brandenburg Gate and outside the chancellery resounded with the thud of thousands of boots, the streets echoed with the roars and singing voices of a seemingly endless column of Nazis, the city's darkness pierced by a snaking parade of twenty thousand torches, accompanied by bands blaring the martial tune "Siegreich wollen wir Frankreich schlagen" ("Triumphant we shall conquer France")—"an endless sea of brown," as Bella Fromm described it.[99] It was truly a "night of deadly menace."[100] The singing and marching lasted for six hours, until 1 A.M., when most Berliners, including Jews, were sound asleep.

4

Facing the Unthinkable

On January 30, 1933, the same day that Adolf Hitler came to power, Hans-Joachim Schoeps had his horoscope prepared. The horoscope predicted that the favorable movement of the planets that had recently brought him notoriety as a published essayist and religious thinker would continue. Indeed, more achievements lay ahead for him by the end of February and in the fall. It was not until 1942 that Schoeps could expect an unfavorable turn of events.[1] These predictions must have buoyed his spirits. Like Germany's new Führer, Schoeps was wont to put his trust in what the stars foretold.

That evening members of a Jewish craftsmen's union met in a Berlin café to discuss their common economic problems. A liberal representative rose to condemn the Zionists' approach to these matters. When his counterpart from the Zionistische Vereinigung für Deutschland (ZVfD) (Zionist Organization for Germany) responded by pointing out that all these differences among Jews no longer mattered, now that Hitler was in charge of the government, he was ignored. The others attending this meeting did not appreciate this "alarmist hyperbole."[2]

In its first public reaction to Hitler's takeover, Robert Weltsch's Zionist newspaper *Jüdische Rundschau* (Jewish Observer) tried to look on the bright side. Weltsch's anticipated "elimination" of Jews from German life would have occurred even if the Nazi leader had not been named chancellor, the newspaper argued, somewhat lamely, because this anti-Semitic tack had been endorsed by other parties as well. It was an inevitable part of Germany's national reawakening. Now, as before, the Jews' best defense was not to fight back, against the tide, but to "keep the spirit of Judaism active and alive."[3]

Liberal-minded Jews had no such upbeat advice to offer. They were still in a state of shock. The unthinkable had happened, not at the voting booth, but through the unilateral decree of a Reich president whom they had trusted to stop Hitler. The dreaded enemy they had fought so long had suddenly slipped into power through the back door, and the Jews were powerless to do anything about it. The best they could do was to salvage some embers of hope from what looked like a dire situation. In his first official remarks after Hitler was appointed and named his cabinet, Ludwig Holländer, the director of the Centralverein deutscher Staatsbürger jüdischer Glaubens (Central Organization of German Citizens of the Jewish Faith), set the tone for the assimilated, middle-class Jewish community:

Under the given circumstances we can do nothing but wait and see. We look with confidence to the Reich president—sure of his sense of justice and his adherence to the constitution. Apart from this, we are convinced that no one will dare to deprive us of our constitutional rights. Our slogan is "Wait and See."

Jews, Holländer concluded, "trust in the ultimate victory of truth and reason."[4] This was essentially the same message conveyed by the de facto spiritual and moral leader of assimilated German Jewry, Leo Baeck. In his first public remarks after January 30, the Berlin rabbi sounded reassuring. There was no hint of panic, no call for a mass exodus. What his fellow Jews heard was a firm if concerned voice calling for patience and forbearance. On February 11, the Berlin lodge of B'nai

B'rith, celebrating its fiftieth anniversary, went ahead with its scheduled evening of music and speeches. The crowd filling the lodge's temple listened expectantly to a concert of violin and harmonium music and then hushed as the stern-faced, fifty-nine-year-old Baeck rose to his feet. If his audience was looking for a forceful response to the Nazi takeover, they were to be disappointed. Instead, the rabbi took the long, historical view of what had just transpired. Speaking in the thin, high-pitched tone that was his trademark,[5] Baeck referred to the enduring strength of B'nai B'rith—a "community within a community" for Germany's Jews—offering his hope that it would remain such a linchpin for the foreseeable future, renewing itself by attracting younger members. Rather than bemoan the end of an era, he hailed a "new beginning" for the organization. In his address Baeck voiced the same sentiments of abiding attachment to the German fatherland that he might have uttered on any occasion at the lodge. When he asked his listeners for financial contributions, it was not to help Jews flee from Germany or to cope with the strains of this unsettling situation. Rather, it was to assist the victims of a recent natural disaster in the Saar.

When Baeck turned his attention to political matters, it was not to comment on the new regime or to predict its policies, but to caution Jews against succumbing to a "proletarianizing" trend, a left-wing class consciousness that was fundamentally at odds with Judaism. Reelected president of the lodge later that Sunday evening, Baeck was honored with a standing ovation that lasted over a minute. He closed the session by expressing the confident hope that those attending would reconvene, as scheduled, four years hence, "in better times."[6]

These remarks were delivered ten days after the dissolution of the Reichstag, during a period of great anxiety about Hitler and the likely consequences of his rule. Many thousands of Jews were not prepared to wait and see what would happen. To them, Hitler posed a direct threat. They elbowed into visa offices in Berlin and other major cities, seeking a fast exit from Germany. All told, over fifty thousand German Jews—or one-tenth of the entire community—left the country within the first weeks after Hitler came to power. Most of them had more reason to flee than their Jewishness. In the main, they were politically active Jews, who had fought the Nazis and lost and who now had every expectation of retribution. Some were prominent writers, artists, and musicians, now declared enemies of the people. A few were ordinary Jews who foresaw no viable future under Nazi rule. They headed mostly for neighboring countries, intending to wait out the storm and then return when Germany got back to normal. Some Jews sought to emigrate to the United States, but because of a stringent State Department policy, revived during the Great Depression, that denied visas to persons judged "likely to become a public charge"(LPC), many of them were discouraged from filing the required papers.[7] (It should be pointed out that few would-be immigrants who actually *applied* for U.S. visas failed to pass the so-called LPC test. Between 1930 and 1933, for instance, of the 1,409 German nationals who filed for visas, only 10 were turned down on the grounds that they were likely to become "public charges.")[8]

But while these Jews were hurriedly packing their bags, the overwhelming majority held back. Like Baeck, most were loathe to rush for the border, at least not until the present unstable situation was clarified and they could see where they stood. For the time being, they were immobilized, fearful of taking any precipitous action that they might soon regret. They were—in the compelling metaphor of the Brazilian writer Moacyr Scliar—shipwrecked passengers sharing their lifeboat with a jaguar: On balance, it was better to sit still and hope nothing would happen than to jump into the ocean.[9]

In the meantime Jews could at least take steps to settle their internal differences and band together to meet the Nazi threat. The day after he accepted the applause of his fellow B'nai B'rith members, Leo Baeck turned his attention to just this task. He huddled with representatives of the regional Jewish organizations and drew up a blueprint for a central body that would speak and act on behalf of all German Jews in this time of crisis. This was the beginning of an effort to defend themselves through a show of solidarity and pride. Thanks to the Nazi movement, Jews were rapidly becoming more conscious of what made them different from other Germans—and what bound them together, regardless of politics, as Jews. As the editor of the *Vossische Zeitung* observed: ". . . from a higher standpoint anti-Semitic oppression has perhaps turned out to be a boon, in that a far greater number of German Jews than ever before are becoming more mindful of their traditions and their great past."[10]

This was an outlook that stirred Robert Weltsch's idealistic passions about Jewish identity. In recent years he had brooded despondently over how noble German impulses were being perverted into fascism—a trend he saw corrupting even Jewish youths through their being exposed

to nationalistic propaganda in school.[11] Off by himself on a skiing holiday high in the Austrian Tirol in December 1931, he had written to
Martin Buber bemoaning the seductiveness of "national romanticism"
and the grim fate its racial exclusiveness held for Germany's Jews. With
liberalism now discredited and "dead," German Jews had no strategy for
protecting themselves. Even Zionism, he confessed to Buber, had nothing practical to offer in this "fateful hour."[12]

If German Zionists like Weltsch were looking for a way to rally the
Jewish community around a higher purpose, the Nazis gave it to them.
Literally overnight Hitler's rise to power convinced tens of thousands of
Jews of the truth of what the Zionists had been arguing, in vain, for
years—namely, that "emancipation" was a sham; that non-Jews would
never accept Jews as equals; that anti-Semitism was the inexorable by-
product of commingling two distinct races whose history, nature, and
destinies pulled them apart. With the power of the German government
invested in Adolf Hitler, all the liberal assumptions about "social
progress" and "constitutional protection" exploded like a punctured
balloon. All previous Jewish efforts to assert and defend their rights in
the courts and to shed their overt Jewishness for the promise of parity
in a secular, enlightened German democracy were invalidated. It was all
a lie, and the Jews were now paying the price for having believed it.

Some staunchly assimilationist Jews, like the Centralverein leader
Alfred Hirschberg, gamely sought to portray the dawning Nazi era as a
"heroic phase in the emancipation struggle of German Jewry,"[13] a struggle it would ultimately win because Jews "believe in the future of the
true Germany."[14] But these words rang hollow in light of harsh, brutal
facts: Hitler was chancellor, parliament was suspended, anti-Semitic violence was spreading, and the Nazis promised worse to come if they won
the upcoming Reichstag election in March.[15] What mattered now was
how, because they happened to be Jewish, their lives were going to be
altered by this unforeseen and once unimaginable turn of events. German Jews were searching for a way to reorient themselves, for a forum
in which to air their concerns, for a voice that offered hope without
illusion.

The *Jüdische Rundschau* offered all these things. After years of marginal
obscurity, advancing views on Jewishness that few happily "invisible"
Jews cared to read about, its editorials had finally been vindicated. It was
hard for Weltsch and other Zionists to resist feeling a smug "inner sat-

isfaction" at the collapse of liberal Jewish thinking brought about by Hitler's triumph.[16] At the same time they were invigorated. They could sense that the shift in Jewish fortunes was playing into their hands. Now, at last, Jews were ready to listen to them: Zionism, not liberalism, held the answer for Jews in a Nazi-run Germany. Zionists, like the Nazis, accepted the premise that race defined a nation. Perhaps now Jews would be emboldened to build their own *Volksgemeinschaft* (national community), emulating the Germans'.

The tightening Nazi hold on power only heightened Jewish fears and made many realize they would need more than fervent declarations of patriotism—as the Centralverein urged—to see them through this unprecedented predicament. Matters were quickly getting out of hand. On the night of February 27, 1933, the Reichstag was set ablaze, probably by Hermann Goering and his henchmen, who conveniently put the blame on a Dutch Communist named Marinus van der Lubbe. The Reichstag fire handed Hitler a ready-made excuse for suspending most civil liberties and cracking down on his remaining left-wing opponents. It was to be they—not the Jews—whom the Nazis would go after first. Several thousand Communists and Social Democrats were seized in their living rooms, dragged off to SA dungeons, and badly beaten. The left-wing press was banned. A pent-up zeal to eliminate all political adversaries goaded the Nazis into a wide-sweeping rampage. On the evening of March 1, a large number of SS invaded the headquarters of the Centralverein, on the Emser Strasse. They arrested several officials and confiscated election materials and other documents purportedly linking the Jewish organization to the Communists. This eight-hour-long raid—the first flexing of Nazi muscle against a mainstream Jewish group—sent a shiver through assimilated Jews, who could never have imagined a German government ever sanctioning such illegal actions.[17] The head of the Centralverein, Ludwig Holländer, was so distraught that he suffered a nervous collapse and had to be relieved of his duties. Even though Goering, in a meeting the following day with Centralverein representatives, conceded it was "absurd" to conceive of any collaboration between their organization and the Communists, apologized for this "mistake," and promised that the new regime would protect Jews as it would protect all German citizens,[18] many Jews got the point. In a steady stream, they headed for the frontier, led by such prominent Nazi targets as Bertolt Brecht and Kurt Weill. Those who were not so conspicuous chose to hold their breaths until the Reichstag election, hoping it would check Hitler's excesses. Typically, Leo Baeck urged his fellow Jews to look beyond the vagaries of the moment for guidance. The wheel of fortune may go up or tumble down, he wrote in an article that appeared in the *Centralverein Zeitung* the day after the Nazi raid, but this should not shake Jewish convictions about justice and duty. These convictions remained intact. "Fear God, and honor His commitments," the rabbi wrote. "That is the [obligation of the] whole man!"[19]

If most Jews were inclined to follow such advice, others saw a chance—as the Zionists did—to turn adversity to their advantage. In the middle of February, Hans-Joachim Schoeps returned from Leipzig, where he had hoped to take his state examination certifying him as a teacher, to his parents' apartment in Berlin. His plans to oversee the publication of a second volume of Kafka's papers and then go on an extended tour of the Orient were now derailed. He was in need of other outlets for his considerable intellectual energies. What proved enticing to him was organizing a Jewish youth response to the Nazi revolution— a response that would repudiate the effete and misguided strategies of established Jewish groups (mainly the Zionists) and propose a new, more appropriate, solution to the "Jewish problem" now that Adolf Hitler ruled Germany. Schoeps assessed the situation this way: As long as the Nazis were going after the Left, those Jews who were firmly opposed to communism and even democracy and staunchly backed a nationalistic renewal might well find their own niche in the new German order.

In Kassel Schoeps convened a small band of similar-thinking friends from the earlier youth movement. His goal was to use this nucleus of Germanic-oriented Jewish youths to initiate a dialogue with the country's anti-Semitic rulers and then reach out to other young Jews, forging a kind of intellectual vanguard. In fact, he called his assemblage the Deutscher Vortrupp (German Vanguard), adapting its military-sounding name from a pre–World War I faction of the original German youth movement.[20] Schoeps envisioned the Deutscher Vortrupp initially as a discussion group, which would seek to make sense out of the historically changed situation now confronting Germany's Jews. But the group was also designed to assume active leadership in the Jewish community. It represented, in a Jewish context, the fulfillment of the youth movement's aspiration to break the grip of "bourgeois" values and restore a deeper commitment to Judaism without undercutting the movement's German patriotism.

The Deutscher Vortrupp drafted, rather pretentiously, eight "theses," including a frontal attack on the Zionist movement for preaching a "humanitarian social ethic," instead of spirituality, and for trying to build a *Machtstaat* ("a state based on power") in Palestine that ran counter to the Jews' true historical mission. This mission, according to the Deutscher Vortrupp, was to live in banishment in the Diaspora until the coming of the Messiah, remaining loyal to the countries in which they happened to live, even to a Nazi state that wanted to throw them out. Accepting the Nazi-decreed separation of the races—as the sons of Japhet and Shem were rent asunder in the Bible—Schoeps and his followers stoically shouldered a responsibility to "bear witness" to their dual identity as Germans *and* Jews, even as the calumny of the Jew haters rained down on them. This was the ultimate test of their allegiance, to which they were willing to submit.[21]

But Schoeps was not really prepared to be merely a "passive object" of Nazi mayhem, calmly waiting like a martyr for the ax to fall. Along with other politically conservative (and nationalistic) Jewish groups, the Deutscher Vortrupp had hopes of currying favor with the Nazis and their allies at the expense of more "dubious" elements within the Jewish community. These elements were, on the one hand, the Zionists, who made no bones about their higher commitment to Jewish nationalism, and, on the other hand, the liberals, who incensed German radical nationalists by masquerading as authentic Germans, claiming that their Jewishness was inconsequential. Schoeps was trying to analyze the "Jewish problem" in political terms, thus bypassing the sticky question of race, and to offer a solution that would mean a Nazi accommodation of Jews who shared his beliefs. Like other conservative Jews, he was also trying to reach out to the non-Nazis in Hitler's cabinet (eight of its eleven members), to bolster their influence at a time when the Nazis had not yet gained full control of the government.

To build his case, Schoeps pursued contacts with the one-million-strong veterans' group, the Stahlhelm (Steel Helmet). During the Weimar era, this right-wing group had called for a "strong hand" or "iron broom" to rid Germany of its parliamentary fiasco.[22] The Stahlhelm shared Schoeps's anachronistic enthusiasm for restoring the monarchy and counted among its card-carrying members Prince Wilhelm of Prussia.[23]

Although it kept Jews out, this powerful interest group was only mildly hostile toward them. Its members were known as "armchair anti-Semites,"[24] and its vice president, Theodor Duesterberg, turned out to be the grandson of a rabbi.[25] Therefore, Schoeps and his Deutscher Vortrupp comrades thought there might be enough common ground to build an alliance with the Stahlhelm. But nothing ever came of it.

Schoeps stood a better chance of joining forces, defensively, with other right-wing Jewish groups. One of these groups was the Verband nationaldeutscher Juden (VndJ) (Association of Nationalistic German Jews), headed by Max Naumann. Since its formation in 1921, the VndJ had opposed any Jewish group, but especially the Zionists, that wished to preserve any vestige of Jewish identity. Its members regarded their fellow Jews from eastern Europe as nothing more than a blight on German soil. Politically, the group subscribed to a völkisch philosophy that imitated the Nazis' and heavily stressed the need for German renewal. In 1932 Naumann had gone so far as to endorse the Nazi Party—the only head of a Jewish organization ever to do so.[26] Like the Deutscher Vortrupp, the VndJ hoped to ingratiate itself with Germany's new rulers, playing up to such non-Nazis as Franz von Papen; Konstantin von Neurath; Alfred Hugenberg; and Franz Seldte, head of the Stahlhelm. For these groups, the best line of defense against an anti-Semitic government was to subordinate their Jewishness and to raise the national colors even higher.

They had allies, of a sort, in another nationalistic Jewish organization: the Reichsband jüdischer Frontsoldaten (RjF) (Reich Association of Jewish War Veterans). Dedicated to combating anti-Semitism by keeping alive the memory of Jewish war sacrifice, the RjF emphasized both patriotic service and the defense of Jewish rights. Among the activities it sponsored were physical fitness and sports competitions, as ways of perpetuating the pride and solidarity so many young Jews had discovered two decades before in the trenches. Unlike the VndJ, the Jewish veterans' group was not willing to play down its Jewishness to placate the new government. It did, however, share the antipathy of these other right-wing Jewish groups toward those downtrodden "ethnic" Jews who had immigrated to Germany from the East. (In 1933 between 20 and 25 percent of the Jews living in Germany had come from eastern Europe.) To the veterans, the Ostjuden were essentially second-class Jews who, if need be, were expendable. In any event, these Jews were not *German* Jews.

Schoeps had tried to put out feelers to philosophically kindred Jewish groups before Hitler came to power and had written an article in late 1932 entitled "The New Face of Politics," in which he argued that hatred of the Jews stemmed from their perceived support for leftist politics. True Judaism, he declared, could not be liberal. Only through a return to its real roots could the Jews find their place in a Nazi state.[27] (After January 1933 this article was brought to the attention of the Gestapo, which found its contents objectionable, declared Schoeps an enemy of the state, and placed him on their list of dangerous dissidents.)[28] Schoeps was prone to defining "true Judaism" in language that approximated the requirements of the German nationalist Right: It was to be authoritarian, led by an elite that embodied its ideals and was willing to sacrifice personal freedom and pursuits for these ideals.

With Hitler now ensconced in the chancellery, the twenty-three-year-old Schoeps embarked on a similar route, establishing an "action committee," together with the VndJ and the Schwarzes Fähnlein (Black Squad), an amalgam of right-wing Jewish youth groups roughly analogous to the Hitler Youth. This committee was torn by a clash of philosophies and egos (Schoeps could not stand Naumann and later branded the VndJ "fascist");[29] thus it is not surprising that its ambitions of negotiating successfully with the government on behalf of all German Jews eventually came to naught. But in the first months of Hitler's rule, many conservative Jews agreed with Schoeps's position that active accommodation with Germany's "national renewal" gave them the best chance of surviving inside the Third Reich. This position was soon to be sorely tested.

Max Warburg, a thoroughly assimilated Jew, finally aroused to the dangers posed by the extreme nationalists, was more inclined to view the Nazi takeover from a pragmatic, political perspective. Taken aback by the events of January 30, he remained convinced that Hitler, the product of backstage machinations, would not last long in power. Therefore, the proper Jewish reaction was not to tag along with the vaunted "revolution" or stand helplessly on the sidelines, but to fight back, in the belief that doing so would hasten Hitler's demise. Warburg thus favored pumping more money into Jewish efforts to refute Nazi propaganda about the Jews and to back non-Nazi candidates in the upcoming March election. One of his first acts under the new regime was to join the Centralverein in appealing to the American Jewish Committee for additional funds for defensive literature.[30] Warburg also realized that the

Nazis were going to force some Jews, namely the Ostjuden, out of the country, so he quickly began to draw up a plan for exporting capital to assist them.[31]

Warburg's guiding credo was "Weiter machen"—keep going. He was determined not to allow any fear of what the Nazi-led regime *might* do to interfere with how he went about his business. The inheritor of a 135-year-old family-owned bank, Warburg saw himself primarily as a guardian of that treasured institution. He would protect the position and assets of what had been entrusted to him and secure the bank's future for generations of Warburgs to come. He vowed to shield his firm "like a fortress."[32]

Sharing this historical long view with Leo Baeck, Warburg put the Nazi takeover in a larger, assuaging context. In the past, Jews had faced periods of oppression and endured them, and they would do so this time. He, Max Warburg, would certainly survive. (Warburg even tried to rationalize away the Nazi victory. "Foreign pressure" on Germany dating from the infamous Versailles treaty was to blame for Hitler's rise, not anti-Semitism, he wrote.)[33] Hitler could not possibly last long at the helm of a civilized, modern society like Germany. Still, his bank was already feeling the affects of the change in power. On March 14, 1933, Warburg received a letter from a non-Jewish Hamburg banker, saying he would no longer seek financial advice from the firm of M. M. Warburg and Co.[34] Indirectly, pressure was applied to the bank by letters directed to city officials complaining about its "dictatorship" in financial circles.[35] The mayor of Hamburg informed Warburg, through an intermediary, that he would not be able to consult with the banker as much in the future as he had in the past.[36] Courteously and discreetly, old friends and colleagues were sidling away from one of the most obvious symbols of "Jewish power" in an emphatically anti-Semitic Germany. In 1933 the bank's list of clients plummeted to 1,875 from 5,241 in 1930.[37]

Personally, Warburg did not feel in any immediate danger. His political views hardly qualified him as a left-wing radical. On most topics Warburg held moderately conservative positions, nothing unusual for a well-to-do German, Jew or non-Jew, in his profession. During the previous Reichstag election, he had contributed funds both to a middle-class party, the Deutsche Volkspartei (German People's Party), which was founded by Gustav Stresemann, and to the Deutsche Staatspartei (German State Party), largely because of their compatible economic programs.[38] He had refused to back Alfred Hugenberg's more conservative Deutsche National Volkspartei (German National People's Party), since it had inserted an anti-Semitic plank in its platform.[39]

In Jewish affairs Warburg also stuck to the middle of the road, torn between loyalties to his persecuted people and to his resurgent country, just as Leo Baeck was. Like Baeck, he was sympathetic to building a Jewish homeland in Palestine, moved by the "heroic efforts of brave pioneers" he had observed there.[40] Also like Baeck, he had lent his name to the cause of Palestinian development, accepting the argument that Jews in the Diaspora faced a "double task" in their current predicament—to build a new Jewish base for the future while maintaining the one in Germany they already had.[41] For this reason, Warburg—the most cosmopolitan and assimilated of German Jews—had commissioned and hung in his Hamburg office a portrait of Moses longing for the Promised Land.[42] Warburg's divided sense of Jewish obligations did not sit well with either outspoken Zionists, such as Kurt Blumenfeld, or with outspokenly German nationalists, like Max Naumann or Hans-Joachim Schoeps. During the early months of 1933, the Hamburg banker reluctantly found himself more engaged in an unwanted intra-Jewish ideological struggle than in warding off the Nazis. On the one hand, he chided Blumenfeld for capitalizing on the anti-Semitic climate to further his Zionist ends. On the other hand, he accused nationalistic Jews of being "obstinate" in their denial of any Jewish identity or responsibility.[43] Neither group, Warburg thought, understood his position or desired the sort of unified Jewish response the present crisis demanded.

Warburg's optimism issued not only from his upbeat personality and view of history but from who he was and who he knew. He was a towering eminence in Germany's economic affairs, an intimate of its most powerful elites. If the kaiser was no longer there to vouch for him (having gone into Dutch exile after the war), Warburg could still look for protection to a personage like Hjalmar Schacht. In mid-March Warburg had joined with two other Jewish bankers in signing Schacht's reappointment as president of the Reichsbank.[44] A recent convert to the Nazi cause—an "incurable turncoat"[45] and "ruthless opportunist" was what Bella Fromm called him[46]—Schacht had ascended to prominence with the help of several Jewish bankers and financiers, and many of them, including Warburg (who had known Schacht for twenty years), now looked to him to return the favor. For the time being, the wily Reichsbank president appeared to be their ace in the hole.

Bella Fromm could well afford to disparage Schacht's character and steer clear of him, for she could count on more honorable but equally powerful non-Jewish friends in Berlin to be her guardian angels. General Kurt von Schleicher may have been out of office, and another mentor, Paul von Hindenburg, tottering toward the grave, but she still enjoyed the confidence and friendship of several current and future personalities of consequence, including the aristocratic General Werner Freiherr von Fritsch, the commander of the Berlin military district who was soon to be named chief of the Army High Command.[47] Fromm was on cordial terms with leaders of the Stahlhelm (even though she privately considered the veterans' group myopically and dangerously pro-Nazi).[48] And Papen, the vice chancellor—another "traitor" she despised for his total lack of principle—knew and liked her.

On top of this, the popular society columnist could depend on her many admirers in the foreign embassies—men who by a phone call or a whispered word on a receiving line could save her from any looming calamity ("Nobody is going to do any harm to our Bella," the ever-charming, newly arrived French ambassador André François-Poncet, greeted her at one afternoon tea. "They know that the diplomatic corps protects her.")[49] Aside from these official "sponsors," Fromm was romantically involved with Herbert Mumm von Schwarzenstein, an aristocrat who had just been appointed vice chief of protocol in the Foreign Ministry. A close friend since childhood days in Bavaria, Mumm was a tall, blond ex-army officer, the son of an Austrian duchess. He left Germany shortly after helping to put down the Hitler putsch in 1923 and came back only in 1932, eager to embark on a diplomatic career.[50] An astute observer of top Nazi leaders, "Rolf" (as she referred to him in her diary) could both help her stay abreast of and interpret the regime's thinking and—in a pinch—come to her rescue.

Sooner than she might have thought, Fromm found herself in need of such help. On March 10 she hosted one of her semimonthly cocktail parties at her quiet, suburban home at Hohenzollernkorso 40, in Tempelhof, to which the usual mixture of diplomats and German government officials were invited. It was just five days after the Nazis had failed in their bid to win an outright majority in the Reichstag election, spurring hostility toward the Jews, who were somehow at fault. (The

Nazi Party not only had to depend on its allies in the conservative Deutsche National Volkspartei to form a government, but it fell far short of the two-thirds parliamentary majority needed to recast the German constitution along its ideological lines.) There was growing pandemonium in the streets, with SA hoodlums burning Weimar's despised black, red, and gold flags, as well as in Berlin's political circles. But Bella Fromm was not one to let her festive afternoon be ruined by such distractions. One by one, the gleaming black limousines pulled up outside her house, disgorging dignitaries from Egypt, France, Romania, Czechoslovakia, and the German Foreign Ministry (including Herbert Mumm). The embassy vehicles had to maneuver their way through angry Nazi "hordes," who at one point set upon the elegantly dressed wife of a Belgian baron because they mistook her for a Jewess. At first, "Frau Bella's" sprawling music room sheltered her guests from the loutish rabble—but not for long. A mob of Brownshirts collected outside her front door. Fromm was told they had seen guns and ammunition being brought into the house. There were spies hiding in this Jew's home, and the Nazis were going to "fumigate" the premises. A panic-stricken Fromm telephoned the police, but they only alarmed her more by demanding to search the house for evidence of "political agitators" and by refusing to interfere with the SA crowd milling outside.

Fromm then resorted to her connections. A phone message to Mumm's superior in the protocol office was relayed to the Foreign Ministry's secretary of state, Dr. Bernhard von Bülow (an anti-Nazi), who, in turn, alerted the vice chancellor, Papen, and offered to run over to Hitler's office to tell him as well. The chief of protocol also rushed over to Hindenburg's palace and informed the aged president, who "cursed and thundered" at this outrage.

In no time four black sedans carrying men on Hitler's personal staff, wearing SA uniforms, drove up and chased the crowd away. Fifteen mounted police, dispatched by Papen, then appeared in a superfluous show of force on the now-deserted Hohenzollernkorso. Fromm, who had not lost her sense of decorum during all this turmoil, then slipped into an evening gown, pinned on her Iron Cross and her other decorations, and drove "with slightly wobbling knees" to a reception at the Hotel Adlon for the departing American ambassador, Frederic Sackett. Papen was expecting her. He kissed Fromm's hand unctuously in the writing room and offered his apologies for the "unpleasantness" that had occurred earlier in the day. He then asked if she would mind using her influence to keep the diplomats whose national flags had been ripped from their limousines from making an international incident out of this happening.[51]

This ordeal taught Fromm an ambiguous lesson: Either no Jew was now safe from a Nazi mob, or she could still expect her well-placed friends to take care of her. Subsequent events would lead her to believe the latter—that she remained a kind of untouchable among Germany's Jews. This conclusion would allow her to confront the deteriorating situation in the Third Reich without becoming fearful of her own safety.

In late March, at a time of continuing anti-Jewish violence and talk of a boycott of Jewish businesses, Fromm was presented with a "most peculiar proposition." Felix Tripeloury, secretary of the Reich press office, approached her at a reception in the Peruvian legation and revealed that the Foreign Ministry was worried that further anti-Jewish measures would alienate foreign governments. (Press reports of physical abuse of Jews were already causing the German government considerable embarrassment.) She was asked to go to Hermann Goering, the newly named Prussian minister of the interior, escorted by a pair of Jewish war heroes, to present a plan, concocted by Konstantin von Neurath, that would entail the expulsion of "undesirable" Jews (those from eastern Europe) while permitting the remaining, "respectable" German Jews to stay.[52] Although she inwardly dismissed this proposal as a "farce," Fromm agreed to inform leaders of the Jewish community about it and see what their reactions might be. Leaving the party, she went directly to the Oranienburgerstrasse synagogue, looking for Leo Baeck, only to be told he was out of town. She then walked back down the darkened street feeling disheartened, not at having failed to reach Baeck, but at the thought that Jews were now, pressured by the Nazis, turning against each other, saving their own necks at the expense of the poor, unfortunate Ostjuden. "We will never get anywhere," she wrote that night at her desk. "The Jews will never be in the same boat."[53]

She had to admit that this statement was true of her, too. She was sui generis. Fromm had a unique role to play in the Nazi capital as a conduit between powerful groups that found the access she could provide them indispensable. The Nazis needed Fromm, or so they thought. They would therefore tolerate her presence across the dining room tables they frequented, Jewess that she was. For Fromm, this special status bestowed a sense of immunity: She could empathize strongly with the plight that other Jews faced, but it was not *her* plight—not yet anyway.

Instead of being hounded out of the country, Fromm had her hand kissed by Adolf Hitler. This bizarre event occurred at the Palais Prinz Friedrich Leopold. Franz von Papen was hosting a reception under dazzling crystal chandeliers, when the Führer unexpectedly made an appearance. Hitler headed straight across the room to greet Frau von Papen, who was standing next to the ubiquitous Fromm. Fromm tried to beat a retreat, but the attractive female journalist could not elude Hitler's grasping hand. "Why do you wish to avoid me, *gnädige Frau?*" the master of Germany asked. "Why can't I wish you a good evening?" Not realizing he was in the presence of a Jew, Hitler then pressed her fingers to his lips, fixing on her his legendary hypnotic gaze. He asked if Fromm was enjoying herself. He then inquired about her medals, much to the amusement of her diplomatic friends standing nearby. Slightly disgusted with herself, Fromm spent the rest of the evening pursuing this "plain looking little man" with her gaze, noting his social awkwardness and his servility toward the attending German nobility. Later she sat at the same table with Propaganda Minister Joseph Goebbels— the man who was planning a massive nationwide boycott of Jewish shops, scheduled to start in two days. In a hysterical voice, Goebbels ranted about the Jews. Finally, the Romanian ambassador attempted to calm him down by pointing out that some Jews—like the lady sharing his table—were politically conservative. The diminutive Goebbels then flew into a worse rage. "There is nothing worse than rightist Jews," he shrieked. When it was all over, Fromm went home and wrote about the evening for her newspaper, *BZ:*

> Very much to the surprise of the guests, Adolf Hitler appeared at about ten o'clock. This constituted his first formal social appearance at a large party since his assumption of his duties as chancellor. He was warmly welcomed by the hosts. They used the occasion to present those diplomats whom he had not yet met, especially the ladies of the international set.[54]

That was for public consumption. She then recorded her fears in her diary: the "baiting of Jews continues incessantly. It has become accepted practice for Jewish victims to be dragged from their beds before dawn and taken away."[55] The next day Fromm jotted down the warning given her by a well-meaning baron: The Jews were soon to be driven out of their restaurants and shops, out of the press and cultural life. They were going to be herded back into the ghetto. It was time to get out of Germany.[56] Secure where she was, unafraid, Fromm chose to disregard this piece of friendly advice, as she would ignore many others like it.

In Munich, cradle of the Nazi revolution, Richard Willstätter was spared many of the alarming details of what the Nazis were starting to do to the Jews—the nightly raids, the bloody beatings, the naked threats. With his daughter now married and living elsewhere, and with his last administrative tie to the university severed through Hitler's assumption of power, Willstätter heard little of what was going on.[57] What he did hear came in the form of watered-down, second-hand reports from professorial colleagues who dropped by now and then but did not wish to upset him. Everyone understood that Germany had undergone a fundamental change. The universities had no choice but to go along with it. What else could they do? In his cocoon, Willstätter was not all that discontented, at least not professionally. The severing of external bonds and obligations had freed him to focus more exclusively on his research. However, the funds he had been receiving from the Rockefeller Foundation were now running out. Therefore, on March 26—the day before Goebbels announced a "mass action" against German Jews in retaliation for "atrocity stories" allegedly being circulated by sympathetic Jews in England and the United States—Willstätter applied for a renewal of his grant, to further what was a pioneering study of the biochemistry of enzymes.[58] The fact that Jews were coming under such attack did not deter him from completing his paperwork. First, he did not believe that the German people or their government could ever treat Jews the way Nazi hate mongers were demanding. Second, he defined himself not as a *Jew*, but as a scientist, a scholar. He was not a political radical, but a patriot who had served his kaiser well in time of war. He was merely a shy, courtly, white-haired man with a Vandyke beard, who was content to stay out of the public eye and tend to his garden of roses and collection of fine paintings. He was also one of his nation's most eminent scientists. Why should he have anything to fear?

Most German Jews were more worried. They tried to see the good side of their country's new Führer. During his first weeks in the chancellery, Hitler had been occupied with consolidating his power, offering mollifying words to the non-Nazi conservatives and moderates while eliminating all opposition on the Left. Such "radical" groups as the Communists and the Social Democrats were linked, in the minds of many Germans, to social and economic upheaval and were thus seen as inimical to the country's well-being and alien to its values. As a whole, the German people—including the Jews—desired peace, order, and stability, and Hitler's vision of a Volksgemeinschaft under strong, unified Nazi rule promised them as much—and more. The new order Germans saw emerging from a transitional violent crackdown on the Left and sporadic attacks on Jews appealed to deep-seated national longings for a restored sense of pride and achievement after so many years of international humiliation and economic despair.

With this still fluid and ill-defined Nazi state, most Jews, excluding those on the Left, had hopes of working out some kind of mutually acceptable compromise that would allow them to continue to live under this totalitarian regime, as Italian Jews had managed to do under Mussolini.[59] Various groups in the loosely structured Jewish community came up with their own interpretations of what "national renewal" meant and sought to make their separate peace with it. Many well-to-do Jews had found in the Nazi triumph reason to hope for an economic upturn and greater personal prosperity. Comfortable, middle-class Jews, sick of street fighting and revolving-door governments, looked to a strong ruler to impose law and order and end the Communist threat. Well-assimilated, patriotic Jews responded to the same yearnings to restore Germany to its rightful place among the nations of the world that the Nazis had cultivated among their non-Jewish friends and neighbors. Liberals still clung to the hope that if the Nazis managed to hold on to power (which they doubted), they would eventually become more "reasonable" and accept a legal solution to the "Jewish problem" with only minor restrictions placed on the rights of German Jews.[60] (What might happen to the Ostjuden was another matter, but that was *their* problem.) The Zionists saw in the Nazi triumph the counterpart of their own nationalist cause achieving a historic victory, perhaps a harbinger of the establishment of a Jewish state in Palestine. In the short run, the Zionists had reason to believe their movement would benefit from a Nazi-imposed "siege mentality" because it would draw Jews together qua Jews and reintroduce them to their common identity.

Yet none of these groups spoke for German Jewry, any more than any one political party had during the Weimar years. Indeed, there was no "Jewish reaction" to Hitler taking over control of Germany. Jews simply did not exist as a monolithic bloc in 1933—except in the minds of the most rabid anti-Semites. Rather, they were separated from one another by their country of origin, economic status, depth of religious belief, observance of traditions, occupation, appearance, ties to other Jews, and place of residence—differences that were of great significance and, in their minds, irreconcilable.

The Nazi regime encouraged this diverse Jewish response by sending out mixed signals. It did so because its leaders did not yet have a "Jewish policy," any clear idea about what to do with the Jews. They only had an amalgam of shrill campaign rhetoric and hatred. So what now emanated from the government was unsettlingly inconsistent. One day Hitler's Storm Troopers would beat up Jews on the Kurfürstendamm, the next day the Führer would plead for calm and a halt to such "spontaneous attacks." Hermann Goering guaranteed the "safety of life and property of Jewish citizens"[61] the same day the SA besieged Bella Fromm and her guests. While Hitler declared that he intended no actions against the Jews, only against the Marxists—and Heinrich Himmler, head of the SS, promised to protect Jewish rights[62]—Goering refused to have the police intervene to guard Jewish shops set upon by mobs of Storm Troopers. Meanwhile, acts of anti-Semitic violence and intimidation multiplied. Was the government behind them? Could it curb the wanton brutality of its own minions?

As Jews pondered these life-and-death questions, the Nazis began to formulate their own answers. Although Hitler realized that extreme anti-Semitic measures were not popular among the German people and were giving his new regime a bad name abroad, he could not resist pressures from radical elements within the Nazi Party to go after the Jews for long. To balance his need to appear statesmanlike, acting within the law, against this pent-up desire to strike at the demonized Jewish enemy, Hitler moved toward a more organized and coherent policy toward the Jews.

In spite of their efforts to keep a low profile and avoid provoking the regime, German Jews unwittingly handed the Nazi leaders the excuse they needed to launch their first anti-Semitic measures—the first government-sanctioned persecution of German Jews in centuries. It happened in

March 1933. Reports of Jews being beaten and forced to emigrate were now trickling out of Germany. On March 14, the new American ambassador, William E. Dodd, wrote to a friend in Washington that many Jews were "terror-stricken" by Nazi brutalities and dreaded an imminent midnight knock on the door.[63] In this strictly confidential letter—Dodd was worried he would lose his job if its contents leaked out—the ambassador advocated an American boycott of German goods, so as to not repeat the mistake of German Jews, who had naively "trusted to the intelligence of the German people" and not fought the Nazis.[64] This and other stories of "atrocities" suffered by Jews reached Stephen Wise, a Zionist leader who was the founder and longtime president of the American Jewish Congress. Wise was also convinced that the Jews in Germany had made a fatal blunder by not raising their voices in time against Hitler. He was determined that the same charge would never be laid at his doorstep. Therefore, he resolved to unite American Jews—and their fellow citizens—behind the proposed anti-German boycott, using a planned rally in Madison Square Garden as his forum. Other protest events against the Nazi government were organized in some three hundred American cities, as well as in Poland and Romania, to be held on March 27.

The German government was deeply troubled by the prospect of such unfriendly acts. Aside from the damaging political fallout, the economic repercussions of an American or British trade boycott would be disastrous to a Germany just getting back on its feet after the prolonged worldwide depression. To defuse the proposed boycott, the Nazi regime tried to stem the flow of negative information seeping out of the country. In particular, the Jewish press—still free to publish without any official censorship—was instructed to tone down its reporting of anti-Semitic incidents.[65] Simultaneously, the Nazis slammed "foreign atrocity propaganda" as lies and distortions, pointing the finger of blame directly at Germany's Jews. As many of them had feared, they were now to be punished for besmirching the nation's good name in the eyes of the world. A Gestapo official told one German Jewish leader that since the Jews had not done anything to squelch the "atrocity" stories, if an anti-German boycott resulted from them, a pogrom would likely follow. And the government would not do anything to stop it.

Meanwhile, other anti-Jewish steps were being considered. Many within the Nazi hierarchy wanted to punish the Jews by declaring a counter boycott of their businesses. At cabinet meetings, the Jew-baiting editor Julius Streicher together with Goebbels urged Hitler to authorize a protracted boycott, with the goal of driving Jews out of the economy, but Schacht, Papen, Neurath, and other non-Nazis cautioned against this plan, arguing that Germany would suffer economically, both at home and abroad.[66] In the end, the non-Nazis' position prevailed. The boycott would be limited, symbolic, but it would still make the Jews suffer.

As the date set for the anti-German rallies approached, Jewish groups in Germany joined the Nazis in deploring this "campaign of lies" against their country. (The Jewish veterans' association, RjF, sent a letter to the American embassy in Berlin denouncing the atrocity stories on the day that Ernst "Putzi" Hanfstaengl, Hitler's foreign press chief, told Bella Fromm over tea at the Italian embassy, "All the rumors about the persecution of Jews . . . are cheap lies and absurd tattertales.")[67] Jewish organizations did so partly because of Nazi intimidation and partly because of a genuine belief that these foreign demonstrations would only backfire against their people.[68] Those who did not speak out voluntarily were persuaded by Goering to do so. On March 26 the same portly former flying ace who earlier in the month had cordially received two liberal Jewish leaders and reassured them that their rights would be protected by a Nazi-headed German government now issued a blunt warning to a Jewish delegation: Anti-German propaganda and talk of a boycott must cease; otherwise he would "no longer be able to vouch for the safety of German Jews."[69] There would be a pogrom. When Max Naumann, representing the VndJ, complained about anti-Semitic violence in the Third Reich, Goering brushed it aside. "When you use a plane," he said, "shavings will fall." The Prussian interior minister then went on to "suggest" that the various Jewish groups should issue a statement opposing the mass rally planned for the next day at Madison Square Garden. As it turned out, this was the last time a high-ranking Nazi official would ever meet with a group of German Jews. Leaders of the Centralverein and ZVfD took the hint and dispatched a cable to Stephen Wise and other American Jewish figures, expressing their strong opinion that Monday's protest should be canceled. Some American Jewish groups then agreed to back out of the rallies, but Wise would not budge. Three Jewish spokesmen also traveled across the Channel to London, to plead against anti-German measures in light of these scarcely veiled threats.

Of those present, all but one of the British Jews shook their heads in disbelief: Apparently, their German coreligionists had lost their reason.[70] In a statement issued in Berlin, the ZVfD repudiated all "anti-German" campaigns abroad: Other nations did not have the right to make German Jews their concern.

Stephen Wise was not impressed. Speaking before the American Jewish Congress assembled in Carnegie Hall, he mentioned the cables from German Jewish leaders, but he also cited other letters smuggled out of Germany telling of swastikas being carved into the flesh of Jews and other hyperbolic horrors. "Do not believe the denials," a German Jew now in France had cautioned him. "Nor the Jewish denials."[71]

Back in Germany, under the Gestapo's nose, Jews were afraid of anti-Semitic rioting and further acts of violence. "Irresponsible and absurd exaggerations" about their plight only fanned the fires of hatred, they believed.[72] Nevertheless, the mass protests in New York and other cities went ahead as scheduled. The anti-Jewish zealots in the Nazi Party were enraged. Goebbels took to the airwaves, announcing a "mass action" that, in fact, had already been planned for some time. In front of her radio, Bella Fromm scribbled down his frightening words without adding comments of her own: "We are going to take our revenge. The Jews in America and England are trying to injure us. We shall know how to deal with their brothers in Germany."[73]

In response, Robert Weltsch's *Jüdische Rundschau* reiterated what the ZVfD had already stated: Anti-German propaganda only hurts German Jews. His newspaper would continue to fight against the spread of "horror stories" about the situation in Germany.[74] This statement echoed Weltsch's earlier declaration that "there have not been any pogroms in Germany."[75] A brand-new Jewish organization, which unified the various *Land* (regional) associations, joined the Berlin *Gemeinde* (Jewish community) in making a similar pledge, reminding Hitler and Hindenburg of the Jewish "blood sacrifice" to the fatherland during World War I. (This new National Representation of the Regional Associations— Reichsvertretung der Landesverbände—was cochaired by Leo Baeck.) The entire Jewish community should not be economically ruined for the "transgressions" of a few, these groups argued.[76] (The outspoken, New York-based *Jewish Daily Bulletin* labeled this statement a "pathetic appeal.")

By now it was too late. The Nazi leadership had made up its mind.

The Jews of Germany were to be punished. There would be a one-day boycott against all Jewish businesses, to take place on Saturday, April 1, 1933, commencing at 10 A.M. If "international Jewry" did not cease its anti-German propaganda, the boycott would resume the following Wednesday. This action, the official communiqué said, was to be carried out with strict German discipline. Nevertheless, it would teach the Jews a lesson.

5

"Now We Are All Jews"

Something terrible was going to happen. Amid the flurry of government threats and reassurances, with Storm Troopers prowling the streets and placards hastily pasted on Berlin kiosks, it was hard to say exactly *what* lay in store for Germany's Jews, but this was no bluff. Something *was* going to happen to them. The Jews sensed it, and accepted it as inevitable in a way they had not accepted the likelihood of Hitler ever ruling Germany or of tens of millions of their fellow Germans ecstatically flocking to the rippling swastika banners and shrill slogans of a party that preached hatred of the Jews and insisted they could have no place in their "community of the people." By now, German Jews had witnessed enough of the improbable—the inconceivable—to be braced for this next hammer blow to their self-esteem and inner security.

What would happen? What would this officially decreed boycott—

the first organized assault on Jews in the Third Reich—bring? Who would take part? Would the government keep it under control? Would it lead to more violence? The ominous signs were already creating a flurry of panic in the Jewish community. Reports of Jews being dismissed from public offices—from schools and law courts, from opera houses and governmental bureaucracies—fed these fears.[1] This anxiety was driven to new heights by a morning radio broadcast on March 29, 1933, which declared that all Jews were about to be fired from their jobs.[2] This announcement was soon retracted, but the fears did not subside, and with good reason. When the Nazi Party manifesto for April 1 was made public, it demanded that the number of Jews in the fields of law, medicine, and civil service be reduced to the percentage of Jews in the overall German population. The same *numerus clausus* was to be applied to Jewish students in the universities.

Because of these new restrictions and a growing unease about their future, more Jews resolved to leave Germany. The crush of would-be émigrés seeking a refuge in neighboring countries like Holland and Switzerland forced the Hilfsverein der deutschen Juden, the welfare agency headed by Max Warburg, to relocate to more commodious offices in the headquarters of the Berlin *Gemeinde* (Jewish community), on the Oranienburgerstrasse.[3] Then, on the eve of the boycott, Hermann Goering's nasal voice filled German living rooms, announcing the news. "I have been appointed to destroy . . . ," Bella Fromm caught him saying. That day she happened to be preoccupied with other matters. Earlier she had received a "frantic call" from the Foreign Office: Why hadn't *die gnädige Frau* mentioned the chancellor's first public appearance in her story this morning? It turned out that some politically naive or empty-headed Ullstein editor at *BZ* had simply cut the paragraph out. Having dealt with that crisis, Fromm turned to confront the more pressing danger. "Won't you move into our house for a time?" a gracious Venezuelan envoy implored her. "Things may be pretty nasty the next few days." Fromm said thanks, but no thanks. By profession she was a journalist, and there was a big story in the making.[4] SA men armed with carbines were taking up positions outside Jewish-owned shops along the elegant Kurfürstendamm. The windows were already smeared with tar.[5] The city's police were instructed to stand back, out of the way, and not to restrain the protesters.

Robert Weltsch was a newspaperman, too, and though being a Jew might have dictated that he stay at home on April 1 behind drawn curtains, as other Jews were doing, his professional curiosity got the better of him. He phoned Kurt Blumenfeld, his fellow Zionist, and talked him into sharing a taxi, to drive around the city to see the face of this new Germany firsthand. Weltsch and Blumenfeld rode with widening eyes eastward, from the Kurfürstendamm toward Berlin's epicenter, down the Leipzigerstrasse, turning toward Hausvogteiplatz and then on toward the Spittelmarkt, where Jewish shops were the most thickly concentrated. Through the taxi's windows, the two men gawked helplessly, outraged by this public spectacle of Jewish abuse. But this day of boycott was oddly grotesque and even humorous. The "fat, brown, robotlike" Storm Troopers looked like trolls out of *Peer Gynt* as they monotonously dipped their brushes in buckets of white paint and sketched long-nosed caricatures of Jews on shop fronts. The literatus in Weltsch could not resist wryly admiring some of the Nazis' more poetically inspired inscriptions: "Jede Mark in Judenhand/Fehlt dem deutschen Vaterland" ("Every mark in a Jew's hand is one less for the fatherland").

Most comforting to him was the indifference, if not disdain, that Berliners displayed toward this official persecution of Germany's Jews. Shoppers brushed past SA guards and obliviously strolled into premises defaced with the crude slogan "Juden 'raus." The Jewish store owners showed quiet courage, maintaining their dignity and poise in the face of taunts and invective. In Weltsch's eyes, this represented an ironic moment of triumph: The "inferior" Jews were revealing their inner superiority over those who were tormenting them. For him, the boycott was not so much denigrating Jews as it was elevating them, by bringing out, under duress, their finer qualities.[6]

As soon as the taxi dropped him off outside his apartment, Weltsch raced up the steps to his desk and began to write. The words that flowed out of him would form the lead essay in the next issue of the *Jüdische Rundschau*. They would constitute one of the most celebrated expressions of Jewish opinion under the Nazis—published opinion still condoned by a regime that had not yet fully turned its attention to the "Jewish problem" and to the question of how to deal with a Jewish presence in an otherwise "Aryan" state. For now—and for some years to come— the Jewish press would carry on with Nazi acquiescence, in accordance with Nazi logic. Unlike *German* publications, Jewish newspapers, books, and magazines could not be forced into line—*gleichgeschaltet*—with party doctrine because the Nazis considered the Jews to be racially incapable of conforming to such (higher) standards. Instead, it was a natural, if somewhat irritating, consequence of racial separation and exclusion that Jews should be left to do what they wanted within their own cultural sphere—another kind of ghetto. What this strange but consistent thinking gave the Jews was a channel for reaching out to each other when other lines of communication were broken. It was an opportunity that Robert Weltsch was about to seize with relish.

On April I Bella Fromm ventured out on the streets of Berlin, despite her secretary's pleas that she stay at home. At the Ullstein publishers' offices, everyone was on edge but otherwise going about his or her business as usual until the heavy thud of SA boots resounded outside. The mob, Fromm noted, included the building's doorman, to whom she had given an overcoat as a gift a few days before. He, too, was now chanting "To hell with the Jews!" at the top of his voice. The Nazi throng continued down the street without seeking to enter, and after a while Fromm requested that her car be brought around. It was—by the same doorman, dressed once again in his dignified gray livery, "his face a full moon of good-natured innocence." Twice, she observed later in her diary, he had changed color within two hours—emblematic of the fickle German populace.[7]

In the days leading up to the boycott, Leo Baeck had not escaped the Nazi pressure to speak out against those Jews who were supposedly spreading tales of "atrocities" abroad. Before April I Julius Streicher, Germany's leading Jew-baiter, had headed an ad hoc "Central Committee to Defend Against Jewish Atrocity and Boycott Propaganda,"[8] which had sought—and gained—the backing of most German Jewish groups for his efforts to denounce the "lies" and "distortions" picked up by and repeated in the foreign press. Baeck had agreed to join this protest, perhaps only half unwillingly. He genuinely did not wish to see his country internationally defamed for anti-Semitic acts that had never happened. (And many of the published stories were exaggerated fictions.) Nor did he wish to court a confrontation with Germany's new masters by refusing to cooperate with Streicher. Prudence seemed to dictate a more tempered course of action. Publicly, Baeck would simply affirm the truth—and the truth was that Jewish corpses were not turning up in cemeteries and Jewish girls were not being raped in Berlin back alleys. His true feelings—for example, his endorsement of an anti-

German boycott—he would reveal only in private. So Baeck added his name to those of other Jewish leaders, such as Max Naumann of the Verband nationaldeutscher Juden (VndJ); the opera director Kurt Singer; and Ludwig Freund, a top official in the Reichsbund jüdischer Frontsoldaten (RjF), condemning the foreign "atrocity propaganda."[9] Just before April 1, he had arranged to have a copy of the statement of the Reichsvertretung der Landesverbände (National Representation of the Regional Associations) denouncing any foreign boycott of German goods and proclaiming steadfast loyalty to the fatherland, delivered to Adolf Hitler in the chancellery. At this point Baeck still hoped to sway the Führer's mind, or at least to stay his hand from making any further anti-Jewish moves.

In his Munich "inner exile," Richard Willstätter was not personally affected by the boycott of Jewish businesses. Few Jews lived in the city—only about nine thousand out of a population of over three-quarters of a million—and fewer still were the targets of Hitler's men this particular Saturday. Some six hundred shops were boycotted, but peacefully. The easygoing people of Munich looked on phlegmatically.[10] At his home along the Isar, the eminent chemist would scarcely have noticed anything unusual even if he had bothered to look out his window. His attention was still focused on his research into enzymes—work for which he had just applied for a grant from the Rockefeller Foundation. As a scientist and an "inactive" Jew, he still felt safe, removed from this upheaval. On the day of the boycott, his good friend Fritz Haber, a convert to Christianity since his student days, now despairing of the future of Jewish scientists under the Nazis, wrote Willstätter a cautionary note: No longer should the two of them expect to be spared from persecution or loss of their prestigious posts. The one-day boycott, as he observed it from the outlying Dahlem section of Berlin, was exposing the unmistakable outline of future Nazi policy toward the Jews. "Race" was what defined them now, Haber thought, and no disclaiming of religious belief or practice would satisfy a political movement bent on exorcising this "alien" element from the German volk. Willstätter could not escape the Nazis' wrath much longer, Haber said. But the two Nobel laureates were in a bind: If they resigned any of their remaining public posts (Willstätter was still secretary of the Bavarian Academy of Sciences), they might well be attacked for promoting anti-German propaganda—the ostensible reason for the boycott.[11] So, for the time being, Haber and Willstätter would follow the lead of Jew-ish leaders like Baeck and Weltsch and do nothing that might possibly be construed as unpatriotic. (Several weeks later, the two scientists took steps to dissociate themselves from a more openly hostile profes-sional world: Willstätter resigned from the German Chemical Society, and Haber, the organization's vice president, followed suit out of sym-pathy with his friend.)[12] This "doing nothing" included not making plans to leave Germany. Instead, Willstätter dug in his heels. He vowed to stay in the Bavarian capital as long as it was possible to do so "with dignity."[13]

In Hamburg—a former "red" city inhospitable to Germany's "brown" rulers—a somewhat unnerved Max Warburg could take comfort in the fact his bank had not been attacked by the SA. Indeed, the boycott had taken place without incident. Nazis had picketed Jewish shops and forced some to close their doors for the day, but aside from the pres-ence of uniformed men armed with bayonets and revolvers and throngs of curious onlookers straining for a peek, "one would hardly have real-ized that a serious boycott was in progress," as the American consul put it.[14] The Jewish-owned department store Karstadt had even stayed open all day, after having dismissed all its Jewish employees the day before. Warburg and several other Jews had also agreed to step down from the store's board of directors.[15] In hindsight, his resistance to pleas from family members that he emigrate and from his brother Felix, in New York, that he liquidate the bank now seemed fully justified. The Nazis clearly had no intention of destroying M. M. Warburg and Co. The firm's importance to any German government, even a fanatically anti-Semitic one, could not be underestimated, particularly if it was bent on financing a massive military buildup. (Hadn't Warburg stood next to Hitler when he had certified Hjalmar Schacht as head of the Reichs-bank?) For now, his "fortress" remained secure. More pessimistic views, like those of his close adviser and friend, Carl Melchior, Warburg smugly disregarded.

His supreme confidence would weaken in the coming weeks as, one after the other, his leading posts in the financial and business commu-nities were summarily taken away from him. A junior official with whom Warburg was not even acquainted informed him curtly that he was being removed from the board of the Hamburg Board of Trade (Wirtschaftsdienst), which Warburg had built up through his own efforts.[16] The city's chamber of commerce, which, in better years had bestowed its gold medal on this native son, also had him resign. So did the advisory board of the Reichsbank—his "protector" Schacht broke this sad news to him as gently as possible.[17] In fact, all these unpleasant surprises were conveyed to him "in good form," in marked contrast to the damning verbiage that kept cropping up in the pages of Nazi newspapers like the *Völkischer Beobachter* (National Observer). To make up for these restrictions on his public service, Warburg plunged with fervor into Jewish affairs, dealing with the growing needs of would-be émigrés and displaced persons who turned to the Hilfsverein in their despair. This assimilated Jew, who had once believed that invisibility offered the best protection against German anti-Semites, now identified more and more openly with the cause of his own people. Warburg, too, was now a Jew.

Hans-Joachim Schoeps did not allow the smearing of the Star of David on Berlin shop windows to discourage him. After the initial shock of the boycott, he was pleased to see life quickly return to normal.[18] If the Nazis were bent on excluding Jews from Germany's social, cultural, and political life once the boycott ended, he was equally determined to weather this longer storm. The period of oppression might not soon pass, he told his fellow members of the Deutscher Vortrupp the week of the boycott, but they would have to "stand by our country" and not succumb. His and their Germanness was now being tested, and they would pass the test: "No one can tear Germany out of our hearts," he said.[19] Schoeps continued to believe that conservative-minded Jews with a strong attachment to their country would be acceptable to the Nazis, could participate in the coming "national regeneration," and would not be treated the same as either foreign Jews living on German soil or those identified with the radical Left. The government would be willing to negotiate and reach a compromise with someone like himself. The challenge that he and his followers faced was how to achieve this modus vivendi. "Today," he wrote, "we are liquidating the epoch 1812–1933, and at this historic turning point commences the struggle for the entry of German Jews into the new Germany."[20] One way of appeasing the Nazis and preventing the wholesale exclusion of Jews from German life was by acknowledging their grievances. Schoeps saw some validity in the nationalists' complaint that Jews were too numerous in the fields of law, medicine, and academia. He supported a reduction of the Jewish presence in these and other professions, even if it meant that his own career path would be sabotaged. Rather than expel the Jews (as the Nazis were now threatening to do), the new Germany simply needed to carve out an enclave for them—a kind of Jewish "national park," as he put it.[21] The twenty-four-year-old Schoeps, who spoke for only a handful of Germany's Jews, drew up the outline of a plan to guarantee the Jewish populace minority legal status in the Reich and then had the temerity to submit it to Hitler.[22] In making this kind of direct appeal to the Führer, he would be joined by the Jewish veterans group, the RjF, which also asked for a role in "rebuilding" Germany.[23]

Speculation that the Nazis would make good on their vow to expunge Jews from certain professions and the civil service prompted the Reichsbund's leaders to direct a plea for special treatment to their old comrade-in-arms, Hindenburg, reminding him of their war sacrifices.[24] This ploy worked. The Reich president implored Hitler to exempt Jewish World War I veterans from losing their professional positions, and the chancellor, still dependent on the backing of Hindenburg's conservative allies, gave his consent. When the new Law for the Restoration of the Professional Civil Service was promulgated by the Reich interior minister Wilhelm Frick on April 7, authorizing the "retirement" of all non-Aryan civil servants (including schoolteachers, university professors, judges, and public prosecutors, as well as career bureaucrats), Jews who had served during the war were exempted, as were those who had held their posts prior to 1914 or who had lost a father or son on the front. The brunt of the law thus fell most heavily on younger Jews and those who had entered the country from eastern Europe and the Soviet Union. For the moment, this stratagem of conservative Jewry appeared to be successful. By turning against other, less desirable Jews, they had gained a temporary foothold in Hitler's "new order." (After 1933, it is not surprising that the RjF gained popularity, increasing its membership from thirty thousand to nearly fifty-five thousand.)[25] For this gain, the sacrificing of less "Germanic" members of their race was a price worth paying.

Many Jews were dismayed by the raw expressions of hatred that marked the April 1 boycott—the curses hurled at them, the slogans scrawled on their windows, the Storm Troopers' brazen violation of their lives and livelihoods. The *Centralverein Zeitung* solemnly noted the "deep, angry shame" that the community felt.[26] Bella Fromm ran into some of this anti-Semitic animosity when she drove that evening to a

Berlin train station to pick up her teenage daughter Gonny, who was returning from a ski vacation. Beside each arriving train, an SA company came to a halt and belted out in "animal cadence" its vile cry: "To hell with the Jews! Shameful death to the Jews! We won't have any more Jews!"[27]

These sounds and sights left indelible scars on Jewish memories, but what left an even deeper impression was the contrasting attitude of the German public. They were clearly *not* anti-Semitic zealots. In the big cities German passersby had either looked on impassively or walked right past the Storm Troopers into Jewish-owned shops.[28] Some went out of their way to show kindness to Jews singled out for denunciation.[29] Most Germans who witnessed any of the abuse directed at Jews on April 1 found the spectacle absurd, mildly amusing. It was like watching a gang of drunken, disorganized college fraternity brothers making fools of themselves in public. Toward the Jews, many onlookers felt only indifference: They did not overly sympathize with the Jews' predicament, but neither did they wish to worsen it. Mostly, they wanted things to return to normal.

It was a reaction that swayed the powers that be. Apprehensive from the start about how the boycott would be received, the Nazi leadership had watched anxiously as prices on the Berlin stock exchange plummeted after the announcement of their one-day anti-Jewish protest. The long-term economic consequences of hounding the Jews out of business were spelled out to Hitler by Schacht and other non-Nazis in the cabinet: Germany's recovery from the depression was threatened. On the political front, foreign denunciations of the German government's actions had been embarrassingly vociferous, a blow to the Nazi regime's frail mantle of legitimacy. In the United States the official reaction was diplomatically muted, but many private citizens, especially Jews, were outraged. Within the Reich the lukewarm response of the German man in the street confirmed Hitler's concern about the lack of popular backing for a crackdown on the Jews.[30] Sensing that the boycott was causing too much damage, the government backed down from its earlier threat to resume it in a few days. The boycott was called off after only fourteen hours, with Joseph Goebbels, the propaganda minister, lamely trying to put a good face on this retreat by claiming it was due to a curtailment of anti-German propaganda abroad—which was patently untrue.[31]

The plain, inescapable truth was that this first large-scale organized

move against Germany's Jews had ignominiously failed. It was a setback
for the Nazi radicals who had urged it and for a party program based
on anti-Semitism. This move against the Jewish community was painful
for many individual Jews who faced the loss of their jobs under the new
civil service law; however, the boycott brought not widespread despair,
humiliation, and defeatism, but, ironically, a more positive outlook—a
sense of pride and hope for the future. Rebounding from this first blow
that was intended to strike them down, many Jews would proclaim a
psychological victory.

On the afternoon of April I Robert Weltsch sat at his desk uplifted
by what he had just witnessed on the streets and sidewalks of Berlin.
The essay he wrote summed up his emotions in its hortatory headline:
TRAGT IHN MIT STOLZ, DEN GELBEN FLECK! ("Wear the Yellow Badge
with Pride!"). It began on a note of historical significance, a stepping
back from the passions of the moment to assess weightier matters:
"The first of April 1933 will remain an important day in the history of
German Jewry, indeed in the history of the entire Jewish people. The
events of this day do not have only a political and economic dimension,
but a moral and spiritual one as well."[32]

It was necessary for all Jews to reflect on these aspects because the
boycott had clearly defined them as a distinct, ineluctable group. No
longer could Jews harbor the illusion that they were anything but Jews
in German eyes—the National Socialist revolution had ushered in a
"new age" that presented German Jewry with a fundamentally altered
situation. To react appropriately under attack, Jews ought not, as they
had done in the past, camouflage themselves as Germans, but instead
affirm their Jewishness—by which Weltsch meant the Zionist credo
spelled out by Theodor Herzl in his seminal *Judenstaat*, where the "Jewish question" was confronted openly. According to Herzl, the differences between Jews and other European peoples lay at the heart of anti-
Semitism. The unwillingness of German Jews to admit these crucial
differences—in effect, their betrayal of Judaism—Weltsch believed, had
contributed to their "degradation" by the Nazis, who despised such a
"lack of character." Thus, the Jews were partially to blame for what had
now befallen them: They were hated because they had pretended to be
what they were not. No such disguise could work any longer; the Nazis
had stripped it away. Only racial Jewishness mattered to the Nazis: All
Jews were marked with the same symbolic yellow badge and would share
the same fate under it.[33]

This badge, recalling the actual one Jews had been forced to wear in medieval times, was intended to shame and ostracize, but would, like Hester Prynne's scarlet letter, admit the Jews to a deeper appreciation of a common human bond. It would give them a redeeming feeling of pride, matching what the Nazis had imparted to the German people. In fact, Weltsch argued, a ringing affirmation of Jewish identity would emulate the Germans' national renewal and thereby earn Jews the respect and acceptance they had lost by seeking to be assimilated. For shattering this delusion, Jews actually owed the Nazis a debt of thanks: Hitler had awakened them to their true being. According to Weltsch, Nazism was not the Jews' damnation, it was their salvation: "We recall all of those who for 5,000 years have been called Jews, who have been stigmatized as Jews. We are reminded that we are Jews. We say 'Yes,' and we wear it [the symbolic yellow badge] with pride."[34]

It was a curious interpretation of misfortune, to see in it not impending calamity but an opportunity for Jewish self-rediscovery and rebirth, but the *Rundschau* succinctly articulated Weltsch's belief that the German Jews had erred in craving acceptance on others' terms.

Because of his publisher's worries about how an article affirming Jewish pride might be received by the Reich minister for public enlightenment and propaganda, Joseph Goebbels, this April 4 issue of the *Jüdische Rundschau* was distributed at sidewalk kiosks, instead of being mailed to subscribers, as usual.[35] No Jewish newspaper had ever been sold this way or had been so openly available to readers. It was a risky gamble for Weltsch. Until now Goebbels had taken no steps to harass or shut down the Jewish press, but this issue clearly might provoke him to do so. In fact, this edition of the Zionist newspaper did set off an explosive reaction—not in the Propaganda Ministry, but among Germany's Jews. The few thousand printed copies were sold out in a rush. Weltsch himself handed out papers to vendors near the Bahnhof Zoo, and when all these copies were gone, he managed to convince his reluctant publisher, Betty Frankenstein, to bring out a special edition, reprinting the "yellow badge" essay, of five thousand copies. These, too, were quickly snatched up. Thousands of Jews—Zionists and assimilationists alike—wrote letters to the editor praising the piece and expressing their agreement with it. The demand for subscriptions to the *Jüdische Rundschau* skyrocketed.[36] Kiosks up and down the Kurfürstendamm were suddenly plastered with front page articles for all to read. The newspaper had found—as a pensive Weltsch explained to Martin Buber later that month—an "unprecedented echo" in the Jewish community.[37] On the strength of this one essay, the *Jüdische Rundschau* had been transformed from a pesky fringe voice, ignored by all but the most committed Zionists, into a chief spokesman for all German Jewry.

By contrast, when an assimilated Jew like the scholar Ismar Elbogen urged stoic forbearance, telling readers of the *Centralverein Zeitung* to work hard and help one another,[38] his words rang hollow and anachronistic, in light of the stunning news that Jews were to be dismissed from the German civil service. Leo Baeck's agreement to chair a new Central Committee of German Jews for Welfare Assistance and Development, to meet the material needs of Jews whose incomes had been abruptly cut off, likewise seemed hardly adequate to meet this extraordinary emergency. The crisis that German Jews were experiencing was a spiritual as well as a material one, and only the Zionists were fully responding to its challenge.

So, within the Jewish community, dividing lines were being drawn once again. Anxious to nip this divisiveness in the bud, Baeck proclaimed Jewish unity under the banner of the Reichsvertetung he headed, but day after day it was the shrill cry of an unrepenting liberal Jew assailing the Zionists, and a Zionist retorting, that set the tone among his fellow Jews. When, for example, one assimilationist essayist sought to respond to the Nazi policies with a quotation from Goethe's *Wilhelm Meisters Lehrjahre* (Wilhelm Meister's Apprentice Years)—"If I love you, what business is it of yours?"—Robert Weltsch fired back that such self-deprecating platitudes could never be Jewry's "only salvation." This salvation lay in affirming their Jewish being. Weltsch advanced such an opinion while, almost in the same breath, insisting that he was not interested in engaging in "inner-Jewish polemics."[39] In this war of words, he did not hesitate to adopt German nationalist phrases for his own ends. "National" Jews, he said, also affirmed the value of the "*Volkstum* and blood for the individual and for a people as a whole."[40]

Weltsch's advancement of Zionism as a Jewish variant of Nazism played on the shifting political tides of early 1933 as the Hitler regime was institutionalizing its ideology. His appeal to Jewish racial identity and destiny was at once an accommodating response to and a reflection of the dominant nationalistic ethos in Germany. Jews were drawn to the unifying, affirmative message in Weltsch's editorials as the prospects for German Jewry grew daily more uncertain and the old faith in law and order fell away.

The short-lived April boycott did not mark the end of this new wave of anti-Semitic actions. Physical attacks on Jews continued,[41] as did the forcing of Jews out of their positions. The Berlin offices of the American Jewish Joint Distribution Committee were raided.[42] The Gestapo interrupted a meeting of the Centralverein deutscher Staatsbürger jüdischer Glaubens (Central Organization of German Citizens of the Jewish Faith) in Berlin.[43] Meanwhile, Jewish lawyers lost clients as many non-Jews allowed themselves to be persuaded not to seek their services. Jews were being excluded from the literary, musical, and theatrical worlds. German universities were similarly being purged of Jews—as Fritz Haber had predicted to Richard Willstätter they would—and giants of German science like James Franck were resigning out of protest. (Haber chose to retire in May, rather than to have to commit the ignominy of firing some of his Jewish colleagues.) Jewish physicians, except those who had been in practice before 1914, lost many of their patients. According to the *Jewish Daily Bulletin*, the number of unemployed Jews standing on breadlines jumped thirty thousand in a single week in April—to eighty thousand.[44] One British visitor found German Jews living in "one continuous state of mental agony and nightmare," like persons trapped at the base of a volcano waiting helplessly for it to erupt.[45]

With its boycott and dismissal of Jewish civil servants (an estimated five thousand out of a total of six thousand),[46] the government had launched a staggering attack on the nation's Jews. Reeling off balance, the Jews were waiting to see what would happen next. The April 7 Law for Restoration of the Professional Civil Service and the setting of a numerus clausus for Jews were alarming developments, devastating to those individuals who were directly affected and their families, but not devastating to the community as a whole. Many Jews, in fact, were willing to agree with Hans-Joachim Schoeps that they *were* too overrepresented in these professions. They could live with these new laws as long as the restrictions signalled a legal clarification and resolution of their status in Nazi Germany, instead of more beatings and name-calling. In the aftermath of the less than wholly successful boycott, they could now hope that Hitler would rein in his radicals and steer a more moderate course. But this was by no means a sure thing. What the Jews had experienced in early April might also foreshadow even worse officially sanctioned repression. Who could tell?

With the direction of Nazi policy so unclear, many Jews fell prey to psychological fears. Others rallied behind time-tested defensive strate-gies. "We are defending our rights as best we can," a shaken Max War-burg confided to Chaim Weizmann. "It is again a difficult time, but over the last 20 years I have become used to trouble and will fight again."[47] The theme of rising to meet adversity, as Jews had done time and time again in the past, was articulated by other moderate leaders. Leo Baeck called in public for a greater community effort to help the less fortu-nate and to build a long-term future for Jews in Germany. More educa-tion and social welfare would carry them through this unsettling time, he said.[48] Deep within, Baeck was far more pessimistic. At some point in April, this rabbi, whose life so aptly embodied the historical symbio-sis of German and Jew, grimly conceded: "The end of German Jewry has arrived."[49] This was a starkly unequivocal pronouncement, coming from the lips of a religious scholar who had always managed to take the long view and who had found consolation for Jewish suffering in the experiences that lay both behind and ahead of them. It was this message of historical continuity, of enduring faith and truth, that Baeck had always espoused. It was this message that he had given to cold and weary German Jewish soldiers on the eastern front during World War I, recall-ing in their hearts the homeland they had left behind and to which they would soon return. Who better than he knew of the centuries of rejec-tion, hostility, ostracism, and violence that Jews had endured on Ger-man soil and yet prevailed? Who better than he could see beyond the vicissitudes of the Third Reich and envision a better Germany for Jews after its demise? Who better than he could offer his people reason for hope? And yet Baeck could not help but realize that this threat to Ger-man Jewry's one-thousand-year existence was without precedent. Ger-many was going through a radical metamorphosis, and if it continued to evolve in this way, there would be no place in it for Jews. This was the simple truth Baeck could not evade. But it was also a truth that a man of his stature in the Jewish community could not openly proclaim. While accepting it inwardly, Baeck could not allow this bleak prognosis to deter him from doing what he could to help those Jews who remained with him in Germany, unwilling or unable to leave. They were his chief responsibility, and they now looked to him for guidance and sustenance, not for words of doom and despair. As long as Baeck was able, he would try to fulfill that obligation, to make their lives as bear-able as possible.

To strengthen a community under assault, Baeck and others who were committed to fighting for its survival had first attempted to open a dialogue with the government, requesting meetings with Hitler and stressing their patriotism. In this bid Baeck even went so far, in a May 1933 statement, as to declare that German Jews joined with the Nazis in rejecting communism and to affirm that "the renewal of Germany is an ideal and a desire within the German Jews."[50] But, aside from Hindenburg's intercession on behalf of Jewish war veterans, this strategy of appeasement failed. The German Führer simply turned a deaf ear on the professions of loyalty and ingratiating letters mailed to him by Jewish leaders, refusing to sit down with them or to disclose the full dimensions of his Jewish policy.

Thwarted in this approach, many of these Jewish leaders turned their attention to bolstering German Jewry internally.[51] A more cohesive, self-supporting, and resilient community, encompassing *all* Jews, seemed to offer the best alternative way of helping those individuals in need, boosting their morale, and building a bulwark against any future Nazi hostility. Stronger, interdependent ties among Jews could best be fostered by a single all-encompassing organization, to which Jews could look for direction and that could speak to the government for all of them. Since the Jews lacked real power in Germany, unity was the strongest weapon in their limited arsenal. It could provide a collective "inner resistance"[52] for the large majority of Jews for whom leaving Germany was not a realistic or attractive option.

By now, Baeck and other community leaders had concluded that emigration could save only a small minority of German Jewry. The Jewish community was aging, and relatively few of its members had the skills or desire to quit their homeland and forge a new life abroad. Furthermore, the logistics and finances involved in relocating half a million Jews were staggering, even if welcoming host nations could be found. (And no ready candidates were coming forward, eager to absorb a mass exodus of refugees.) For these reasons, emigration had to be seen as desirable mainly for younger, unattached Jews, who were just starting their careers, or for the politically persecuted. For the rest, some kind of tolerable arrangement would have to be worked out within the hostile confines of the Third Reich. (Shortly after Hitler came to power, close to sixty thousand Jews had left. Of this number, some ten thousand returned to Germany by the end of 1933, either homesick or convinced that the Nazi leader's days were numbered.) There was no other choice.[53]

Bringing Jews more closely together also inevitably deepened the Jewish identity and distinctiveness that assimilationist groups like the Centralverein had long opposed and the Zionists had endorsed. Now Nazi oppression was proving more persuasive than these Jewish arguments. Jews who, like Haber and Willstätter, had rarely thought of themselves as Jews were being made to do so, pushed against their will into communal solidarity. If they could not yet bring themselves to wear Weltsch's celebrated "yellow badge" with pride, they could be induced to do so out of feelings of powerlessness and vulnerability.

For Leo Baeck, in particular, Jewish unity was essential to prevent the community from destroying itself through internecine strife. In the aftermath of the boycott, the Zionists were daily picking up strength, demanding more power in the various Gemeinden, especially in Berlin, and putting the dismayed liberals on the defensive. These revived antagonisms had to be defused and laid to rest. Furthermore, the tremendous public response to Robert Weltsch's appeal to Jewish pride showed Baeck and others that Jews now wanted and needed to feel connected to one other, as members of a community under siege, rather than remain separate and invisible individuals. Unity had a powerful psychological rationale.

For all these reasons, liberal Jewish leaders like Baeck began, during the summer of 1933, to discuss seriously the creation of a central organization. This body would strive to accomplish what previous attempts had failed to do, namely, to end the factional squabbling among Jews and give them all a legitimate, equal place in the same ethnic community, albeit apart from other Germans. This desire to organize defensively grew out of several emerging realizations. First, it was becoming obvious that Hitler and his cronies were not the least interested in holding a dialogue with any Jewish groups to hash out some compromise solution to the "Jewish question." The fawning letters that emanated in May from bodies such as Baeck's Reichsvertretung der Landesverbände (National Representation of the Regional Associations) and the right-wing VndJ were ignored as brusquely as earlier ones had been.[54] (As Hitler remarked in June: "I cannot find any interest in seeing Jews.")[55] The Nazi leader wanted to treat the Jews as objects of his policies, not as opponents deserving of a modicum of respect or acknowledgment. In the absence of any vocal defenders in non-Jewish circles, the Jews would have to depend on internal solidarity to sustain them.

Second, although Baeck and most Jewish leaders thought that their future in Germany was bleak, they also believed it was inescapable, a future that had to be accepted as best they could. Except for the young and the unattached, most German Jews were simply too settled and too dependent on their German homeland, its language and culture, to leave in great numbers even if they had the means and the necessary papers to emigrate—which few did. Himself a member of the older Jewish generation, Baeck (now nearing his sixtieth birthday) looked at the predicament from his coevals' perspective and resolved to concentrate his energies on helping those Jews who, like him, were not inclined to flee Germany. As a rabbi, Baeck saw that the crisis his fellow Jews faced demanded more of him as a spiritual and moral leader than had ever been the case in the past. He was ready and willing to gird up his loins to meet these additional burdens, through the inner strength that his faith gave him.

Baeck was encouraged to play a more prominent role in the Jewish community under Hitler by what he and other sanguine Jews perceived to be a moderating of Nazi policies in light of the boycott's lack of success and the general unpopularity of anti-Semitic violence. The *Jüdische Rundschau*, for instance, ran an editorial in May—ironically right after books by "un-German" authors had been tossed on bonfires in Berlin and other cities—citing speeches by several governmental ministers hinting that the "revolutionary phase" of the Nazi rule was now over.[56] Jews would be allowed, Robert Weltsch believed and hoped, to continue their lives in Germany in a legally circumscribed, but also protected and largely autonomous domain—a Jewish oasis in a Nazi desert not unlike Schoeps's "game park."

If Leo Baeck was swayed by the pressing material and spiritual needs of the community, Richard Willstätter, a less consciously Jewish figure, justified staying in Germany on purely patriotic grounds: He was not about to abandon his country just because its rulers were now openly hostile to his race. Inside his Munich villa, Willstätter did not experience any of the verbal or physical abuse being inflicted on other Jews, and even the burning of the works of world-famous authors did not shake his determination to defy the Nazis, stubbornly and passively, simply by remaining where he was, waiting for their vaunted "revolution" to run out of steam. Instead of readying himself to go abroad, Willstätter expressed his contempt for the Nazis by resigning from another public post, as head of the mathematics and natural science branch of the Bavarian Academy of Sciences.[57]

The premature retirement of his good friend Fritz Haber depressed Willstätter, but did not shake his resolve. From Berlin Haber wrote bitterly about the callous treatment he had received after two decades of outstanding scientific service to his country. ("From the circle of I.G. Farben there has been no one who has talked to me, or visited me, concerning my offer of resignation.")[58] Willstätter empathized deeply but still did not believe he would be touched by the forces that were ruining the careers of Haber and other Jewish scientists and scholars. In a sense, he had already sacrificed a large part of his career by resigning his professorship in 1924. This act had spared him much of the indignation that Jewish academics were now enduring. It had also given him a feeling of immunity. To Chaim Weizmann, Willstätter conveyed his optimistic belief that now, after the initial riots and anti-Semitic hysteria, Nazi moves against the Jews would abate, and he would ride out this dwindling storm, clipping his roses along the banks of the Isar.[59] (As a frustrated Kurt Blumenfeld blurted out: "This man will never understand the Jewish problem.")[60]

In the fall of 1933 Willstätter finally came out of his shell-like exile to travel abroad—not to emigrate but to accept a prestigious international honor, the Willard Gibbs Medal awarded by the American Chemical Society for outstanding distinction. It was only the fourth time this medal was being presented to a non-American. Arriving in New York by steamer Willstätter paid a brief visit to relatives in Westchester County before catching a train to Chicago for the awards ceremony. It was a hugely uplifting, triumphant moment for this world-renowned scientist who was scorned and abused in his own land. Some forty of Willstätter's former students converged on the Midwest city to greet and praise him, and on the evening of September 13 over a thousand persons crowded into a lecture hall to hear him speak. It was an introspective address, reviewing his career and paying tribute to mentors like Adolf von Baeyer. In it, Willstätter spoke of the love of scientific inquiry that had sustained him all his life, through good and bad:

To delve into Nature's secrets is something beautiful beyond description; it is an enviable privilege of the scientist to conquer obstacles when all known devices were deemed inadequate for their circumvention, and to penetrate far enough to lift Nature's veil a little more and more from her hidden treasures. This sensation of felicity in the struggle for knowledge is not dimmed by age. Today, in a study of ferments in blood cells, I live through similar suspense and equal fascination as a beginner forty years ago.[61]

As he basked in the adulation of his colleagues, in a city then celebrating "A Century of Progress" in technology and science, the courtly mannered Bavarian chemist could not help but be struck by the growing contrast between such impressive scientific progress and frail human nature, which seemed doomed to repeat the same terrible blunders, generation after generation, in Sisyphean futility. "Oftentimes we ask ourselves, with severe scruples," Willstätter concluded in his stilted and heavily accented English, "is mankind really becoming wiser, better, and nobler? Has the power of religion grown to render impossible hate and strife between races and nations?"[62]

The answer, Willstätter knew, was No—the cruel nightmare of Nazi Germany had taken hold across the Atlantic, hurling his ancestral homeland back to the brink of barbarity. That was the reality he faced, the reality to which he would still choose to return in a few days. If philosophy had served as consolation to the imprisoned Roman thinker Boethius a millennium and a half before, science would assume this role for Willstätter now, its inexorable and independent development rewarding his life's commitment to serve the "common weal of mankind." Content in this faith, he could endure the humiliations of being a Jew under Hitler as a great athlete might put up with the taunts and jeers of an angry crowd blinded by its petty, demeaning passions. Willstätter did not "play" to please the multitudes. They would not stop him from going back to Germany, where he belonged.

The thought of leaving Germany weighed on Bella Fromm's mind, too. People kept coming up to her and whispering warnings: *It was time to get out.* Frederick T. Birchall, correspondent for the *New York Times,* implored her to take an "extended vacation": A lot more trouble lay ahead for her inside the Third Reich.[63] Where she sat, at the epicenter of Berlin social life, trouble sought her out. The same day as her conversation with Birchall, Adolf Hitler recognized Fromm at a celebration of "National Socialist People's Welfare" and sat down on the empty chair beside her. "We have met before, *gnädige Frau,* haven't we?" was his opening line. Trapped, Fromm raised her arm stiffly and rendered the now obligatory salute to the Führer of the German people. A moment later she had to stand in bitter silence as the strains of the infamous Horst Wessel song wafted across the ballroom.[64]

The signals she picked up were mixed. On the heels of her friends' promise to protect her came the announcement of governmental measures that imperiled her livelihood, if not her person. One day, she was summoned to Goebbels's office, to listen to the minister of propaganda incongruously mutter his approval of her society columns. Two days later, her employer, Ullstein, announced that all Jewish employees were to be fired. (This did not actually happen.) In her diary Fromm gave more free play to her darker thoughts: "Not a day goes by without the arrest of some 'unreliable' colleague through the Gestapo," she noted in May. "The very ringing of the doorbell has a shattering effect on all of us."[65] On balance, Fromm came to conclude, she had a good chance of surviving as long as she kept her privileged position as the darling of the diplomatic corps. The Nazis would not dare incense foreign opinion by going after her. Besides, she could use her contacts for the benefit of less fortunate Jews—those being herded into concentration camps because of their leftist views or driven out of the country because of their race. By the middle of the summer of 1933, Fromm could tally up the names of several hundred Jews and other persecuted Germans she had helped rescue from dire straits and bring safely over the frontier.[66] Politically close to the conservatives whom Hitler had displaced, Fromm kept hoping they would mount a challenge to Hitler's rule. Her dear friend General Kurt von Schleicher, now living in seclusion outside Potsdam, might step forward to lead the veterans' group Stahlhelm in an uprising against the Nazi regime.[67] Hitler, she felt, was still vulnerable, still not firmly in the saddle. Things might still take a turn for the better.

Max Warburg was also hopeful—at least for the long run. As he surveyed all the anti-Jewish actions that Germany's new masters had either tolerated or orchestrated in just a few months, he saw no immediate letup looming. Pressures on Jews to quit their posts, sell their homes, and leave the country would only grow. More and more Jews would emigrate, and the government would encourage them to do so. Jewish organizations, such as the Hilfsverein, could try to assist this exodus as best they could, offering job training to would-be émigrés and working with the government on an agreement to allow Jews to transfer some of their wealth abroad.[68] Still, emigration would have to proceed slowly, cautiously, to calm any fears abroad of a mounting flood of undesired Jewish refugees. Warburg would work in his low-key, behind-the-scenes manner to facilitate this kind of gradual emigration. Assessing the situation dispassionately, he agreed with Leo Baeck and other leaders of assimilated German Jewry that emigration could not be the antidote to deprivation and humiliation for the great majority of Jews. These Jews would have to stay behind and fight a rearguard battle to preserve what diminished rights they still had and to win back those they had already lost. "We must steel ourselves for a struggle that will last many years," he told Chaim Weizmann.[69] Warburg was not prepared to say that the Jews would fail in this endeavor. There was still cause for optimism. It was not yet a time to yield to panic.

Over the next few months, Warburg's belief that the Jews could hold out was badly battered. Nazi officials showed themselves to be untrustworthy when he attempted to negotiate with them about a "liquidation bank" that would ease the transfer of Jewish assets overseas to Palestine and other countries.[70] And there was some speculation, reported by the American diplomat George Messersmith, that the German government would take over the country's private banks, including M. M. Warburg and Co.[71] Furthermore, contrary to what he and many like-minded Jews had expected, the level of anti-Semitic persecution was rising, not falling. This increased persecution seemed to be occurring despite the government's wish to appease foreign opinion by curtailing acts of physical violence against Jews. (The regime realized, Messersmith recounted, that mistreatment of the Jews had led to an effective boycott of German goods in many countries and that these trade sanctions could well have "disastrous effects" on the German economy.)[72] On the evening of June 15, for example, a band of some forty SA men, acting entirely on their own, raided a meeting of young Berlin Jews, beat them with rubber clubs, kicked them, and held them in custody until early the next morning, when the police found and freed them.[73]

At the end of June, Warburg sent his young friend Wilfrid Israel, owner of a department store that bore his family's name, to London to brief British Jews on a "new wave of terrorism" that was "continuing unremittingly and . . . likely to increase in extent and ferocity." Jews were being taken from their homes and badly beaten. Warburg was concerned that the Nazis might now shut down all Jewish organizations and seize their assets, and he was accordingly seeking to have their funds trans-ferred abroad as soon as possible for safekeeping.[74]

The tragedy of German Jewry struck those close to Warburg. On June 9, while Warburg was in Amsterdam, his eighty-year-old uncle, Moritz Oppenheim, and his aunt committed suicide, despairing of what the future held in store for them.[75] Gamely, Warburg sought not to let such tragedies drain his spirit or energies. When his friends on the stock market refused to shake his hand, he did not condemn their behavior. When he was asked to step down from the board of directors of the Hamburg-American Line, he did so graciously, even completing the farewell speech that the emotionally overcome chairman, Max von Schinkel, could not bring himself to finish, with Warburg recalling his accomplishments for the shipping line in the third person.[76] Like Bella Fromm, Warburg still had friends in high places, and realizing this gave him some comfort as the situation around him deteriorated. For the moment, he could afford to hold his ground, help less fortunate Jews get out of the country, and otherwise serve the community to which he was now closely linked. Like so many of his fellow German Jews, War-burg had been changed by being tarred with the epithet "Jew." If he was no longer "Max Warburg, Hamburg banker," but rather "Warburg, the Jew financier," then he would fight back on those terms, as a proud, unbowed Jew. He would fight on tenaciously, ignoring the pleas of his family that he leave Germany while emigration was still possible.

To Jews on both the Left and the Right, the Nazi assault on their community presented opportunities along with travails. The Nazi-imposed definition of Jews as separate from, and inferior to, an Aryan Volksgemeinschaft was not wholly unwelcome. Indeed, it strengthened the hands of groups that had formerly been on the periphery of the Jewish community, bestowing on them more credibility and inner con-fidence. For a profoundly conservative German patriot like Hans-Joachim Schoeps, the present adversity could be seen as a test of Jewish loyalty to the fatherland. Out of this trial by fire, those Jews whose Ger-manness was pure, unalloyed by any taint of Jewish nationalism (unlike the Zionists), would emerge worthy of acceptance by this revolutionary Third Reich. By aligning themselves philosophically with the tenets of German renewal, even as practiced under Hitler, these Jews expected that the violence and hatred directed at them would decrease. "Our task," Schoeps proclaimed, "is to wait until we are again accepted in the

Gemeinschaft; in the meantime we must seek to adjust to new events, not yield to resentment."[77] The vehicle for his Jewish version of Gleich-schaltung would be the Deutscher Vortrupp (German Vanguard) he had formed earlier in the year, in the hope that other young Jews, searching for a new guiding lodestone, would flock to it. To gain a foothold in the Nazi state—always preferable to being expelled from it—Schoeps was willing to accept second-class minority status for the Jewish community.

In so openly courting the Nazis and meeting nearly all their demands (except that the Jews leave Germany), Schoeps was playing a dangerous game, seeming to cozy up to an enemy that despised Jews while staying aloof from those Jews who did not agree with him and whom he deemed insufficiently Germanic. It should thus have come as no great shock to him when a Zionist publication, the *Jüdisches Volksblatt*, accused him of "swastika assimilation." Not so, Schoeps protested to his editorial collaborator Max Brod: "We are no Nazis."[78] It was more accurate to describe him as a German conservative in a totalitarian state, whose patriotic love was as yet unrequited.[79] Schoeps desperately wanted to honor his two overarching passions—for "eternal Germany" and for "eternal Jewry," as he put it hyperbolically to Martin Buber.[80] That these two had already been officially decreed not only irreconcilable but antithetical and inimical was a recognition that Schoeps was not willing or able to make.

In positing Judaism as an analogue to National Socialism and in stressing Jewish cultural and spiritual roots that had long been neglected, Schoeps sounded strangely like the Zionists.[81] Schoeps heaped wrath upon Zionism for "betraying" Germany and for promoting a historically distorted notion of Judaism, based on politics instead of abiding moral and religious values. However, he shared the Zionists' contempt for discredited Jewish liberalism, which had claimed that Jews were not really different from their German Christian friends and neighbors and had shed Judaism as an embarrassing remnant of a bygone era. Both he and the Zionists believed that German Jews could be true to their identity only by openly attesting to their Jewishness.

While presenting his Deutscher Vortrupp as a means of achieving a political rapprochement with the Nazi regime, Schoeps continued to advocate his affirmative view of Judaism without sensing any incompatibility. As he informed the Protestant theologian Karl Barth, Schoeps was still formulating a "systematic theology of Judaism," an outgrowth of his earlier published analysis of contemporary Jewish faith, *Jüdische Glaube in dieser Zeit*. His goal was to define a Jewish approach to life that rested on a belief system, rather than on political goals or cultural patterns. This was, he believed, what German Jews cut adrift from their liberal credo sorely needed.

Professionally, Schoeps fell victim to the Nazis' "legal" moves against the Jews in the spring of 1933. The numerus clausus imposed on Jewish teachers thwarted his plans to launch an academic career.[82] By late spring, he was still hopeful, however, of having his dissertation published and of making a name for himself—if not a livelihood—in this way.[83] (Schoeps, then in his mid-twenties, could still count on financial support from his comfortably well-off parents.) Schoeps was also inspired by the movement—made necessary by a Nazi decree limiting Jewish children in public schools to 1.5 percent of the total enrollment—to open more Jewish schools, fostering a greater awareness of Judaism. Martin Buber was taking the lead on this front, setting up a number of *Lehrhäuser* (literally "teaching houses") to provide young Jews with a unifying moral center during what he foresaw as a long period of oppression and subjugation by Hitler.[84]

Although Buber and Schoeps disagreed on the importance of Zionism and of a Jewish homeland in Palestine, they shared an interest in reviving the spiritual core of Judaism. (Buber also had somewhat similar views as Schoeps's on the essential nature of the Jewish people, recognizing that their common bond was based on race and the notion of volk. That is, Jews constituted a "blood community" of their own, akin to the Aryan one.)[85] With his prospects in the German public schools dimming, Schoeps renewed his earlier acquaintance with Buber by letter, inquiring about the possibility of becoming, as a representative of "German-conscious Jewry,"[86] a docent in history, the history of religion, or philosophy.[87]

In pursuing these options, Schoeps sustained an unshaken optimism about his—and most Jews'—future in the Third Reich. Unable to see that anti-Semitism was central to Hitler's worldview, the politically naive Schoeps held out hopes of the Jews being treated by the Nazis as they were under Mussolini's fascist regime.[88] He was strengthened in this belief by a response he received to his accommodating letter to the SA leader (and fellow homosexual) Ernst Röhm. Röhm told Schoeps that the Führer's ranting about the Jews was only "demagogic nonsense."[89] Throughout the remainder of 1933, Schoeps put out other such feelers to high-ranking officials, asking that his small band of "German-conscious" Jews—the Deutscher Vortrupp—be granted a place in this new German Reich. By and large, the letters were not answered. To the government of Adolf Hitler, Schoeps was just another Jew. If he attracted their interest at all, it was to have the Gestapo keep a close watch on him, to see that his message—that some Jews were willing and eager to be absorbed into Germany's new state—did not catch on.

While Richard Willstätter, Max Warburg, Bella Fromm, Leo Baeck, and Hans-Joachim Schoeps were weighing the odds of survival inside Hitler's Germany, each believing he or she had something important to contribute by staying, Robert Weltsch was churning out editorials rhapsodizing about a "Jewish renaissance." Daily his readership was growing larger and larger. It was a heady time for Weltsch, with Jews of all persuasions now turning to the pages of the *Jüdische Rundschau* every Tuesday and Friday for the latest information and guidance, thirsting—as he put it to Martin Buber—for a message that would uphold their souls.[90] For Weltsch, caught up in the swirl of Zionist publicizing, like an orator on a soapbox who has finally gathered an attentive crowd around him, it was easy to confuse the tragedy faced by the Jews with the Zionist ideological victory that was its by-product. Yes, Jews were suffering, bereft of their sense of belonging in Germany, wandering around helplessly and in despair, like lost campers in a darkened forest. But, in Weltsch's eyes, the good being born out of this wrenching rejection overshadowed the anguish. On May 16, 1933, he summed up these sentiments in an essay entitled "Ja-Sagen zum Judentum" ("Saying 'Yes' to Judaism"):

Nowadays the Jews' sense of belonging together is being strengthened. Jews who until recently passed by each other without a word of acknowledgment or mutual recognition have been drawn closer to each other. One thinks of another Jew as someone who shares the same fate, as a brother. Jews can speak to each other once again. Some part of the wall that in everyday life separated one human being from another and blocked entry to the soul has crumbled away. A moment like this is a fruitful, a holy moment, which can lift our hearts and create a community. The commonality of an ancient inheritance of blood and history, of destiny and mission, once again returns to our consciousness as having significance. To affirm this, with all our heart and a clear mind, this alone is the Jew's worthy answer to this moment.[91]

This realization that they were all Jews together was an intoxicating elixir, the emotional equivalent of what millions of "Aryan" Germans felt under wind-tossed swastikas, hearing the hypnotic chant *"Ein Volk, Ein Reich, Ein Führer!"* that introduced Adolf Hitler. These powerful feelings, to which Weltsch gave such eloquent testimony, infused the Zeitgeist. They were hard to resist, for Jew and non-Jew alike. That they were also blinding, as illusory for German Jewry as was the bourgeois-assimilationist myth they supplanted, was scarcely discernible. A generation before, the kaiser had proclaimed all his people Germans, and the Jews had marched off gladly to die in the trenches for the nation that so acknowledged them. Now branded *Juden* by a movement that loathed them, German Jews gravitated toward each other, resolved once again to prevail through solidarity. Once again, they would be proved wrong.

6

Suffering the Slings and Arrows

As time passed, ambivalence about leaving Germany only deepened. For many remaining German Jews, fear about what *might* happen to them—midnight arrest, the loss of a job—gave way to muted hopes about what they could do to endure this ordeal. Rather than think selfishly only of themselves, Jews began to take care of other Jews. Being part of a community under attack was emotionally and spiritually uplifting but also a trap. Once forged, bonds of solidarity could not easily be broken. It was harder for a communally entangled Jew to say, "I will leave all this behind and go my own way." For the time being, a stronger, culturally assertive Jewish community seemed to be a safe haven, a refuge from the hatred that swarmed around it.

Most Jews were still waiting, in the months following the April 1933 boycott and the attendant rash of violent incidents, for the other shoe to drop. There was much talk that summer about a coming "second revolution" to purge Hitler's remaining conservative opponents as the Gestapo and the SA had rid Germany of Communists and Social Democrats a few months before. If this purge was to happen, the Nazis would have few inhibitions about going after the Jews more relentlessly and systematically; then Jewish patriotic and nationalistic pledges would not make any difference.

But miraculously, the shoe did not drop. Hitler held back, keeping his street brawlers on a short leash. Order was what the German Führer needed now to "legitimate" his rule and consolidate his hold on power. "The revolution is not a permanent state of affairs," he lectured Nazi Party officials in July. "The stream of revolution released must be guided into the safe channel of evolution."[1] Hitler went on to offer what many Jews might be forgiven for interpreting as an olive branch: "We must therefore not dismiss a businessman if he is a good businessman, even if he is not yet a National Socialist, and especially not if the National Socialist who is to take his place knows nothing about business. In business, ability must be the only standard."[2]

And, indeed, the hardship inflicted on Jewish academics, professionals, and governmental officials by the so-called Law for the Restoration of the Professional Civil Service was not as devastating as the Jewish community might have feared. Only some 25,000 families were directly affected, and the roughly 200,000 Jews who were engaged in commerce of one kind or another were still able to earn their livelihoods as before.[3] Even within the professions, Jews were helped by the Nazis' concession to Paul von Hindenburg that exempted those who had begun their careers before 1918, who had fought in the wartime army, or whose fathers or sons had been killed in battle. Hitler and his cohorts were dismayed to discover that fully 53 percent of Jewish judges and prosecutors and 70 percent of Jewish lawyers were thus not covered by the so-called Aryan clause of a law enacted on April 10 covering the legal profession.[4]

As the realities sank in, Jews came to conclude that life under Nazi rule was perhaps not going to be so terrible after all.[5] Perhaps Hitler would be content to browbeat them now and then but otherwise leave them alone. Perhaps his real enemies were the leftist Jews and the decidedly un-Germanic Ostjuden. Perhaps Hitler understood, as Hjalmar Schacht and other moderates kept pointing out, that he really *needed* the Jews. Perhaps the worst was over. Perhaps the Nazis would not stay in power for long. Speculations like these stayed the steps of many Jews who were thinking about emigration. Leaving one's country—the home of one's father, grandfather, and great-grandfather, in some cases—was seen as a final, desperate act. And so far, few members of the German Jewish community had reached the point of desperation. Uncertainty about what was to come induced inertia. (This inertia was deepened by the "flight tax," equal to 25 percent of a would-be émigré's wealth, which had been imposed two years before the Nazis came to power.)

If Jews wanted to leave, they found doors abroad relatively open to them. Around the world, the severe economic impact of the depression was abating and with it, the pressures to keep out job-seeking immigrants. For example, many persons who were previously deemed "likely to become public charges" (LPC) in the United States and therefore ruled "temporarily" inadmissible were now free to apply for visas and, in a number of cases, received them. The Jewish beneficiaries of this changing situation were mainly those with relatives in the United States who were willing to support them or those with definite prospects of employment—still a small minority.[6]

After lobbying by American Jewish groups, President Franklin D. Roosevelt had instructed the U.S. State Department to ease the entry of persecuted German Jews into the United States, and in August a directive was cabled to all U.S. consulates, urging that Jewish visa applicants be shown the "utmost consideration."[7] It was not clear that these instructions were universally heeded, however. Individual consuls still exercised their right to interpret the LPC clause as they saw fit, and many did so as strictly as before. In Germany, the Berlin consulate was judged by some to be overly zealous in keeping the number of visas issued low—under 10 percent of the annual quota.[8] The extent to which inhospitable American officials deterred Jews from applying and Jews refrained from seeking visas because they did not want to emigrate to the United States is difficult to sort out. Clearly, many Jews were daunted by the paperwork and other requirements (perceived and otherwise) for entry into the United States. It is equally clear that for the great majority of German Jews in 1933, the United States was simply too remote a land, too alien, too great a leap for them to make. Furthermore, because of its continuing high rate of unemployment, the United States was not widely thought of as a "land of unlimited opportunities" for prospective émigrés. In any event, harsh anti-Semitic measures did not translate into a great upswing in German Jewish immigration to the United States during that year. All told, only 535 Jews crossed the Atlantic with valid U.S. immigrant visas,[9] even though the quota for Germany in 1933 stood at close to 26,000.

Compounding this hesitation to leave was the desire expressed by numerous Jewish émigrés—scattered around the neighboring European countries of France, Poland, Czechoslovakia, and Holland—to return home, now that the Nazi "revolution" appeared to have ebbed. Nearly ten thousand German Jews who had fled abroad earlier in 1933 changed their minds before the year's end, packed their suitcases again, and boarded trains back to the Third Reich.[10]

Richard Willstätter was one of those who chose to come back of his own free will—twice, in fact. Of course, he was not really an émigré, only a scientist traveling outside Germany to fulfill certain professional obligations. His heart did not travel with him. The United States impressed Willstätter with its scientific and technological energies and open manner, but it was not a country suited to him, even if he were thinking of settling somewhere outside Germany, which he was not. Seven months after he returned from New York, he accepted Chaim Weizmann's invitation to travel to Palestine for the opening ceremonies of the Daniel Sieff Institute for Agricultural Chemistry. Weizmann was to head this research center (funded by his brother-in-law and fellow Zionist, Israel Sieff), later to become world-famous as the Weizmann Institute.[11] He was a special admirer of Willstätter, having hung the chemist's photograph in his Rehovot office, next to one of Fritz Haber.[12] Weizmann had collaborated with Willstätter on a project involving a vegetable foodstuff a few years before,[13] and Weizmann was now eager to have his valued colleague honor this momentous occasion by his presence. As a secondary thought, the British Zionist leader may well have hoped that seeing the work of Jewish settlers firsthand would sway Willstätter to support Palestinian development more actively.

If so, he was to be disappointed. Willstätter caught a steamer to the shores of the Jewish ancestral homeland in April 1934, delivered a speech before some five hundred dignitaries at the Sieff Institute, and then toured factory where salt was being extracted. Weizmann also took him to his mother's home, in Haifa, for a Passover seder. An exuberant crowd of some two thousand surrounded the house, singing Hebrew songs and dancing the hora. The two European professors were dragged down into the midst of the dancers, and they clapped their hands and tried to keep in step the best they could. Willstätter was touched by this experience, as someone who had lived a decade in solitude might be, but he was not emotionally seduced by the promise of a Jewish nation. What moved him most about Palestine were the "living and speaking stories of the Bible" he had seen being enacted around him;[14] this historical legacy of Judaism had meaning for him, but not its visionary future in the desert. Palestine would not become his adopted home either. Urged to become director of the new institute, Willstätter declined with this argument: "I know that Germany has gone mad, but if a mother falls ill it is not a reason for her children to leave her. My home is Germany, my university, in spite of what has happened, is in Munich. I must return."[15]

Coincidentally, Robert Weltsch also set sail that spring for what he hoped would become the Jewish national homeland. Almost a year after his now famous "yellow badge" editorial, the Zionist newspaper editor wanted to see for himself what concrete progress was being made toward fulfilling his longtime dream. In his youth, as a member of Bar Kochba, Weltsch had entertained some naive, idealized notions about Palestine, epitomizing it in his mind as a settler with a cotton-white beard and pipe standing in front of a lingering sunrise.[16] In 1923 he confronted the harsher reality for the first time, when he spent four weeks with a fellow Bar Kochba member in Tel Aviv. In those days everything was primitive and unfinished. Palestine was truly the frontier; it was like visiting a friend whose house was being built, and only the frame was finished. Instead of paradise, Weltsch found himself besieged by flies and mosquitoes in the "sand desert" that was supposed to be Israel's future capital.[17]

This time—his fourth trip to Palestine—Weltsch was hopeful of finding a genuine new home for the Jews, arising from the toil of committed Zionist settlers that would uphold Jewish ideals. Still, like Willstätter, he was going to Palestine only to visit, with no intention of finding a haven there from Nazi Germany. After over a year under Hitler, Weltsch still believed that Jews could find a niche within this "new order."[18] He was not alone in this belief. The fear of Nazi-incited violence was receding in some quarters, and pro-German Jewish groups clung to their public optimism about defending their rights in the Third Reich. The German government seemed more focused on addressing the problems of unemployment and economic revitalization than on attacking Jews. Yet, to those German Jews who did want to emigrate, Palestine was proving more attractive: Roughly one-third of all Jewish refugees were now headed there.[19] Weltsch was eager to file a report for his readers on the impact of this recent exodus as a kind of journalistic bulletin from the front.

It was Passover, and Weltsch responded to the celebration he encountered in Jerusalem with the idealist's fervor that had never really left him since his youth. He boldly titled his first report for the *Jüdische Rundschau* "The Way to Freedom." In it, he discussed the development of Palestine as "the essence of Judaism." In the coming era Palestine will play "a central role in Jewish life," he accurately prophesied.[20] As he traveled around the country, Weltsch could not help but be struck by what a wave of German Jewish immigrants had accomplished in such a short time. Everywhere, fields were being planted, crops harvested, buildings erected, cities built.[21] (It is not known if Weltsch ventured to Rehovot to hear Richard Willstätter speak at the opening of the Sieff Institute.) In Palestine, before his very eyes, Jewish ideals were being transformed into a vital, dynamic, thriving community. It was an enthralling sight for a dedicated Zionist to behold. Weltsch may have wondered if there was a role for him in this burgeoning land—a land of sunshine and hope compared with the hellish Germany he had come from. In the mid-1920s he had toyed with the idea of putting out an edition of the *Jüdische Rundschau* in Palestine, but concluded that his first loyalty was to Germany and its Jews.[22] He came to the same conclusion in 1934, in spite of the increased allure of this promised land. His place was back in Berlin, at his desk, tapping out words of encouragement and pride for his newspaper's disoriented and distressed Jewish readership. Weltsch would point the way to Palestine but not follow it himself, like Vergil in Dante's *Divine Comedy*. He would only bring back the good news for others' benefit. Weltsch himself had another role to play.

Max Warburg became a convert to the cause of Palestine during his 1929 excursion to the Middle East. Moved to tears by what he saw then, he remained skeptical about Zionism. He grew convinced that Jews belonged in Palestine, although—for both practical and philosophical reasons—not *all* Jews. Warburg was ideologically divided with regard to his obligations as a Jew. The development of Palestine and the plight of his fellow Jews in the Diaspora had equally strong claims on him. This was the dilemma of being a Jew with deep roots in northern Europe. Warburg felt not that these two loyalties warred within him but that they had attained a healthy equilibrium. Thus, he lashed out at Zionists like Kurt Blumenfeld for berating the assimilationists and arguing that only Palestine held the solution to the now acute "Jewish question."[23] Palestine simply could not absorb all German Jewry, Warburg thought. What was important for those Jews who were unable—or unwilling—to emigrate was to affirm their spiritual solidarity with the building of a Palestinian homeland. In returning to time-honored Jewish values for inner strength and orientation, the Hamburg banker, once considered among the most assimilated German Jews, was taking a position not all that different from that of Weltsch and Weltsch's mentor Martin Buber. In trying to peer beyond the crisis of the moment for deeper meaning and spiritual sustenance, Warburg sounded much like the man who was emerging as the moral anchor of German Jewry— Rabbi Leo Baeck. In a five-page letter to Buber written in October 1933, Warburg struck a note that might have come word for word from one of Baeck's speeches: "How do I strengthen Judaism within me so that I can enter into the world, in order to fight for a betterment of humanity . . . for the realization of God's teaching in everyday life . . . to prepare for the coming of the Messiah?"

Palestine, he went on to say, cannot merely be a place of refuge for those who are driven from their European homes. It must be a land inspired with "new fire" for the old Jewish teachings, a mecca of Jewish renaissance.[24] Having expressed these opinions, Warburg then defended those Jews—including himself—who did not opt to ignite these flames in the Holy Land. "There ought to be no sadness about being a Jew in Germany," he said, indirectly responding to the Zionists who were portraying the Jews as poor unfortunates. Jews had attained an "inextinguishable achievement" during the Enlightenment, but their emancipation had not been complete in "flesh and blood." Now a great task stood before them—a new struggle for freedom and dignity, based this time not on denying Judaism but on avowing it.[25] Judaism would restore Jews under Hitler as it elevated those living in Palestine.

Judaism was also a roof beneath which all remaining German Jews must now gather, for their ability to survive depended on togetherness. On a practical level, Warburg was determined to forge unity through the creation of a central organization of German Jews—the Reichsvertretung der deutschen Juden (National Representation of German Jews). Having come to believe, by mid-summer 1933, that a fruitful dialogue with the German government would not materialize in the near future,[26] Warburg threw his considerable organizational talents and personal influence behind the effort to stop the back stabbing among various Jewish groups and bring them together for their common good. This was the only way Jews stood a chance of winning the protracted struggle both to regain their rights and maintain their economic foothold that Warburg foresaw. (Warburg's conviction about the need for internal Jewish cohesion was confirmed by the rebuff he received when he headed a German Jewish delegation to London in August, seeking financial help from their British coreligionists.[27] Germany's Jews, he realized, would have to depend on each other.)

"Unity" was replacing "go about your business" as the slogan on many Jewish lips as more and more of them accepted that the liberal era of legally protected rights was gone for good.[28] (In private Hitler was now saying he wanted to see the Jews "wiped out.")[29] Entirely changed circumstances called for a new kind of collective response, even if Jews huddling together smacked of the old ghetto mentality. To gain this unity and "coordinate" themselves with the new order, Jews were willing to contemplate the same authoritarian leadership their Aryan countrymen had welcomed in Hitler. In the August 15 issue of the *Centralverein Zeitung*, the moderate Werner Senator proposed just such a "dictatorial" realignment, "putting the Jewish community in order within the new state to ensure our existence, with pride, as Jews."[30]

There was a widespread feeling that the Jews' present leaders, spending their time squabbling over petty issues, were not up to such a task and that other, truly forceful personalities would have to step forward and perform it. Warburg's name was one that frequently surfaced in this search for a paramount Jewish spokesperson. In August 1933 three prominent Jews in Cologne wrote to Warburg, inviting him to provide the missing "strength" in the German Jewish leadership: He was a figure honored in all camps, acceptable to both Zionists and assimilationists.[31]

But Warburg was not interested in such a visible, guiding role. He was, after all, a banker—a master of discreet negotiation and gentle persuasion—not a person who was at ease dealing with the inflammatory passions of large public gatherings. (Warburg was also worried that the Nazis might attack him for his close ties to Weimar political figures.)[32] At a meeting of twenty Jewish leaders held in an Essen synagogue on August 20 Warburg firmly turned down the leadership of the proposed Reichsvertretung der deutschen Juden and recommended a man who was already widely respected for his moral authority—Leo Baeck. Three heads of the Essen Jewish community—Georg Hirschland, Ernst Herzfeld, and Hugo Hahn—had arrived at the same conclusion a few days before, deeming Baeck the only leader sufficiently independent of the liberal-led Berlin *Kehilla* (Jewish community) who was unlikely to become its tool for dominating the rest of German Jewry. They also admired Baeck's broad outlook (his support for Palestine as well as his stature among liberal Jews) and conciliatory manner, which outweighed some concerns about his being too burdened by other responsibilities and not possessing the "necessary resoluteness" of a strong leader.[33]

So, at the four-hour meeting on August 20, attended by representatives of the major Jewish organizations—except the Zionistische Vereinigung für Deutschland (ZVfD)—Hirschland, Herzfeld, and Warburg (representing the Hilfsverein der deutschen Juden) succeeded in persuading Hermann Stahl, head of the Berlin community, to accept Baeck's leadership. Baeck had already declared his willingness to take on this enormous challenge and to forgo his other duties if need be. He also agreed with the Reichsvertretung's overall strategy, which was to emphasize training and emigration for Jewish youths, who clearly had no future in Germany.[34]

In his mind, Baeck had neatly divided his fellow Jews into two groups. There were those who, like himself, were over thirty years old, were settled in their lives and professions, and had families and other commitments in Germany. By and large, they would remain there, no matter what indignities or outrage the Nazis heaped on them, because this was their home. Starting all over, in some alien, distant land, was simply out of the question for Jews of their generation.[35] They would live out their days on German soil, the final vestiges of a once-vibrant thousand-year-old Jewish presence. Then there were the younger Jews—perhaps a third of the total community.[36] They were a dwindling group within an aging community, still unformed, unattached, and unafraid. For them, Palestine beckoned like a lighthouse in a storm. On board the German "ship," they had virtually no hope of finding a job or building a life. In fact, Nazi policies were costing them jobs, in favor of older Jews with families. For these younger Jews and for the community's survival, emigration and the creation of a national homeland was a powerful aspiration. The problem would be how to get them out—without provoking an anti-Semitic reaction abroad.[37]

Because he saw the community split along age lines, Baeck envisioned a dual-track response to the Nazi threat. The older Jews would fortify themselves by drawing together, keeping the anti-Semites at bay, while the younger ones made good their escape abroad. Thus, when the Zionist leader Arthur Ruppin came to Berlin from Jerusalem in mid-August and outlined his scheme to resettle 250,000 Jews in Palestine, Baeck, Stahl, and other German Jewish leaders (including Robert Weltsch) all endorsed it, at least in principle.[38]

This conclusion about the community's fate was reached in light of the Nazis' tightening of their grip on the reins of power over the summer, and the attendant rise of anti-Semitic incidents and exclusionary policies. Conservative groups like the Stahlhelm (Steel Helmet) allowed themselves to be absorbed into the Nazi fold, and hopes of restraining Hitler faded. (As Bella Fromm noted in her diary: "The disintegration spreads. All camps and classes change color to brown.")[39] The Führer's declaration that the "revolutionary" phase of the Nazi movement was over, supplanted by an era of "order," brought a diminishing fear of violence, but this relief was offset by Hitler's affirmation of the inseparability of nation and volk. In Hitler's "total state," Jews would be gradually, but firmly squeezed out.[40]

The expulsion of Jews from the elite professions was now followed by other, similar measures. The Deutsche Arbeitsfront (German Labor Front) barred Jews, depriving them of most blue-collar jobs, by adopting an Aryan clause, and so did the German film industry. The property of émigré Jews could now be legally confiscated by the government. The naturalization of Jews (after 1918) was revoked. There were reports of another economic boycott in the offing.[41] Jews were now excluded from public parks, and the American diplomat George Messersmith passed on rumors to Washington about a new law under consideration that would deny Jews German citizenship.[42]

The support of Baeck and other assimilated Jews for emigration to Palestine grew out of their sober assessment of prospects in Germany. But it was also based on clear signs from the Nazi Party and the German government encouraging this exodus. In July 1933, for example, the *Völkischer Beobachter* (National Observer) ran an article endorsing the Zionists and their policy of increasing the flow of emigrants to Palestine.[43] (About this time, Leo Baeck told a visitor that the Nazi regime would "welcome" a Jewish exodus.)[44] This article was followed, about a month later, by a directive from the Economics Ministry permitting Jews to take more money with them to Palestine than the minimum-required £1,000 ($4,000).[45] Apparently, committed to denying Jews a place within the Third Reich, the Nazis were prepared to make some concession to get the Jews out, even to apply pressure toward that end, if necessary.[46] Up to this point, a consistent Nazi policy toward the Jews had not existed. The Nazis had denounced the Jews, arrested them, driven them from their jobs, and boycotted their businesses, but none of these actions arose from any clear plan about how to treat the annoying anomaly of a racially alien and inimical minority living in a country that staked its identity—and its claim to allegiance—on racial lines. It was one thing for radicals in the Nazi Party to call the Jews "vermin" and to wish to rid Germany of them, but quite another to figure out how to attain this goal. And the party's leaders continued to disagree about the economic wisdom of expelling the Jews. Furthermore, they were afraid of the negative diplomatic consequences of such a drastic move. The "Jewish question" was still much in need of a solution.

Oddly, it appears that it was Jews who first proposed one. On June 21, 1933, the ZVfD issued a statement outlining its position vis-à-vis the new regime: The Zionists, too, embraced this renewal of *Volksleben,* or racially conscious life. What was right for the Germans was also right for the Jews. Although the German Zionists argued that the Jews should be free to engage in "fruitful activities for the Fatherland" and remain loyal (and tolerated) citizens, they held out the long-term solution of "normalizing" German-Jewish ties by a mass exodus of Jews to Palestine.[47] During a transitional phase leading up to this exodus, Jews would be granted protection under the law and the right to earn a living. (It is interesting that in an essay entitled "The Special Position of the Jews," which appeared a few days later, Robert Weltsch's *Jüdische Rundschau* did not urge that Jews leave their native land; instead, it sought the regulation of the Jews' status that would be "in accordance with the character of the new state" and that would give the Jews "an irrevocable opportunity for existence" within it.)[48]

Plans for the emigration of Jews appealed to the Nazis, since they would eventually produce a *judenfrei* Germany. But the "eventually" was still a major hitch: The logistics (and immigration barriers) to be surmounted in relocating several hundred thousand Jews abroad (not to mention overcoming their reluctance to depart) were formidable, and no government office was about to step forward with a feasible, affordable scheme for accomplishing it. So the best the Nazi regime could do for the moment was to encourage emigration by making life in Germany even more unpleasant for its Jews and the conditions for leaving more enticing.

In the meantime, the energies of the Jewish leadership were directed toward a more immediate concern—the "preservation and strengthening" of the Jewish presence in Germany, as the Zentral Ausschuss der deutschen Juden für Hilfe und Aufbau, (the Central Committee of German Jews for Welfare and Development), led by Leo Baeck, phrased it in a July 1933 appeal for support to the Central British Fund for German Jewry.[49] Many, if not all, Jewish leaders (including Baeck and Max Warburg) preferred that emigration take place in an orderly manner, to avoid any repetition of the "chaotic" rush abroad that had occurred immediately after Hitler came to power. Those Jews who had panicked and caught the next available train for the frontier had soon discovered they were utterly unprepared for life on foreign soil. The transition had not gone smoothly. This fact contributed to the return of so many émigrés during 1933. If future emigration to Palestine and elsewhere was to succeed, Jews would first have to learn new skills, new professions, and new languages. Their leaders would have to reassure prospective host countries that a wave of Jewish refugees was not about to inundate their shores. (Baeck was among those who feared that the "worst kind" of Jews would be too prominent in any such massive exodus.)[50]

It was natural for Baeck to become deeply involved in meeting the needs of his beleaguered community. In private he may have concluded that the Jews were finished in Germany, but on another, philosophical, level Baeck still believed in historical continuity, in the recurrent cycles of persecution and renewal Jews had experienced through the ages, and he felt obliged to call it constantly to mind as a consoling thought. As a scholar of Judaism and a rabbi, Baeck could not readily repudiate the teaching that human beings are shaped by their unbroken links to earlier generations and by their responsibilities to succeeding ones. This was the belief he chose to espouse in public. In an April 1934 lecture at a Munich synagogue on "The Meaning of History," he made this credo explicit: Jews could not break this endless chain of generations any more than they could sever their bonds to God.[51]

Baeck accepted this teaching on a personal level. He saw himself as a spiritual leader confronted by an extraordinary historical crisis. The fate of German Jewry was being entrusted to him, and he had to see that he served this trust well by delicately balancing necessary change with tradition, just as he blended his Germanic ways and attachments with his growing commitment to a Jewish homeland in Palestine. In a real sense, Baeck was the prisoner of the conciliatory, fatherlike role he had played in the Jewish community until then. Among a Jewish people divided by ideological disputes and personal rivalries, Baeck stood apart as a man of intellect, moral force, personal dignity, compassion, and humility, who was disposed to put the welfare of others ahead of his own and willing to listen to all points of view and find common ground among them. With his carefully trimmed beard; imposing, nearly six-foot stature; formal attire; and mien of an Old Testament prophet, Baeck embodied a muted pride that met the needs of his fellow Jews for self-respect in the face of their daily humiliations in Hitler's Germany. At heart, he was also sanguine about human nature and, therefore, about the Jews' long-term survival. He conceived of Judaism as a "religion of ethical optimism"[52] and believed that those German Jews who had once shamefully hidden their spiritual roots would find a fountain of regenerating strength in it. In Baeck, these same Jews had an exemplar both of this faith and of their own tragic predicament—bound to Germany by temperament, history, and patriotic feelings, yet propelled toward a separate identity and place in the world by circumstances imposed upon them. In this role Baeck spoke most directly for Jews who had been born in imperial Germany. These older Jews had served their kaiser in uniform a generation before; had taken advantage of the Weimar Republic's opportunities to advance professionally and entered and prospered in the ranks of the bourgeoisie, only marginally conscious of—and impeded by—their Jewishness; had established families and seen them grow; and now—in just a few incredible months—had watched their secure, almost idyllic world and their belief in it disappear in a puff of smoke, as if, all along, it had been only a tantalizing mirage. Now, barren of any hope and vision for tomorrow, they longed for the steady, soothing words of Leo Baeck. Come what may, he would stand by his flock, and they would stay with him.

As the de facto leader of German Jewry, Baeck was not without his faults. His ability to reconcile intra-Jewish conflicts also made him somewhat diffident, reluctant to impose his own opinions or lead the way. His personal modesty could at times be mistaken for a lack of self-confidence. His manner in public was formal and distant, his speaking voice strained and squeaky. Furthermore, Baeck was a scholar and a religious man, not a political one. He had little experience with the day-to-day headaches of running a large organization and little of the strong personal charisma that could help a leader overcome the current divisiveness and forge the unity that had eluded Germany's Jews for so long. Certainly, Baeck fell short of the Hitler-like model of a "towering Führer" that Robert Weltsch told Martin Buber the Jews needed if they were ever going to end their pointless bickering,[53] but he was the closest approximation of it they had.

The Berlin rabbi considered Judaism a religion of deeds: God's teaching was fulfilled through individual human actions. It was an obligation he did not now shirk. In a sense, it was an extension, on a larger stage, of all that he had done with his life thus far. On September 17, 1933— the same week that Richard Willstätter was being feted by American chemists in Chicago—the Reichsvertretung der deutschen Juden came into existence, and Leo Baeck confidently set about realizing its chief objectives. The first was to bring the Jews together. Two major Jewish groups had already voiced their unhappiness with this new central organization and its leadership. They were the Zionists, who saw the Reichsvertretung as reimposing a discredited assimilationist thinking on the Jewish community, and the heads of the Berlin Gemeinde, who thought they did not have sufficient power within it.[54] (Orthodox Jews—a tiny minority in Germany—and the right-wing Verband nationaldeutscher Juden also refused to join the organization.) The Zionists' position was ironic because the ZVfD had long sought to unite German Jewry in one organization, to affirm their common identity and to build a common defense against anti-Semitic attacks. Now, with interest in Jewishness and Zionism soaring (to handle all the Rosh Hashanah celebrants in 1933, thirty-three theaters and halls had to be rented in Berlin),[55] the German Zionists wanted to press their claim to be the dominant force in German Jewish life, not jump on someone else's broken-down bandwagon. Baeck tried to accommodate the Zionists by adopting some of their agenda. For instance, the Reichsvertretung supported the creation of more Jewish schools, to immerse young

Jews in their heritage, and of vocational programs to train them for a
new life in Palestine.[56] As construed by Martin Buber, the schools were
also supposed to be spiritual havens, fortifying Jews against the hostile
world around them.[57] On top of all these concessions, Baeck ceded the
Zionists two seats on the Reichsvertretung's advisory council (*Beirat*)
and announced that he was willing to "respect philosophical differences" while striving for the common good.[58] The Zionists accepted this
olive branch and came on board. Despite personal antipathy between
Baeck and its head, Hermann Stahl, the leadership of the Berlin
Gemeinde reluctantly followed suit, with Baeck promising to yield them
more power, but not overall control.

In its first public proclamation, the Reichsvertretung sounded a
somber note. Noticeably absent was any Pollyannaish assimilationist
rhetoric about a "return to normalcy," to the status quo ante:

> At a time that is as hard and difficult and trying as any in Jewish his-
> tory, but also significant as few times have been, we have been
> entrusted with the leadership and representation of the German Jews
> by a joint decision of the National Representation of the Jewish
> Communities, the major Jewish organizations, and the large Jewish
> communities of Germany. . . . We must understand [the new regime
> in Germany] and not deceive ourselves. Only then will we be able to
> discover every honorable opportunity, and to struggle for every right,
> for every place, for every opportunity to continue to exist. . . . There
> is only one area in which we are permitted to carry out our ideas, our
> own aims, but it is a decisive area, that of our Jewish life and Jewish
> future. This is where the most clearly defined tasks exist.[59]

Jews were asked "with all passion for Judaism" to join together
behind the new organization and help it achieve its goals. Given the
wide spectrum of Jewish views the Reichsvertretung encompassed, these
aims were necessarily eclectic—ranging from furthering the development of Palestine to proving their worth, as employees and employers,
to the German economy to reaching out a hand "in love and loyalty to
Germany" to non-Jews.[60]

The establishment of the Reichsvertretung fixed Leo Baeck's fate
inside Germany: His assumption of the leadership of the Jewish community meant that he would never leave until, as he later vowed, he was

the last Jew left on German soil. His life and that of the community were now merged. He stood upright like the captain on the bridge of a slowly sinking ship, steadfast and unbending, deaf to the nearing waves.

Max Warburg took a post on that bridge, too. He was also intimately engaged in putting the Reichsvertretung together. Behind the scenes he helped overcome the resistance of some community leaders, as well as Stahl's dislike of Baeck. He persuaded Baeck to become president, steered through the election of the Reichsvertretung's governing council, and accepted (as did the absent Richard Willstätter) a spot on that body. All this negotiating and organizational planning seemed to reinvigorate Warburg, to rekindle some of his old optimism, bruised after his personal setbacks of the past few months.[61] Like Baeck, Weltsch, and most leading Jews, Warburg understood that strong, centralized, even dictatorial leadership was essential for the community's survival. Because of his concomitant work with the Hilfsverein, he believed that German Jewry would continue to exist no matter what happened in their country. The Hilfsverein's attempts to obtain immigration papers for Jews were proceeding slowly, however. At this rate, which Warburg prudently preferred to an exodus "in waves," there would still be a sizable contingent of Jews in Germany for years, if not decades, to come. In working for the Jewish community, Warburg was salvaging something positive from what had befallen him, seizing a new purpose from the jaws of adversity. Driven from company directorships, ostracized by non-Jewish financiers, vilified in the Nazi press, threatened with violence, and held up to public ridicule,[62] the sixty-six-year-old banker still adamantly refused to heed the pleas of his relatives that he get out of Germany. For him, leaving would be an act of cowardice.[63] His newfound religiosity fortified Warburg as much as it did Baeck, Weltsch, and many others. A true Jewish renaissance—a second emancipation—which would shield and save the race, could come only through a rebirth of religious faith, he told Martin Buber. In the task they faced, the Jews were not unlike the German people, Warburg believed: "As the Germans had to fight against false accusations of guilt, so must the German Jews fight against the charge of being at fault for events for which they are not responsible."[64] Religion would be the foundation of Jewish unity, Warburg wrote to Georg Hirschland.[65] Jews had to reach back to the teachings of the old prophets and apply them to their present situation.[66]

By helping to revive communal bonds among the Jews who would remain under the Nazis and, at the same time, clearing the path for those whose future lay overseas, Warburg was performing the "double task" he felt the Jews' historical fate obligated them to accept. But in pledging these two equal allegiances, he invited condemnation from the opposing camps in the Jewish community. Neither the Zionists nor the hyper-Germanic Verband nationaldeutscher Juden could tolerate this kind of ambivalence. As a would-be builder of a broad Jewish consensus, Warburg—like Leo Baeck—had to find a way to respect these great differences of opinion without letting them tear the community apart. This daunting task weighed more heavily on his mind than anything the Nazis might have in store for him. From the latter danger Warburg still felt protected by his association with some of Nazi Germany's most powerful figures.

Like many other Jews, Warburg experienced a feeling of freedom in participating in community-based activities. When they had racially excluded the Jews from the Volksgemeinschaft, the Nazis had logically ceded them a degree of autonomy and independence that was highly improbable in a modern totalitarian state. Inside the fences of their "Jewish game park," the ostracized Jews of Germany were relatively free to run their own affairs. To preserve and further their separate cultural life, they were allowed to form the independent Kulturbund der deutschen Juden (Cultural Association of German Jews) in June 1933, as a counterpart to the Nazis' ideologically correct Kulturkammer. An outlet for Jewish artists who were no longer permitted to perform on German stages or in German orchestras, the Kulturbund promoted an awareness of Jewish values and themes that was oddly incongruous in the Nazi state.[67]

The Jewish press was another case in point. True, the government had put pressure on Jewish newspaper editors, such as Robert Weltsch, to tone down reports of "atrocities" allegedly inflicted on Jews,[68] and, as a result, these editors had come to discern—as had foreign correspondents—the boundaries of permissible reporting and editorial opinion beyond which they would venture at their own peril.[69] But, aside from respecting these loose guidelines, Jewish newspapers could print what they wanted, in stark contrast to the nazified "Aryan" press, which had to toe the party line slavishly.[70] No topics were officially taboo, and an editor like Weltsch simply had to follow his instincts about what stories he could run without incurring the wrath of Joseph Goebbels's Propaganda

Ministry.[71] What he could print was far more factually accurate than what appeared in the German press. Partly for this reason, circulation of the *Jüdische Rundschau* rose sharply during the early years of the Third Reich, with thousands of readers, Jews and non-Jews alike, who were hungry for real news taking out subscriptions.[72] By September, the newspaper was selling forty thousand copies of each issue—up tenfold in the five months since the famous "yellow badge" editorial.[73]

Closer to Weltsch's heart was the news his newspaper could disseminate about a Jewish renewal in a time of fearfulness and betrayed (assimilationist) values—a message that his readers were eager to receive; the *Jüdische Rundschau* provided their daily spiritual bread. It was only by affirming this "new spirit" of fundamental unity that Germany's Jews could transcend the petty, "egotistical" disputes that were turning them against each other.[74] Along with his fellow Zionists, Weltsch perceived many parallels between their nationalistic philosophy and that of the Nazis. Both movements defined a nation in terms of race, history, *Volkstum* (literally, "national traditions"), and cultural cohesion.[75] Many Zionists, Weltsch included, chose to interpret the Nazi conquest of Germany not as meaning the end of German Jewry (because it was racially incompatible) but, rather, as inviting a modus vivendi between the two peoples based on strict separation, mutual respect, and shared values. Within their own sphere, the Jews would deepen their special identity through revived religious and cultural traditions by developing their own schools, fostering their own forms of artistic expression, and creating their own communal organizations.

Weltsch was particularly interested in promoting Jewish education, especially at the elementary level, to instill pride and Jewish consciousness at a young age.[76] Paradoxically, this stance put him, a lifelong Zionist, in the position of *not* advocating the mass exodus of Jewish youths to Palestine—an exodus that was urged by assimilated leaders, such as Baeck and Warburg. Indeed, Weltsch was more interested in nourishing hungry Jewish souls with Jewish values than in rescuing them from material want and physical degradation. Nazi Germany was a laboratory in which this process of rebirth was rapidly taking place, and Weltsch was its chief publicist.

From an ideological standpoint, the Nazi racial state was a long-denied vindication for Weltsch. It had exposed the lie of "false assimilation"—Jews selling out for the illusion of acceptance in the Diaspora, acquiring a corrosive inferiority complex. Finally, Weltsch could declare with some quiet satisfaction that liberalism had failed. Finally, the Jews were listening to what he had been saying all along: The only way to solve the "Jewish problem" was by proudly proclaiming that they were Jews. Only by asserting this common identity could they overcome the petty, "egotistical" preoccupations that were turning Jew against Jew.

Weltsch's mood of exaltation and triumph made it difficult for him to detect the ominous tone in Nazi speeches, the refrain about "getting rid of" the Jews. He was not able to see, as Kurt Blumenfeld and more Palestine-oriented Zionists were, that the Zionist flowering under the Nazis could only be an ephemeral side effect, shortly to be crushed. To his idealistic mind, this Jewish revival was *the* consuming reality from 1933 onward. It kept him from objectively scrutinizing Nazi hatred of the Jews and from realizing there could be, ultimately, no compatibility between these two "revolutions" unfolding within the same country.

Instead, Weltsch continued to press the case for Jewish coexistence within the Third Reich. He refused to be deterred from pursuing this goal by Nazi abuse and rejection. In an essay ("On the New Emancipation") published in June 1993, he recalled that the *Jüdische Rundschau* had been the first Jewish newspaper (that is, ahead of both the right-wing nationalists' and the assimilationist *Centralverein Zeitung*) to declare that an event like the April boycott could not cut the ties binding German Jews to their fatherland.[77] To protect the rights of Jews under Hitler, Weltsch sought a separate legal status that would grant them "complete respect as human beings and as Jews"[78] and "a legitimate sphere of existence" in Germany,[79] without turning them into hunted pariahs. For these rights, he was willing to give up many previous "liberal" rights and concede the justness of the Nazis' racial reasoning.[80] Jews *should* be willing, he confided to Martin Buber, to yield their leading positions in German cultural life and their visible presence in the civil service and academia. They *should* forgo sexual relations with "Aryans" to keep the two races unsullied.[81] They *should* retreat to the periphery of German life, outside the Volksgemeinschaft, yet still be able to remain (illogically) within the state.

Weltsch's desire to carve out this sanctuary (and not to antagonize German anti-Semites) led him to urge his readers to vote yes in the November 1933 plebiscite on Hitler's plan to withdraw Germany from the League of Nations and his implicit goal of rearming Germany to regain the military might stripped away at Versailles. As "citizens," Jews had no choice but to rally around their government, as they would rally around *any* German government, the *Jüdische Rundschau* declared a week before the vote.[82] In taking this stance, Weltsch was echoing the public sentiments of many other Jewish leaders. Leo Baeck's umbrella Reichsvertretung issued a similar plea on the plebiscite[83] (in part, as the result of a meeting between German Jewish spokesmen and Reich officials, ostensibly aimed at preventing any postelection hostility toward the Jews).[84] The Jewish community clearly felt compelled to display its patriotism with enthusiasm, even if it did so involuntarily. In the end Hitler got the near-universal backing he had wanted for this first bold step toward rearmament and war. Jews joined in the 95 percent who voted yes, just as overwhelmingly as did the inmates of the Dachau concentration camp.[85]

For now, Weltsch was free to wage his editorial campaign for a Jewish enclave inside the Reich. Aside from a raid on his offices in mid-June that resulted in the confiscation of two issues, the *Jüdische Rundschau* (and the rest of the Jewish press) was little affected by the restrictions imposed on the Jews' rights in other spheres. On the contrary, business was booming.

On a personal level, Weltsch managed to circumvent the January 1934 directive limiting the working press to certified "Aryans" by arguing that as a Jew writing for a Jewish publication, he should be exempt from these guidelines.[86] After nearly a year of inconclusive correspondence with the nazified Reichsverband der deutschen Presse (Reich Association of the German Press), Goebbels interceded and granted Weltsch the right to practice his profession, albeit on a restricted basis. (Although he could still enjoy free access to the Propaganda Ministry, Weltsch could no longer attend press conferences or fraternize with foreign reporters.)[87] That he was thus able to go on earning a living figured as much, if not more, in Weltsch's decision to remain in Berlin as did his conviction that this was where he properly belonged. (Weltsch formed another tie in the fall of 1934 that may well have deepened his commitment to stay. After being a widower and sole parent to his two young children for three years, he remarried, moving with his bride Suse to a garden apartment on the Charlottenbrunnenstrasse in fashionable Grunewald.)

Across town, Bella Fromm was nearly as successful in dodging the descending Nazi ax. She was still benefiting from the high esteem of her diplomatic friends, their devotion to her, and the weight their influence carried with the Nazi leaders. For their part, the Nazis still thought her potentially useful, as a source of casual insights into foreign attitudes toward the regime.[88] But neither her "usefulness" nor her friendships gave Fromm true peace of mind. As early as March 1933, she had intimations that "sooner or later they [the Nazis] will throw me out of the press."[89] When Nazi functionaries infiltrated the *Vossische Zeitung* to "coordinate" it with party doctrine, easing out Jewish writers and editors,[90] she was spared. Fromm continued to produce her breezy columns about the doings of Berlin high society, the formal banquets and cocktail parties to which she still received invitations, and celebrities like Magda Goebbels, even though it was a secret to no one in power that these intimate accounts of Nazi social life were being written by a Jewess. (When Goebbels once summoned her to his office, it was not to berate or intimidate her, but only to remind her that her coverage of an upcoming fashion show had to have a sufficiently Germanic focus.)[91]

In utter disregard of all the barriers Germany's new masters had erected between Jews and "Aryans," the popular and vivacious Fromm continued to mingle with what passed for Berlin's elite in those days, sitting next to President Paul von Hindenburg during a Palm Sunday service;[92] meeting Hermann Goering's mistress (and future wife) at an embassy dinner;[93] chatting with her old friend, the Nazi filmmaker Leni Riefenstahl, at the racetrack;[94] and attending a pre-Christmas reception for the National Socialist Welfare Agency at the insistence of a party friend who pointed out: "We take care of the Jews, too."[95]

The Nazi policy limiting membership in the Reich press association (and, hence, the right to work as a journalist) to Aryans did have an impact on Fromm. Threatened with a January 1, 1934, end to her journalistic career, "Frau Bella" was reassured by none other than Minister of Defense General Werner von Blomberg, Foreign Minister Konstantin von Neurath, and the papal nuncio, Cardinal Eugenio Pacelli, that this simply would not happen.[96] (Frau Neurath suggested that Fromm make her life less stressful by being baptized.)[97] Fear of what lay ahead for her under this new press policy induced Fromm's close friend, the journalist Vera "Poulette" von Huhn, to commit suicide by overdosing on sleeping pills. Stricken by this loss and afraid she might one day meet a similar end—"Whom will these beasts kill next?" she scribbled in her diary[98]—Fromm kept a level head. "I don't want to run away, but I am convinced that one day we will have no other choice—the necessity of emigrating draws ever nearer."[99] Instead, she vowed to fight for her job, to put up "stiff resistance," feeling it was her "mission" in Germany to "stick it out" for the sake of the Jews who turned to her for help in acquiring visas and escaping from the Third Reich.[100] At the end of the year, while most Berliners were gearing up for their Christmas festivities—the first under Adolf Hitler—Fromm spent countless hours waiting to see officials at the Reichsverband and dashing off requests that she be exempt from the "Aryan" clause.[101]

But Fromm did not have as much luck as Robert Weltsch, who could rightly claim that he wrote solely for the "Jewish press" and was, therefore, a special case. On January 3, 1934, her editor at the *Vossische Zeitung* curtly informed her that the newspaper had been prohibited from running any more articles under her byline.[102] Another flurry of letters, coupled with pleas by Franz von Papen, Werner von Blomberg, and others, failed to reverse this decision. Goebbels himself intervened to say that the Reichsverband was not going to change its mind.[103] Realizing that she faced unemployment, Fromm thought briefly of quitting Germany, but her feelings of obligation to other Jews held her back. "After all," she confessed in her diary, "I have the duty to stay as long as I am able to assist those poor who are without connections."[104]

In the spring of 1934 her former employer, the *Vossische Zeitung*, went out of business, and Fromm succeeded in finding work as a correspondent for a society weekly, publishing under the aristocratic pseudonym "Hubert von Eltville." Goebbels apparently knew who the real author was but did nothing because he liked her stories. Later on Fromm would help support herself and her daughter by writing short pieces for the British and Austrian press. Even Nazi papers approached Fromm, offering to pay her handsomely for articles on Berlin's diplomatic corps, but she turned them down.[105] She did not need that kind of work.

An unattached woman with many powerful admirers, "Frau Bella" felt she could take care of herself, even under these trying circumstances. Sixteen-year-old "Gonny" (Grete Ellen) was another matter. An expert skier and aspiring Olympic swimmer (the Nazis would not let her compete because she wasn't a party member, her mother believed), Gonny was also a photographer and was shepherded around, under her mother's protective wing, to snap pictures at elegant social gatherings.

But the tensions of life as a Jew in Hitler's capital were taking their toll on Gonny. In the spring she tearfully told her mother she had to leave.[106] George Messersmith, the American consul general, agreed. After a send-off party at the French embassy, Gonny boarded a liner bound for the United States, with a downcast Fromm left behind to brood: "Life has no more meaning for me until I have my child with me again."[107] Still, Fromm found some solace in being able to help others in distress who were following Gonny abroad.

Fromm continued to hope that conservative circles outside the Nazi Party might somehow be emboldened to depose Hitler. She went around, like a dutiful camp follower, to their social affairs, only to be depressed by their fervent "Heil Hitler!" greetings.[108] Few, if any, of her friends among the aristocracy or military still resisted the seductive promises of the Führer or cared for the plight of his enemies. (For some who did, a bloody fate lay in store a few months later.) Of course, "Frau Bella" was different. They would always stand behind her, no matter what. "Nobody is going to do any harm to our Bella," the French ambassador had once told her,[109] and the refrain of those words, like an oft-repeated bedtime prayer, had a way of soothing her days, of making her believe it was true. It would be safe for her to stay. Even when Fromm visited her family's tomb at Kitzingen and found it robbed and disfigured by swastikas, with a sign outside the Jewish cemetery sneering "One-way Street to Palestine,"[110] she did not seriously consider changing her mind.

Hans-Joachim Schoeps, a more vulnerable Jew, also thought he would be sheltered from the coming crackdown. His shield was political, rather than social, and he deemed it sturdy enough to deflect whatever blows the Nazis might hurl at "the Jews." Like Fromm, he pinned his hopes on right-wing German nationalism—not as an (anti-Nazi) anti-dote to Hitler, but as a movement close enough to his own political and philosophical views to embrace him and his Deutscher Vortrupp (German Vanguard) as kindred spirits, their undeniable Jewishness notwithstanding. During 1933, Schoeps had put out feelers to the Stahlhelm, whose soldierly Prussian conservatism he approved of and in April, believing that he might become a "negotiating partner" with the Nazis, he had drawn up his scheme granting Jews legal minority status in the Reich.[111] The attention this plan brought him fed Schoeps's dreams of leading a nationalist Jewish avant-garde, modeled along the same *bündisch*, comradely lines as German nationalism, prepared for the day when Nazi anti-Semitism would abate sufficiently to admit Jews into the "community of the people."[112]

In the meantime Schoeps would seek to distinguish himself and his followers from other Jews, both those who had called for "assimilation at any price"[113] and the Zionists, who talked of "flight" and a new homeland in Palestine. Compared with these Jews, his bond to Germany was unbreakable. "Our suffering today does not change this one iota," he wrote stoically in an August 1933 article. "We will not leave Germany and go to Erez Israel before the day the prophets sound the trumpets."[114] Schoeps contended that his small band of Jewish youths recognized the "truth" of the Jewish situation under the Nazis in a way no other group could grasp. Only his German Vanguard stood "ready for Germany" as obedient soldiers eager to go forth into battle, only they were ready to "prove our Germanness through suffering and self-development."[115] Only they would remain loyal to Germany under any circumstances, at any price. To spread this message and win broader support among Jewish youths, Schoeps put out a newsletter, *Der Vortrupp*, which reiterated the idea that only Jews who congregated under his banner could possibly hope to reach an accommodation with Germany's anti-Semitic rulers.

In thus positioning himself, Schoeps was walking a thin line. In aping the Nazis so openly (Schoeps even adopted the title "Führer" for himself),[116] he courted the charge of *being* a quasi-Nazi. Indeed, Schoeps was more than once attacked on these grounds. In January 1934 he ran into difficulties obtaining a research grant from the Academic Assistance Council, based in England, when a Cambridge professor of rabbinics declared of him: "That man is a Nazi!"[117] Schoeps was taken aback by this accusation and indignantly replied to the professor: "If the German Jews are falsely addressed and unjustly treated by the present regime, that is certainly very painful, but this is something we have to settle with our government, and no one can interfere with our doing so; we will not be released from our loyalty to volk and Fatherland even if injustice is committed against us."[118]

On the other hand, Schoeps risked antagonizing the Nazis for attempting to reach out to them in defiance of their racially segregationist Jewish policy. In fact, he was not only rebuffed by Nazi officials (Interior Minister Frick refused to meet with him in October),[119] but his articles, such as "The New Face of Politics,"[120] earned him the scrutiny of the Gestapo. According to Schoeps, he was interrogated on several occasions by the secret police, which considered him a dangerous enemy because he was trying to make Jews look like the willing allies of Aryan Germans.[121]

This special attention did not cause him undue anxiety. Schoeps may well have relished the status bestowed on him by the Gestapo. And he certainly did not think about emigrating. He still wanted to make his case that at least some Jews deserved a place in Nazi Germany and that he was the person to create it. While pursuing this agenda, Schoeps made further overtures to Martin Buber about teaching in one of the latter's proposed Lehrhäuser for educating Jewish youths.[122] Barred from employment in German public schools, he was greatly in need of work. Schoeps was forced to return to his protective parents' Berlin apartment, on the Hasenheide, to make ends meet.[123] But even this "defeat" did not dampen his spirits. At age twenty-four, his self-confidence was keen, as were his belief in the rightness of his views and his desire to communicate them.

Like Leo Baeck, Robert Weltsch, Max Warburg, Bella Fromm, and Richard Willstätter, Hans-Joachim Schoeps had defined a clear mission for himself in the Third Reich and steeled himself to carry it out. The first Nazi attacks on Jewish rights and well-being had jolted each of them not into headlong flight, but into constructive action. Now they were gamely rising to the occasion, rededicating their talents and energies to defending whatever sphere of activity remained open to them, adapting to a harsh and demeaning environment in ways that matched their philosophy and hopes. For Richard Willstätter, the response was essentially private and introverted—to fasten with even greater self-discipline on the scientific questions that had fascinated him all his life and that offered him the surety of progress in a time of barbaric political retreat. He opted for "inner emigration." But for all the others, the roles they chose had a communal dimension: They opted to help guide German Jews through the greatest calamity in their history, to succor the needy, to prepare Jewish children for a new life, and to draw Jews together in a revitalized community, so one day, they could cross the threshold that lay beyond Hitler. There was no sense yet that such a threshold might not exist, that the German Jews were trapped in a room without doors, only bars. These six figures had absorbed the first blows aimed at them and stood their ground. If anything, this initial experience with the Nazis had intensified their resolve to persevere, to endure. They found meaning in doing so. As Leo Baeck reflected in an essay titled "Days and Life," human existence is more than a succession of daily vicissitudes; a deeper significance shines through, and the travails fade into the background. Recognizing that one was a Jew yielded a solid, fortifying core of self-awareness, giving German Jewry more inner strength than it had ever had before.[124] If the Nazis had meant to break the Jews' will by heaping adversity on them, they had so far achieved only the opposite effect.

7

Testing the "New Jews"

The first year of Adolf Hitler's rule ended on a sad note for Germany's beleaguered Jews. On January 29, 1934, Fritz Haber, burdened by a weak heart and a broken will, died in Basel. It was a tragically symbolic death—not just of one eminent Jewish scientist, but of the German-Jewish symbiosis that Haber epitomized and that destroyed him. "I was German to an extent that I feel fully only now," he wrote pensively to his friend Richard Willstätter just after he decided to resign his post in Berlin in the spring of 1933.[1] "In my whole life I have never been so Jewish as now," he confided proudly to Albert Einstein a few months later.[2] A Jew who had affirmed his patriotic allegiance by converting to Christianity, Haber was a man torn asunder, unable to go on living as a divided soul or to start a new life. Shortly before Haber's death, Willstätter visited Haber in Switzerland, finding his old colleague "weary of suffering"[3]—a phrase that could be equally applied to both men. More accustomed to exile and "passivity"[4] and more inwardly resilient, Willstätter mourned Haber but did not follow him into the abyss of despair. He could endure this wrenching death as he had endured others, more painful, closer to his heart, in the past.

For the Jews it was a season of deaths. The day after New Year's Max Warburg lost his close associate and financial adviser, Carl Melchior— a man of great self-restraint and discipline who had rediscovered his Jewishness with gusto during the April 1933 boycott and thereafter worked himself literally to death for the good of the community. His passing left a void at the bank and in Warburg's confidence. Melchior and he had suffered through many setbacks together. Now Warburg would have to face an uncertain future by himself. On January 1, a larger tree had crashed in the pruned German-Jewish forest: The writer Jakob Wassermann, whose entire life was shaped by a vain attempt to gain the acceptance of his fellow Germans. (He had once written: "It is futile to show them loyalty, be it as a comrade-in-arms, or as a fellow citizen. They say—he is Proteus, he can be anything. . . . It is futile to live for them and to die for them. They say: he is a Jew.")[5] Wassermann's novelistic quest for peace between Christians and Jews had not surmounted anti-Semitic hatred. His death, like Haber's and Melchior's, seemed to toll the knell of the assimilated era.

Yet there was life after death, in spite of death. After a full year of Hitler, the German Jews were still very much alive, very much in evidence. Out of a community of 525,000, less than one-tenth had left the country for good. Most hesitated to follow in the émigrés' footsteps, believing they had passed the Nazis' baptism by fire. What they had, in fact, survived was this: 319 new laws and regulations restricting how Jews could live—from where they could bathe, to whom they could sleep with, to where they could work. They had been arrested in the night, taken away, and beaten senseless; they had been called "Jewish pigs" and had swastikas smeared on their windows and cut into their hair.[6] Some had been shot to death, others dragged out of their homes or driven from their places of business. (By 1934, some 75,000 Jewish businesses had been liquidated.)[7] Many, in utter despair, had taken their own lives.

But on the plus side of the ledger, many Jews were going about their daily lives as before. The anti-Semites had singled out certain groups of

Jews for abuse—Communist Jews, Social Democratic Jews, eastern Jews—but gone after the community as a whole only sporadically, almost desultorily. The aborted April boycott had shown that most Germans did not approve of broad anti-Jewish measures; they stuck by their corner jeweler or pediatrician out of personal loyalty, if not heartfelt sympathy. Hjalmar Schacht's argument that expelling the Jews from the economy en masse would both offend foreign opinion and sabotage an economy that was poised to make a full recovery after the worldwide depression carried weight in the Nazi inner circles, even with the Führer himself. Generally left alone by the regime, large Jewish businesses benefited from the upswing in prosperity that flowed from Germany's stabilization and economic expansion under Hitler.[8] (For example, until 1935 Jewish firms were still receiving contracts to do business with the Nazi government.)[9] A good part of this prosperity was due to Germany's expenditures on armaments: Jews, too, reaped profits from the buildup of the Luftwaffe, the Wehrmacht, and the German navy.

In sum, the Jews had lost their sense of security as coequal (if not beloved) German citizens, but not their livelihood. To fill the vacuum created by the demise of assimilationist liberalism, the Jews had found comfort in each other's company, in their Jewishness. This bond fortified them and gave them a quiet pride. Twelve months after Adolf Hitler moved into the German chancellery, the Jews had fashioned new psychological weapons to ward off a brazen, implacable foe. They were not crushed, not by any means. Having recovered from the shock of the first blows directed at them, the Jews hoped to appease their oppressors by behaving as meekly and agreeably as possible. More blows might still fall, but they would fall less frequently, and with less force, they believed, if the Jews did nothing to provoke them. Calm forbearance seemed a better strategy than counterattack. So had persecuted German Jews reasoned for centuries, and with a good measure of success. History argued for taking the same course now.

Full of pent-up rage but not well-thought-out plans, the Nazis had no clear idea how to deal with this racial minority they despised so deeply. They ranted and raved about the Jews and then abruptly turned their attention elsewhere—to consolidating their power and rebuilding the German economy. "Spontaneous" moves against individual Jews were followed by soothing talk about respecting the law and citizens' rights. Regulations limiting Jewish influence and contact with "Aryans" implied the Nazis might settle for a lasting, second-class status quo for the Jews. The vile sputterings of Joseph Goebbels or Julius Streicher, among others, gave way to the rational arguments of those like Schacht, who said that the Jews should be left alone. In the Jews' minds, this inconsistency in policy produced more confusion—and inertia.

Over the next two years, uncertainty would gradually become a condition of life for Germany's Jews. It was an uncertainty that the Nazis engineered for effect. As a Jewish visitor from Paris noted: "It is becoming ever clearer that the German government wants to keep all German Jews in a state of continuous uncertainty, so that they will remain in permanent ignorance of their fate."[10] The Jews would adjust to this state of affairs as best they could as the unpredictably fluctuating rhythm of persecution and neglect became "normal," not exhausting their hopes but creating the expectation that this was how their lives would continue to be, indefinitely. Over these two years, they would suffer more attacks and indignities, and the nightmare through which they groped would darken. These attacks hinted of worse to come, of a Germany plunging headlong into madness. For the Jews, the fear of jumping off before this plunge would coexist with the fear of what might happen to them if they did not. The thought that some might be lucky enough to survive the Nazi nightmare mingled with a belief that fate had bound them all helplessly together.

At the beginning of this period, there was much talk about finding an "honorable" solution to the "Jewish problem."[11] Such a solution meant making do with less by striking a bargain with the National Socialists: In exchange for withdrawing from those spheres of German life where their presence was deemed offensive, the Jews would be spared further degradation and violence. It was a policy of appeasement and retreat toward a relentless foe—a strategy soon to be adopted by foreign governments as well. It would assume many forms, call itself by many names. It would be undertaken by various groups among Germany's Jews, each convinced it had the best chance of striking a bargain with the Nazis, each claiming for itself the savior's role. Each, in turn, would be thwarted.

On the far Right, the Jewish organizations that spoke up most vociferously were those linked to National Socialism by kindred feelings of manly camaraderie, a shared World War I front experience, a disdain for democracy, and a patriotic hunger for self-sacrifice—all of which, they felt, counted for more than a difference in race. As the leader of the Reichsbund jüdischer Frontsoldaten (RjF) (Reich Association of Jewish War Veterans), Leo Löwenstein, summed up, the Jewish issue should be settled on a "soldierly basis." In this grand, nationalistic campaign to renew Germany, loyal Jews would volunteer as gladly as they had in past wars for the good of the Fatherland, even if all they were allowed to do this time was bring up the rear of march.[12] In arguing for inclusion on these grounds, the RjF and the even more fervent Verband nationaldeutscher Juden (VndJ) were willing to cast to the winds those Jews who could make no such claim to trench brotherhood—namely, the eastern Jews. The Ostjuden could be expelled, if the Nazis so insisted, as long as truly "patriotic" Jews were given a place in the Reich. To emphasize the differences between themselves and Jews of more dubious loyalty, the RjF and the VndJ also blasted the Zionists (who happened to be gaining Nazi support for their scheme for Jewish emigration), saying that they, unlike these would-be émigrés, would resist any dissociation from the "German homeland."[13] The RjF also distanced itself from the Reichsvertretung der deutschen Juden, which was asserting that it, alone, spoke for all German Jewry.[14]

Jewish veterans' groups drew attention to their frontline sacrifice to the Fatherland[15] by having their members light candles in windows on Heldengedenktag (Heroes' Memorial Day), February 25, and by celebrating their war dead in other ways. (The Reichsvertretung advised this practice as well.)[16] By doing so, they hoped to refute Nazi allegations that Jews had shirked wartime duty.[17] They pleaded, in letters to the old field marshal, Paul von Hindenburg, for the right to serve in the German army, even if it was in Hitler's Third Reich.[18] They sought, through sports and other group activities, to instill in Jewish youths the same bond of camaraderie they cherished and that would protect the young people.[19] In the face of Nazi goads and insults, they maintained a stoic silence.

Hans-Joachim Schoeps and his Deutscher Vortrupp (German Vanguard) tried the same approach. Over the New Year's holiday of 1934, this tiny band of young, conservative Jews convened in the Hessian winter resort of Gersfeld to ski and declare it stood for inclusion in the German Fatherland "under all circumstances"[20] as much as it opposed the actions of both assimilationist Jews and Zionists, who were committing nothing less than a "crime against Judaism."[21] The German Vanguard,

Schoeps wrote a few months afterward, would become a "leadership echelon," paving the way for all German Jews to enter the new German order by "conscious acknowledgment and affirmation."[22] Schoeps laid out his position more fully in a pamphlet entitled *Wir deutschen Juden*, some six thousand copies of which he had printed and distributed in the spring of 1934. In this pamphlet, he praised the Nazi revolution as a "complete novelty," a radical cure for a sick society on the verge of collapse.[23] If Jews would only accept this new Germany, in spite of its anti-Semitism, then would "sound the great hour of their new incorporation" into it.[24] In this essay and other writings, Schoeps was charting a new path (or "third way") for Jews who were unable to endorse either Zionism or the discredited liberal credo.

To spread his gospel, Schoeps spoke to gatherings of Jewish war veterans, who found him—despite his obvious youth and lack of war experience—a compatible voice. They applauded the parallel he drew between the plight of Germany's Jews and Job. ("We suffer a martyrdom for the truth," he told veterans in Hamburg.)[25] They accepted his linking the World War I generation with the German youth movement. In 1935 Schoeps would further bolster this intergenerational bond by publishing for the RjF a collection of letters written by Jewish soldiers subsequently killed in battle.

The problem for Schoeps and other ultra-patriotic Jews was that they represented exactly what the Nazis did not want—a Jewry so in love with Germany they could not bear the thought of leaving it. (Even the Jews who *were* bent on quitting the Reich could not readily discard their deep-seated German identity. In October 1934 the American consular official in Berlin, W. Ware Adams, reported that it was difficult to compile accurate statistics on Jews seeking U.S. visas because Jewish applicants "insist upon declaring their race as German even after the difference between race and religion is carefully explained to them, often even when they give racial discrimination as the reason for their desire to emigrate.")[26]

Because of their intense loyalty, these nationalistic Jews were hostilely spurned by the Nazis. When the Jewish war veterans commemorated their dead, the Nazi press howled that it was all a lie—the Jews had been conscripted against their will, and those who had died while serving were largely victims of disease.[27] To the RjF's numerous petitions asking that a "special status" be granted its members in the Nazi state,[28] the regime gave no response. When nationalist-oriented Jews hung swastikas on the front of their homes and stores to display their allegiance to Hitler's regime, the government issued a decree banning such acts.[29]

But in rejecting the advances of Jewish patriots, the Nazis had to be careful. Blind devotion to the Fatherland was a quality that Hitler wanted to nurture among his people for his own ends, not disparage. The ties binding World War I veterans of different religions were emotionally strong, and as long as the German army and powerful groups like the Stahlhelm (Steel Helmet) remained independent of the Nazi Party, Hitler had to respect and defer to their sensibilities. (The Stahlhelm was dissolved by SA leader Ernst Röhm in May 1934, when Hindenburg was in failing health and unable to do much to stop him.) That deference was embodied in the person of President Hindenburg. The immense (6 foot, 5 inch) ancient warrior, the hero of German victories at Tannenberg and the Masurian lakes, evoked a glorious imperial era. He was a father figure to a nation now being wooed and won by an electrifying political leader of another generation and another class (a "Bohemian corporal"), yet reluctant to cast aside the old-fashioned values the old field marshal stood for—honor, devotion to country, and uprightness. Hindenburg's sticking by these values had saved the jobs of Jewish veterans back in April 1933, after the RjF had appealed to him to exempt them from the newly enacted "Aryan" clause. Ex-soldiers and other Jews still looked to Hindenburg as their protector, as perhaps the one person in all Germany who stood between them and the forces of darkness and destruction.

Then, on August 2, 1934, Germany's Memorial Day—the twentieth anniversary of the outbreak of World War I—the eighty-six-year-old Hindenburg died. (Jews were not permitted to fly flags in honor of their war dead that day—bitter proof of their diminished status.)[30] The same day Hitler assumed the field marshal's position, taking the official title Führer and Chancellor of the Reich. Shorn of their guardian, Jewish war veterans had every reason to fear that the special status they had enjoyed until then would be taken away.

They were right. In short order, the names of Jewish soldiers were chiseled off war monuments around the country, as part of the Nazi campaign to rewrite German history and erase any positive Jewish role in it.[31] From then on, the situation of conservative Jews only worsened.

Patriotic Jewish leaders like Hans-Joachim Schoeps kept voicing views
that might ameliorate Nazi rage and check these actions, but they could
see that their time was running out. The German Vanguard continued
to hold periodic "leadership sessions," to expand its ranks and refine its
message for Jewish youths. At a Christmas 1934 gathering in the
Thuringian forest, Schoeps found out that a group of enthusiastic
Zionists was dancing around a tree in the village. Incensed, he raced to
the home of the local Nazi Sturmbannführer, a cobbler, and woke him
at three in the morning by pounding on his door. Schoeps apologized
profusely for the Zionists' behavior to this bleary eyed and dumbfounded Nazi functionary, handed him some leaflets about the German
Vanguard, and melted back into the wintry night.[32]

Always a tiny faction (at its peak, in 1934, the Deutscher Vortrupp
had only 1,300 names on its mailing list),[33] on the far Right fringe of
the Jewish community, Schoeps's German Vanguard had entertained
lofty notions of forging a new, pro-German youth movement. But, again
and again, efforts to enlarge its narrow base failed. A brief alliance with
other conservative groups had collapsed because of personality clashes
and philosophical differences: Schoeps was not willing to repudiate his
Jewishness for the sake of an arrangement with the Nazis. (He insisted
he could serve Germany only by adhering to his Jewish identity.)[34] And
the organization had also not succeeded in attracting young German
Jews with its message of hostility toward the bourgeois, older generation. In following a rigidly conservative, authoritarian line, Schoeps had
alienated his band from nearly all the rest of German Jewry (except for
the war veterans). The self-proclaimed "leadership echelon" had not
inspired Jewish youths. This was a fact that Schoeps candidly acknowledged at the Deutscher Vortrupp's gathering at the mountain spa, Bad
Orb, in late December 1934. The group had not found any positive
echo, he said: "We have been defeated so thoroughly along the entire
front [in our assault] against German Jewry that our question today
must be: Do we want to be accepted into the Jewish community at all?"
Schoeps wrested a kind of Pyrrhic victory from this defeat, contending
scornfully that the Deutscher Vortrupp's attempt to renew German
Jewry had been directed at an "unsuitable object" and that the proper
course of action for its "revolutionary" impulses was to withdraw from
any such engagement into isolation, to retreat into the woods like the
Wandervögel of an earlier era.[35]

What he was proposing was that the Deutscher Vortrupp should suspend its activities until a more propitious day dawned. Politically unsophisticated and narcissistic, Schoeps had miscalculated the appeal of his volatile mix of nationalistic fervor and intellectualized Jewish faith. The contradictions between being a German and being a Jew had only intensified over the past two years, not found some higher, Hegelian synthesis. At the same time, Schoeps and his followers were feeling pressure from the regime's secret police. Schoeps continued to be questioned by the Gestapo in an atmosphere of half-imagined danger and self-glorification. (Some years later, Schoeps would characterize these encounters as "more exciting than a novel.")[36] The Nazis were seeking to force right-wing Jewish organizations out of existence and their members out of the country. As a devout Prussian, Schoeps would resist this pressure as long as he could.

His last hope for an accommodation with the Nazis hinged on the German military. If Jews could be admitted to its ranks, then they could still claim to be serving the Fatherland as they had done during World War I. In March 1935 Hitler ushered in this possibility by reinstating universal military service (in defiance of the Versailles Treaty) to defend Germany against what he called its "bellicose" European neighbors. Within two weeks, the German Vanguard had responded to this clarion call to arms. From Berlin, Schoeps issued the following statement:

In this historic moment, in which the German Reich restores its military sovereignty, we young German Jews feel compelled to express our satisfaction over this step. Just as our fathers fulfilled their duty to the Fatherland in 1914–18, so are we, too, prepared today for military service, in loyalty to our motto: "Ready for Germany."[37]

The offer was flatly rejected. After having received assurance from army officers he knew that this would not happen, a stunned Schoeps learned, in September, that the government was going to ban Jews from military service. This decision punctuated the failure of Schoeps and the RjF to reach out to a nazified Germany.[38] Henceforth, the conservative Jewish Right was headed down the road toward extinction. To soften the pain of defeat, the RjF leader Leo Löwenstein urged his followers to choose "inner emigration" after the September ban was announced.[39] Schoeps talked of a "journey inward"[40]—an evocative romantic metaphor recalling the halcyon days when bands of towheaded youths hiked whistling into the forest to commune with nature and restore their souls. The problem now was that the metaphor was dead: For Germany's Jews, there would be no more sanctuaries, either inner or outer. Schoeps did not realize that he was only conjuring up ghosts.

Self-delusion was not the exclusive property of the far Right. The vast majority of essentially apolitical, middle-class, assimilated German Jews clung to a chimera of their own. This was the belief that the restraints of law would hold the Nazis in check. It was a belief that only the kind of persecution that had befallen Jews in the past was being repeated now and that they would endure this animosity as they had then. It was a belief that Jews survived anti-Semitic attacks by banding together, by returning to the fold. It was a belief that inner resolve and quiet faith could defeat material suffering and want. It was a belief that the agonies of the day were subsumed and justified within the long sweep of human history.

This belief Leo Baeck promulgated, in public, even as he privately accepted the futility of any long-term Jewish existence in Hitler's Germany. In his opening remarks before a meeting of the governing body (Rat) of the Reichsvertretung at the Berlin lodge of B'nai B'rith on Sunday, February 4, 1934, Baeck compared the Jewish community's current ordeal to the hostility and ostracism it had faced following World War I. Then, as now, patience, waiting, and immersion in the challenges of each passing day would be the watchwords, coupled with the assurance, Baeck told his audience, "that what we do is done for generations" to come. The judgment of history lent greater weight (and worth) to the actions of individual Jews now.[41]

Baeck's view of how his fellow Jews should react to Nazi provocation and vilification was also influenced by his scholarly and theological outlook. Rather than give up hope or grow defiant, he believed, German Jewry ought to draw inward and gain strength and composure from spiritual values. In an essay that appeared a year and a day after Hitler assumed power, Baeck urged "restraint"—staying within one's own self—as a way of accepting one's destiny.[42] This mollifying advice contrasted markedly with what the Berlin rabbi was saying privately. For instance, in March 1934, Wilfrid Israel, the young Berlin department-store owner and liaison to Jewish groups abroad, forwarded a report on the "general situation" inside Germany that revealed a much more pessimistic outlook. Described as being "in the closest touch with Dr. Baeck,"[43] Israel conveyed a mood of "greater distress" than in recent months, characterizing Jewish leaders' view of the future as "fairly hopeless," despite the upbeat pronouncements of pro-German Jewish groups.[44] He did not mention Baeck's name, but the description fit.

Realizing that emigration "was not the real solution"[45] for his people, Baeck focused on consoling the community and helping the Jews who would remain in the Reich. He called the Jewish community a "protective house," in which no Jew could feel alone, and that could sustain each one through this period of crisis. The work of the community—education, retraining, and welfare assistance—was bringing Jews together, "closer than ever," Baeck said. It was this "practical work" that the Reichsvertretung enthusiastically supported, to divert despondent Jews from their inertia and angst, as well as from their ideological clashes.[46] (At the Reichsvertrung's February 11, 1934, meeting, Max Warburg, Martin Buber, and several others introduced a resolution stressing this theme of community building; their ultimate goal was to secure some Jewish Lebensraum inside Germany. Among those who voiced their unanimous approval were such unlikely associates as Robert Weltsch and Richard Willstätter.)[47] Accepting a fate in the Jewish community was a theme to which Baeck returned again and again, as he did to herald the Jewish New Year in September 1934, saying that what was needed now was "the will to common purpose and the will to sacrifice,"[48] or as he did in April 1935, praising the *Gemeinde* (Jewish community) as the "fortress of our future"—the "roof over our heads."[49]

In the fall of 1934 Baeck would use the occasion of the Reichsvertretung's first anniversary to look back on the Jews' initial response to Hitler: "We have passed a decisive test," he declared in his opening address. "We have been and remain loyal citizens of the state" by remaining reserved and humble in manner, while refusing to be dehumanized by the Nazis.[50] "In the ties between soil and spirit lie the richness of German Jewry," he went on. Such a bond to a country cannot be lost as long as one does not give it up. "When there is a will there is a way," Baeck said.[51]

But what was also needed was a German government that would respect the principles of law and order that still protected Jews as citizens of the Reich. Baeck's advocacy of a calm, inner solidarity was based on these principles being inviolable. In his overtures to governmental officials, he emphasized that the abuse suffered by his people was illegal, as if pointing this out might bring them to their senses. Writing to cabinet ministers on behalf of the Reichsvertretung in January, Baeck contended that violence and chaos harmed the new Reich as well as its Jews. It would benefit both to work out some kind of reasonable arrangement, sparing the Jewish community additional "psychological pressure" and economic hardship. For such an arrangement, Baeck was prepared to concede some of the Nazis' points—for example, that the large number of Jews in academia and in German cities was "unhealthy."[52] In taking this approach, he was like an animal tamer mouthing soothing words to a chained but menacing tiger—all his instincts told him there was no real danger as long as the tiger did not become enraged. And, even then, the chain would hold it back. There was a firm restraint keeping the beast from its prey.

Baeck's confidence in German law was sorely tested during 1934. First came the death of Hindenburg. This loss was as devastating for a liberal Jewish leader like Baeck as it was for the more conservative Jewish veterans. Hindenburg had been a key link in the chain of legal protection. When Baeck rose in the Regentenstrasse synagogue to deliver the eulogy for Hindenburg on Sunday, August 5, in a service sponsored by the RjF, he did not conceal his anguish. Standing above politics, the towering field marshal had exemplified steadfastness and uprightness to Germany's Jews, Baeck said. The Jews had looked to him as a "rock" of security and belonging, as another Abraham. Baeck ended his moving remarks with these words:

> Deep, painful sorrow for his departure overflows among us German Jews, together with all in the German Fatherland. Many years will pass in the German nation during which many will long for Hindenburg—will regard him with yearning. That which he was will remain as an everlasting certainty, as an unwavering exhortation: "Look there at the rock!"[53]

At the end of the memorial service, Baeck and the other Jews who were packed in the synagogue joined in singing the sentimental old-soldiers' song, "I Had a Comrade."[54] (Bella Fromm, who had "venerated the old soldier in the Old Gentleman," attended Hindenburg's funeral in Tannenberg with equally heavy a heart.)[55]

Terrible as this loss was, it was overshadowed by the shock to Jewish faith in law and order that had occurred in June 1934. Back then, with Hindenburg's health rapidly declining, vice chancellor Papen had been persuaded by his conservative, non-Nazi allies to make one last bid to rein in the Nazi government.[56] He did so in an outspoken speech at Marburg University that denounced the violence and radicalism of the regime. Enraged and determined now to crush his lingering right-wing opposition, Hitler and his henchmen plotted a retaliatory strike—one that would also, conveniently, eliminate the rowdy, paramilitary SA and its defiant leader, Ernst Röhm. A former comrade-in-arms, Röhm now represented the last remaining bona fide challenge to Hitler's power.

From her web of informants within and outside the Nazi Party, Bella Fromm discovered what was being planned. To tip off her dear friend General Kurt von Schleicher—who was a prime target of the plot—she hosted a small dinner party on June 25, 1934. But, as he had in January 1933, the general only laughed off Fromm's whispered warning.[57] (Coincidentally, on the same day, Röhm's adjutant met Fromm at a diplomatic tea and gave her his leader's photograph.)[58] On the morning of June 30, Fromm was urgently summoned by Herbert Mumm, her lover and longtime Nazi Party confidante who worked in the Foreign Ministry. He had horrifying news: At 9 A.M. six SS men in plainclothes had arrived on the doorstep of General Schleicher's villa, on the Wannsee, rung the bell, and shot the fifty-two-year-old retired army general when he opened the door. Elisabeth, his bride of only eighteen months, was gunned down just as cold-bloodedly. Mumm was now worried about Fromm. "It's known that he came to see you only a short while ago," he told her. "You'll have to be careful, Bella! There is a wholesale butchery in full swing."[59]

Fromm was terrified. After having taken over power without violence or bloodshed, the Nazis were now brutally settling scores with "enemies of the state," executing several hundred SA leaders and other opponents on the Right, including some in the military. There was no telling where the slaughter would end. An intimate of Schleicher, befriended by Papen (who had been placed under house arrest), she had good cause to fear for her own safety. Instinctively, Fromm drove over to a friend's house, to hide, but then, afraid that she might only call attention to herself by behaving suspiciously, she slipped into an evening dress and pinned on her medals for a gala in honor of the prince and princess of

Japan. With her two best friends in Berlin lying dead on the outskirts of the city, she did her best to go through the motions of making social chitchat during the reception.[60]

Following the "Night of the Long Knives," Fromm retreated to the countryside for a few days and then returned to Berlin. Soon she was back at her desk, drafting articles for her society newspapers. "I know what is in store for me," she had written in her diary earlier in the year, concerned mainly about her journalistic career. After watching SA and SS thugs storm an aristocrats' ball in January, she had carried a concealed revolver for a time, then heaved it into a canal. Now her feeling of vulnerability intensified. But so did her sense of obligation to the Jews who were still in Germany, defenseless, in need of her help. For them, she would stay on. Even though she now fully realized what the Nazis were capable of, she would not give up. As long as the Gestapo did not come and cart her away, she would not leave the country.

The Röhm putsch reduced Jews everywhere to silence. It seemed their best ploy while the Nazis destroyed other enemies. The Jewish press did not dare to print a single word about the SA massacre. Judging from the columns they did publish, it was as if the event had never transpired. Typically, in its July 1, 1934, issue, the *Bayerische-israelitische Gemeindezeitung* admonished Jews to show more reserve, tact, and dignity and to behave impeccably in public places so as not to offend.[61] Such genteel advice had not been of much help to the late General Schleicher. Robert Weltsch's *Jüdische Rundschau* devoted its front page to recalling another death—Theodor Herzl's, thirty years before—in order to advocate the creation of a Palestine homeland.[62]

In public, mainstream Jewish leaders kept up a facade of indifference, turning their attention to other matters. Leo Baeck chose to direct his first remarks after the Night of the Long Knives at the RjF, which had again accused the Zionists of not being sufficiently "patriotic."[63] No one group could claim a monopoly on love for the Fatherland, the rabbi chided. (Behind the scenes, Baeck and his deputy at the Reichsvertretung, Otto Hirsch, were meeting with the Zionist Arthur Ruppin, to discuss the possibility of Jewish emigration to Palestine, the United States, Argentina, and Brazil.)[64] About the same time, Max Warburg conferred with the Baltimore rabbi Morris Lazaron, in Amsterdam, and impressed the visiting American with his "extraordinary combination of strength and humaneness" in spite of all that had just taken place. Warburg opined that he expected the situation in Germany to be "quiescent" for the next week or so.[65] In Cologne and other cities in mid-July 1934, three thousand German Jews gathered to honor their war dead, even though more recent slaughter preoccupied them.[66] The *Jüdische Rundschau* ran a short piece by Baeck, solemnly recalling the beginning of World War I thirty years before and the Jewish sacrifices made for Germany in it.[67] In his words was only the faintest hint of past as prologue.

In private, the Jewish leaders were more candid. Until the SA massacre, Hans-Joachim Schoeps had kept alive his hopes of an "arrangement" with the Nazis. He had also dreamed of forging an alliance with larger, more influential conservative groups, such as the Stahlhelm. Now the Stahlhelm was dissolved, and the regime had shown, with one sudden flash of steel, that it was not to be trusted or guided by law. As much as more moderate Jews, Schoeps had to admit that the chances of achieving a Nazi-Jewish concordat were virtually nil. Personally, Schoeps now had greater reason to dread Germany's masters. Seeking to justify the bloody June 30 purge, the Nazi hierarchy had seized on the SA's "moral corruption" and "pervert dispositions," most evident in the flagrant homosexual practices of many of its members, including Röhm. Hitler could present himself to a distressed German public as the guardian of conventional morality, even though he and his associates had blithely tolerated such "abnormal" behavior for years. Indeed, homosexuality had been deeply embedded in paramilitary groups like the SA and the German youth movement since their inception. Male eroticism was often what brought young men together in these groups.[68] Yet homosexuality was not condoned by German society. It was treated as immoral and a criminal offense long before Hitler came to power, and it had thus become a kind of open secret within these renegade groups, as well as another indication of their divergence from the bourgeois world.

Schoeps was no exception in this regard. Although he sometimes boasted about having "girlfriends"[69] (and would even marry during World War II while in Swedish exile), he preferred the company and affection of young men. The periodic retreats of the Deutscher Vortrupp provided him with the perfect setting to cultivate intimate friendships and love attachments. He had to do so discreetly, of course, to avoid a scandal. (In 1935 the other members of his group learned that Schoeps had been having an affair with another of their comrades;

the news exploded in the tightly knit circle like a bombshell.)[70] After the Night of the Long Knives, homosexuality was considered a more serious vice (anathema according to the puritanical norms of the Volksgemeinschaft), to be punished more harshly. Homosexuals formed another classification of prisoner in Nazi Germany's burgeoning concentration camps. Thus, Hans-Joachim Schoeps had another good reason for fearing the scrutiny that he and his small band of German enthusiasts were receiving from the Gestapo—reason enough for him to reconsider the wisdom of remaining so politically visible, but not enough of one for him to conclude that he would be better off living in some other country.

The violence and slide toward lawlessness marked by the purge of the SA and accelerated by Hindenburg's death took its toll psychologically on Germany's Jews—the victims-apparent. The normally sanguine Max Warburg traveled from Hamburg to Berlin in August to meet with the new American ambassador, William E. Dodd. On his face Warburg wore "the effects of his troubled life" over the past year. He confessed to Dodd that his—Warburg's—life would be in danger if the Nazis ever learned of his political views.[71] His tireless work on behalf of the Reichsvertretung and Jewish unity had also drained his energy and resilience. Warburg was depressed to see his fellow Jews failing to put the common good ahead of their continuing back stabbing.[72] Yet he was still determined to fight for Jewish survival—according to his brother Felix, *struggle* and *must* remained his favorite words[73]—but conditions in the community, particularly economic ones, were growing worse despite all his efforts.[74] To gain leverage with the government and ease the international friction created by anti-German boycotts in the United States, Warburg was now trying to convince the American Jewish community to send over a representative as a go-between with the government. This indirect approach seemed to offer more hope of lessening the community's material suffering, since the German Jews themselves had no influence on Nazi policy. (Rudolf Hess, the deputy Führer, declared on August 16 that no Nazi Party officials were henceforth to have dealings with Jews.) The American consul general, George Messersmith, endorsed Warburg's proposal.[75] However, Ambassador Dodd was more cautious, concerned that any foreign Jewish attempts to promote a more "sensible" policy might cause more harm than good.[76]

Previously Warburg had hoped—along with Baeck, Weltsch, Schoeps, and others—that a concordat might be hammered out between the German Reich and its Jewish population, similar to what had been negotiated with the Vatican in July 1933, granting the Catholic Church the right "to regulate her own affairs" in Germany. On board the SS *Europa,* bound for New York in December 1933, Warburg had articulated this desire in a letter to Weltsch. If Jews were allowed to oversee *their* own affairs, it would preclude the need for legally defining and treating them as a separate minority. In the long run, Warburg thought, this solution would better safeguard Jews from exclusion and expulsion from Germany.[77]

But the notion of an agreement with the Nazis had suddenly lost much of its appeal: Who could any longer expect them to keep their word? The next time Warburg—accompanied by his Gestapo "shadow"—boarded a steamer for the United States, in the middle of October 1934, it was primarily with the goal of raising funds to spur German Jewish emigration across the Atlantic. (Thus far only five thousand Jews had left Nazi Germany for a new life in the United States.)[78] However, he had not completely discarded more positive thoughts—a "second emancipation of the Jew" might still occur under Nazi hegemony, he told his American Jewish friends, which would constitute the basis for a new Jewish life once Hitler had passed from the scene.[79] He did not appear to have any doubts that the Jews would outlast the Nazis.

In Warburg and many of his contemporaries, such contradictory views produced a psychic stasis: revulsion and fear caused by anti-Semitic and antidemocratic policies or acts balanced by stoic forbearance and Jewish solidarity and pride. The outcome of the Nazi era was by no means clear, but for the moment, the idea that there would be some kind of an outcome—a life after Hitler—was mildly reassuring.

It was easy to be reassured, even about the current state of affairs in Germany. On the surface, much of daily life remained as it had been before Hitler came to power. Nazi attacks on the Jews were like summer thunderstorms that came and went quickly, leaving an eerie calm. A typical visitor to Berlin in the summer of 1934 would find much to praise. The British Zionist leader Selig Brodetsky was surprised by the courteous treatment afforded him in Berlin shops and by the number of Jewish stores still doing business. When he met with Leo Baeck, the latter conceded that life was not all that bad for Jews who lived in Germany's cities. It was only in villages and small towns, where they were more visible, that Jews were living "on the edge of a volcano."[80] Baeck's granddaughter, Marianne, was still happily enrolled in a German public school. But Baeck stressed to Brodetsky that there was no future for Jewish youths inside the Third Reich. Young people would have to go to Palestine.

In August 1934 the newly appointed American consul general in Berlin, Raymond Geist, reported back to Washington that conditions for Jews in German cities, including Jewish merchants, was generally "satisfactory." Although the harassment and boycott of Jewish stores were commonplace in smaller towns, these measures were increasingly opposed by non-Jews. Many Germans believed "there would be better times" for them if Jews were allowed to conduct their business freely. Jewish professionals were "desperate" to find new jobs or emigrate, but the number of Jews directly affected by Nazi dismissals amounted to only about seventeen thousand, Geist estimated. He did sense fears of coming "political or economic disasters," which would be blamed on the Jews and for which they would pay dearly. But for the time being, Geist believed that "the German government wishes . . . to maintain an armistice with respect to the Jewish question, owing to the pressure of other problems."[81]

In this time of mixed signals, Jewish ambivalence only deepened. Wrenching crises had been endured, but the lessons to be drawn from these experiences were unclear. Bella Fromm had lost the right to work as a journalist for German newspapers, lost her daughter to America, lost her best friend to suicide, and lost other friends to assassins' bullets, but then found other employment, with the help of Ambassador Dodd, writing for English and other foreign publications.[82] (In May 1934, she sailed for the United States—not to stay, but to be reunited briefly with her daughter.)

Robert Weltsch had faced a similar career obstacle, but had gotten around it with the argument that a Jew ought to be free to write for the benefit of his own people.[83] So he was permitted to publish more essays exhorting Germany's Jews to persevere. ("We Jews today are in the fortunate position of having the future of the Jewish people unfold before our very eyes," he wrote.)[84] Weltsch even successfully locked horns with Goebbels, the propaganda minister. In July the Zionist editor ran an essay making the modest but brave assertion that "The Jew Is a Human

Being, Too,"[85] in response to a speech in which Goebbels had labeled Jews subhuman "fleas." Weltsch's retort prompted Goebbels to shut down the *Jüdische Rundschau* and deliver a second speech ridiculing the newspaper's position.[86] But the ban was lifted a month later, and Weltsch could find some satisfaction in having held his ground.

Max Warburg came back to Germany from the United States to face more discouraging developments—the Nazi threat to bar Jews from the army and demote them to second-class citizens. The Baltimore rabbi Morris Lazaron reported in May 1935 that Warburg was more "depressed and done in" than he had ever seen him.[87] But, as the situation worsened, the Hamburg financier metamorphosed into "a lion at bay," resolved to fight the Nazis every step of the way and resist expulsion from Germany. The Jews, he told Lazaron, had nothing to lose by standing up for their rights as citizens, even if it was a hopeless cause. "Now is the time to act," Warburg said, and Lazaron pronounced him "magnificent."

In Munich, the spring of 1935 saw Hitler Youth nail up signs on the outskirts stating Jews Not Welcome, and there were anti-Semitic demonstrations in the city's center. These incidents did not especially perturb Richard Willstätter. He remained an "outsider" preoccupied with the intricacies of enzyme function "too difficult for me, if not for our time"[88] and so absorbed that he had little time or energy left over to scan the daily headlines or speculate on the eventual fate of Germany's Jews. (Willstätter was more concerned about obtaining fresh animal livers from Munich slaughterhouses for his experiments.)[89] The Jews' plight was still not his, safeguarded as he was "by his own reputation and by the devotion of his Munich audience."[90]

Hans-Joachim Schoeps may have blanched when he learned of the Night of the Long Knives, but his fear did not stop him from maintaining a busy schedule of speeches to Jewish war veterans on the subject of "German-Jewish consciousness";[91] from writing on the "tragic position" of Franz Kafka;[92] or from attending an international conference of scholars in Rome. (Passing en route Italian troop trains bound for Ethiopia, Schoeps caught a glimpse of Germany's military future.)[93]

Leo Baeck could look back on a contentious but ultimately fruitful period of unity building by the Reichsvertretung under his leadership. Social welfare for needy Jews was now consolidated under its authority.[94] Zionists and assimilated Jews were now cooperating, with the

Reichsvertretung's blessing and through the offices of Max Warburg's Hilfsverein der deutschen Juden and the Jewish Agency, in accelerating the exodus to Palestine.[95] (Still, the number of German Jews emigrating there did not exceed eight thousand a year.) Baeck's appeal for more "practical work" within the community, circumventing ideological conflicts, had been generally heeded, even while various Jewish groups continued to jockey for a special relationship with the Nazi government. On the first anniversary of the Reichsvertretung's founding, Baeck had withstood a bid by Berlin community leaders to take over control of the organization and shape it more in accordance with their liberal views.[96] As a result, he gained confidence that his leadership—and his program for steering German Jewry through this crisis—had broad community backing.

As he cemented his role as the spokesman for all German Jewry, Baeck also altered his message. It was a sign of the times. He no longer spoke as a liberal Jew, proud of the long process of acculturation in Germany. His words now, reflecting the dominant tone in the Jewish community, had a decidedly Zionist accent. When the chief rabbi of Berlin rose to speak on "The Existence of the Jew" before an attentive audience in the Berlin Lehrhaus one May evening in 1935, he described his people as a race whose historical existence in the Diaspora had always been endangered, seen as they were as "a different people" living among suspicious neighbors.[97] Their plight now was not really different from what they had faced before. Only belief in God and solidarity with these earlier generations could guide the Jews of today to a more secure future.

With the direction of Nazi policy still a mystery, the German Jews lived anxiously from day to day, salvaging what they could, protecting what they could. After two years of Nazi rejection and abuse, loyalty to the Fatherland was still seen as a necessary, anchoring virtue. Thus, when the people of the Saarland had the opportunity to vote on rejoining the Reich in January 1935, the German Jewish community felt obliged to support a yes vote, even if it meant that some five thousand more Jews, until now living in freedom and peace, would thereby be placing their heads under the Nazi yoke.[98] In fact, the Jewish vote in the Saar in favor of returning to the Reich was thought to be important, since local supporters of the Social Democrats and the Center Party favored the continued autonomy of Saarland. German Jewish leaders traveled to the Saar region to lobby their coreligionists.[99] When the desired result was achieved (over 90 percent of the Saar voters backed absorption into Germany), these leaders welcomed their returning neighbors like long-lost brothers. Leo Baeck spoke for practically the entire Jewish community when he hailed the Saar Jews out of a "warm sense of solidarity." He pledged: "We will stick together, loyal to the precepts and hope of our German Jewishness."[100] To a neutral observer, this statement had the ring of a passenger on a foundering ship embracing a person just plucked from dry land.

Beneath all these affirmations of patriotism, unity, and communal pride lay a hope and a growing consensus: Despise the Jews as they might, the Nazis could not rebuild Germany's economy without them. As much as they might be driven out of public life, legal and medical practice, swimming pools and beaches, schools, restaurants, the theater, the civil service, and the army, the Jews would retain an important niche in commerce and industry. It would be suicidal for the Nazis to do otherwise, to disregard what Hjalmar Schacht and other moderates were saying. In spite of all they had suffered since January 1933, the Jews of Germany could not help but be heartened by what the Reich commissar for Berlin, Julius Lippert, had to say early in 1935. Addressing a meeting of the U. S. Chamber of Commerce on February 26, Lippert, hoping to squash an anti-German economic boycott, declared that anti-Jewish measures by the German government would be confined to professional and cultural spheres. Jews could continue with their economic activities as before. This policy, Lippert said, would remain in effect as long as Jews served the state loyally.[101]

The Jews were not sure how seriously to take this pledge. It had come only from a Nazi bureaucrat, not from Hitler himself (who had little to say about the Jews). And even the Führer was not to be taken at his word. Jews had grown used to sifting through the language of Nazi speeches to extract a kernel of truth. Pessimists could infer from some remarks that the Jews were finished. Optimists could be buoyed by declarations like Lippert's. Jewish newspapers pondered the merits of each point of view on their editorial pages.[102] Individual Jews reached their own conclusions. When William E. Dodd, the American ambassador, dined with Max Warburg a few days after Lippert's speech, he found the banker more sanguine than he had been the summer before.[103] Warburg still belonged with the optimists.[104] He was, after all, chief officer of a bank that continued to do a considerable amount of business in the wholly nazified German state.[105]

And many others shared Warburg's outlook. The success of a large number of Jews in holding on to their jobs or their businesses through the middle of 1935 bolstered the conviction that they would be able to survive in Germany. For now, this relative economic security offered enough reason to stay put. Indeed, it was largely because of this nebulous perception (as well as tighter restrictions on the amount of money that emigrants could take with them)[106] that the number of Jews leaving the Reich did not increase significantly during the years 1933 to 1935. The exodus did not swell despite a loosening of the once strictly enforced "likely to be a public charge" policy that had kept Jews and other would-be émigrés from obtaining visas to the United States.[107] It appeared that only if their economic circumstances changed drastically for the worse would the Jews seriously question their ties to Germany and their future in it.

What they did not fully realize was that the Nazis were gradually formulating a new Jewish policy—one that would "legally" force the Jews into a more marginal and tenuous position, undermine their status, and imperil their existence. Sooner than they were prepared to deal with it, another Jewish illusion was about to be shattered.

8

Second-Class Citizens

By the summer of 1935, a Jew living in the Third Reich could still be forgiven for hesitating to emigrate. The long-range outlook was still cloudy. After watching in dismay as an anti-Semitic government was installed and fervently embraced by their fellow Germans in 1933, after being expelled from some professions and having their businesses boycotted, Jews rightly sensed a moderating of Nazi policies. Over the past year or so, no more nationwide anti-Jewish boycotts had been attempted. Far fewer Jews had been beaten in the streets or dragged into prison. The number of anti-Semitic regulations and laws enacted in 1934 dropped sharply. The Nazis were distracted by more pressing matters than persecuting the Jewish minority. Radical elements in the Nazi Party who were keen to go after the Jews with hammer and tong had, again, lost out to cooler heads who preferred an indefinite truce until the economy recovered. Adolf Hitler had tacitly agreed to tolerate Jewish businesses when he appointed Hjalmar Schacht economics minister on August 2, 1934—the day General Paul von Hindenburg died. Therefore, it was not unreasonable for an employed Jew or a Jewish store owner to conclude that life, under drastically diminished but bearable conditions, might go on this way for some time to come.

True, the flow of Jews abroad did not diminish, encouraged as it was by both the German government and the Zionist movement, which was eager to populate Palestine. (The overall emigration of Jews averaged 24,000 a year after 1933.)[1] This exodus was boosted by the Transfer (*Haavara*) Agreement, reached in August 1933 by the Economics Ministry, the Jewish Agency, and the Zionistische Vereinigung für Deutschland (ZVfD). Under this arrangement, Jews were allowed to transfer some of their assets to Palestine in the form of currency. First, Jewish funds were placed in blocked accounts of the Reichsbank. Then they were used as credits, to purchase German goods for export to Palestine. Eventually the émigrés recovered their assets, in local currency, from the proceeds of these transactions. The transfer of Jewish assets was managed by a Treuhandelgesellschaft, or trust company, made up of a consortium of banks, including M. M. Warburg and Co. (Approximately one-third of the German Jews emigrating to Palestine got around the British-imposed quota by bringing with them, thanks to the Haavara agreement, assets worth 1,000 thousand pounds—$4,000—or more. Classified as "capitalists," this group of Jews was not seen as undesirable by British authorities.) The transfer scheme was popular with the German government because it promoted emigration and German trade at the same time—circumventing the foreign boycott of German goods. Among Jews, the Transfer Agreement was more controversial; many saw it as undermining the international boycott and forging an unholy alliance with the Nazi regime. (Max Warburg, however, argued that this arrangement could help as many as a third of Germany's Jews escape the Reich.)[2]

Gradually, the Zionist urging that Jews fulfill their destiny by settling Erez Israel was being heeded. In 1934 alone, a third of the roughly 23,000 Jewish émigrés from Germany elected to go to Palestine, taking advantage of the Haavara pact.[3] This trend was slowed in May 1935 by the British government, which was worried about the consequences of a flood of European Jews arriving on Palestinian shores; it placed a cap of 75,000 on the number of Jews who could be admitted into Palestine over the next five years.[4] The reluctance of many middle-class and well-to-do Jews to give up their material possessions and way of life further limited emigration—more than the Nazis wanted.

Psychological and emotional ties to each other were also keeping many Jews from leaving. Within the Jewish community, a philosophical shift was taking place. A people once proudly "more German than the Germans" was now compelled to confront its Jewishness and make a virtue out of this necessity. To be a Jew, symbolically to wear the "yellow badge," engendered a pride as powerful as any previous pride in Germany's greatness or their own achievements. The Zionists, who had preached the virtues of Judaism to an indifferent audience for decades, were now riding the crest of this wave of ethnic and religious reawakening.[5] Politically, the Zionists wanted more of the power that they had been previously denied by the liberal majority. They deeply resented the whiff of suspicion that had previously hovered over them because of their perceived dual allegiance to Zionism and to Germany. Now the tables were turned. The Nazi triumph enabled a Zionist triumph. Both movements saw the Jews and the "Jewish problem" similarly. Both had grown with the Zeitgeist—with the rise of racial politics. Both could now legitimately lay claim to their people's hearts and souls—if with radically different goals in mind.

The ZVfD brought its case for leadership out in the open in May 1935, when it publicly demanded "the right to influence decisively the entire Jewish life in Germany"[6]—a declaration published in Robert Weltsch's *Jüdische Rundschau.*[7] The Zionists were seeking to capitalize on a change in Nazi attitudes toward the Jewish community. Having first attacked the less "Germanic" Ostjuden (taking away their professional posts in 1933 while sparing those of native-born and more "patriotic" Jews), the Hitler regime was now toughening its stance toward conservative and moderate groups. A ban on placing wreaths on Jewish veterans' graves had recently been imposed, and the law barring Jews from the German army was about to go into effect. And, at about the same time, the SS announced it intended to suppress "assimilationist tendencies" within all branches of the Jewish Kulturbund. The government was also becoming more interested in what the Zionists had to say. (Around this time, a Foreign Ministry official told the Zionist Martin Rosenbluth that the Nazis found the Zionist movement "ideologically very closely related.")[8] Adolf Eichmann, the bespectacled Nazi functionary and onetime traveling salesman who later claimed he had been "converted" to Zionism after reading Herzl's *The Jewish State*,[9] had joined Section II-112 of the Sicherheitsdienst (Security Service), which was responsible for Jewish affairs, in 1934.[10] He began to promote Zionist activities and policies at the expense of the assimilationist groups, which he despised. Foremost among the goals Eichmann shared with the Zionists was emigration.

While various branches of the German government were quietly tilting toward the Zionists, other Jews were less inclined in that direction. The *Centralverein Zeitung*, in an editorial entitled "For Work—Against Resolutions," took the ZVfD to task for saying that its views now predominated in the Jewish community. At heart, the assimilationist newspaper said, there was an aura of expediency about all these "new Jews."[11] Within the Reichsvertretung der deutschen Juden, the Zionist demand for greater power caused a major crisis, testing, once again, its fragile unity.[12] Leo Baeck and his colleagues on the *Beirat* (governing body of the Reichsvertretung) already had their hands full rebuffing the bid of the Reichsbund jüdischer Frontsoldaten (RjF) for special, protected status under the Nazis and opposing an even more Germanic group, the Erneuerungsbewegung der jüdischen Deutschen (Revival Movement of the Jewish Germans). Now they had to contend with a reinvigorated Zionist challenge, not only to their broad, middle-of-the-road strategy, but also to specific policy directions. For example, the Zionists, via Weltsch's editorials, were advocating that Germany's Jews be treated as a separate legal entity, whereas the Reichsvertretung leadership would have no truck with such an officially segregating proposal.[13] And, in the *Gemeinden* (Jewish communities), especially in liberal Berlin, Zionist spokesmen were demanding a greater say in the running of community affairs.[14] (This new assertiveness grew out of a greater numerical strength: Membership in the ZVfD had risen from a mere 7,500 in 1931–32 to 43,000 in 1933–34 to 57,000 in 1935.)[15]

As the Nazis attacked or repudiated other Jewish groups, the Zionists vigorously advanced their own agenda, as evidenced in the headlines of the *Jüdische Rundschau*: "No Resignation!" "Only Through Our Own Work."[16] But their elation would be short-lived. Another major onslaught was being planned against German Jewry, and this time the Zionists could not expect any gain from it.

Bella Fromm, on a radio speaking tour in the United States, 1943. Because of her web of high-level connections in German government and diplomatic circles, Fromm felt that mounting anti-Semitic hostility would not affect her. By 1938 her protectors could no longer help her, and Fromm reluctantly boarded a westbound train out of Berlin, headed for exile in America. (*Bella Fromm Collection, Boston University*)

Hans-Joachim Schoeps, age 25, in 1934. Because he fervently embraced many of the same values and policies espoused by right-wing German nationalists during the 1930s, Schoeps and his small Deutscher Vortrupp (German Vanguard) of conservative Jewish youths were accused of being pro-Nazi. In order to be allowed to stay in the Third Reich, he proposed an accommodating *modus vivendi* that the Hitler regime flatly rejected. *(From Julius H. Schoeps, ed.,* Im Streit um Kafka und das Judentum, Briefwechsel: Max Brod–Hans-Joachim Schoeps *[Königstein/Taunus: Jüdischer Verlag bei Athenaeum, 1985]. Courtesy of the Leo Baeck Institute, New York)*

Richard Willstätter, circa 1930. Although the Nobel Prize–winning chemist was so outraged by anti-Semitism that he resigned his prestigious Munich professorship in 1924, he steadfastly refused to leave Germany until it was nearly too late. Willstätter maintained that Jews should not abandon their country just because it behaved badly toward them. *(Courtesy of the Leo Baeck Institute, New York)*

Leo Baeck, 1933. A leader of considerable moral authority, Baeck saw his duty as ministering to the needs of those older Jews who, like himself, were too deeply rooted in German culture to contemplate a life in exile. Through his own stoic perseverance, he reinforced their unwillingness to leave. *(Courtesy of the Leo Baeck Institute, New York)*

Robert Weltsch, Berlin, 1930s. Because the Nazi rise to power strengthened the Zionist position in Germany vis-à-vis assimilated liberal Jews, Weltsch devoted most of his journalistic efforts to lauding this ironic "Jewish renewal" under Hitler. Consequently, he underestimated the grave threat that the regime posed to all Jews, regardless of their ideology. (*Courtesy of the Leo Baeck Institute, New York*)

Max Warburg, 1930s. Because the Nazi government was initially dependent on his family-owned bank to help Germany's economic recovery, Warburg felt he could best aid his fellow Jews by working out agreements that would allow émigrés to take some of their wealth abroad with them. To his detractors, in Germany and the United States, Warburg was trying to strike a deal with the devil. *(Courtesy of the Warburg Archives, Hamburg)*

Jewish student members of the Zionist group Bar Kochba (Son of the Star), Berlin, 1902. Inspired by Martin Buber, this branch of the Zionist movement appealed to many intellectuals and writers, including the Czech-born Robert Weltsch, because of its emphasis on building a Jewish homeland based on the ideals of Judaism. *(Courtesy of the German Information Center, New York)*

German Jewish soldiers celebrating Yom Kippur on the western front, 1915. Germany's Jews flocked to military service when World War I broke out, to demonstrate their loyalty to the kaiser. Eleven thousand of them died, yet their sacrifice was discredited by right-wing nationalists who claimed the Jews had shirked military service. *(Courtesy of the Leo Baeck Institute, New York)*

An extensive Dortmund family observing Passover during the pre-Nazi era. As German Jews prospered under the Weimar Republic, their ties to Judaism grew more tenuous. But to the Nazis, none of this mattered: they defined the Jews in racial terms, not by their religious observance. *(Courtesy of the Leo Baeck Institute, New York)*

German Jewish youth having lunch at a camp sponsored by the Jewish veterans'
organization Reichsbund jüdischer Frontsoldaten (RjF) (Reich Association of
Jewish War Veterans), circa 1930. The RjF sought to instill in the post–World
War I generation the same feelings of patriotism and camaraderie that Jewish
soldiers had experienced at the front. Hence, the group strongly supported
Germany's nationalist revival in the 1930s. *(Courtesy of the Leo Baeck Institute,
New York)*

Faculty and students at the Institute for the Scientific Study of Judaism, Berlin, circa 1933. (Leo Baeck, who taught there for nearly thirty years, is seated on the far right.) Offering a university-level education to rabbis, as well as to non-Jews and Jewish women, the institute made a significant contribution to the flowering of assimilated, bourgeois German Jewry. Tolerated by the Nazis as part of a segregated Jewish educational system, the institute remained open until June 30, 1942. *(Courtesy of the Leo Baeck Institute, New York)*

Young Nazis guard the entrance to a Jewish-owned department store in Berlin during the April 1933 boycott. Designed to teach the Jewish community a lesson, this one-day protest was met with only a lukewarm public response and helped build solidarity among Germany's beleaguered Jews. (*Courtesy of the German Information Center, New York*)

A benefit concert for the Jewish Winter Relief, late 1937. While many Jews lost their jobs as a result of anti-Semitic laws and pressure, the community continued to take care of its needy members through such fund-raising efforts. One of the most prominent welfare organizations was Max Warburg's Hilfsverein der deutschen Juden. *(Courtesy of the Leo Baeck Institute, New York)*

Berliners gather outside a Jewish-owned clothing store looted by a Nazi mob on Kristallnacht, November 1938. This well-orchestrated pogrom convinced many remaining Jews that it was time to emigrate. Unfortunately, by then many doors had already closed overseas. *(Courtesy of AP/Wide World Photos)*

The synagogue in the Bavarian city of Bamberg ablaze during Kristallnacht. The destruction of so many houses of worship shocked the world and reminded German Jews of medieval atrocities their ancestors had endured. (*Courtesy of the Leo Baeck Institute, New York*)

The interior of a fire-gutted Berlin synagogue a few days after Kristallnacht. This first incidence of full-scale violence aimed at the Jews grew out of the Nazis' frustration with the slow rate of Jewish emigration. *(Courtesy of the German Information Center, New York)*

Since the murder of Ernst Röhm and the elimination of the more violence-prone SA, elements of the Nazi Party who were inclined to deal with the Jews on a legal basis had gained influence. These forces, headed by Heinrich Himmler and Reinhard Heydrich in the SS, interior minister Wilhelm Frick, and economics minister Hjalmar Schacht, wanted to devise a policy that would control and restrict the still numerous Jews on German soil for the foreseeable future. Their desire to create a legal framework took on greater urgency during the spring and summer of 1935 when Jews were subjected to more acts of violence. In Munich, several Storm Troopers broke into and wrecked Jewish shops.[17] A meeting of the Kulturbund in the Bavarian capital was broken up by an SS gang, which forced the Jews in attendance to walk out of the building to taunts of "Throw the Jews Out of Germany" and "Perish the Jews."[18] In Berlin, there were anti-Jewish riots and property attacks on July 15.[19] A few weeks later, a group of Nazis marched down the Kurfürstendamm, frightening Jewish customers out of the cafés.[20] These acts were followed by rumors emanating from the German provinces of a plan to expel Jews, through a "wave of terror" or starvation.[21] Further anti-Semitic rioting broke out in Wiesbaden. These scattered, "spontaneous" acts were fueled by speeches delivered by the Jew-baiter Julius Streicher (before fifty thousand cheering Storm Troopers in Berlin's mammoth Sportpalast) and by Joseph Goebbels, the propaganda minister, warning that the Nazis would soon show the whole world what they intended to do with the Jews.[22]

At first, Hitler himself did not give a clear indication of the course he would take. At an August 20, 1935, meeting of the party's top leaders, he listened to Schacht argue for an end to anti-Jewish violence to protect German trade and avoid putting "the economic basis of rearmament at risk."[23] He also listened to one of Goebbels's deputies insist that Jewish businesses be immediately confiscated.[24] Schacht's reasoning prevailed. The Führer preferred an approach to the Jewish problem that would not alarm or offend foreign nations, especially since Germany had been chosen to host the Olympic Games the following summer. Therefore, Hitler authorized the drafting of a set of laws designed to appease his rabidly anti-Semitic cohorts and to placate opinion abroad at the same time. But he also made it clear that if this legalistic approach did not satisfactorily bring the Jews under control, the party would devise its own "final solution" to the Jewish problem.[25]

Hastily formulated over a twenty-four-hour period during the annual Nazi Party convention in Nuremberg in September, the new legislation consisted of two major parts. Under the first, the Reich Citizenship Law, Jews were demoted to the status of "subjects of the state," denied the full political rights of citizens. This law meant, in effect, that Jews could no longer look to German law or the courts for protection. The second of the so-called Nuremberg laws addressed the long-unresolved question of how to formalize relationships between the Aryan and Jewish races. To guard the "purity of German blood," this "Law for the Protection of German Blood and Honor" prohibited any sexual relations or marriage between Jews and non-Jews, banned the flying of the German national flag—the Nazi swastika—by Jews (as a legally distinct people, they could hoist only the blue-and-white Zionist flag outside their homes and synagogues), and made it illegal for Jewish households to employ German women under the age of forty-five as domestic servants.

Made public on September 15, 1935, in Hitler's first speech on the "Jewish question" since he became chancellor, the Nuremberg laws were presented as a way of preventing further beatings and demonstrations against the Jews.[26] They were also rationalized as a response to the recently adopted resolution of the World Zionist Congress, which had recently convened in Lucerne with thirty-four German Jews, including Robert Weltsch and Leo Baeck, in attendance. (The congress expressed international Jewish solidarity with the oppressed German Jewish community and condemned its oppressors, affirming that the racial ties binding Jews were stronger than national differences. In debating this resolution, Weltsch took the American Jewish leader Stephen Wise to task for dwelling excessively on the negative aspects of the German situation, instead of stressing the work that Jews were accomplishing in Palestine.[27] But, in private conversations during the congress, Baeck echoed this pessimistic note: The situation in Germany was hopeless, and Palestine offered the only real solution.[28]) If the Jews were blatantly trumpeting their worldwide bonds, then how could the Nazis be blamed for codifying German Jews as a separate race, not deserving of German citizenship?

The Nuremberg laws did not take the Jewish community by surprise. For months, there had been telltale signs of a move in this direction. In July the Gestapo had arrested a number of Jewish men and Aryan women, charging them with "racial disgrace," even though no law then prohibited such sexual relationships. In early May interior minister Frick, long considered a "moderate" on Jewish policy, had prophesied that, in the future, German citizenship would be determined not by birth, but by the decree of the Führer—a true citizen must embody the will and way of thinking of the state.[29] And, just a few days before the Nuremberg laws were adopted, the minister of education, Bernhard Rust, had announced in a speech that, starting the following Easter, all German public elementary schools were to be racially "cleansed" (of Jews).[30] (Weltsch's *Jüdische Rundschau* lamented this step as a major blow to Jewish participation in German life, yet also saw it as a boost to Jewish schools—one of the "most important building blocks" of Jewish life.)[31]

Public reaction in the German Jewish community tended to divide along ideological lines. Even in their hour of relegation to second-class citizenship, German Jews were still unable to deal collectively with their common plight, interpreting Nazi policies in accordance with their differing views of what response was correct. The Reichsvertretung, reflecting the conciliatory nature of its leader, Leo Baeck, almost immediately issued a blueprint for "planned Jewish life" in light of the new laws.[32] It wanted to convey to the government the Jews' willingness to abide by a set of rules that, while exclusionary, at least formed a framework within which Jews might remain in Germany without fear of further intimidation, oppression, or violence. Boycott and defamation would cease, and a more independent, if limited, Jewish community would develop, the Reichsvertretung believed.[33] The organization would work toward this goal by supporting schools that taught the religious values and traditions of Judaism; by promoting emigration, particularly for the young; by backing the rapid settlement of Palestine; by helping the needy in Germany; and by helping to secure the economic well-being of the remaining Jews.[34] The Reichsvertretung's leaders wrote to Hitler, asking that their organization be given official recognition to speak for the entire community, but they received no reply.

The liberal newspaper of the Berlin Jewish community, the *Gemeindeblatt der jüdischen Gemeinde zu Berlin*, took up the same general theme. Its editorial of September 22, 1935—"Lift Up Your Hearts"—characterized the Nuremberg laws as marking the end of 125 years of Jewish development on German soil. The task for Jews now was not to mourn the passing of this era, but to reorder their lives in accordance with these laws. The essay cited Hitler's promise, in a speech to the Reichstag, that the Nuremberg laws would make possible a "tolerable relationship" between Jews and non-Jews.[35] The strict legal segregation of the Jewish community would allow Jews to develop their own way of life more freely than in any other country, the editorial argued. Furthermore, Jews could now hope that their economic livelihood would be protected.[36]

Patriotic Jewish groups could not muster as much enthusiasm. Coming on the heels of their exclusion from the military draft, the Nuremberg laws felt like the final nail in their coffin. They were a setback that the veterans could overcome only through their deep sense of duty. "We must not let the feeling of being abandoned overcome us," the RjF newspaper, *Der Schild*, pleaded with its readers.[37] At the other end of the spectrum, Robert Weltsch's *Jüdische Rundschau* directed Zionist unhappiness not at the new laws, but at those Jewish groups that were mouthing "empty words" and advocating only "soothing means" of dealing with what was, actually, a radically altered situation.[38] These laws necessitated a "new beginning" in the Jewish community. Emigration to Palestine should now be a top priority because it represented the future for German Jewish life. The *Jüdische Rundschau* also urged Jews to obey the new laws and to seek guarantees for their economic and cultural life under them.

Within a few days, the various Jewish organizations realized that it was pointless and counterproductive to point fingers at each other. If nothing else, the Nuremberg laws were a great leveler of differences. Jews who had sought a special status because of their wartime service or long-standing ties to Germany now stood on equal terms with those who had emigrated from Russia six years before. The Nazis' legal definition of the Jews as a distinct race unified them more than all the work of Leo Baeck, Max Warburg, and their unity-minded Jewish colleagues had achieved in two years of tireless labor. On September 25, 1935, over two dozen German Jewish organizations, including the Reichsvertretung, the Centralverein deutscher Staatsbürger jüdischer Glaubens, the ZVfD, and the RjF, signed a statement saying they were prepared to work together for a new relationship with the German people. They affirmed the right of the Reichsvertretung to speak for all German Jews and their hope of maintaining their economic sphere of life under these new conditions.[39] (An "impoverished community" could neither adequately support its needy members nor expedite emigration, the groups reasoned.)[40]

Without a doubt, the Nuremberg laws represented a watershed for the Jewish community in Nazi Germany, but the tantalizing question was: What kind of watershed? Was the outlook now better or worse for the Jews? If they were now legally denied the rights of citizens, did it mean that more draconian steps lay ahead, or were these laws the basis for a prolonged, "protected" coexistence, similar to what Jews had known, as *Schutzjuden,* prior to their emancipation?[41]

Listening to a broadcast of Hitler's Nuremberg speech at the Uruguayan minister's home, Bella Fromm was shaken by this "hymn of hate." She had been tipped off that such laws would be enacted even before Hitler came to power, but this foreknowledge did not make it any easier for her to accept them.[42] Fromm had recently spent two months in the United States, seeing her daughter Gonny, and quietly spreading the word about what was happening inside Germany. After this extended respite abroad, she listened to the Führer's words with a deeper pessimism. She harbored no illusions about Germany's "national renewal."

For her personally, however, life did not change much in the wake of the Nuremberg laws. She still received and accepted invitations from Berlin's diplomatic corps. She attended one reception hosted by the new Spanish ambassador at which she was presented to German "special ambassador" Joachim von Ribbentrop, decked out in his SS uniform. When Ribbentrop gave her one of his intense kisses on the hand, she blurted out: "Oh, Herr von Ribbentrop . . . the hand is a non-Aryan one."[43] The embarrassed future foreign minister awkwardly snapped to attention with a firm "Heil Hitler!" and turned away. Fortunately, Fromm did not suffer any fallout from this chance encounter. She was as established a fixture at these social occasions as was Ribbentrop and much more highly esteemed. The Nazi diplomat may have realized how impolitic it would be for him to tell his host not to include "Frau Bella" on his next invitation list. The halo of immunity surrounding her was not diminished by the Nuremberg laws.

Fromm had another excellent reason for feeling she was still safe in Hitler's Germany. Her lover, Herbert Mumm von Schwarzenstein, occupied a sensitive post in the Foreign Ministry that made him privy to developments in the government and party long before they were officially announced. He was able to keep Fromm advised of what lay ahead. For instance, in late October 1935, just eleven days after a tense, overflow crowd had jammed into Berlin's Fasasenstrasse synagogue to hear of the Jewish community's plans to send Jewish children abroad without their parents, in light of the Nuremberg laws,[44] Fromm took a stroll with "Rolf" through the Tiergarten. In the course of their conversation, he revealed Hitler's decision to occupy the Rhineland by March.[45] In this, as in many other predictions, he was to be proved correct. Thus, Fromm could always count on having enough advance notice about changes in Nazi policy to take the necessary steps to protect herself.

Other prominent Jews, deprived of such inside information, were more worried about what passage of the Nuremberg laws implied. Hopes raised at the Reichsvertretung offices that the Nazis might open a dialogue with Jewish leaders were now rudely dashed. The new laws might curtail economic harassment, but the Jews were still persona non grata, still pariahs. The Nuremberg legislation appeared to provide Nazis officials with a basis for further discriminatory, "legal" actions. Indeed, the somewhat hyperbolic Jewish Telegraphic Agency ran a report on September 23, 1935, saying that local authorities in the Nazi Party would now feel free to impose anti-Semitic measures of their own.[46] Many Jews reached the conclusion that the time had come to get out of Germany. (The number of Jews who received visas for the United States jumped from 347 in September to 442 in October to 627 in January 1936.[47] This increase occurred after President Franklin D. Roosevelt's decree that German Jewish applicants were to be extended "the most considerate attention and the most generous and favorable treatment possible under the laws."[48]) And a crackdown of sorts did ensue. Its target was the most prominent German Jew—a leader thought to be untouchable.

It was Yom Kippur, a time of atonement. A speech by Joseph Goebbels denouncing anti-Semitic violence[49] had given Jews cause to believe they would be able to spend a quiet, peaceful holiday. But beneath this surface calm, Jews were deeply disturbed by this latest assault on their rights. The Nuremberg laws took away, in one fell swoop, almost all semblance of equality that Jews had struggled for over the past one hundred years. They were a cruel defeat.

Until now, Leo Baeck had done his best to avoid a confrontation with the Nazi regime. His sense of duty toward his community had stayed him from taking any steps that might result in his arrest or removal from office.[50] At the nineteenth World Zionist Congress, held in Lucerne, Baeck and other attending rabbis had decided that the deteriorating situation in Germany, particularly Goebbels's hate-filled remarks over the summer, required a more outspoken response on their part. Jews needed to be given courage for the tougher times ahead of them. With this thought in mind, the Jewish religious leaders drafted a Kol Nidre ("All Vows") prayer to be read in synagogues on the eve of Yom Kippur.[51] It was a declaration that minced no words, that expressed the long-simmering indignation German Jewry felt toward the country's masters:

> At this hour every man in Israel stands erect before his Lord, the God of justice and mercy, to open his heart in prayer. Before God we will question our ways and search our deeds—the acts we have committed and those we have left undone. We will publicly confess what sins we have committed and beg the Lord to pardon and forgive us. We stand before our God. Acknowledging our trespasses, individual and communal, let us despise the slanders and calumnies directed against us and our faith. Let us declare them lies, too mean and senseless for our reckoning.[52]

Adoption of the Nuremberg laws gave the prayer a sharper edge. The rabbis agreed to go ahead and read it from the pulpit. The prayer would affirm their faith and refusal to submit meekly to Nazi tyranny. Before the start of Yom Kippur, officials at the Interior Ministry obtained a copy of the prayer, and the Gestapo moved swiftly to suppress it. Rabbis were told they faced arrest if they persisted with their plan. But they were not dissuaded. Public reading of the Kol Nidre prayer took place in synagogues all over Germany. However, in the end, the only rabbi who was picked up and taken to prison was Leo Baeck. Presumably, he was chosen to make a point for the entire community. Even so, the Gestapo were uneasy at taking on a figure of Baeck's international stature. The arresting official asked him, with apparent regret, "Why did you not show us that?"[53] Taken into custody on the morning of October 10, 1935, Baeck was held for a while at Gestapo headquarters, on the Prinz Albrecht Strasse, then transferred to a cell in Columbia

House, at the Tempelhof airport, where he was treated decently and offered sweetened rice after declining the prison's nonkosher food. Finally, after being held about twenty-four hours without being charged with any offense, Baeck was released. The Nazis had intimidated him as much as they dared to do. Even this brief arrest had brought down the wrath of American Protestant leaders on the government's head, in the form of a written protest, and earned the regime unfavorable press coverage in the London *Times* and other foreign newspapers.[54] This condemnation, coupled with the efforts of Julius Seligsohn, a Berlin Jewish lawyer who was active in the Reichsvertretung, gained Baeck's release. The Nazis' unwillingness to punish Baeck more severely showed how sensitive they remained to foreign opinion. Nearly three years after taking power, Adolf Hitler could still not silence with impunity the nation's most eminent Jew for daring to accuse the government of spreading lies about his people.

Stymied, the regime tried another tack. Baeck's second-in-command at the Reichsvertretung, Otto Hirsch, was arrested upon his return from abroad and held, in isolation, for a week. There were some reports that he was being kept in detention to pressure the Reichsvertretung into officially endorsing the Nuremberg laws.[55] In this matter, too, Baeck seems to have gotten the better of the Nazis. He informed the Gestapo that the Reichsvertretung could not continue to function without Hirsch. Without charging Hirsch with any crime, the Gestapo then relented and let him go.

Despite the positive outcome of this first direct clash between Germany's most respected Jew and the Nazi regime, it was clear that the Nuremberg laws were setting in motion many fundamental changes in the relationship between the Jewish community and the rest of German society—many of which did not bode well. The very fact that Jews were now legally defined as a separate and inferior entity dealt a tremendous blow to Jewish self-esteem and inner security. The Jews believed deeply in the law, in a society ruled by laws that afforded them equal justice. Now the law was being turned against them. From now on, they would have no recourse for seeking redress for any wrongs that might be inflicted on them.

The Nuremberg laws pushed the Jews into a segregated cultural ghetto. A week before they were ordered out of German schools, Hans Hinkel, the newly appointed Interior Ministry commissar for Jewish matters, announced that all "non-Aryans" were also to be expelled from the Kulturkammer, the umbrella organization for all sanctioned "Germanic" artists. Jewish newspapers could no longer be sold openly on street corners, where they might end up in the hands of Aryan readers.[56] Jews would have to organize their own winter relief program (Winterhilfe).[57] Their names were to be stricken from German war memorials.[58] They could no longer sit in Berlin concert halls and listen to Mozart and Beethoven. Under pressure from Hinkel, the Reichvertretung der deutschen Juden (German Jews) was obliged to change its name to the Reichvertretung der Juden in Deutschland (Jews in Germany), to reflect the Jews' more tenuous foothold in Germany.[59]

For all the brave talk about a more "regulated" existence under the new racial laws, large numbers of German Jews were seriously thinking about emigrating. More than ever Palestine was their destination of choice. This was only logical, in light of the growing belief that the Jews constituted a people unto themselves—a people uniquely disadvantaged by being scattered all over the globe, on inhospitable soil, a people now rebuilding its historical homeland. Three days after his release from a Gestapo prison, Leo Baeck spoke before a gathering of Berlin Jews to urge them to leave the country "since there is no alternative left."[60] This was the first public assembly devoted to emigration—an unmistakable sign of a shift in Jewish thinking. One can only speculate how much Baeck's exhortation to flee the Reich had been influenced by his incarceration: The Gestapo may have hinted at more persecution if the Jews did not leave Germany and pointed out to the sixty-two-year-old rabbi that it was his responsibility to help save his people from disaster by espousing this course of action.

This change in attitude played well into the Zionists' hands. In their view, the Nuremberg laws marked the final defeat for liberal Jewish thinking and another boost for their own dream of a national homeland. Instead of regretting a lost assimilationist past, the Zionists enthusiastically hailed "a new Jewish existence in the future."[61] Along with reports on Jewish athletic events, the pages of the *Jüdische Rundschau* were devoted to propagandizing about the desert nirvana of Palestine, with a new pictorial supplement ("Youth in Jewish Land") displaying idealized scenes of a "new home for our children."[62] Feeling vindicated in its policies, the ZVfD revived its claim to a greater leadership role, demanding that half the representatives to the Reichsvertretung be

Zionist. This time, they were able to make their argument stick: Within two weeks, Leo Baeck and the rest of the advisory council had agreed to these terms, as did the once staunchly assimilationist *Vorstand* (governing board) of the Berlin community.[63] A tiny minority before Hitler's rise to power, the Zionists had expanded their ideological base to encompass over a hundred thousand German Jews.

In his editorials Weltsch continued to drive home the point that Zionism alone properly explained the perennial "Jewish problem" and offered the only lasting solution to it. He went on to attack those Jews who had pretended that the "Jewish question" did not exist and who, even after the Nuremberg laws, insisted on seeing matters "in a false perspective"[64]—in other words, as Jewish Germans, not as Jews. Weltsch's argument was beginning to get across. The liberal counterpart to the *Jüdische Rundschau*, the *Centralverein Zeitung*, introduced a regular feature on developments in Palestine. The organ of the RjF, the *Schild*, began to focus on preparing Jews for emigration, now that many veterans were planning to leave Germany.[65] If right-wing Jews needed any more proof of the futility of their patriotic course, it came when the Nazis disbanded the Verband nationaldeutscher Juden on November 22, 1935, and arrested its leader, Max Naumann, the next day. The editor of the *Schild*, Hans Wollenberg, was also prohibited from making speeches in favor of Jews staying in the Reich. And, in an election fraught with symbolism, Leo Baeck was elected head of Keren Hayesod, the Zionist Foundation Fund for Palestine.

It was not just the Nuremberg laws that were changing so many Jewish minds. It was also an alarming new threat. After numerous assurances from governmental officials that the new anti-Semitic legislation would not impinge upon Jewish economic activities, interior minister Frick gave a speech in the now-reabsorbed Saarland, in which he obliquely referred, for the first time, to "restrictions" in the private economic sphere.[66] Frick later balanced those ominous remarks during an address before the party faithful in Berlin. Yes, Jews were going to be completely "retired" from the civil service (the previous exemptions would be revoked), but once a "clear separation" of the two races by "legal means" had been achieved, the Nazis would be satisfied. "National Socialism," he emphasized, "has no intention, as is often said, of tormenting Jews to the point of bloodshed."[67]

But pressure on Jewish businesses was mounting,[68] apparently the result of an intense struggle within the Nazi Party about the wisdom of driving Jews out of the German economy.[69] Schacht's power was waning and along with it, the material well-being of the Jewish community. Jews were now barred from working on the stock exchange, in public hospitals, and in the legal profession, as well as in other occupations.[70] Sensing that the economic foundation for Jewish life in Germany was crumbling, Robert Weltsch appealed to the League of Nations' emigration committee to "open the gates" to more Jews because a "large part of the Jewish community has no chance of preserving its economic existence in Germany."[71] Weltsch saw the impact of the Nuremberg laws on Jewish economic life as the final straw needed to break the community's back and to overcome whatever resistance there still was to quitting the Reich.

The Zionist editor and his newspaper were not spared from this concerted governmental effort to break Jewish intransigence. When Weltsch described the Jewish home as the last refuge for his people in Germany, the *Jüdische Rundschau* was immediately, if only briefly, shut down.[72] (In this editorial he had stated: "Does not a time of blossoming follow each epoch of decline? Jewry understands the lessons of nature. . . . Our way leads, in spite of all obstacles, upward. Providence and history are our leaders.")[73]

While some Jews were close to despair, others—like Weltsch and Max Warburg—refused to give up. The Nuremberg laws simply were a goad to fight on more tenaciously. Warburg seemed to thrive on greater adversity. Shrugging off feelings of hopelessness, he immersed himself in helping to find safe havens for young Jews abroad, investigating the prospects in Cyprus, Egypt, and Syria. (Yet, at the same time, he quietly urged older Jews to stay, convinced they would "survive the storm.")[74] Warburg was strengthened in his resolve to continue his work for the Hilfsverein der deutschen Juden by a sympathetic (and protective) Schacht, who told the Hamburg banker that the Nuremberg laws would apply only to a small minority of Jews—farmers, shopkeepers, and small businessmen—but would leave those in the banks, large firms, and major commercial holdings alone.[75] (Schacht also conceded he had not been able to "relieve" the Jewish situation in any significant way.)[76] Although Schacht's words may have colored his personal outlook, Warburg pressed ahead with his efforts to secure safe passage abroad for the many thousands of Jews who saw there was no future for them in Germany. His focus remained the financial aspects of emigration.

In November 1935 Warburg laid out a proposal for Schacht to consider and present to the appropriate governmental officials. This was the outline for a "liquidation bank"—a means for Jews to transfer all their assets abroad preparatory to their leaving Germany. The proposed bank was an expansion of the transfer agreement worked out in 1933 to promote emigration to Palestine. Warburg envisioned that a total of 250 million reichsmarks (or over $100 million) would be transferred outside Germany, mainly to Palestine but also dispersed to Jews in North and South America and elsewhere in Europe. However, he did not provide Schacht with any timetable or indicate how much longer Jews might be expected to remain inside the Reich.[77] By proposing a legal way of transferring a vast amount of Jewish wealth out of the country, Warburg was seeking to satisfy both the Nazis and well-to-do Jews. The Nazis could regard such a financial agreement as the carrot required to get Jews to leave the country. (The scheme also included lifting the foreign boycott of German goods, and it implied that funds placed at the government's disposal in the liquidation bank, known as Altreu, could be used to finance Germany's rearmament.)[78] Jews with large sums of money at stake could see the liquidation bank as their best hope of preserving their standard of living abroad.

But the German government did not exactly jump at Warburg's idea. The diminution of Jewish rights and status under the Nuremberg laws had made officials less willing to negotiate with Jews. Talks between Warburg and Schacht, who was now busy readying the German economy for a massive military buildup and eventual war, dragged on for months without much real progress.[79] On the government's side, most officials felt that the Jews ought to be forced out without the advantage of their wealth;[80] the regime should simply confiscate this money and put it to better use expanding Germany's war machine.

Among his fellow Jews, Warburg's plan also found its critics. In the United States, Stephen Wise, a fierce opponent of most German Jewish reactions to Nazi policies (and of Warburg's in particular), denounced the liquidation bank as a "dastardly plan"[81] designed "for the rich only."[82] Other foreign Jews shared his misgivings and doubted the wisdom—and morality—of striking any kind of agreement with Adolf Hitler. In Germany, most Zionists objected to the "Warburg plan" on the grounds that it encouraged Jews to cast themselves to the winds, seeking refuge in all corners of the globe, rather than head toward Palestine. Chaim Weizmann condemned Warburg's "arrogance" for coming up with this kind of emigration scheme.[83] (Even an American observer like the diplomat George Messersmith thought that the Hamburg banker was one of those German Jews who were acting as "instruments of the government"; Warburg's search for credits for the Reich from countries such as the United States did not "increase the confidence which can be felt in anything which he says for the present concerning the German situation.")[84] Warburg himself wondered if the liquidation bank would really speed up the Jewish exodus, referring to his plan, in a letter to the exiled Jewish financial expert Hans Schäffer, as nothing more than "a drop of water on a hot stone."[85]

Nonetheless, Warburg pressed ahead, asking officials in London to increase the quota of Jews allowed to enter Palestine to set an example for other prospective host countries. Sensitive to the charge that he was concerned only about well-to-do Jews, he also urged that some 30,000 working-class Jews emigrate over a four-year period, with half going to Palestine and the other half dispersed around the world. (The economic plight of less affluent German Jews was growing worse; one in five was now on relief.)[86] Aid from abroad would finance their departure. Warburg hoped to raise $15 million to bring as many as 250,000 Jews out of Germany.[87] Despite the attacks leveled at him and his plan, Warburg displayed his usual resilience and optimism. After seeing him in London at the end of February 1936, Warburg's cousin Siegmund was surprised how much the elder Warburg was maintaining "his balance and even his sense of humor" while economic conditions for Jews were deteriorating.[88] Three months later, Siegmund reported that the Warburg bank was still "remarkably untouched by the Nazi situation . . . the business is doing very well"[89]—no doubt a partial explanation for Max's upbeat mood. Warburg also persisted in his attempts to convince American and British Jews to dig deeper into their pockets for their impoverished brethren in Germany. Some of this money, in the form of badly needed foreign exchange, would go to the German government in exchange for the transfer of Jewish assets abroad.

Still, thanks to Warburg's initiative, several thousand German Jews were able to bring as much as 50,000 marks ($20,000) with them to Palestine during the first six months of 1936. The belief that a return to their ancestral homeland was now the Jews' best option received a jolt in April when anti-Jewish rioting erupted in Palestine. Jews were pummeled in the streets of Jaffa and in their quarter of Jerusalem, with nearly a dozen being killed in one day as their Arab neighbors demanded an end to Jewish immigration. The Arab demonstrators proclaimed a general strike to vent their outrage at the anticipated wave of Jewish refugees from Nazi Germany and to force the British government to stop it from happening. This news made headlines in the German Jewish press, spreading fears of further violence and of Britain's caving in to Arab pressure. In Berlin the measured but firm voice of Leo Baeck denounced the uprising and declared that the Jews would not be deterred from building a nation on Palestinian soil.[90] "The Jews of Germany," he stated, "are firmly bound to the work of developing Palestine."[91]

But this time Baeck's words were not sufficiently reassuring. The number of German Jews bound for Palestine continued to taper off during 1936, extending a trend begun the year before, as would-be refugees chose more secure and attractive destinations such as the United States. (All told, some 30,000 Jews emigrated to Palestine between 1933 and 1936.) In fact, emigration did not increase appreciably after the Nuremberg laws and the subsequent loss of more Jewish jobs. A mere 25,000 left in 1936, up only 4,000 from the previous year;[92] of this number, approximately 6,700 went to the United States—a one-third increase over 1935 but still far below the annual visa quota of 25,957.[93]

There were several reasons for this leveling off of emigration. Preparing to host the nations of the world for the eleventh Olympiad, the Nazis had curtailed the most flagrant forms of anti-Semitic persecution, and many Jews took this period as an opportunity to catch their breaths, rather than to flee, even though there were signs that conditions for them would only worsen once the games were over. In addition, Jews who still owned businesses or other property or were otherwise well-off remained reluctant to part with much of their material wealth, despite the possibility of transferring their assets abroad that was now open to them.[94] Many Jewish capitalists now regarded Palestine as a risky proposition[95] and generally were inclined to stay put, reaping profits from the upswing in Germany's economy spurred by the Nazis' vigorous rearmament program. This renewed prosperity seemed to outweigh their loss of rights and the likelihood of more repression further down the road. Consequently, the great majority of Jewish émigrés before 1937 came from the lower socioeconomic classes and were young.[96] (Most refugees were between twenty-one and thirty-five years old, an age group that constituted only about one-fourth of the Jewish community.) Left behind was a well-attached residue of Jews who were either too old or too unwilling to give up what they still had for an uncertain life in a new and strange land.[97] (Only one in every hundred émigrés was over age 65.[98] Partially as a result of this emigration pattern, the percentage of the Jewish community aged 60 or over would rise from 16.3 in 1933 to 27.49 at the beginning of 1938.[99]) Leo Baeck, himself in his early sixties, epitomized this deep bond of his generation to the German fatherland and spoke for it.

For leading Jews who were involved in community affairs, such as Baeck, Robert Weltsch, and Max Warburg, this was a time to concentrate on expediting the departure of other Jews from Germany. Warburg, for example, joined Otto Hirsch and several other Jewish leaders in London for a conference on emigration during the second week in March—the same week that thirty thousand German soldiers marched unopposed into the Rhineland.[100] In April, his Hilfsverein presented a plan for annually resettling twelve thousand German Jews, from all social classes, outside Palestine, at a cost of $1 million. Contemptuous of what he called the "wild emigration projects of the past year,"[101] Warburg promised an orderly, well-planned exodus. This would be the new goal of his welfare agency.

Robert Weltsch thought that one important service he could render his readers was to report directly on the opportunities and pitfalls that might await them abroad. In early May 1936 he booked passage on the steamer *Westerland,* bound for the United States—a destination more German Jews were considering now that Palestine was experiencing violent upheaval.[102] On the other side of the Atlantic, Weltsch could not help but be impressed by the openness and friendliness of the Americans he met.[103] Yet he saw the United States through Zionist eyes. (Weltsch used his visit to solicit support for Zionist activities in Palestine from such American Jewish leaders as Supreme Court justice Louis Brandeis and Stephen Wise.) Its vitality, dynamic flux, and economic opportunities strongly reminded him of the Jewish homeland; thus, his journey westward turned into a reaffirmation of the promised land to the east.

In August 1936, Weltsch published a piece in the *Jüdische Rundschau* in which he declared Palestine to be "the only land that can lead the Jewish people into a new future, in so far as it will ensure the existence of the volk."[104] (This essay appeared less than two weeks after the rival *Centralverein Zeitung* reported that fewer than a third of all 100,000 Jewish émigrés since 1933 had resettled in Palestine.)[105] In unequivocal terms, the article in the *Jüdische Rundschau* told German Jews: "Our people [volk] is threatened with destruction: The moral, material, and intellectual basis of our life [in Germany] has been shattered." But Weltsch's attention—and concern—was directed less at this dire domestic situation than at the obstacles to emigration to Palestine. Palestine was where the Jews' future lay; they need not be so preoccupied with what happened to Germany. As Leo Baeck said, the Jews must look beyond today and create "a new form and new content of life . . . [the] man of the future."[106]

Less prominent Jews had more personal problems on their minds. Hans-Joachim Schoeps was one of them. As part of the government's drive to suppress and eliminate conservative Jewish groups who were opposed to emigration, the Deutscher Vortrupp was forced to break up in December 1935 after the Gestapo banned the last two issues of its newsletter.[107] The members of this small organization came together for the last time at Bad Orb, a west German spa, where Schoeps confided he was on the Gestapo's list of Jews who were not to be allowed out of the country. He vowed, like the captain of a sinking ship, to be the last member of the group to quit the Fatherland.[108] Not ready to give up his coterie of young, idealistic Jewish intellectuals, Schoeps arranged a series of clandestine meetings in various Berlin apartments during the winter of 1935–36, to discuss plans and distribute copies of the Deutscher Vortrupp's now-illegal newsletter.[109] Somehow a Gestapo informant succeeded in infiltrating these sessions, supplying his superiors with a distorted account of this would-be "Jewish Führer" that resulted in Schoeps's arrest on a charge of high treason. Along with his comrades in the Deutscher Vortrupp, he was taken to Gestapo headquarters and made to stand all day facing a blank wall.[110] Then, just as abruptly, they were released.

What galled the Nazis about Schoeps and his followers was their pig-headed insistence that German Jews be accepted into the Third Reich. In a memorandum written in response to the Nuremberg laws, Schoeps outlined a scheme that would grant Jews a protected legal status and ensure them "an equal share in both the duties and rights of all German citizens." In return for this legal protection, Schoeps stated, "German Jews, too, will put into effect the Führer principle, valued through-out the Reich," through a rigidly authoritarian self-governing principle. The head of a German Jewish community reconstituted along these lines was to be a "highly intellectual leader" (a person resembling Schoeps) who would bear the title of *"Oberrabbiner,"* or "chief rabbi" of Germany. The remaining Jewish community would be divided into three distinct groups—"non-Aryans," who did not, from a religious stand-point, regard themselves as Jews; believing Jews, the majority in the community; and Zionists. The latter were to be treated as a "Palestin-ian minority in Germany" and encouraged to emigrate. The core group of religious Jews would be led, in the Gemeinden, by rabbis, and would exclude any Jews not born in either Germany or Austria, as well as any categorized as Marxists. This "rump" community would enjoy freedom from persecution (as would the excluded Jews, or "non-Aryans"), as well as the right to run their own schools and economic activities.[111]

This was precisely the kind of live-and-let-live arrangement the increasingly hostile Nazi regime, determined to push Jews out of the Reich, now abhorred; thus, it is no wonder that the Gestapo came down on Schoeps and his clique as hard as they did. And Schoeps was fortu-nate. The charge of high treason against him was dropped. He was tailed around Berlin by a Gestapo "shadow" and questioned now and then in the infamous Prinz Albrecht-Strasse building, but he stayed out of prison.

Schoeps was free to focus on other matters. One of these was the publication of his academic writings. Prevented from pursuing a con-ventional scholarly career, Schoeps was keen to find an audience for his distinctive views on Judaism and Jewish philosophy. A principal vehicle was the publishing firm Vortrupp Verlag that he had founded in 1934 with money borrowed from his parents. Early in 1936, the firm issued Schoeps's *Gestalten an der Zeitenwende* (Turn-of-the-Century Figures), a collection of three essays on Nietzsche, Kafka, and the historian Jacob Burckhardt. Schoeps's continuing interest in Kafka was intensified by his personal identification with the Czech writer and his predicament. Like Kafka, Schoeps longed for the old gods but was forced to accept they had disappeared for good. This was the great tragedy of twentieth-century man, Schoeps believed.

Aside from a desire to publicize his views on these intellectual giants, Schoeps was also trying to acquire some credentials in the academic world, to make himself more attractive to foreign universities. As early as June 1933, he had concluded that his chances of obtaining a teaching or research post in Germany were decidedly slim and had begun to cast an eye abroad, even as he was advocating a "patriotic" Jewish accommodation with the Nazis. He had turned for help to Max Brod, his collaborator in publishing Kafka's posthumous papers. After the Nuremberg laws were enacted, Schoeps renewed his appeal for Brod's assistance in locating a teaching post in Prague.[112]

The dissolution of the Deutscher Vortrupp and the treason charge against Schoeps gave greater urgency to his wish to escape Germany, despite what he had pledged his erstwhile comrades about being the last to "abandon ship." In August 1936 he tossed his net wider, applying for a research grant at Manchester College, Oxford, to write a thesis on "The Religious Renewal of Judaism and the Modern World"[113]—work he claimed he could not carry out as a Jew in Germany. For a letter of recommendation, he appealed to the Protestant theologian Karl Barth, who obliged Schoeps—to no avail.[114] Brod was no help either, and so this unemployed, twenty-seven-year-old Jewish intellectual had to resign himself to staying in Berlin, at least for the time being. Until he found suitable employment outside Germany, Schoeps would continue to write, publish, and present his views in lectures as conditions allowed. In November 1936, for example, he was invited to give a talk on Kafka's *The Castle* at the Zion Lodge in Hannover. During the 1934–36 period, Schoeps also worked on various publications that were promoting an interfaith dialogue, asking Barth, Martin Buber, and other leading theologians for contributions.[115] He produced a book of his own on this theme: *Jüdisch-christliches Religions-Gespräch in 19te Jahrhundert* (Jewish-Christian Religious Dialogue in the 19th Century).

On top of all these writing projects, the tireless Schoeps kept up a busy schedule of speeches before local chapters of the Jewish veterans' organization, the RjF. He remained philosophically close to this deeply nationalistic group, even though he was a generation younger than its members. When he addressed RjF chapters, Schoeps spoke of their shared love of country, their Germanic roots. But, according to what he claimed many years afterward, he made use of these occasions to level attacks at the regime. In one of his speeches Schoeps might describe Nazism as "nihilistic aggression against everything that was German." If a Gestapo agent should happen to slip into the hall during his remarks, Schoeps would simply substitute the term *Bolshevism* for *Nazism*.[116]

If this claim was true, it meant that Schoeps was taking extraordinary risks for a Jew already labeled as "treasonous." By contrast, Richard Willstätter was innocuously conducting his scientific inquiries in Munich. On April 27, 1936, he wrote to inform W. E. Tisdale of the Rockefeller Foundation about his work on the effects of insulin and adrenalin on the "enzymatic hydrolysis of carbohydrates," acknowledging in a self-deprecating aside that the foundation might prefer to give money to younger scientists with more "promise."[117] This appeal was mailed the same week that word reached Germany's Jews about the Arab uprising in Palestine and its likely impact on emigration there. Yet these faraway events intruded on Willstätter's world as little as had the promulgation of the Nuremberg laws the previous fall: To a chemist wrestling with the most fundamental questions of nature, what difference did German citizenship make?

Of more concern to Willstätter, as he revealed in his letter to Tisdale, was an insidious feeling that he was growing old and obsolete in his field. As he approached his sixty-fourth birthday, he was as keenly curious about the mysteries of organic chemistry as he had been as a young man at the turn of the century. In his Bavarian "inner exile," he closely followed the latest advances of his former colleague and fellow Jew, the Czech chemist Felix Haurowitz, in investigating the properties of hemoglobin.[118] But the success of his onetime pupil only made the contrast between them more painfully evident. Twenty-four years Willstätter's junior, Haurowitz, then conducting research in Prague, was still a rising star. Surveying his friend's published findings, Willstätter had to admit that the discoveries of the younger scientific generation were surpassing his own. Continued international recognition of his achievements could not assuage this intimation of decline and fall.[119]

Age was not just a psychological state of mind. Willstätter had never been a vigorously healthy man, and each passing year seemed to weaken him perceptibly. He was weary of life, weary—like his late friend Fritz Haber—of putting up with humiliating conditions, yet too weary to escape from them. He envied the "youth" of a scientist like Kasimir Fajans (aged forty-eight), who had managed to start a new life in foreign exile, at the University of Michigan, after he quit his Munich post when the Nuremberg laws had been made public.[120]

What some like Fajans could do, many others were as unable, or unwilling, as Willstätter to undertake. In April 1936 Bella Fromm had seen the American diplomat George Messersmith off to Washington, taking with him her information about the unpublicized persecution of the Jews, but this violence and oppression still seemed remote to her personally. In July Messersmith offered to obtain a visa for her, but Fromm had politely declined. She was not interested. The same month a longtime friend of hers Moritz ("Pappi") von Carnap, the last chamberlain to Germany's last kaiser, had taken her aside and whispered: "You'd better leave Germany now, my child. It's going to be terrible here. Soon nobody will be able to protect you any more. Look for a new home while you are still young enough to adjust yourself. Take along the memory of our Germany as a kind of beautiful dream. Everything that is in Germany now will die."[121]

Within two weeks Carnap was dead, but Fromm did not budge. She had watched the "noisy pageant" of Nazi enthusiasts outside the Reichstag in March when Hitler's troops had marched unopposed into the Rhineland and heard her lover "Rolf," who had foretold this event, pronounce war "inevitable."[122] Yet the prospect of a European conflict had not weakened her resolve to stay either. In August she grimly endured the "colossal" spectacle of Hitler's "supermen" at the Olympics,[123] then enjoyed a brief visit from her daughter Gonny returning from the United States. The Nazis gave Gonny some of the special treatment her mother cynically accepted from them, knowing full well it was only to curry favor with her diplomat friends.[124] But accept she did. She still deigned to clasp the hands of men like Hjalmar Schacht and Franz von Papen, concealing her contempt for their hypocritical fawning over the Führer.[125] These social ties still gave Fromm the feeling she was safe. Her role as liaison to Berlin's diplomatic corps had not yet reached its final performance. She would continue to play it as long as she could so that, off-stage, she could still assist other Jews escape. Time was running out: There were indications that their plight was about to become much worse.

9

Tightening the Noose

The Olympic hoopla was barely over when, as predicted, a new anti-Semitic campaign was launched. Berlin, the city of international brotherhood in August 1936, turned ugly and spiteful in September, covered with posters spreading more poisonous lies about the Jews.[1] And these posters were merely the prelude to the drumroll of invective rumbling out of Nuremberg as the faithful of the Nazi Party reconvened to hear Adolf Hitler rant and rave about the "shameful Jewish system of world hatred."[2] Only a year before, a more restrained Führer had said of the Jews: "The only way to deal with the problem which remains open is that of legislative action."[3] This statement had ushered in the so-called Nuremberg laws. But much had changed in twelve months. Revitalizing the German economy to arm the military had gained urgency with the prospect of an inevitable European war. In this accelerated, highly mobilized, and relentless campaign

183

to spur economic growth, Jews were eyed with greater suspicion: Could the Nazis *really* trust them to contribute unstintingly to this national effort? As a warning, Hitler promulgated laws making it a crime punishable by death to harm the German economy and promising to punish all Jews for any damage done by any one of their number.[4]

At the same time the Führer shuffled his economic advisers. Hjalmar Schacht, the voice of moderation on the "Jewish question" and confidante of Max Warburg, lost power in September 1936. Hermann Goering replaced him as the plenipotentiary who was charged with implementing the Nazis' second four-year plan, gaining virtual dictatorial control over the German economy. This was the same Goering who had previously shown no compunction about intimidating the Jews and forcing them out of the country, so it was likely that he would soon take steps to reduce the still-considerable Jewish role in the Reich's business, commercial, and financial affairs.[5] There was a palpable anxiety among the 425,000 or so Jews still living in Germany—a feeling that, as a correspondent for the Jewish Telegraphic Agency put it, the Nuremberg laws were by no means "the last word" in officially sanctioned anti-Semitism.[6]

At the end of September 1936, the government took a swipe at Jewish economic activities by ordering all Jewish companies and public organizations to fire any Jews on their payrolls who held foreign passports.[7] This was a way of eliminating the presence of undesired aliens in the völkisch Reich as well as weakening the Jews without passing any more racially based laws. More rumors of an economic crackdown against the Jewish community circulated, concomitant with a move by Robert Ley's Deutsche Arbeitsfront (German Labor Front) to drive Jewish firms out of business.[8]

On October 25, without any provocation, the Nazis banned meetings of all Jewish organizations "until further notice." The government also prohibited any face-to-face contact between Jews and the Gestapo (thus making it nearly impossible for relatives to obtain news about arrested husbands or fathers).[9] Two days afterward, the property and other assets of the Berlin-based Suhler rifle factory were confiscated—the first expropriation of a Jewish firm to take place under the Nazis. This seizure was followed by a none-too-subtle warning from Joseph Goebbels, the propaganda minister, that Jews would face new restrictions if they became "fresh."[10] Without waiting for any such justification, German banks announced they were calling in Jewish mortgages, with the result that many homeowners lost whatever real estate they had left.[11] More blows fell in quick succession. On December 4, 1936, banks were instructed not to extend any further credit to Jewish customers.[12] On December 9 Jewish charitable organizations were stripped of their vital tax-exempt status, and the next day the government made public a demand that all large Jewish commercial firms be handed over to "Aryan" owners by the coming spring.[13] Then, in February 1937, Ley stated that a chief goal of Goering's new four-year plan was to eliminate Jews from German economic life.[14]

These repressive economic actions against the Jews were accompanied by increased anti-Semitic pressure in other spheres, constituting an orchestrated Gestapo campaign to accomplish what nearly four years of harassment and denial of rights had failed to achieve—the mass departure of Jews from the Reich. After the initial emigration of some 60,000 Jews in 1933, the steady trickle abroad had remained at about 25,000 a year. At this rate, it would take an interminable sixteen years for Nazi Germany to become *judenfrei*, and this was simply an unacceptable amount of time for party zealots. In January 1937 Section II-112 of the Sicherheitsdienst (Security Service), which was responsible for Jewish affairs, issued a report pointing out that emigration offered the only real solution to the "Jewish problem" and that steps taken to promote it had thus far been inadequate. As new barriers to emigration had arisen around the world, including Palestine, a certain "weariness" had set in among the remaining Jews, that made them disinclined to leave. Gestapo officials ventured their opinion about how to overcome this inertia: (1) Jews would have to be forced out of the economy, (2) political pressure on them would have to be increased, and (3) the "technical possibilities" (or job skills) for émigrés would have to be improved.[15]

To make Germany less attractive to the Jews, the Nazis tried to undermine their communal solidarity and belief that they were being legally protected by the Nuremberg laws. In early October 1936, Hans Frank, the chief Nazi jurist, declared that the Nazis aimed to recraft German criminal law to fit more closely with their ideology—in other words, to nazify it.[16] Also in October, the government revealed that all Jews (and half Jews) were to be prohibited (starting in 1937) from serving in the German army and, ironically enough, barred from displaying photos of Hitler and other Nazi leaders in their windows and affixing the swastika emblem to any merchandise they sold.[17] The rabidly anti-Semitic Julius Streicher, editor of *Der Stürmer*, publicly demanded that any Jews who were found guilty of "racial disgrace" in their sexual relations should receive the death penalty. The Gestapo's surveillance of Jewish organizations was stepped up, not only to keep tabs on what was said at their meetings, but to identify and punish any Jews who continued to advocate that Jews be granted a place in the Third Reich. This move followed the November 1935 ban on speeches promoting such a position.[18] Early in 1937 the Gestapo suspended Jewish organizations for two weeks, commencing in February, in retaliation for their alleged role in spreading word abroad about new anti-Semitic regulations.[19] In January 1937 the government decreed its intent to liquidate all Jewish bookstores as of the end of March.[20]

The conditions faced by Germany's Jews were decidedly worse than a year before. In Berlin, where more and more Jews were congregating, seeking a haven from the persecution that was sweeping the more exposed countryside, it was estimated that some thirty thousand persons, or one-fifth of the entire Jewish community, was on relief.[21] The loss of jobs and income was deepening the mood of desperation. Jews sensed that Nazi Jewish policy was no longer being mollified by "realists" like Schacht, but driven headlong by radicals in the Gestapo and other police and security agencies who were bent on getting their way without making any compromises or concessions. The cumulative effect of all the anti-Semitic steps taken from the fall of 1936 through early 1937 was to create the impression of a rapidly deteriorating situation. More Jews than ever were convinced that it was utterly hopeless for them in Germany: They had to leave. As the once-staunchly assimilationist *Centralverein Zeitung* conceded, emigration was now only a question of "when" and "where."[22]

But just as this realization was dawning, the gates overseas were beginning to close. The violent Arab protests (including a 175-day general strike) against Jewish emigration cost eighty-eight Jewish lives and caused the British government to cut its visa quota in half. In 1937 the number of German Jews who were issued visas to Palestine fell from a yearly average of between 6,800 and 8,400 to 3,286.[23] (Illegal immigration was a way of getting around this reduced quota.) Meanwhile, another country with a sizable Jewish population—South Africa—was tightening the requirements for entering its territory; under its new Aliens Bill, which took effect on February I, 1937, all incoming foreigners would have to possess entry visas.[24] The Jewish Telegraphic Agency reported that fully 93 percent of the German Jews who requested this visa were turned down.[25] Canada and Australia raised similarly effective barriers by stipulating that all would-be immigrants had to be farmers.

In the wake of these developments, the United States—the land of unlimited opportunity across the Atlantic—might have taken in many potential émigrés, but did not, in spite of increased interest in going there.[26] One reason why it did not was economic: Many Jews lacked the prerequisite financial resources. (American policy still required visa seekers to prove they had "adequate means of support" before they could enter the country.[27] Virtually all Jews who were granted visas during this period had relatives in the United States who could provide such support; restrictions on the amount of money that émigrés could legally take with them from Germany made this financial backing essential.[28]) These requirements kept the number of German Jews who were admitted into the United States at approximately seven thousand during 1936, filling less than a third of the openings set aside for German immigrants.[29] (The number of German Jews who applied for visas was this low despite the special priority given to them by American consular officials, acting on instructions from the State Department.)

Compounding this economic hurdle was a perception that the United States was not willing to let in more Jews. Several visa officials were accused of anti-Semitic prejudice. In June 1937, for instance, a Jew named Goldsand, then living in Paris, claimed that the American consulate in Stuttgart made a practice of expressing its animosity toward Jews by rejecting 90 percent of their visa applications. The examining physician at the consulate was alleged to have rejected nearly all Jews on the trumped-up grounds of physical unfitness. In responding to these charges, the U.S. consul general, Samuel Honaker, produced documents showing that during 1936 and the first half of 1937, only between three and nine percent of the formal Jewish applicants were actually refused visas. However, these figures did not include the much larger—and undocumented—number of Jews whose lack of "assurances of support" prevented them from even being considered for visas.[30]

The other side of the coin was that the United States was simply too far away, too culturally alien, and too unknown a land to attract tens of thousands of Jewish refugees. And even if there had been a sudden rise in the demand for U.S. visas, an isolationist Congress, backed by popular sentiment, would not have been prepared to increase the number of émigrés who could be admitted from Germany.

So, just as the pressures and inducements for leaving mounted (in October 1936 the Nazi government offered to let impoverished Jews take half their assets abroad with them if they emigrated within two months),[31] the opportunities for doing so were diminishing. Caught between a rock and a hard place, the leaders of the Jewish community struggled to convince their people that all was not lost. There was no reason to panic or to attack each other. There was still consolation and safety within the community, within the ring of common suffering and common purpose. On several occasions Rabbi Leo Baeck delivered this message of endurance through unity in his usual soothing and fortifying manner. To mark the Jewish New Year, he and other top officials of the Reichsvertretung der Juden in Deutschland penned an open letter to German Jews on September 16, 1936, reminding them of the strengthening ties that linked each individual Jew to the *Gemeinde* (Jewish community).[32]

But Baeck and these other mainstream Jewish leaders could not avoid a depressing dilemma. Just as much as they had come to accept that salvation for Germany's Jews lay in escaping the German Fatherland, so did they fully comprehend the logistical, financial, diplomatic, and psychological barriers that blocked this route. For one, not all Jews had yet made up their minds that it was necessary for them to go. Well-to-do Jews were still attached to whatever businesses or wealth they had left. Older Jews, an ever-growing percentage of the community, remained as intractable as ever, resigned to awaiting the fate the Nazis had in store for them in the familiar, *gemütlich* surroundings of their own homes. Squeezing middle-aged Jews out of jobs to make life in Germany untenable for them had had the opposite effect: Poverty deprived them of the financial means they needed to qualify for visas to many countries and sapped them of their will to emigrate. Even for Jews who were willing and able to leave, the way out was not easy. Many attractive destinations were beginning to follow Palestine's example, reviewing their visa policies and making them more stringent to head off the large-scale social turmoil an influx of German Jews might ignite. There was a limit to the world's capacity to absorb such refugees and, in the context of aftershocks from the worldwide depression, resurgent nationalism, and undiminished anti-Semitism, this capacity was shrinking.

Baeck, speaking for the Reichsvertretung, chose not to spell all this out. Heightening fears about the long odds of fleeing Nazi Germany seemed as ill advised to him as heightening fears about what the Nazis might do to those Jews who remained in their clutches. As a spiritual and moral leader, Baeck still saw his task as steeling his fellow Jews for the ordeal that lay ahead for them in the Third Reich. Typically, Baeck took this tack in a speech before the members of the Berlin lodge of B'nai B'rith on October 15, 1936. He spoke not of present travails, but of the transcendent, messianic ideal in Judaism. One of the great achievements of their faith, he reminded his listeners, was that it had freed humanity from a traditional fear of the future. For believing Jews, the future was not a matter of what "will be," but of what "ought to be." The collaborative efforts of Jews could hammer this ethical vision into a reality, even in times as bleak as these.[33]

An equally reassuring message came from Baeck's lips the following month when he spoke to a gathering of Berlin Jews who had come to the lodge hall to hear several speakers discuss "Emigration, Security, and Development [*Aufbau*]." This meeting took place two weeks after the British colonial minister William Ormsby-Gore had announced a significant cut in the number of working-class Jews allowed to enter Palestine and a little over a month after the end of the Arab general strike. In the aftermath of the strike, the British government had authorized a royal commission, chaired by Viscount Peel, to review its policy on Palestine and recommend changes in its constitution. (This commission was an outgrowth of a more limited inquiry begun earlier in 1936.) After the orchestra of Berlin's Kulturbund had played, fittingly enough, the overture to Saint-Saëns's opera *Samson et Dalila* (the story of a Jewish revolt against another oppressor, the Philistines), Baeck rose to dispel whatever anxiety his audience might have about the outcome of the royal commission's work. He had every confidence in Viscount Peel's wisdom, courage, and fairness, Baeck said. There was no reason to assume that Jews were about to lose the right to return to their ancestral homeland that had been promised to them by Lord Balfour nearly twenty years before.[34]

In Karlsruhe, shortly after New Year's Day, 1937, Baeck returned to the loftier philosophical plane he preferred. He gave a talk on "Security

and Certainty," contrasting the longing of nonreligious Jews for the former with the peace of mind the devout found in the latter. In dark
hours, a feeling of security will desert us, Baeck said, whereas "certainty
about what the hand cannot touch nor understanding grasp" gives life a
deeper meaning—a dimension of "the mysterious and the hidden . . .
that is above everything" and that offers each Jew "a grasp of the infi-
nite in his daily life."[35]

Robert Weltsch was as much of an idealist as Leo Baeck, but his particular brand of idealism revolved around making a lifelong dream—a
Jewish national homeland in Palestine—a concrete reality. Since the
Nazis had pushed the Jews into an ethnic enclave and thereby revived
their Jewishness, his vision had attracted a considerable following.
Declining living conditions and the Nazis' eagerness to accelerate the
flow of Jews abroad, particularly to Palestine, had reinvigorated his
Zionist ambitions. The dangers lurking ahead for Jews on the sidewalks
of Berlin or Munich were of less concern to him than were Arab unrest
and tightening barriers to emigration to Palestine. Tackling these problems consumed most of his long days, spent in the cramped editorial
offices of the *Jüdische Rundschau* on the Meineckestrasse.

Weltsch saw the Arab violence as a sad vindication of his long-held
belief that a Jewish homeland could be created only after some kind of
accommodation was reached with the other peoples of the region. (For
example, in a 1930 letter to his fellow Zionist, the attorney Felix Rosenblüth, Weltsch had chided German Zionists for putting forth a program
for Palestine that provoked Arab hostility.)[36] The Arabs were no more
amenable to having a horde of "alien" Jews living in their midst than
was a volk like the Germans. Indeed, for Weltsch, the two situations
yielded a striking parallel. If they were to survive as a people in Europe,
as well as in the Middle East, the Jews had to form their own separate
(that is, nonintrusive) sphere and respect the rights of others to preserve
their own nation-states along racial or ethnic lines. A "Jewish island in
an Arab sea" would be quickly engulfed unless the Jews first came to
terms with the Arabs' bona fide fears and rid themselves of what he saw
as "anti-Arab chauvinism."[37]

Now Weltsch was worried that Jews emigrating from Germany had
pushed too hard, too fast, to stake their claim to precious Palestinian
soil and, in the process, had stirred up hatred that might destroy his
dream of a Zionist homecoming.[38] From New York, at the height of the

Arab general strike, Weltsch confessed to Martin Buber his fears that Jews and Arabs might never reach an understanding. "How can one not despair?" he asked rhetorically.[39] At almost the same time that Leo Baeck was uttering his sanguine thoughts about the Peel commission, Weltsch addressed a Berlin conference on the "problems of Palestinian policy," and expressed some of his far more pessimistic feelings. The British, he said, were afraid of instability in the Middle East; they saw Arab nationalism as a potent force sweeping the region—a force they would have to reckon with. In acceding to Arab demands for better treatment and equality, Weltsch argued, the British would not necessarily be bound by past agreements, namely, the Balfour Declaration.[40] The entire premise of the Zionist movement over the past twenty years was endangered.

The only way to salvage their national home was for Jews to press for a territorial solution that gave both them and the Arabs their own independent states, so constituted that neither would pose any threat to the well-being of its neighbor. Since the mid-1920s, the themes of "reconciliation," "compromise," and "equal rights" with the Arabs had distinguished the Berit Shalom (Peace Covenant) society, to which Weltsch belonged, from the rest of the Zionist movement; he and such founding members as Arthur Ruppin were lone voices on the fringe. Weltsch had been reminded of the unpopularity of his position during his June 1936 visit to the United States. Attempts to convince American Zionists like Justice Louis Brandeis and Stephen Wise of the wisdom of treating the Arabs fairly had failed abysmally. Weltsch came away disappointed with the narrowness of their thinking and their unwillingness to see his point of view.[41]

Just as Hitler's coming to power in Germany had bolstered Weltsch's position four years before, now he was given a second boost by the Arab revolt and consequent formation of the British royal commission. The Peel commission was impelled by instability in the region to give serious thought to Berit Shalom's notion of a binational Palestine. Indeed, when Viscount Peel presented his final report to Parliament in July 1937, its chief recommendation was to partition the country into two sovereign states, one Jewish, the other Arab, with a small remaining area to be left under British mandate. (The plan also called for placing an annual cap of twelve thousand on Jewish émigrés over the next five years.)

The Peel commission report sparked a volatile debate among both Zionists and non-Zionists. A deep, acrimonious gulf separated those who viewed it as a realistic, albeit imperfect, way of achieving a Jewish homeland from those who dismissed it as a betrayal of Zionist ideals. Weltsch and the *Jüdische Rundschau* naturally threw their weight behind the commission's proposals. When the Zionist Congress convened that August in Zurich, the intra-Jewish debate came to a head. Chaim Weizmann, recently reelected head of the World Zionist Organization and a strong backer of British policy, gave a speech tentatively endorsing the Peel report, and his view carried the day. When a vote was taken, three-fourths of the 458 delegates (including Weltsch) backed "in principle" the partitioning of Palestine into two states, while withholding formal endorsement of the plan itself.[42] The congress also rejected the view that Jewish and Arab aspirations in the region were "irreconcilable" and committed the Zionist movement to seeking a peaceful resolution of the Palestinian conflict.

Back in Berlin, Weltsch resumed his editorializing on behalf of the Peel report, believing it offered Jews the best—if not the only—hope for establishing a state of their own.[43] Weltsch was not naively swept away by Viscount Peel's proposal; he realized well that it represented a compromise of Jewish territorial aspirations. He also understood that Palestine could not be the sole salvation for all the millions of Jews scattered—and oppressed—throughout the Diaspora. This small, largely barren and inhospitable country could at best absorb 10 percent of the world's Jewry. Nonetheless, the building of a homeland in Palestine was deserving of support from Jews everywhere: It was their symbolic reunion. Over the next two years, preoccupation with this goal prevented Weltsch and many of his Zionist associates from perceiving the trend toward war in Europe and the peril it would pose to millions of Jews.[44]

When he surveyed conditions facing the Jews in Germany, Weltsch was prone either to turn a blind eye or to laud the "Jewish renaissance" that had occurred under the Nazi shadow. In a major retrospective on the first four years of Hitler's rule published in the *Jüdische Rundschau*, Weltsch dwelt at length on the positive developments that the Jews had experienced: Before January 1933 most had ignored the central importance of Jewishness in their lives and had existed blithely under the illusion of assimilated security. Jews had lost sight of their origins, their values, their religion. Nazi-fueled anti-Semitism had induced a radical introspection: *What is it to be a Jew?* As Weltsch saw it, this revived interest in Judaism was now producing exciting, specific results: training and other types of preparation for emigration to Palestine and education of Jewish youths in their traditions and culture. Although he had to admit that the past four years had cost German Jewry a great deal of pain and suffering, he was more passionately eloquent about what they had gained as a people.[45]

The fourth anniversary of the April 1933 boycott provided the Zionist editor with one more opportunity to accent the positive. Being singled out and castigated because of their Jewishness had awakened Jews to their essential being—their "national feeling" (*Volksgefühl*)—to a degree that otherwise might never have occurred. Weltsch went on to argue, in an essay in the *Jüdische Rundschau*, that "Most [Jews] realized that the time had come not to complain or accuse, but for us to confront anew the eternal questions of Judaism and humanity and their protection [of us]."

Although much of the initial euphoria about Jewishness and hope for a "genuine, creative" rebirth of the community had faded since then and many of the so-called new Jews were now plainly running out of enthusiasm, Weltsch took heart from the fact that so many German Jews were now marching happily under the Zionist banner, bound, at least in spirit, for the promised land of Palestine.[46]

A series of setbacks in the spring of 1937 battered the public optimism of Weltsch, Baeck, and other Jewish leaders who were now united in assigning top priority to emigration from Germany. Impatient with the rate of departure, Nazi officials stepped up their attacks on Jewish groups and their leaders, intervening in the internal affairs of the Jewish community to a greater extent than they had done until now. The regime had apparently decided it no longer sufficed to apply pressure from without. They needed to force Jewish organizations to become their active instruments in purging the Reich of Jews as rapidly as possible.

Having already singled out conservative and patriotic groups, such as the Reichsbund jüdischer Frontsoldaten (Reich Association of Jewish War Veterans) and Hans-Joachim Schoeps's minuscule Deutscher Vortrupp (German Vanguard), the Hitler regime now took aim at a far more broad-based and influential Jewish body, the Reichsvertretung, and at the voice of liberal, assimilated Jewry, the Centralverein deutscher

Staatsbürger jüdischer Glaubens (Central Organization of German Citizens of the Jewish Faith). At first, the Nazis merely issued warnings to the Jewish organizations about failing to promote emigration aggressively. This attitude would no longer be tolerated.[47] But such a relatively restrained strategy did not work. In early March the Centralverein sponsored a meeting in Berlin on the "spirit and form of Jewish work," which was intended to emphasize German Jewish unity. The meeting attracted an overflow crowd. Among those attending were several agents of the Berlin Gestapo, including the head of its "Jewish section." Ignoring their presence, the Centralverein's Ernst Herzfeld, a lifelong proponent of German-Jewish ties, stuck to his theme: The Centralverein, once concerned about the rights of individual Jews, was now helping the entire community through spiritual, material, and legal assistance. Younger Jews might be embracing another future in foreign lands, but the older ones in Herzfeld's audience could rest assured that the Centralverein would stand firmly beside them in this hour of great need; the centuries-old German Jewish community was not about to be "dissolved."[48] (Leo Baeck had been slated to speak that evening, but his wife, Natalie, had fallen gravely ill. Stricken by a stroke, partially brought on by Nazi attacks on her husband, she succumbed early the next morning, leaving Baeck deeply bereaved, deprived of the companion who, in her own quiet, unobtrusive way, had sustained his life for the past thirty-eight years.)[49]

A few weeks after this meeting, Herzfeld and some sixty other mainstream Jewish leaders (minus Baeck) were "invited" to report to Gestapo headquarters, where they were told to surrender their passports, and then subjected to a "wild harangue, full of curses," by the head of the "Jewish section," before being allowed to go. Adding more clout to this verbal browbeating, the government imposed a ban on all public Jewish meetings for two months.[50] Under orders from Heinrich Himmler, SS and Gestapo units then initiated a nationwide crackdown against a Jewish organization that they had scarcely bothered until now—B'nai B'rith. Shortly before 7 A.M. on April 19, 1937, Gestapo agents entered the Berlin lodge on the Kleiststrasse, seized files and other property, and rounded up some five hundred persons who were connected with the fraternal Jewish society, including Baeck, in the meeting hall. These individuals were forced to remain sitting in the hall, without being allowed to speak, until early in the afternoon, while Gestapo officials interrogated each person separately in another room.[51]

Baeck and several dozen other B'nai B'rith members were then taken to Gestapo headquarters and held under arrest for two days. Defiant, Baeck refused to sign a statement ceding all the society's property to the government and attempted to argue that B'nai B'rith was a religious, not a political, organization; there was no reason to suspect it of fomenting opposition to the Nazi regime. He was ignored. The Berlin lodge was ordered permanently closed. Chairs, tables, cutlery, and oil paintings were carted away to help stock an anti-Semitic museum in Munich.[52] Similar moves were made against other lodges throughout Germany; all told, 103 were raided and shut down on the grounds of being "hostile to the state." Children and elderly Jews were evicted from B'nai B'rith-run sanitariums, and the organization's financial assets were confiscated. The official, improbable reason given for this abrupt suppression and dissolution of what had previously been considered an "apolitical" body was its purported links to German Communists.[53] The real reason was the Nazis' wish to destroy a financially strong, politically influential,[54] and culturally unifying Jewish body, in order to hasten the community's demise. The following week the Gestapo made this objective clear by hauling Baeck and some fifty other Jewish leaders down to Berlin police headquarters. An official named Flesch cursed them, took away their passports (this time because of some anti-German atrocity propaganda that had surfaced abroad), and berated the silent band of Jews for being "too cocky." Emigration was proceeding too slowly, Flesch said. Only the Zionists were earnestly pushing in that direction—the only "right" direction for Germany's Jews—and they were making only a "halfhearted" effort.[55] The one Jewish group "worth anything" in Flesch's opinion was the revisionist Zionist faction, headed by Georg Kareski.

Kareski was an ambitious maverick in Jewish political life. A banker originally from Poznań, in eastern Prussia, he had helped found the Zionist Jüdische Volkspartei (Jewish People's Party) in 1919 and then used it to advance his own conservative, antisocialist agenda and wrest control of the Gemeinden away from the dominant liberals. In developing a Zionist political base within the Jewish community, Kareski diverged from the rest of the movement, which believed in staying out of domestic politics and concentrating its energies on Palestine. The Jewish People's Party achieved a considerable electoral breakthrough in the November 1930 election for the Berlin Gemeinde's executive board

(*Vorstand*) when its candidates amassed over 25,000 votes (versus nearly 42,000 for the Liberal Party).[56] On the basis of this showing, Kareski was elected head of the Gemeinde. At the time of Hitler's takeover, he held one of the two Zionist seats on the community's governing body.

Sensing that the political tide was turning in his favor under a Nazi regime, Kareski made an aborted and foolhardy attempt to seize control of the Berlin Gemeinde by occupying its administrative offices, but he was forced to back down when no other Jewish faction rallied to his side.[57] After this failure, Kareski established an unlikely alliance with Hermann Stahl, the liberal who led the Berlin community, to challenge the authority of the newly formed Reichsvertretung and its head, Leo Baeck. In 1934 Kareski's policy differences with the Zionistische Vereinigung für Deutschland (ZVfD) led to his being ousted from that organization and joining a state Zionist, or revisionist, group, which was strongly committed to Herzl's original goal of building a Jewish state. This small group (with an estimated one thousand members) at first adopted the then-unpopular position of favoring a legally protected minority status for Jews in the Third Reich. By 1935, however, the state Zionists had switched positions, and Kareski proposed the gradual emigration of twenty thousand Jews a year to Palestine, to dissolve the community and thus end the "Jewish problem."[58] This scheme recommended Kareski to the Gestapo, which supported his unsuccessful candidacy for head of the Kulturbund.[59] When Kareski renewed his attacks on what he claimed was the "politically impotent" and poorly run Reichsvertretung in 1937,[60] joining forces again with the Berlin liberal Stahl (who detested Baeck), the Gestapo decided to push for a state Zionist takeover of the community as a way of accelerating emigration.[61]

Not long after the B'nai B'rith lodges were closed, the same Nazi official, Flesch, met twice with Baeck—treating this acknowledged leader of German Jewry with "embarrassing politeness"—to urge the rabbi to accept Kareski as a member of the Reichsvertretung's five-man ruling body.[62] Both times Baeck flatly refused to do so. At one point he told the Gestapo: "You can force me to appoint Kareski as a member of the presidium. But you cannot force me to continue as president of the Reichsvertretung."[63]

Taking advantage of Baeck's vulnerability after his wife's death and his arrest, Kareski's state Zionists tried to take control of the Reichsvertretung at a June 15, 1937, meeting of its governing council. With four

Gestapo agents looking on, Kareski charged that Baeck and his chief deputy, Otto Hirsch, lacked the trust of all sectors of the Jewish community and ran the organization inefficiently. The various Gemeinden should be given greater autonomy, he said. Armed with cables from the London-based (and financially crucial) Council for German Jewry; its president Herbert Samuel; and Max Warburg's brother, Felix, all expressing dismay at any forthcoming change in the Reichsvertretung's leadership[64] and supported by the Centralverein's as well as the ZVfD's delegates, Baeck managed to beat back Kareski's challenge. However, he did agree to allow Kareski to join a commission to investigate the charges he had brought against the organization.[65]

In July this commission made a recommendation that more power should be given to the Berlin Gemeinde in overseeing the Reichsvertretung's operations. The report gave Kareski a strong power base in German Jewish politics, but only for a short while. The July collapse of a cooperative bank that he directed, owing to his improper lending practices, undercut Kareski's position. He emigrated to Palestine in the fall.[66]

All these assaults on his leadership and personal well-being weakened Leo Baeck. (He was sent on a week's vacation in July to "recover his nerves.")[67] For four tumultuous exhausting years, he had stood at the helm of a foundering Jewish community, holding a multitude of key posts, trying to keep internal fights and Nazi intimidation from tearing it apart, and the end of his ordeal was nowhere in sight. Over the years he had grown larger than life in the eyes of his fellow Jews. Here was a kindly rabbinical father figure who had given them the faith, the courage, and the long-range perspective to come to terms with their persecution by the Nazis. Despite the strains of his numerous obligations to a dwindling and demoralized community, Baeck had lost little of his inimitable energy, remarkable for a man of his age. He still rose each day before dawn to work on his translation of the Gospels from Greek into Hebrew to make clear their Jewish influences.[68] In his apartment overlooking a park in Schöneberg, he continued to host—without his beloved Natalie to help him—regular afternoon teas, during which he would offer his views on the current Jewish situation. Every Friday at 8 A.M. Baeck gave a lecture on the art of preaching at the Hochschule für die Wissenschaft des Judentums (Institute for the Scientific Study of Judaism). To countless Jews whose lives had been shattered by acts of hatred or ostracism, the loss of a job, or the emigration of loved ones, he offered daily counsel and consolation. He was one of the few figures of authority these remaining Jews could count on.[69]

Baeck had an immutable belief that the Jews of Germany would somehow survive the Nazis as they had survived rejection and repression in the past—a belief, as Robert Weltsch would later characterize it, "in the ultimate victory of goodness even under the most terrifying circumstances."[70] Baeck once told his friend Heinz Warschauer, fresh from witnessing anti-Jewish riots in Palestine: "Hitler and his like cannot turn back history. We Jews will suffer. Some of us may die. But we will survive. We Jews have old eyes."[71] Shrugging off a suggestion by the Indian leader Mahatma Gandhi that German Jews all commit suicide, Baeck replied simply: "We Jews know that the commandment of God is to live."[72] A restoration—a final salvation—would be the reward for Jews once this frightful period had finally passed into history.[73]

Baeck's optimism about the ultimate outcome in Germany was also based on his assessment of his Aryan countrymen and their values. During the twentieth World Zionist Congress in August 1937, he gave Arthur Ruppin his opinion that as many as 80 percent of the German people actually opposed persecution of the Jews but were afraid to say so.[74] The Nazis may have won the Germans' votes, he thought, but they had not corrupted their hearts.

If Leo Baeck could find the moral resolve and religious conviction to carry on under growing pressure from all sides, Hans-Joachim Schoeps had more difficulty doing so. He had lost his leadership base, the cadre of naive young Jewish conservatives who were anxious to participate in Germany's national "renewal." By 1936, he had confronted his own bleak situation: He had virtually no hope of finding a teaching post in Germany or otherwise earning a living there.[75] Seeking more opportunities abroad, Schoeps succeeded in arranging a series of lectures in Amersfoort, the Netherlands, in April 1937 on "the crisis of the Christian consciousness in the Western world." Afterward Schoeps traveled to England and Belgium to inquire—in vain—about possible academic openings. Outside Germany his intellectual talents could find no outlet. Schoeps had more confirmation of this fact when he ventured northward for an eight-week "study trip" to Denmark and Sweden in June and July. Getting a visa allowing him to stay in these countries was also a problem. Later in the year he pursued a vacancy at the University of Leiden, in the Netherlands,[76] but this, too, came to naught.

Schoeps blamed his interrupted, incomplete education for his failure to find a university post. To rectify this deficiency, he made up his mind to do one of two things: locate a teaching post at a Jewish high school in Berlin or become a university docent while completing his studies. But neither option worked out. Jewish schools in the Dahlem and Grunewald sections of Berlin informed him that they had no openings.[77] And, according to what Schoeps asserted after the war, the Gestapo blocked him from taking a post at the Institute for the Scientific Study of Judaism.[78]

The Gestapo appears to have taken an active interest in Schoeps's leaving the Reich. In December 1937 the secret police required him to prepare a report detailing his efforts to obtain employment abroad.[79] It is not clear how actively Reinhard Heydrich's minions were encouraging Schoeps to quit Germany, but their periodic "interviews" with him had an intimidating impact. To appease the Gestapo, Schoeps submitted all the requested information just before Christmas, claiming it was not possible for him to migrate to most northern or central European countries because of their climate, which acerbated his asthma. He added that he could not go to England either because he needed access to German-language materials in archives and libraries.[80] (What Schoeps did not tell the Gestapo was that his search for a haven outside Germany was also hampered by governmental restrictions on the amount of money he could take with him: In response to his query in late October, the Gesellschaft für die Förderung wirtschaftlichen Interessen [Society for the Advancement of Business Interests] informed Schoeps that after subtracting a Nazi-imposed "flight tax," he could not take more than 50,000 reichsmarks [$20,000] with him to any country other than Palestine. And, for Schoeps, Palestine was not an option.)[81]

In spite of the bleak outlook for him in the Third Reich and the Gestapo's pressure on him to leave, Schoeps remained unenthusiastic about abandoning his native land. In a letter to Martin Buber, mailed in October, Schoeps confessed that he had undertaken his summer odyssey around Europe really to convince himself that, "despite everything," he was in the "best hands" in Germany, where he truly belonged.[82] He was going through the motions because he had to, Schoeps said, but his heart was not in it.

Max Warburg's heart was still very much in his welfare work for the impoverished and needy Jewish community. His chief concern was still to help Jews to emigrate in an orderly, prudent fashion. But, like Baeck,

Warburg was under fire for running an allegedly inefficient and incompetent organization. At a March meeting of the Jewish Colonization Association in London, he had to deflect charges that the Hilfsverein der deutschen Juden was being poorly managed and not getting the job done. Warburg admitted there was truth in these criticisms but offered a plausible excuse: The Hilfsverein, like all other Jewish organizations in Germany, was simply overwhelmed by the demand for its services.[83]

The task of finding suitable destinations for Jewish émigrés took up a great deal of the welfare agency's time. In January 1937 the French colonial minister suggested that German Jews might be allowed into such scattered and remote outposts as New Caledonia and New Hebrides in the Pacific; French Guyana; and the island of Madagascar, off the eastern coast of Africa. The latter site had been mentioned in earlier schemes for resettling the excessive population of Ostjuden in Germany and was now favored by the Polish government, which was seeking to reduce the number of Jews under its jurisdiction.[84] But the Hilfsverein, taking a close look at the island's tropical climate and largely mountainous, forested terrain, was not so enamored.[85] Nor, after numerous international debates about the proposal, were many other Jews; it did not strike them as a practical or attractive destination. (During the war, in the summer of 1940, Himmler would revive this plan, and Adolf Eichmann would go so far as to draw up a blueprint for transporting 4 million of Europe's Jews to Madagascar.)

The Hilfsverein was more partial toward the tiny Central American nation of Costa Rica, where a small number of Jews had emigrated at the end of the nineteenth century and in a second wave—coming from Germany, Poland, and Turkey—after World War I. But the Hilfsverein's worsening balance sheet threatened to make any exploration of this refuge short-lived. While taking the waters at Karlsbad, as he was accustomed to doing, in June, Warburg received some more bad financial news from his associate, Arthur Prinz: the organization could not stay in operation longer than six months.[86] Warburg hurried back from the Czech spa to deal with this cash flow crisis, but first he had to take time out to help defend Leo Baeck's leadership of the Reichsvertretung. At a late morning session of its governing body, Warburg listened patiently to a progress report by the commission set up to improve the Reichsvertretung's representative makeup (it was adopted with only minor changes) and then introduced a resolution of his own, supporting the work of Baeck and Otto Hirsch.[87] The resolution was approved.

The meeting ended quickly after that, with a new spirit of Jewish unity in the air, largely thanks to Warburg.

The banker then shifted his attention back to rescuing the Hilfsverein. He dispatched an urgent request for $250,000 to the Council for German Jewry in London, saying that without it, the welfare agency would have to abandon its policy of assisting all Jews to escape from Germany.[88] Since "Palestine" was now the word on so many Jewish lips, Warburg encountered strong opposition trying to convince affluent British and German Jews to contribute to an organization that was proposing to disperse refugees to such improbable places as Costa Rica. He could only make his case with hard facts. He told the thirty-sixth annual meeting of the Hilfsverein in October that the number of Jews allowed into Palestine that year amounted to only one-fifth of all the émigrés.[89] The Middle Eastern nation simply could not absorb all the Jews who might wish to go there. But the emotions attached to the ancient Jewish homeland were not so easily dispelled.

Warburg had just celebrated his seventieth birthday in June 1937—a major milestone for German Jewry's most eminent financier and philanthropist. In the Jewish press he was praised for his many years of support for Palestine, for his role in creating the Reichsvertretung and leading the Hilfsverein, and for his promotion of economic growth in Hamburg and throughout Germany following the World War I.[90] Whatever differences Warburg may have once had with the Zionists concerning Judaism and the importance of Palestine to Jews in the Diaspora were now glossed over. So much had the positions of this former spokesman for assimilated, secular Jewry and Theodor Herzl's devout followers narrowed that they hardly seemed worth dwelling on.

Warburg did not, however, think of Palestine as the only appropriate home for the world's Jewry. He had not given up his ideal synthesis of Judaism and patriotism—a patriotism that could take root in the Jews' new homes around the world at the same time it was being extirpated in Nazi Germany.[91] It is understandable that Warburg was not an admirer of the Peel report, which he saw as a "pretty game," full of "hypocritical objectivity," designed only to free the British from their obligations under the Balfour Declaration. He believed that the commission's report, with its "binational" solution, was really sounding the death knell for the Jews in that corner of the globe—soon the Arabs would throw them back into the sea. Germany's Jews would be wiser to turn their gaze elsewhere.[92]

As for the future of his own bank, Warburg had reason to remain somewhat sanguine, even during this period of accelerated "Aryaniza-tion" of Jewish firms and businesses. What Hjalmar Schacht, the Reichsbank president, had predicted had come true: The Nazis were forcing small companies and shops to liquidate but leaving large Jewish-owned concerns, including banks, alone. The powerful consortium of banks that lent money to the Reich government and stoked Germany's expanding, war-oriented economy still counted several Jewish banks among its fifty members. M. M. Warburg and Co. was one of them. The usefulness of these financial institutions and their considerable assets to the Nazi regime could not be overstated. The Warburg bank and others like it also provided the government with a supply of sorely needed for-eign currency.[93] Thus, throughout 1937 the family-owned firm was spared most of the impact of the Gestapo's orchestrated move to stifle Jewish economic life. Even with Schacht now less able to guarantee the bank's immunity from confiscation, Warburg could not help but feel that it enjoyed a privileged status.

Although it was subject to Gestapo suppression at any moment, for any reason, Robert Weltsch's *Jüdische Rundschau* went on printing two issues per week, filled with information and editorial comment to the Jewish community (and other Germans) who were starved for news. Earlier, brief bans imposed by either Joseph Goebbels, the propaganda minister, or the Gestapo had been merely slaps on the wrist—a way of punishing the newspaper for stepping out of line and offending Nazi sensibilities, as when Weltsch had dared to contend, back in 1935, that Jews were also human beings. These sudden crackdowns had drained the morale and stamina of the newspaper's staff, but a keen sense of their historical mission to uphold an imperiled German Jewry kept them going. Since the newspaper was almost exclusively focused on the fluid situation in Palestine (a "new wave of terror" struck in September),[94] the work of Aufbau there, and the fate of Jews elsewhere in the Dias-pora, its editors had good reason to believe they were generally going along with the Nazis' wishes—promoting Jewish emigration and ignor-ing anti-Semitic policies and practices in Germany—and thus ought to be protected from a permanent suspension. Weltsch himself had not been prohibited from working as a journalist, since he was employed by a Jewish publication. The Nazi doctrine of strict separation between the Aryan and Jewish races continued to make them condone a surprising autonomy within the Jewish community.[95] Weltsch was well aware of this dividing line and, as a Zionist who had long believed that Jews should concentrate on their own affairs and collective destiny, he was not tempted to cross it. He kept his personal outrage about what was happening to Germany's Jews at the hands of a brutally hostile regime from spilling over on to the pages of his newspaper, for he knew the price he would have to pay for such invective—arrest, imprisonment, and the closing down of the *Jüdische Rundschau* for good. It was a price he was not willing to pay for one brief moment of triumph. His continuing usefulness to the Zionist cause, he believed, outweighed any impulse to play the martyr's role—or to get of Germany. Thus, when the publisher Salman Schocken asked Weltsch to join his firm in Jerusalem, Weltsch declined.[96] The *Jüdische Rundschau* was too close to his heart for him to walk away from it until the time came when he would have no other choice.

By the fall of 1937, the *Centralverein Zeitung* was probably accurate when it stated that practically all Germany's Jews, except the elderly, were now thinking of emigrating. The Reichsvertretung was redoubling its efforts to achieve that goal, and even the RjF was giving its wholehearted backing to it.[97] But it was equally true that many countries of refuge were now off-limits. Others were unappealing in that they were too primitive for sophisticated, worldly German Jews. Palestine was again beset by violence, and the prospect of further visa restrictions was looming.[98]

Richard Willstätter was one Jew who does not appear to have wrestled with the question of emigration. At age sixty-five, he belonged to the older generation of German Jews who could not be enticed away from their beloved, comfortable homes and neighborhoods by the lure of a better job, a more secure future, or a Zionist dream-in-the-making. More than ever, he seemed content to live out his days on his own terms, doing the scientific work that still fascinated him, in the only home he could really call his own. Willstätter celebrated his birthday in August, alone as usual (his daughter having emigrated), by finishing an article on enzymes. He was not well, and he must have had thoughts about the dwindling number of days left to him.[99] His slow, "modest" progress in figuring out how sugar was broken down in the blood, with help from his loyal laboratory assistant, Margarete Rohdewald, offered some solace—the sense that he could still accomplish something

important and thereby justify his existence. Willstätter was still bothered by the "difficulties and restrictions" of his self-imposed "inner
exile," yet he could not conceive of a better set of circumstances for carrying on his research.[100] He regarded his present experiments as his scientific "swan song."[101] His career and German Jewry appeared to be
waning together, drowning in a mutual embrace that he did not have the
power to resist or to escape. If Germany's Jews were destined for some
kind of eradication, then he might as well disappear with them.

Aside from his research, Willstätter still derived pleasure from the
beauty with which he had surrounded himself in his Munich sanctuary.
He tended the lush roses in his garden with great care. He browsed
through his extensive personal library, with volume after volume of
reproductions of the works of the great European artists like Corot and
Cézanne whom he admired so greatly.[102] Willstätter's ceaseless need to
understand whatever appealed to him aesthetically (the works of human
beings as well as the works of nature) would impel him to make one of
his infrequent journeys from the Bavarian capital in the dead of winter
in 1938, when he would take a train to Paris to view the oeuvre of the
French impressionists. His artistic tour of that city would precede by
two and a half years the pilgrimage of another great admirer of French
art, Adolf Hitler.

Bella Fromm's world was wider and more open than Willstätter's.
While he mused in solitude over his books and paintings beside the
banks of the Isar, she still ventured regularly into the dizzying maelstrom of Berlin high society, her Jewishness presenting no obstacle to
receiving the engraved invitations that cascaded into her mailbox. One
evening, she dined in "Babylonian splendor," elbow to elbow with the
elite of the Nazi Party and their esteemed guests at the opening of the
new Reich chancellery, guarded by three companies of SS and SA men
extravagantly dressed as courtiers.[103] Another night, in the Finnish legation, she sat uncomfortably close to the table of the most infamous
anti-Semite, Alfred Rosenberg. Sipping her wine, she could not help but
feel equal disgust at the entrance of Hans Frank, architect of the nazi-
fication of German law.[104] Yet she did not get up and leave her table.

If barriers were placed in her way, Fromm did not accede meekly but
raised a strong protest. Denied an extension of her passport, necessary
for trips to Switzerland and France (only Jews intending to emigrate
could now obtain passports), she took her case to police headquarters,

presenting a family "pedigree" of seven generations on German territory as proof of her patriotism.[105] Ultimately, with help from her old party friend Eva von Schroeder and after enduring some rudeness by the police, she got her passport renewed for another six months.[106] True, there were stories going around about an imminent Nazi move against her. The Egyptian minister warned Fromm in his impossible German that the Propaganda Ministry was unhappy with her appearance at so many diplomatic receptions and implored her to leave the country at once.[107] However, Fromm continued to accept the invitations. She was like a tightrope walker suspended high above a cage of lions, fully aware that only her poise and cool nerves could save her. She dared not think of making any sudden, rash moves, let alone look down.

For the moment her safety net was intact. Hjalmar Schacht, whom Fromm secretly despised, continued to lend his good name on her behalf—the highest ranking member of Hitler's government willing to stand up for a Jew, at least in principle.[108] Some Nazi leaders still considered her a useful go-between to a diplomatic corps the regime wanted to court and keep tabs on, and nothing could be gained by blackballing her except reproach and chilly silence from these foreign dignitaries. Goebbels himself was not oblivious to Fromm's "usefulness," and tolerated her despite the distastefulness of having to depend on favors from a Jewess.[109] But when Schacht resigned as economics minister in November 1937, Fromm could see the net below her part. She began to think more seriously about getting out for good.

Abroad offers of asylum and work beckoned. If Fromm did decide to emigrate and if she could overcome bureaucratic snags in the passport and visa offices, there was a future waiting for her. Her feminine charm further enhanced her prospects overseas. In June 1937, just before the Peel report was released, she met the visiting president of the International Business Machines Corporation, Thomas J. Watson, at a Chamber of Commerce reception, and he promptly promised her a secretarial post the moment she set foot in the United States.[110] The American ambassador, William E. Dodd, made a similar pledge to her not long before he was recalled to Washington in December.[111]

Even the more serious offers did not persuade Fromm to change her mind about staying. She simply wavered back and forth. On the one hand, her influence was still strong, and it could be brought to bear effectively to help others take the route of escape that she was reluctant to take. On the other hand, her spirit was starting to crack. With autumn approaching, Fromm sought to get away from Berlin's incessant gossip and claustrophobia by taking an excursion boat to Finland, courtesy of a friendly shipping company agent. The ship stopped at the free city of Danzig, which was decked out in billowing swastikas that made it more painful to behold than the German capital she had just left.[112] Clearly, enthusiasm for the Nazis reached across international boundaries; if anything, like other empires, the Reich was the strongest on its far-flung fringes. Flight from it seemed futile. At least in Berlin, Fromm knew where she stood, knew what to expect, knew whom to turn to for help.

But the noose was tightening around her. Fromm could sense that the time for her to leave was fast approaching. Her health was not good. The strain of her glib social masquerade and the constant fear that lay just beneath its facade had worn her down. She was not sure how much more of this make-believe she could take. To recharge herself, she sought, at the year's end, another temporary escape, far from the boisterous "Heils!" of close-cropped Hitler Youth and the ever-watchful eyes of the Gestapo. (Fromm knew that the secret police regularly tailed her. Thus, for safe keeping, she entrusted pages of her diary to the American journalist Louis Lochner.)[113]

Over the Christmas holiday Fromm chose her beloved Alps for a ten-day vacation, even though the "devil" himself—Hitler—was staying not far from her hotel, admiring the same snow-blanketed peaks that Fromm longed for.[114] Unconsciously, perhaps, she may have been drawn to the Führer's Bavarian retreat as she had been transfixed these past five years so near his seat of power in Berlin; her journalistic inquisitiveness, her urge to be close to the action, drew her to the Nazis who repulsed her. The great jutting beauty of the Allgäu moved Fromm deeply. She had resolved that this would be her last visit to these mountains, since she saw matters coming to a head over the next twelve months.[115] On Christmas Day she looked southward at the Alps and wondered how Adolf Hitler, who had already secretly revealed his blueprint for a European war,[116] could fail to be moved by their splendor, how he could see the world only through hate-filled eyes.[117]

When she returned to her apartment on the Augsburgerstrasse, Fromm found, not to her surprise, that it had been ransacked.[118] Although no damning evidence had been found—Fromm was too careful for this to happen—the violation of her home shook her. Somehow the wrecking of her apartment was more devastating than fending off a mob of Brownshirt rowdies on her doorstep had been back in 1933. In the interim she had seen Germany slip deeper into the abyss, seen the Nazis at work up close, and taken the measure of their cruel inhumanity. Looking ahead, Fromm could discern the signs of war and of more severe measures planned for the Jews. She was frequently depressed by the thought of where this was all leading. She could see that her time was running out. As a Jew Fromm could no longer obtain the permit she needed to sell the wines from her family's vineyards and thus sustain the business that her family had run for generations. This restriction was perhaps the last straw. It was too much, to keep going on. After she had been back in Berlin only two weeks, Herbert Mumm whispered to her the words she was now ready to heed: "Bella, it's getting late. The time has come for you to leave."[119] With a nod she agreed. There were others who still needed her help, whose plight still tugged at her conscience and her heart, but she had to think of herself now. At long last it had come down to that.

10

Rushing for the Exits

In 1937 the urge to escape Germany was contagious. For most Jews, it was no longer to be resisted. The Nazis were applying too much pressure. Having unsuccessfully tried name-calling, harassment, random beatings, midnight arrests, ostracism, vilification, denial of rights, and economic strangulation, the Hitler regime was running out of patience. Five years since it had come to power, its openly proclaimed goal of building a mighty German nation based on the unifying and invigorating elixir of the volk remained frustrated: The "Jewish problem" was still unsolved. As of the end of 1937, a total of 129,000 Jews had left the Reich, but another 371,000, or three-fourths of the 1933 community, had stayed behind.[1] Fully 27 percent of those still living in Germany were aged sixty or older—stubbornly opposed to stuffing their lives into a suitcase and hopping on board a train for somewhere else. Other Jews had hesitated, too bound to Germany by history and temperament, by spiritual and material investments there, to brave a giant step into the vast unknown of *Ausland* (foreign countries). For too long their inaction had been endorsed by leaders who spoke reassuringly of a centuries-old history of Jewish suffering and forbearance, of the comforting strength of a community under siege.

Now the Nazis had tightened the vise to the point of unbearable pain and anguish. With a vengeance Jewish businesses were being seized or squeezed out of existence. Starting in the winter of 1937–38, Jewish-owned factories could no longer receive shipments of raw materials to keep them operating, and Jewish commercial enterprises were prevented from restocking their inventories.[2] At Hermann Goering's behest, this stifling of Jewish economic life took on a greater intensity early in 1938. As czar of Germany's economy, Goering was, in his own pig-headed and single-minded way, trying to carry out the wishes of a truculent Führer who, following the retirement of Hjalmar Schacht from the Economics Ministry the previous fall, had ordered that "the emigration of Jews from Germany be furthered by all possible means."[3] (This dictum had been reiterated several months later, when Hitler had emphasized that Jewish emigration was to proceed at all costs, mainly in the direction of Palestine.)[4] Goering told the party faithful that he intended a "fundamental cleaning up of the Jewish question"[5] and proceeded to speed up the pace of the previously erratic and lethargic Aryanization.[6] By April 1938, over 6,000 Jewish firms had been taken over, another 11,000 were about to be, and 15,000 more had already been forced into liquidation.[7] Yet nearly 40,000 shops and businesses were still in Jewish hands, out of a total of 100,000 back in 1933.[8] But Goering's relentless efforts to make the economy *judenfrei* predictably produced the opposite effect from what he desired: Impoverished Jews were now less able to come up with the necessary funds to leave the country.[9]

In their search for a more efficacious way of getting rid of the Jews, the Nazis soon discovered an impressive model to emulate in the neighboring (and newly absorbed) nation of Austria. Shortly after Hitler's triumphal march into the center of Vienna in mid-March 1938 and the subsequent ratification of the German Anschluss by Austrian voters on April 10, SA and SS units indulged in an "orgy of sadism" on the streets of this stately seat of the Hapsburgs, once the home of Mozart, Beethoven, and Brahms. It was far worse than anything the veteran foreign correspondent William L. Shirer had seen inflicted on German Jews. Men and women were made to scrub signs supporting the ousted chancellor Schuschnigg off the sidewalks and clean public latrines while crowds of onlookers jeered at them.[10] Some 12,000 Viennese Jews, including 150 community leaders, were arrested without being accused of any crime, tortured, and hauled off to the Dachau concentration camp.[11] Their valuable belongings—paintings, silverware, tapestries, furniture—were confiscated.[12] Jewish physicians and lawyers lost their jobs. Other coreligionists were forced to wear placards labeling them Jews and thus inviting attacks on the streets.[13]

These actions proved to be only a harbinger of more draconian measures to come. Head of a special, euphemistically named "Office of Jewish Emigration" in the SS, Adolf Eichmann slipped into the Austrian capital in March tasked with the mission of liquidating the country's Jewish population as speedily as possible. Free of any of the restraints that had held back the German government in dealing with its own Jewish population (out of consideration for world opinion, as well as for Germany's economic recovery), Eichmann, himself a native of Austria, was to carry out the forced expulsion of that nation's Jews without compromise or procrastination. Austria would be thoroughly "cleaned" of its Jews through a series of actions based on three principles: (1) emigration would no longer be a matter of choice, but of necessity, overseen by Eichmann's security police; (2) Jewish organizations would be compelled to help implement this policy; and (3) Jews would be stripped of all economic assets except the bare minimum required for them to get out of the country.[14] Goering made the policy exquisitely clear when he visited Vienna on April 28: The Jews must go—all 200,000 of them, he said. The target date for making Austria "racially pure" was 1942.[15]

Eichmann's machinery for driving out the Austrian Jews was brutally efficient and extremely well organized. Jews were to do as they were told, or else be sent to a concentration camp. Faced with these two unacceptable alternatives, some of Austria's Jews chose a third—they took their own lives. During one week in March alone, 1,700 of them committed suicide. The rest, for the most part, scurried to comply with Eichmann's demand. Within two weeks of the Nazis' entry into Austria, a flood of Jews spilled over its frontiers, some bound for Palestine,[16] others hoping for a refuge in lands as far away as Australia.[17] By the end of 1938 some 55,000 had emigrated. The Nazi assault on Austrian Jewry stunned a world that had been lulled into believing the worst of Hitler's excesses was over. Nothing on this scale, with such ruthlessness and cold-blooded determination, had been seen in modern times. It signaled the beginning of a new stage in anti-Semitic persecution by Germany's racist masters. The effectiveness of Eichmann's measures could scarcely be questioned. As one of Herbert Mumm's friends lamented to Bella Fromm, the Nazis had done more to the Jews in a single day in Austria than they had managed to do in five "ghastly" years in Germany.[18]

And the Nazis were quick to import their success. Within days of the Anschluss, German Jews were feeling the sting of the same harsh whip of oppression that had struck their Austrian counterparts. As of March 18—the day that Austrian Jewish organizations were shut down—all German Jews were required to add the Hebrew name "Israel" (for men) or "Sarah" (for women) to their given names to make their racial identity painfully obvious and to humiliate and depersonalize them. At the end of that month, the Nazi regime stripped German Jewish community organizations of their status as public bodies eligible to levy taxes and receive state support—a mortal blow to their continued survival. (The Jewish organizations were also now subject to paying taxes.) This move was quickly followed by a statement from Hans Frank, Hitler's chief jurist, indicating that the "race question" would receive more "vigorous" attention now that Jewish groups were subject to governmental regulation and control.[19]

To mark the fifth anniversary of the 1933 boycott against Jewish shops, the Propaganda Ministry announced, on April 1, 1938, that henceforth all articles slated to appear in the Jewish press were to be submitted to its offices for review three days in advance.[20] The ministry later ordered the Jewish Cinema Institute to start producing films that advocated emigration.[21] In remarks made toward the end of April, Goering divulged an additional threat to Jewish economic power that would do more to drive out Germany's remaining Jews than any film possibly could: By June 30, all Jewish-owned property and cash holdings worth over 5,000 reichsmarks would have to be registered with the government. With a list of all these assets in their hands, the Nazis would have an easy time seizing Jewish wealth. Fears of this anticipated next step prompted several thousand well-to-do Jews to gather together whatever they could legally take with them and head for the Reich's borders.[22]

Some German Jewish leaders defiantly refused to succumb to panic or despair. They saw the Nazi crackdown in Austria and similar persecution at home as a more intensified phase of the trial by fire they had already been through. At least, this was what they said in public. Leo Baeck had been scheduled to cross the Channel on March 15 to confer with officials of the Council for German Jewry in London about increasing funding for emigration, but events in Austria altered his plans. Rather than react to Eichmann's tactics by pleading for more money to help Jews get out quickly, Baeck extended an open hand to Austrian Jews in dire need—much as he had welcomed the Saar Jews into the Reich a couple of years before. He reasoned, with admirable humanity, that German Jews "must stand up as well for their brothers and . . . make available to them any kind of help that is granted to German Jewry by foreign countries."[23] Baeck was spreading his credo of strength through unity beyond Germany's frontiers as he had extended it to the diverse factions within his own community. At the same time, speaking for the Reichsvertretung der Juden in Deutschland, Baeck responded to the Nazis' new restrictions on German Jewish organizations by making it clear that their mission would continue. Jews' obligations to the community had not changed, and would not change, he declared; their chief tasks of raising money for the needy and organizing for a large-scale exodus would remain as before.[24] Instead of paying taxes to keep the *Gemeinden* (Jewish communities) afloat, Jews would be expected to make voluntary contributions of the same amount.

If Baeck was motivated by a desire to unite Jews in their suffering, Robert Weltsch was still guided by his Zionist longing for a Jewish renaissance—a longing that was finally being fulfilled. As he had in many other editorials since 1933, Weltsch pointed out to his readers in a March 3, 1938, essay in the *Jüdische Rundschau*, "Awakened Strengths," that the Nazi experience had actually not been all bad for German Jewry. Historically, he argued, whenever Jews had grown too comfortable with their existence in the Diaspora, they had been jolted by a flare-up of anti-Semitism into realizing that their lives had a higher—that is, Jewish—dimension. This was exactly what had happened to Germany's Jews under Hitler, Weltsch wrote. Whereas they had lost a great deal—

and worse was yet to come—the "balance [was] not completely negative." In this dark hour the Jews had "developed strengths that we ourselves would never have guessed they had in them."[25] Even the Anschluss
of Austria did not shake his conviction, which was akin to Baeck's, that
the unfolding Jewish nightmare in Europe was subsumed by the more
important insights into Jewish identity that it afforded. Yes, Jews were
understandably staggered by this latest round of oppression, but in their
pain, they should not forget the "higher reality" that lay beyond the
quotidian and the personal.[26] The Jews of Germany, Weltsch added a
few days later, had lost their sense of history and failed to comprehend
that what was happening to them now was a fate shared by all Jews living in the Diaspora and nowhere at home in it. They needed to gain this
insight both to fathom and to survive their ordeal. In the pages of the
Jüdische Rundschau, Weltsch did not slacken his journalistic cheerleading.
Yes, the Jewish community was now in decline, but this was not an
excuse to jump ship. Its new burdens, coupled with its shrinking size,
only increased the need for energy, intelligence, and involvement to
make the community function well.[27]

In private Weltsch was entertaining other thoughts. A recent, month-
long ban by the Propaganda Ministry had "depressed" him and his staff
and financially depleted the newspaper.[28] In early 1938 he confided to
his longtime Zionist friend Hugo Bergmann his wish to visit Palestine
in April, although it was hard for him to see how he could leave the
newspaper for that long a period. Weltsch was also worried about getting his seventeen-year-old son Ruben to safety—possibly in the United
States.[29] He wanted to settle his son's fate first and then his own. Palestine weighed heavily on his mind. He regarded it more than ever as the
salvation for German Jewry[30]—despite what he bemoaned as misguided
British policy there.[31] As a lifelong proponent of a Jewish homeland he
began to envision his own future there. Weltsch's second wife, Suse, was
an ardent Zionist who had a "wild and romantic" image of Palestine
and was encouraging him to emigrate.[32]

In the spring of 1938 Weltsch did manage to get away to the Middle East, to bring himself up to date on the political situation there and
to scout out prospects for resettling. On the way back, in June, he
stopped over in Vienna and witnessed firsthand the abuse and enmity
being vented at Austrian Jews amid a blur of swastikas on the city's
streets.[33] Compared to Vienna, Berlin seemed a "paradise." (His reaction

was not unlike Bella Fromm's in Nazi-infested Danzig.) Weltsch may also have sensed he was catching a glimpse of Germany's future.

That future became crystal-clear to Max Warburg in January 1938. Schacht approached him to say he was sorry that he could no longer keep the bank within the consortium that lent funds to the German government. Warburg immediately grasped the implications: The family concern that had started in Hamburg 140 years ago and that had been given over to his stewardship would now have to be liquidated. He told Schacht what he had concluded, and the Nazis' financial "wizard" replied that this was what he had expected.[34] (This conversation took place about the time that Warburg's cousin Siegmund wrote from London to the exiled financial expert Hans Schäffer, expressing his astonishment that the firm was still able to carry on "a very active banking business" in the face of recent actions aimed at Jewish concerns.)[35]

Actually, the fight had already seeped out of Max Warburg. In December 1937, his younger brother Felix had died in New York at the relatively young age of sixty-six, depriving Max not only of a beloved sibling, but of an indispensable confidante and financial adviser as well. His first thought on learning this sad news was to leave Germany for good.[36] When Schacht spoke to him in January 1938, Warburg was too overcome by this loss to contemplate any more efforts to keep the bank from slipping out of his hands. Furthermore, the financial crisis in the Hilfsverein der deutschen Juden was worsening. Just as a soaring interest in emigration early in 1938 increased the need for its services, the welfare agency was running out of cash. In December 1937 it did receive a modest, stopgap grant of 80,000 reichsmarks ($32,000) from the Jewish Colonization Association in London[37] but no one could say how much longer the Hilfsverein could continue its operations on this kind of a shoestring.

Wracked by these personal and professional setbacks, Warburg gave in to the inevitable: He prepared to liquidate the bank. The Nazis, however, still had need of the Warburg name and the reputation that came with it.[38] They were worried that there would be negative repercussions abroad if the bank was hastily dissolved, and so they agreed to subject it to a "friendly Aryanization."[39] Warburg was able to find a non-Jewish banker, Rudolf Brinckmann, and a Hamburg exporter, Paul Wirtz, who were willing to take over the bank in late May. Under their agreement, the firm would change hands basically intact. Even the words "M. M.

Warburg" were to be retained in the new bank's name, at the request of
a German government that was cognizant of the value of tradition and
continuity in financial institutions.

With the end of his banking career in Germany at hand, Warburg
could still look back with pride at what he, a kind of born-again Jew,
had done for his community by staying in the Third Reich. His ties to
Schacht had helped to slow the Nazi ouster of Jews from the economy.
The transfer agreement worked out by him and the former economics
minister had given many thousands of middle and upper-class Jews a
way to flee Nazi Germany with at least part of their fortunes. (Nearly
40,000 Jews had by now succeeded in reaching Palestine, bringing with
them between $30 and $40 million, largely thanks to assistance from
the Hilfsverein and the American Jewish Joint Distribution Committee.)[40] Warburg's Hilfsverein had helped tens of thousands of well-off
Jews make the odyssey to other foreign lands by investigating potential
host countries, providing temporary living quarters, arranging for visas,
and securing passage on ships across the Atlantic and Pacific.[41] His
fund-raising visits to Great Britain and the United States had netted
hundreds of thousands of dollars to bankroll the Jewish exodus.

Within the Jewish community itself, Warburg had stayed discreetly in
the background, quietly using his considerable influence to bridge divi-
sions and build a unified Jewry within Leo Baeck's Reichsvertretung. In
his native city of Hamburg, he had played a key role in keeping the 126-
year-old Jewish Gemeinde alive. Both he and his brother Fritz, for example, had contributed generously to the construction of a new community center, which opened in January 1938, complete with a theater,
restaurant, and two-hundred-seat lecture hall. Warburg spoke at the
dedication ceremonies, just one week into a new year that had already
been marred by several ominous developments. First, on the French and
Swiss frontiers, Jews had had their passports taken away, as the German
authorities attempted to limit travel abroad only to those who were
emigrating; a special correspondent for the Jewish Telegraphic Agency
reported that this move was part of an anti-Semitic crackdown
"unequaled in the previous history of the regime."[42] Second, German
Jewish groups could no longer talk to foreign correspondents without
permission from the Gestapo, and the German police were beginning to
apply direct pressure on Jewish organizations, such as the Reichsvertretung, to speed up emigration.[43] Third, approximately half the Jewish

workers were now unemployed. Fourth, an increasing number of Jewish firms were being liquidated.[44] Finally, all over the Reich, Jews were being taunted by the Nazi ditty "Junge Juden, Übersee, alte Juden, Weissensee." ("Young Jews [go] abroad, old Jews to Berlin's large Jewish cemetery.")

In spite of these developments, Warburg tried, in his remarks, to put a good face on the current state of the Jewish community. Building the Gemeinde's new home, under such adverse conditions, was an important testimonial, he said, to the fact that Germany's Jews were once again "loyal to our Judaism" after they had neglected their religion and culture for so long. (Warburg might have been speaking about his own transformation into a believer.) "We want to do our share to see that Jews again find their composure and bearing, inner quiet and higher peace," he went on to say. These were not the words of a man entirely devoid of hope. The completed community center represented, to him, a vote of confidence in Hamburg's Jewish community, which he estimated to still number as many as fifteen thousand, down only a thousand since Hitler came to power.[45]

The Nazi Anschluss of Austria did not so much discourage Warburg as it inspired him—as it did Leo Baeck—to act on a broader stage. In late April, Warburg ventured across the English Channel again seeking funds from British Jews to help not only his compatriots, but also beleaguered Austrian Jews, escape. He regarded the shocking events in Austria both as a tragedy and as a trump card that strengthened his hand in these negotiations.[46]

In just over a month, Warburg had to give up his bank, relinquishing all control, together with his fellow partners Fritz Warburg, his son Eric Warburg, and Ernst Spiegelberg, thereby ending fifty-five years of personal affiliation with M. M. Warburg and Co. It was a defeat he had managed to stave off for years—the end of his family's preeminence in German banking and of his own influential role in his country's economic life. Warburg had hoped to slip away from the bank quietly, leaving the chore of saying good-bye to his faithful employees to his son, but Eric had already departed for the United States when the time came. It was a deeply painful occasion for the elder Warburg, to have to stand up in public and admit that he had not, after all, been able to keep this great family tradition going. Warburg tried to salvage some good from this failure. Elegantly dressed, with a white carnation in his lapel, he told two hundred members of the firm's staff, crowded into the bank's cafeteria, how pleased he was that M. M. Warburg was not going out of business, only being handed over to other capable hands. He asked them to transfer their loyalty to these new owners. It was up to these same steadfast employees to "bring the ship through all storms and past all rocks"—into a post-Nazi era. After reflecting on the philosophy of banking that had guided him all these years (a banker is a genuine pioneer, always innovating, prepared to take risks), he wished them luck. Then, one by one, Warburg shook their hands, in a solemn ritual that was reminiscent of a man bidding farewell to friends at his own funeral.[47]

Still Warburg was in no rush to exit the Reich. Much work was yet to be done for the Jews stranded in Germany, and he was not prepared to abandon them at this critical hour. The transfer of the bank had barely been made public when Warburg took a train south, to Stuttgart, to address a meeting of the Hilfsverein's governing body. He spoke of emigration as having ebbed; metaphorically, the train headed abroad had pulled into the station, picked up some passengers, and departed. Most of the Jews who were able to leave had by now done so, and the focus of his organization had to shift to meeting the needs of the ones left behind, unemployed and impoverished. Whatever exodus might still occur should be a slow and steady one—not, he insisted, the sort of herdlike stampede that would only foster enmity toward the Jews. The process also had to be orderly and modest in scale, to forestall a "catastrophe."[48] (Warburg may have been referring to the panicked reaction of Austrian Jews in recent weeks.) In his cautiousness, he echoed the views of Jewish war veterans in the Reichsbund jüdischer Frontsoldaten.

Warburg's tempered approach to emigration was not without its critics, especially across the Atlantic. American Jewish leaders, such as Stephen Wise, had had many disagreements with him on this score and with Warburg's overall response to the Nazi threat. Ever since their falling out over an anti-German boycott back in 1933, many Zionists in the United States had chided Warburg for being all too willing to sit down at the same table and negotiate with Jewry's most hated foes. It was thus not entirely without Schadenfreude that these same American Jews reacted to the news that Warburg's bank had been Aryanized. As the New Yorker Max Brauer wrote to Wise: "Perhaps some day Max Warburg will atone for his error and attitude in the first years of Nazism."[49]

Although American Jews were loathe to be so critical of a revered figure like Leo Baeck, they did find his unflagging optimism a bit frustrating. Even after the post-Anschluss attack on the German Jewish
community, Baeck maintained a benign outlook toward a German people that had condoned, if not applauded, these excesses. Although he
was now committed to building a new life for young Jews outside
Europe, Baeck still could not bring himself to accept Judaism as alien
or peripheral to the Western world. If anything, his knowledge of scrip-
ture and religious philosophy taught him just the opposite. Christianity
and Judaism had been tightly entwined through the ages—the former
was not a flat rejection of the older faith but built solidly on its foun-
dations. To prove his point, Baeck had labored over a major scholarly
work during the past few years, tracing the spirit and philosophy of the
Gospels back to what he depicted as their Jewish origins. A bold affront
to Aryan notions of racially based culture and Jewish spiritual deprav-
ity, his book, *Das Evangelium als Urkunde der jüdischen Glaubensgeschichte* (The
Gospels as a Written Record of Jewish Religious History), appeared in
1938, and due to either inattentiveness or indifference, the Nazis never
got around to censoring it. Baeck's intellectual rebuke was another act of
"inner resistance" that went largely unnoticed by his more practical-
minded oppressors.

German Jews could not afford to be so oblivious to what was happening around them. Matters were reaching a breaking point. How long
before the Nazis dismantled the tottering Jewish community and turned
on its unprotected members with unbridled fury, to drive them out, no
one could say. But the day was fast nearing. All signs pointed to it. The
month of June 1938 brought fresh confirmation. With his diabolical
mind now engaged with foreign matters, namely, bullying the Western
powers into ceding him Czechoslovakia, Hitler wanted the Jewish problem solved quickly, so it would not interfere with his grandiose strategy
for expanding German Lebensraum. During a European war, Jewish
enclaves inside the Reich might act as a "fifth column" undermining
morale and impeding victory. That could not be tolerated.

A week and a half after having briefed his top military and diplomatic advisers on how he intended to conquer the Czech nation, the
German chancellor ordered the main Munich synagogue to be razed—
a stark foreshadowing of what was to come in November.[50] The synagogue in Dortmund was also burned to the ground. Meanwhile, in a bid

to throw Jews into a panic, the Nazis incited mobs to instigate anti-Semitic violence in Berlin and Vienna. On June 13 several hundred Jews were arrested during an early morning sweep through Berlin. Many were merely harangued, charged with minor offenses, and released. But less lucky ones were sent to the Buchenwald concentration camp, just outside the town of Weimar, in a display of naked intimidation that the Jewish Telegraph Agency called the "most intensive police campaign against Jews since 1933."[51] Soon the number behind bars reached 2,000, some 1,500 of whom, all branded "antisocial," were coerced into emigrating directly from their cells.[52] This event marked a shift in Nazi policy: Henceforth, emigration was not going to be a voluntary act, but a forced one, as it was in Austria. To spread fear more pervasively, Jewish shop windows in Berlin were broken or smeared with red paint, and their owners were harassed. The number of synagogues in the Reich was going to be reduced, the government said. A weeklong ban on Jewish meetings was also announced, and all Jewish shops were required to be clearly marked as such. Two synagogues in Berlin were damaged by vandals.[53] During a characteristically ranting speech at the Olympic stadium, where just a year before athletes from all over the world had avowed international brotherhood, Joseph Goebbels told a jubilant throng of 120,000 that the government was considering new anti-Semitic laws: Jews would no longer be able to "flaunt their dirty life" in the Nazi capital.[54]

By June 1938 Bella Fromm was in the midst of her own struggle to escape the Reich before war broke out. It would be a long battle. Her friend at the U.S. consulate, Cyrus Follmer, told her that obtaining the prerequisite papers would take until August. Earlier Fromm had been informed by the passport office that, because she was not popular with the government, her application would take longer than usual to process.[55] Nonetheless, she still found time to help the latest group of Jewish victims. By her own account, she managed to have more than two dozen prisoners freed from Buchenwald, rekindling her guilt about deserting those who were more vulnerable than she was.[56]

On June 28, her journalist's curiosity to witness what was happening firsthand again led Fromm into the streets. Riding in her car down the Kurfürstendamm with a female friend from the diplomatic corps, she saw one sickening sight after another. Crude anti-Semitic cartoons and slogans were smeared on shop fronts, and in the part of the city where

Jewish stores were the most numerous, windows were broken and looted items lay strewn on the pavement. As her friend snapped pictures with a concealed camera, Fromm recorded the scene with her well-trained eye: "Everywhere were revolting and bloodthirsty pictures of Jews beheaded, hanged, tortured, and maimed, accompanied by obscene inscriptions." She watched from the safety of the automobile as an elderly Jewish man was forced by SA troopers to pick up shards of glass with his fingers. (The following day Fromm learned that the man had subsequently taken his own life.)

Out of concern for her own well-being, she did not return home that evening, but stayed with Aryan friends. A week later, while having a drink near a café frequented by Jews, she saw a Gestapo truck drive up and herd the patrons out "like cattle" and take them off to prison. That night all establishments in Berlin catering to Jews were raided and declared off-limits.[57] While shaken by these "scenes of ferocity and misery," Fromm regained her composure in time to attend a Fourth of July garden party at the American embassy. Surveying the ripe flowers and mounds of hors d'oeuvres, she could hardly believe that such an ironic contrast could exist within the confines of one city.[58] Warned by "Rolf" (her lover, Herbert Mumm) that her friends would not be able to protect her any more, Fromm had less appetite for these social outings. Frequently, she declined to attend, finding Berlin's lighthearted revelry a grotesque masque.[59]

The Anschluss—Hitler's first move outside German borders (other than his annexing of the Saarland in 1936)—deepened Fromm's feelings of despair, while her ambivalence about taking the irreversible step of abandoning Germany grew more intense: "I cling with every fiber . . . to my home[land] and yet see clearly that for us there is no way back."[60] It was more and more difficult for her to get by from day to day. Money was harder to come by. Her car was stolen, and a few days later Fromm was briefly arrested, then let go, in what she had to feel was an act of sheer harassment.[61] These experiences heightened her intimations of impending disaster. In May 1938 an old aristocratic friend passed on his informed hunch that Hitler planned to seize Czechoslovakia by October—a move bound to trigger a European war.[62] This tip jibed with the warnings "Rolf" had given her and made Fromm persist doggedly in her quest for exit papers, despite the endless red tape and personal humiliation, which—even with "Rolf" finding "devious shortcuts" through the bureaucracy—she had to put up with.[63] In frustration, Fromm sought out a fortune teller, who predicted she would get out of Germany by mid-September.

Hans-Joachim Schoeps was a more ardent believer in soothsayers, but his preference was for astrologers. Every year since the late 1920s, he had had a horoscope prepared for him by a Bavarian with the odd name of Paris. These surveys of the planets had spotted self-destructive impulses and inner unrest, along with Schoeps's tendency toward "adventures and peculiarity" in his love life. Regularly, they cautioned Schoeps, still a closet homosexual, against entering into marriage.[64] The horoscopes did not, it appears, advise that he leave the country (the astrologer may not have been aware that Schoeps was Jewish), but this did not stop him from mailing off dozens of letters to schools and universities as far afield as Iceland, Philadelphia, and Czechoslovakia, inquiring about possible openings. The hot breath of the Gestapo was still warm on Schoeps's neck. Although, through a temporary waiver of the required civil service examination, he had managed to find a teaching post at a Jewish private high school in the suburban Grunewald section of Berlin[65] (and get himself into some trouble for consorting with a young man outside its grounds),[66] Schoeps could not count on the secret police's patience lasting much longer. They wanted him out of the country, soon.

Even if this anxiety had dissipated, he had other good reasons to leave. New Nazi regulations were squeezing the life out of his publishing ventures. As of October 1937, Jewish bookstores had been told they could sell only to Jewish customers, and the importing of Jewish books and magazines was proscribed. (Still, in that year seventy-nine Jewish firms, including Schoeps's Vortrupp Verlag, continued to publish books—four years after Hitler had come to power.)[67] Schoeps tried to adjust to this new situation by making a shrewd accommodation: He offered to sell the titles brought out by his firm to Jewish schools, at a reduced rate.[68]

At almost the same time, Schoeps realized he would have to move the Vortrupp Verlag abroad if it was going to stay in business. In early January 1938 he began exploring the possibility of transferring the publishing house to Holland.[69] Switzerland, Czechoslovakia, and Sweden were also seen as potential bases. Schoeps approached the London bookseller Selfridge about selling his books in the United Kingdom and proceeded to line up an English translator for them.[70] It was a modest enterprise—Schoeps had only twenty-three titles for sale, including five of his own—but he hoped these might be enough to cover his living costs outside Germany. (At home he was still dependent on his parents for money.) Recently, Schoeps had occasionally lectured on such esoteric topics as Buddhism and "the question of contemporary Jewish religion."[71] But he had failed to convince Leo Baeck to sponsor similar talks at the Lehranstalt.[72] This setback reinforced Schoeps's feeling that life was "scarcely bearable" in the Third Reich as long as there was no proper venue for his intellectual interests.[73] All signs now pointed to the exit, if he could only find his way there.

As of January 1938, approximately 135,000 of Germany's 525,000-plus Jews had safely crossed over the Reich's borders to begin new lives in exile.[74] (Leo Baeck's Reichsvertretung had assisted 70,000 of them.)[75] Once regarded as impetuous by their more prudent and optimistic friends, these Jewish refugees were now seen as the lucky ones—the Jews who had slipped out of the trap. The words of Hermann Stahl, the leader of the Berlin Jewish community, uttered in the Fasasenstrasse synagogue in January, resonated with a cold finality: "To those among our youth who have not yet decided to emigrate, I say there is no future for the Jews in this country."[76] Never before had the truth been spoken so loudly and clearly by a prominent figure in the Jewish Gemeinde.

Richard Willstätter had of late had ample opportunity to behold the stark reality of his situation close up. Adolf Hitler had come to the Bavarian capital to celebrate the eighteenth anniversary of the founding of the Nazi Party and used the occasion to blast Jews for arousing the foreign press against Germany: "We will at any rate proceed energetically against the Jewish inciters in Germany," the Führer thundered. "We know that they are the representatives of an Internationale, and we will treat them accordingly."[77] And then, in June, the Munich synagogue had been set ablaze. Being neither a Communist nor a devout believer, Willstätter may not have felt that these mounting attacks were also aimed at him. As usual, he responded to adversity by burrowing more deeply into his scientific investigations. Conferring each night, with the Gestapo listening in on a taped line, he and Margarete Rohdewald were making progress in unraveling the workings of enzymes in muscle tissue.[78] The thought of completing this last great piece of research blocked out virtually everything else that was happening around him.[79]

As he would later write to his former student and collaborator, Arthur Stoll, "It is my lifelong method, which has made it possible for me to achieve anything by taking on a great workload, by concentrated work and overwork."[80]

But Willstätter was not so absorbed in his research that he ignored the plight of friends and relatives who were less well off than he was. Since 1933 he had made a practice of giving money generously to Jews seeking to flee Germany,[81] and this willingness to help did not abate as the Jewish situation grew more hopeless. If anything, he was too free with his money, giving it away with little thought about his own eventual need for it. Being alone, he did not worry much about the future. His daughter Margarete had settled a few years earlier with her husband in faraway Wisconsin, to raise her children, and no one else in his immediate family was left in the Third Reich. His life seemed overshadowed by premature death and abandonment—his father going off to America during the formative years of Willstätter's life, his own near death from diphtheria as a boy, the death of his wife when he was only in his thirties, the death of his son Ludwig at age ten and a half, and now his only surviving child perversely repeating his father's desertion of him. These losses had hardened Willstätter, reminded him that life could be cruel, turned him more inward, and taught him to rely on his own resources and strengths. Now this same Job-like tenacity was working against his survival, telling him that safety did not lie in joining with all Germany's other Jews—those who were clamoring outside the visa offices—but in staying apart from the fray, in waiting out the storm by himself.[82]

There was a wait, too, for the Jews now determined to get out of Germany. Palestine remained their destination of choice, but these days Palestine was not so easy to reach. In 1937 fear of greater Arab unrest had prompted the British to cap the flow of émigrés, and the Nazis, who had at first encouraged the creation of a Jewish homeland, were now having second thoughts about this idea. These misgivings dated back to the issuance of the Peel Commission report. That a Jewish state might actually become a reality caused some party leaders to worry that it could some day pose a threat to German world dominance. If, as the Nazis professed to believe, the Jews formed an international conspiracy bent on destroying the Aryan people, was it really wise to help them gain a territorial base? In an article that appeared in a governmental publication in July 1937, concern was voiced about a "Jewish state where the power of world Jewry could be consolidated."[83] This view was reinforced by a report prepared by Adolf Eichmann, following his visit to Palestine and Egypt in the fall of 1937. On the basis of his analysis of the political situation there, Eichmann recommended a reversal of Nazi policy: "As far as the Reich is concerned, the creation of an independent state by the Jews in Palestine should be impeded."[84] Hitler himself saw the wisdom of such a shift, not wanting to give the Jews what Roman Catholics already had in the Vatican. So, at the same time that the British were closing the gates to Palestine (emigration dropped to 10,536 in 1937, down from nearly 30,000 the year before and a peak of 61,854 in 1935, owing to the decreased quota of visas),[85] the Nazis were turning against the creation of a Jewish homeland.

Emigration elsewhere was equally, if not more, problematic. Although it was officially willing to expedite Jewish visa applications, the United States government did not, in a domestic atmosphere of widespread public (and bureaucratic) anti-Semitism, take any steps that would have increased the number of refugees who could legally enter the country. The State Department kept the number of annual visa openings for all Germany constant even though it was obvious to officials, both in Washington and in the U.S. consulates abroad, that the predicament faced by persecuted Jews was growing desperate and that the desire to emigrate to the United States was mounting. In mid-January 1938, for example, the American consul general in Stuttgart (responsible for a region that encompassed 45 percent of Germany's Jews) reported that German Jews had concluded that their situation was becoming "more and more hopeless" and had resolved to leave. To many of them, the United States appeared the last accessible haven. In response to this increased demand, the Stuttgart consulate had issued 10,483 visas in 1937, a number approaching predepression levels.[86] But, nonetheless, waiting lists continued to grow longer. Both because of the stringency of the U.S. visa policy and the psychological obstacles Jews had to surmount to traverse the Atlantic, the exodus to America had not swelled during the Nazi era. After a steady rise following Hitler's assumption of power, the number had leveled off in April 1937 at a point significantly below the high point reached in the 1920s. Other countries outside Europe were becoming even less welcoming to Jews now that it appeared a mass emigration was in the offing. Within Europe, new barriers were going up as well. For example, no sooner had the Nazis announced their goal of expelling 30,000 Austrian Jews a year than immigration restrictions were put into effect in the Netherlands.

If refugees from Germany and Austria were to find new homes, it would take a commitment by many nations, distributing the burden among them. The drastic steps taken by Eichmann and his minions in Austria made the need for some kind of international response to the refugee problem more imperative. Indeed, on March 25, 1938, less than two weeks after the Anschluss, President Franklin D. Roosevelt, acting on the recommendation of Under Secretary of State Sumner Welles and under pressure from American Jews, called for a conference of concerned nations to convene to address this crisis. To make the planned discussions more palatable to the participants, Secretary of State Cordell Hull made it clear from the outset that no nation would be asked to take in any more refugees. This concession assured that nothing of real importance to Europe's desperate Jews would emerge from the conference.[87]

Hull's pronouncement did not stop German and Austrian Jews from building up hopes. The first response from the mainstream *Centralverein Zeitung* was to run a banner headline, ARE THE DOORS OPENING?[88] These hopes built up during the spring as the situation in Germany worsened. By early June, a liberal Jewish leader, Alfred Hirschberg, an attorney who worked for the Centralverein, was speculating in print about the outcome of the upcoming conference, to be held in the French spa of Évian-les-Bains the following month. As many as several hundred thousand Jews living in the Diaspora could now look forward to an orderly relocation, new homes, careers, and a sense of security, Hirschberg predicted.[89] (The Institute for the Study of the Jewish Question was estimating it would take another thirty years for all Germany's Jews to leave if the present pace of emigration was not accelerated.)[90]

As the date of the Évian conference drew nearer, this optimism faded. None of the thirty-two governments that were planning to send representatives publicly stated that they intended to liberalize their immigration policies. There was no hint of the United States being willing to open its doors any further. In fact, the White House flatly ruled out any such step.[91] In the weeks before the Évian conference was to take place, the *Centralverein Zeitung* sent one of its reporters to Geneva, to take the lay of the land. His prognosis was more subdued: The highly touted international gathering, the first attempt by the world community to confront the burgeoning refugee crisis, might not actually produce any concrete proposals to aid Germany's and Austria's Jews. A will to accomplish *something* existed, but it was not clear how this will could be translated into deeds.[92] The voice of Jewish war veterans, *Der Schild*, was equally skeptical about the conference.[93] The best "spin" Robert Weltsch could put on Évian in the *Jüdische Rundschau* was to hail the scheduled appearance of Neville Chamberlain's cabinet minister Edward Turnour, Earl Winterton, as demonstrating a high-level commitment to resolve the Jews' plight[94] (even though Winterton was known for favoring Arab over Jewish rights in Palestine).[95] The Zionist newspaper maintained this upbeat mood—at odds with other German Jewish publications—despite the fact that Jewish representatives were not even going to be allowed to address the conference and make a direct appeal for help.[96]

Weltsch was temperamentally optimistic and idealistic. Any event that appeared to support Jewish emigration and help build a Jewish homeland had an immense appeal for him. The Évian conference looked, to him, like the lifeline the Jews so badly needed. Pressure exerted there by other nations would force the British to let more Jews into Palestine. Only large-scale resettlement there could rescue Germany's Jews from what Weltsch described to Chaim Weizmann as their collective state of depression.[97]

Weltsch was committed to departing for Palestine as soon as he could pull together the needed funds and paperwork. His own mood was depressed, the result of struggling to keep his newspaper afloat and enduring years of hostility and insecurity in Hitler's Reich. (In January he and other Jewish journalists had been placed under the authority of the Propaganda Ministry's Hans Hinkel—a move that signaled the imminent end to their years of relative independence.)[98] For all these reasons, Weltsch was inclined to hope for progress at the French town of restorative waters.

Max Warburg was not so eager for Évian to be a smashing success. The last thing he wanted was for masses of European Jews to descend on remote corners of the globe, stirring up trouble—and more anti-Semitism. Even in the wake of the Anschluss, he still wanted an exodus to occur at a measured pace. "Forcing the rate of emigration," he reasoned, "would defeat its own ends."[99] Warburg was so concerned about Jews behaving properly (demonstrating an exemplary "uprightness")[100] abroad so as to not cast aspersion on their race that he sometimes sounded indifferent to the fear and anguish that were driving Jews out of their country. He came across a little like a hotel manager insisting that his guests take off their pajamas and put on coats and ties before exiting a fire-engulfed lobby. In his defense, Warburg realized that it would do the Jews no good simply to get out of Germany unless they had a country of refuge. For this to happen, a lot of delicate diplomatic wooing had to take place first. Évian was part of that process, not a miraculous answer to Jewish prayers.

Many Jews were just as worn down by Nazi persecution and intimidation as Robert Weltsch was. The Gestapo had arrested Leo Baeck several times, in addition to his humiliating encounter in April 1937. Baeck had managed to hold his own in this grim game, but the struggle had cost him dearly. The spiritual head of German Jewry could no longer turn to his devoted wife Natalie for support, and increasingly he felt besieged on all sides. The attacks on his leadership by Georg Kareski and a coterie of Berlin Jews, led by Heinrich Stahl, had robbed him of his energy and usual resilience. Nonetheless, Baeck kept up his daily rituals, writing to friends and colleagues on their birthdays and hosting others on the Sabbath.[101] But these reassuring routines could not really divert his attention from the reality that was pressing in on his people. Baeck had joined in urging President Roosevelt to take up the cause of imperiled European Jewry, and so he was naturally pleased to hear the Évian conference announced. He and the other top officials of the Reichsvertretung approached the proceedings with an earnest resolve to see them succeed. For their part, the Reichsvertretung leaders prepared a seventeen-page report, complete with lists of vital statistics on the German Jewish community, to assist the conferees in their deliberations. They began the report by pledging: "The Jews of Germany are determined to exert all their strength, to place their organizational and financial leadership ability in the service of the progress of a major emigration plan."[102]

The unaddressed question was: "How much organizational and financial authority did these German Jews still have?" As evidenced by their minor role at Évian, the answer was: "Not much." In its report, the Reichsvertretung stated that it was inimical to Jewish families to require a set sum of money to be in the hands of each would-be emigrant; instead, families should be treated as a unit. Furthermore, host countries should be in a position to offer arriving Jews a means of earning a living. The list of recommendations in the report was thorough and sincere. It also bespoke a naive trust in the goodwill of other nations. (As several cynical observers pointed out, "Évian" spelled backwards was "naive.")

Bella Fromm had few such illusions left. She had spent enough time with diplomats to understand the self-serving games they played. Their unwillingness to embrace thousands of helpless, impoverished, undesired Jews was all too apparent. Although these diplomats might respect and genuinely like "Frau Bella" and even go out of their way to help her if they could, their personal interest in her could not be extended to mean a concern for all German Jewry, or a desire to find them new homes. More and more removed from Berlin's high society, Fromm spent most of her time trying to obtain a passport and the other papers she needed to escape from Germany.

Rather than place her trust in international conferences and the words of presidents, she sought her own personal escape route. A friendly SS official she dubbed "Karl" helped her untangle the mass of red tape surrounding her tax records, which had to be cleared up before she could receive her passport.[103] To her application to emigrate, Fromm attached a letter of recommendation from Wolf Heinrich Count von Helldorf—the Berlin police president—that certainly did not hurt her case. She could also give a general in the German army as a character reference.[104] The American consul general in Berlin, Raymond Geist, provided additional help in getting a visa for the United States and vouching for her character.[105] Through the intervention of other friends, the U.S. Chamber of Commerce had agreed to recommend Fromm for a visa, on the grounds that she would be able to sell her family's wines on the other side of the Atlantic.

Despite these formidable allies, Fromm made little headway with the Nazi authorities. In June 1938, six months after she filed her application, she still did not have a passport. A friend in the Gestapo told her that she would eventually get one, but cautioned she would not be able to leave Germany with much else.[106] During a Fourth of July garden party hosted by the new American ambassador, Hugh Wilson, her friend "Rolf" Mumm took her aside and asked:

Have you been in the north of Berlin lately? There's something going on. The concentration camps are being enlarged. Better get out, Bella. . . . Here you can't help much more. Nobody can. If we don't stop interfering for your "public enemies," we'll all land in concentration camps ourselves. Outside Germany, you may be of greater help than within these walls.[107]

Hans-Joachim Schoeps was pretty much on his own in finding a way out of the Third Reich. And he was having no luck in the early summer of 1938. The foreign universities and schools he approached had no place for him. Polite letters of rejection were all that he received. One came from a rural school in southern Sweden, another from the philosophy faculty at the University of Reykjavík (Iceland).[108] There were some encouraging words about his being able to do research in England, but Schoeps would not be allowed to work in that country.[109] Even another trip to Scandinavia in June failed to accomplish anything but make his asthma worse.[110] All this time the Gestapo was pressuring him to leave the country. (In August Schoeps dashed off an appeal for help in gaining an entry visa and work permit for Norway, saying that "compelling external reasons" were forcing him to quit the Reich.)[111] Every time he spoke in public or attended a meeting, he feared that the Nazis might use this particular event as an excuse to move against him—arrest him, or worse. His arrest during the winter of 1935–36, on a charge of high treason, had made him more frightened and more cautious. To lessen his risk, Schoeps dumped most of his writings into the Spree Canal at some point in late 1937 or 1938.[112] Presumably many of these documents detailed his plan for including Jews in the Third Reich's future—a point of view now even less popular with the authorities. Although he often succeeded in giving his Gestapo "shadow" the slip in Berlin's crowded streets, Schoeps was regularly called in for questioning about his activities and associations. According to what he revealed years afterward, the Gestapo was keenly interested in what they believed was a "world Jewish movement." Schoeps's suspected knowledge of this movement intrigued his interrogators enough that they protected him as a source and spared him imprisonment.[113]

While Schoeps was vacationing on the North Sea island of Helgoland before heading back to Denmark in his persistent search for a teaching job, the thoughts of many of his fellow German Jews were turned apprehensively to the French village of Évian, along the banks of Lake Geneva. On July 6, 1938, some 140 representatives from 32 nations (of the major European powers, only Italy stayed away), along with delegates from 40 private aid agencies and a sizable press contingent, congregated for nine days at the Hôtel Royal to discuss the growing refugee crisis. (The conference was taking place in France because the Swiss, wary of offending the Nazis, had declined to host it.) This event was billed as the greatest humanitarian undertaking of the year. To attest to their interest—and to stay well informed—German Jewish groups dispatched their most prominent members to attend, if only to wait expectantly in the wings. The head of the American delegation, Myron C. Taylor, a former president of U.S. Steel and a personal friend of President Roosevelt, raised their hopes by declaring he expected that Évian would produce "the best possible results."[114]

The Reichsvertretung was represented by Otto Hirsch, its second-highest official (after Leo Baeck), as well as by Michael Traub, of the Palestine Office, and Paul Eppstein. Zionist leaders Kurt Blumenfeld and Siegfried Moses journeyed all the way from Palestine to attend. Dr. Werner Rosenberg headed a delegation from Warburg's Hilfsverein. At the start of the conference, Earl Winterton met privately with the Reichsvertretung delegates. He listened to Hirsch express hopes that the German government was prepared to permit those Jews who desired to leave the country the right to take a third of their assets with them. Hirsch estimated that this number would encompass some 200,000 Jews, with the rest either too old or too infirm to leave. He also gave his opinion that the government would be prepared to negotiate terms for this mass emigration with the Reichsvertretung once the Évian conference was over. Hirsch, speaking for Baeck, was playing a shrewd poker game: He clearly realized that three sides had to reach agreement if the Jews were to escape Hitler's clutches—the Nazi government, the Jews themselves, and the prospective host nations. In speaking to Britain's chief spokesman at Évian, Hirsch was signaling the willingness of two of these parties to promote a large-scale exodus. All that was missing was a welcoming destination—namely, Palestine. It would be up to the British to deliver that.

But the British were not ready to do any such thing. Secretly, Neville Chamberlain's government had urged the hosting Americans to keep

Palestine off the agenda at Évian, so Earl Winterton would not have to publicly reject the expansion of Jewish immigration.[115] With the suppliant German Jewish leaders who sought him out, he was unfailingly polite but just as firm: The United Kingdom would offer additional visas only to a few hundred would-be émigrés bound for colonial Africa. He brushed off talk of raising the quota ceiling on visas for Palestine.

When Winterton rose to speak to the conferees, he made the same points: It was next to impossible for a country like Britain to absorb more refugees, either within the United Kingdom itself or in the rest of the vast British Empire. He pointedly made no reference to Palestine. His tone was subdued, restrained. Like the American and French representatives, Winterton did not want to arouse Hitler's ire by making a frontal attack on German anti-Semitic policies and their consequences.[116] His speech mirrored the general tone of the gathering. The Évian conference was taking place amid great expectations, but the mood of the delegates was decidedly low key. No one was going to make big promises. (The American chief delegate, Taylor, did state in his opening remarks that the United States was willing to make all 27,370 quota slots for Austria and Germany available for the first time, but *not* to increase their number. He further warned against "dumping" German Jews on the international market.)[117] Issues were to be talked around. (Instead of mentioning the Jews by name, speakers referred to "involuntary emigrants" and "political refugees.") The Jews had to understand that the refugee problem was complex, politically charged, and not readily solvable. (A July magazine poll in the United States showed just how unpopular any upswing in immigration from Europe was: 67.4 percent wanted to keep the refugees out.)[118] No one should hope for miracles.

When all the speeches and deliberations ended on July 15, 1938, there was little concrete action to applaud. The delegates had agreed to establish an Inter-Governmental Committee for Refugees (ICR), with thirty-two nations participating, to oversee and direct international efforts to aid European Jews. The refugee board was to be led by George Rublee, a seventy-year-old international lawyer who was also a friend of President Roosevelt from their days at Groton. Rublee was given full authority to negotiate on the Jews' behalf with the Nazi government. But otherwise not much had changed. Of all the countries represented, only the tiny Dominican Republic had gone on record as willing to take in a large number of refugees. The others had firmly held their ground. They had decreed that "involuntary emigration" should be financed privately, not by governments. No delegate had risen to plead for funds to assist the Jews before it was too late. No one had hinted that it might already be too late.

In public, the German Jewish groups tried to see these results in a positive light. Conceding that not all their hopes had been fulfilled, Robert Weltsch's newspaper, the *Jüdische Rundschau* reported that the most important thing about the Évian conference was that it had taken place. Finally, the attention of the world had been focused on the Jewish plight ("one of the great public problems of our time"), and the urgency of the Jews' situation had been at least tacitly acknowledged. Now, with the United States taking the lead through the ICR, real progress could occur.[119] Leo Baeck's Reichsvertretung took a moderately optimistic stance: Emigration was not an inextricable problem, but it did require more foreign money.[120] The *Centralverein Zeitung* was also quick to praise the concern expressed at the Évian conference, as well as the leading role played by the American delegation. The newspaper declared that the conference was "the first step" toward ending the Jews' dilemma, even though it remained unclear how matters would move forward. An exodus to undeveloped countries in Africa, Asia, and Latin America seemed financially unfeasible, and no delegation had suggested Palestine as a panacea. The best way to assess the immediate future, the newspaper ventured, was as a time to "pause for inspiration," for thinking and plans to jell.[121] Once again the voices raised on behalf of German Jewry would sadly misread the signs of what lay in store for them.

11

The Night of Broken Glass

The Nazis had watched the proceedings at the Évian closely, too. And they were just as disappointed as the German Jews by the lack of results. For some time now, German officials had noted with consternation how the rate of Jewish emigration was steadily falling, not exactly what they wanted. A report by the Sicherheitsdienst (Security Service) in January 1938 had put the 1937 level on par with that of 1934. It was highly questionable if a continued emigration at this pace could settle the "Jewish problem" within an acceptable period, the report concluded.[1] The impatience evident in this document and in the statements of the more radical anti-Semites in the Nazi Party was only intensified by the results of the Évian gathering. The flat refusal of the attending nations to ease open their borders in the slightest could only be interpreted in one way: The Jews would not be getting out as fast as the Nazis wanted. If Germany was to become rapidly "free of Jews," more drastic steps would have to be taken to push the Jews out, regardless of whether any country was willing to take them in. Normal rules and procedures would have to dispensed with. Within Germany, harassment would have to give way to "shock tactics" and the threat of force. As Adolf Eichmann had demonstrated in Austria, this method worked.[2]

Time was now of the essence for Hitler. He was bent on adding Czechoslovakia to Germany's expanding empire. This exercise in diplomatic intimidation ran the decided risk of sparking a European war. The Nazi leader wanted the Jews out of his way before it came to that.

But in the immediate aftermath of the Évian conference, German Jews faced more demeaning restrictions, not stepped-up violence. Starting July 28, every one of them, even infants over three months old, was required to carry identification cards designating them as *Juden*. In Berlin, Jews could now sit on only the few park benches set aside for them.[3] A law, announced on August 2, 1938, expelled all Jewish physicians (including World War I veterans) from the profession by the end of September, allowing only a limited number to continue to treat Jewish patients in the capacity of "healers."[4] This law ended the careers of nearly all the remaining Jewish doctors in Germany, some four hundred in Berlin alone. A similar ban on Jewish commercial travelers was also promulgated.[5] Starting in mid-August, all Jews were compelled to add Jewish first names to their own, as an earlier proclaimed law came into effect.

In a kind of goal-line stand, organized German Jewry regrouped one more time, finally achieving, as the clock was running out, the real unity that had eluded the community for so many years. With the *Gemeinden* (Jewish communities) and all other Jewish organizations facing the loss of their tax-levying power, the Reichsvertretung der Juden in Deutschland (National Representation of the Jews in Germany) met, in late July 1938, and agreed to reconstitute itself as a private entity, calling itself the Reichsverband der Juden in Deutschland (the National Association of Jews in Germany). This body was to be given a stronger central authority, absorbing the power of the regional Jewish associations, or *Landesverbände*, which were voluntarily dissolved. Zionists were granted an equal share of power with non-Zionists, prompting the *Jüdische Rundschau* to hail formation of this new body as a "milestone" in German Jewish history.[6]

As one might have anticipated, Leo Baeck was chosen to lead this new organization. He accepted this duty by acknowledging that his was a lost cause. In the past, Baeck told his assembled colleagues, he and other leaders had tried to "ban the threatening specter of chaos" from the Jewish community. "We have met all our troubles with trust in God and with our self-respect . . . we have created a new inner order and new forms of spiritual and material self-help." But then Baeck's remarks took a more despondent turn. Even he could not pretend any longer that these years of perseverence would ultimately make any difference. At best, they had sustained Jews while staying in Germany was still an option for them. This era was now ending, as Baeck had privately admitted back in 1933. So, too, was the strength of those who had borne the weight of the entire community on their shoulders. "There can be no doubt that this continuing, extraordinary exertion of our energies has its limits," the gaunt-faced rabbi confessed. "Even more narrow has the realm of our existence become . . . our energies threaten to fail us." In this dark mood Baeck could find some cause for hope only in the little that the Évian conference had accomplished. (A more sanguine Otto Hirsch claimed that one could see "light at the end of the tunnel" after the conference.)[7] This hope was that borders around the world would now open to Germany's Jews. "In us lives the desire for a life prepared for sacrifice in the free air of the world. In us lives the will to link our existence with the work of peaceful [Palestine] development."[8] Exhausted themselves, the Jews would have to depend on help from others to make this happen.[9]

It was a faint hope, articulated without a great deal of conviction. Baeck had closely followed what Myron Taylor, Earl Winterton, and representatives of the other nations had said at Évian a few weeks before, and there was little in their words to make him believe that his people would now be permitted to build a new home in Palestine, or anywhere else in the world. But, as he had declined in the past to bare his innermost thoughts about the fate of the Jewish community under Hitler, so now Baeck glossed over these harsh, irrefutable facts.

His fellow Jews were discovering them for themselves. Hans-Joachim Schoeps had barely returned from a frustrating four-week job hunt in Denmark when he had what he described as a very "unpleasant" meeting with the Gestapo.[10] He had been summoned to secret police headquarters, interrogated about his failed Scandinavian trip, and then been curtly told that he had to leave Germany within six weeks.[11] Schoeps confided to a professor in Basel that he planned to go first to neighboring Switzerland, where he hoped to give lectures on "thinkers of tragic existence."[12] Then, after a few months, he would seek a more permanent sanctuary elsewhere. A month later Schoeps was still waiting to carry out these plans, having sought in vain during the interim to land a post in either England or Sweden.[13] At some point in 1938, he had spoken to Leo Baeck, who had asked him to serve as an emissary to the Confessional Church (a Protestant movement founded by Martin Niemöller that was, to some extent, opposed to the Nazis' treatment of the Jews.)[14] As someone who looked up to Baeck as a "fatherly friend and pastor,"[15] Schoeps had readily agreed to take on this dangerous mission, although it is not clear exactly what it entailed.

That summer Bella Fromm was also stymied in her bid to leave Germany by events beyond her control. But her problems were mainly bureaucratic. Even with Herbert Mumm's (Rolf's) help, the processing of her papers had assumed Kafkaesque dimensions. In early August 1938 Fromm recorded with apparent frustration in her diary: "I simply can't imagine how other emigrants, without any wires to pull, ever manage to overcome the abyss of deliberate difficulties." Among the obstructions was a requirement that she pay all her taxes one year in advance—another type of "flight tax" levied by the Nazis.[16] To speed up matters at the passport office, Fromm appeared there one day decked out in her World War I medals. A week before she was finally due to receive her visa, Fromm had still not succeeded in acquiring all the necessary clearances to quit Germany, and so, heeding American Ambassador William E. Dodd's advice, she reluctantly turned to a powerful personage whom she despised, Hjalmar Schacht. Now holding the position of minister without portfolio in Hitler's cabinet, this self-proclaimed friend of Germany's Jews saw to it that Fromm's paperwork at the foreign exchange office was expedited.[17] An impressed but puzzled customs official asked her: "What have you done that the highest Nazis go to bat for you?"[18]

A week later, on August 18, after waiting in line for almost six hours outside the U.S. consulate, "Frau Bella" was finally handed the precious document. (Explaining to her diplomat friends Cyrus Follmer and DeWitt Warner why she had not told them of her arrival and spared herself the long wait, Fromm replied, somewhat disingenuously, that she had not wanted any "special privileges." She had also wanted to surprise her American friends.) Fromm promptly kissed the official gold seal on the visa, crying with happiness.[19] All she had to do now was book passage and pack her bags for the United States.

Coincidentally, just two days before, Max Warburg had revealed similar plans of his own: He would be heading to New York at the end of the month, but only to stay for one or two months.[20] He would take his wife and daughter Gisela with him, to see American relatives, and then return to carry on his work on behalf of Jewish welfare organizations.[21] Just before he was to depart, Warburg spoke with Earl Winterton about future Jewish emigration. The banker was concerned that the impoverishment of Jews would induce a massive number of them to go abroad—they simply could not live much longer in Germany on diminishing bank accounts alone. The German Foreign Office might wish them to leave, but Warburg thought the result would be counterproductive: Countries that might be receptive to taking in *some* refugees would quickly raise their barriers to such an undesirable Jewish element. (In the aftermath of the Évian conference, it is not easy to imagine what countries he may have had in mind.)

Warburg wanted the newly formed Inter-Governmental Committee on Refugees (ICR) to exert its influence to convince the Foreign Ministry *not* to accelerate the flow of emigrants. To make the exodus successful, he further recommended a plan that would enable Jews to invest in German companies located in "host" countries. This would be the only way, he believed, for Jews to remove any of their wealth from the Reich. The Nazis were no longer amenable to a direct transfer of assets and would not be willing to meet with the ICR's head, George Rublee, to discuss this topic.[22] (Thus far Rublee's group had made no headway in exploring negotiations with the Hitler regime. Initial overtures after Évian had been rebuffed. Furthermore, the British had expressed reluctance to have this subject aired with the Germans, as it might lead to more pressure on Great Britain to increase the number of visas for Palestine. Compounding all this, tensions surrounding the Munich crisis of September 1938 would make talks between the ICR and Germany on the refugee question untenable.) Even at this late date, Warburg had not given up on his goal of reaching some kind of agreement with the Nazis that would give the Jews a good chance of starting new lives overseas. Indeed, his optimism would actually bear fruit several months later. But by then, Warburg would no longer be in the picture. His temporary relocation to the United States would have become a permanent one.

August 1938 also found Robert Weltsch pondering a future for himself outside Germany with greater urgency—and despair. A recent escalation of Arab violence in Palestine had reminded him there was no guarantee that peace awaited Jews wishing to flee Nazi Germany. The German Jews could be seen as jumping out of the frying pan into the fire. Weltsch could foresee Palestine remaining a bloody battlefield for years to come. And, even if this did not happen, he was not confident that he would ever reach Palestinian shores: Visas were hard to come by. An alternative destination, such as the United States, seemed even more remote. (In August, another possible haven, Argentina, tightened its immigration policy due to growing domestic unemployment.)[23] The visa quota for the United States was filled until March 1939. At the same time, matters were growing unbearable for Weltsch in Berlin. The authorities were beginning to make life very "unpleasant" for Jewish newspapers and their editors. Like Baeck and many other Jews who had suffered Nazi persecution for years, Weltsch was now simply too weary to cope with more anti-Semitic restrictions. He felt trapped, exhausted, "horribly depressed."[24]

There was good cause for Weltsch's angst. Toward the end of August, it appeared likely that Hitler would go to war over his claim to the Sudetenland. (The Führer participated in ominous naval war games in the Baltic on August 23.)[25] In such an eventuality, Jews could expect short shrift: The Jewish Telegraphic Agency published a report about ten thousand penniless Jews being "dumped" abroad to save the Reich money if the anticipated conflict materialized.[26] As fences continued to go up around the world (Brazil followed Argentina in forestalling a Jewish influx by setting a quota that limited the number of immigrants to 2 percent of the total which had arrived from a particular country over the past fifty years),[27] some Jewish spokesmen continued to deny the inevitable. When Rublee's ICR convened its first meeting in London at the end of August 1938, the liberal *Centralverein Zeitung* was heartened just as it had been on the eve of the Évian conference. It seemed it would take Rublee another two weeks to get down to business, and the best advice the newspaper could offer its Jewish readers in the meantime was to remain patient, to wait just a little more. The editorial struck the same tone as what many Jewish leaders had been saying back in 1933.[28]

Bella Fromm was not going to wait any more. The day after this edi-torial appeared, an "enormous shipping van" pulled up outside her house, at Augsburgerstrasse 44, just south of Berlin's Zoologischer Garten. She had paid a bribe and the exorbitant price of 2,500 reichs-marks to acquire this means of shipping her furniture and other belong-ings to the United States.[29] After two days of packing, the van was sealed and ready for departure. So was Fromm. At the last minute she found out that she would also need a visa for Belgium because her train would be crossing its territory. This visa was speedily procured. At nine that evening she went down to the same platform at the same railroad station where her daughter Gonny had departed four years before, to catch the night express for Paris. "Rolf" came with her, dressed incon-spicuously in civilian clothes. He had told Fromm that if he ever had to go to battle wearing a German uniform, he would turn around and shoot in the other direction.[30]

It was a brief, sad farewell. After the train pulled out of Berlin, head-ing due west, Fromm managed to fall asleep but was rudely awakened at two in the morning on the German-Belgian frontier. Nazi customs offi-cials entered her compartment, demanding to see what she had in her two suitcases. In their search they discovered some pieces of family jew-elry and accused Fromm of trying to smuggle them out of the country. They called her a "Jewish whore" and bullied her into signing a confes-sion and handing over the jewelry. The statement she had to sign read:

I am a Jewish thief and have tried to rob Germany by taking German wealth out of the country. I hereby confess that the jewels found on me do not belong to me and that in trying to take them out, I was eager to inflict injury on Germany. Furthermore, I promise never to try to reenter Germany.[31]

Then they left her, and with only her purse, a pair of disheveled suit-cases, and a concealed 100-mark note on her person, in the dead of night, five years and nine months after Adolf Hitler had assumed con-trol over her country, Bella Fromm passed over the border to safety. She shed "tears of liberation," noting derisively in her diary that this was a country to get out of even if one had to leave naked.[32]

On September 6, Fromm reached Paris, where she collected all the parcels, trunks, and suitcases, including pages from her diary, that she had sent there through diplomat friends over the past several years.

Three days later, with her papers safe in her hands, she strode confidently up the gangplank of the SS *Normandie,* the "gorgeous boat" that was to take her to her new home in the New World and to her daughter. On deck as the stately but doomed ocean liner cleaved the waves, Fromm could not yet fully relish her good fortune, her freedom, her escape from Hitler. "I find I cannot yet stand fun and laughter," she wrote. "A paperhanger from Austria did that to me."[33]

Fromm was not the only German Jew in transit during September 1938. Many of her race were ignoring the stale advice to "wait and see" and were racing for the exits on the eve of Rosh Hashanah, the beginning of the year 5699 since the Creation, a thousand or so years since Jews had permanently settled in what was now known as the Third Reich. To mark this solemn day in the Jewish calendar, Leo Baeck and Otto Hirsch offered the consolation of history to those still left in their community, nearly overwhelmed as they were by doubt and despair. Their argument was familiar: As in the past, Jews now could take comfort in the inner renewal that always arose from these trials of the spirit. Now Palestine offered this same hope. But it was hope reserved mainly for the young. Representing the Reichsvertretung, Baeck and Hirsch addressed their words more to those who were not going to depart for the promised homeland: "We Jews are a race that is used to waiting," the two men reminded their readers. "Palestine is our strength." This strength came ultimately from faith, and this was unshakable. In it, "we have already stood upright." Perseverance belonged to those Jews who now clung fast to this age-old surety: "We Jews are the race that is sure of eternity. As we are with God, so must God be with us."[34]

But the message of faith was not enough. It was not enough for Robert Weltsch, who suddenly felt himself at great peril. If Germany did go to war over Czechoslovakia—which was still a strong possibility—he might be interned, as a Czech citizen, for the duration. "Detention" could easily become a euphemism for worse horrors. Weltsch knew enough of the Nazis' methods to realize this. So, on the second day of Rosh Hashanah, a day normally devoted to spiritual introspection and atonement, Weltsch booked a seat on a flight for Warsaw, the first stop on his odyssey to the Middle East.[35]

Weltsch left with a bad taste in his mouth, caused not so much by what the Nazis had done to his adopted country as by what his fellow Jews had done, or rather *not* done. Looking back at five years of Hitler's rule, he saw only Jewish blunders, Jewish passivity, and Jewish naïveté about what they had confronted. "It is a bitter recognition that every Zionist brings with him from a European trip," he wrote once he had reached the safety of Palestine. "Jewry has not fought the Nazis in any systematic way." During these five years, German Jews had not made a single attempt to respond to Nazi anti-Semitic slander. Instead, they had played it safe, hoping in this way not to antagonize and provoke their tormentors. But their argument that this strategy would keep things from getting worse was dead wrong because things were already terrible. It was all stupidity, Weltsch realized in retrospect. Even now the Jews had not faced up to the true nature of the danger: A war of annihilation was being waged against them; to say "it can't happen here" was the final act of self-deception.[36]

This was an odd summation for a journalist and editor who had urged Jews symbolically to wear a yellow badge with pride to affirm their Judaism; who had hailed the renaissance of Judaism under the Nazis; who had, in the pages of his newspaper, consistently refrained from sounding the alarm about the mounting anti-Semitism in the early 1930s; and who had focused his editorial output on Jewish culture and the Jewish future in faraway Palestine. It sounded, indeed, like an outburst of self-condemnation, held in check until Weltsch had fled the pressure-cooker world of Nazi Berlin and his public responsibilities to the German Zionist cause.[37]

Religious faith was not enough for Richard Willstätter, either. Willstätter's entire life had been guided by another kind of belief—in the power of the human mind to penetrate and comprehend the mysteries of the natural world. This power was, he believed, immune to the scourge of politics and social upheaval. It had kept him going through the long years of the Nazi nightmare by reminding him that human beings were capable of at least some kind of genuine progress. Now he was being slowed down by the frailties of his own physical being. But Willstätter's work was not yet finished, and he wanted to keep at it as long as he was able. Going into exile abroad would be an unnecessary distraction and a disruption of that essential task; it was as if he were being forced to leave his laboratory because of some small electrical fire elsewhere in the building. Willstätter still felt he was above the fray, sacrosanct, protected by the respect and deference his fellow Germans extended to a scientist of his international stature. This was a notion that made eminent sense to a monarchist like him but had no validity in the raucous, teeming streets.

Willstätter's more worldly friends sized up the situation without any such illusions. From his vantage point in Switzerland, Arthur Stoll, Willstätter's former student, could see that the days of German Jewry were coming to an end. None would escape the Nazis' wrath. To save Willstätter, Stoll invited him to be his guest in the small town of Arlesheim, near Basel, in the second half of September 1938. He intended to keep Willstätter from returning, to make it plain to him what a frightful mistake that would be. Willstätter came, listened, but was not swayed. With Weltsch already en route to Palestine and Bella Fromm reunited with her daughter in New York, he turned back, to the fatherland that wished him gone.[38]

As much as the Nazis wanted to expel the Jews, they were now thwarted by restrictions abroad. Neighboring Switzerland, for instance, invalidated all Jewish passports on October 5 and then issued new ones clearly marked with a red "J" to curb an influx of unwanted German Jews.[39] Willstätter had barely returned to Munich when this policy was announced on the radio. It had the undesired consequence, for Jews and Nazis alike, of making emigration even more difficult.

Meanwhile, in the aftermath of the Munich pact signed by Hitler and British Prime Minister Neville Chamberlain on September 30, giving Germany the Sudetenland, Jews faced more restraints on their already diminished rights. The Nazis hoped these moves would convince them to get out. Jewish lawyers were to be disbarred, except for a few who could continue to represent Jewish clients as legal "consultants."[40] This restriction, coming on the heels of a similar ban on Jewish physicians, was crippling to the community's economic life. And what the Jews did not know was that on October 18, 1938, Goering revealed to top Nazi officials that these measures were merely a prelude to a more systematic and far-reaching suppression of Jewish life. The Jewish problem, he declared, had to be dealt with by all means available. His goal was to drive Jews completely out of the German economy.[41] There was some speculation, in Heinrich Himmler's SS newspaper *Das Schwarze Korps*, that the Jews remaining in Germany would be held as hostages to preclude attacks on the Nazi state by Jews elsewhere in the world.[42]

The renewed crackdown left Hans-Joachim Schoeps helpless. The loss of his passport meant he could not make any further trips abroad in search of employment. "The world—not just Europe—is closed!" he exclaimed in desperation to Martin Rade. France was his last hope, and it was a faint one.[43]

The same week that Schoeps penned this letter, European Jews were buffeted by two major blows that further reduced their options. The first was announcement of the quota for Palestine for the coming six months; 2,000 Jewish "capitalists" (with assets of £1,000 [$4,000] or more), 1,000 workers, and 800 relatives of émigrés would be allowed into the country. That was all. This was the British response to the Évian conference.[44]

The second blow came right after the first. The Polish government proclaimed it was requiring all its citizens abroad to renew their passports by the end of the month or they would forfeit their citizenship. This was seen by the German authorities as a thinly veiled attempt to "dump" these unwanted Jews, numbering in the tens of thousands, in their lap. Deadlocked in negotiations with the Poles as the deadline neared, the Germans took matters into their own hands. On the eve of the final date set for renewing the passports, Gestapo agents rounded up some 17,000 Polish Jews[45] (3,000 in Berlin alone)[46]—the first large-scale action of this kind carried out by the Nazis. The hapless Poles were packed into special sealed trains and shuttled to the border. There they were herded into the "no man's land" that separated Poland from the Third Reich. If the Polish government did not agree to take them back, these unfortunate, stateless Jews would starve to death. Instead, the Poles only tried to push the Jews back into Germany.

After finding temporary shelter in a border town, the expelled Jews were finally permitted to reenter their country, thanks to pressure brought by other Polish Jews. During this time, *Das Schwarze Korps* published a piece calling for the expulsion from the Reich of *all* foreign Jews—an indication that radically anti-Semitic elements in the Nazi hierarchy welcomed this Polish crisis as an invitation to take more far-ranging steps.[47]

Events then took a dramatic, unexpected turn. On November 7, 1938, a teenage Polish Jew named Herschel Grynszpan walked into the German embassy in Paris, claimed he was in possession of secret documents, and asked to speak to a member of the embassy staff. He was shown into the office of Ernst vom Rath, a twenty-nine-year-old legation secretary who happened to be an opponent of the Nazi regime. After sitting briefly in vom Rath's office, Grynszpan suddenly called him a "filthy kraut," pulled out a concealed revolver, and fired five times, striking the embassy official twice and wounding him mortally.[48]

The shooting sent shock waves through the German Jewish community, as Nazi radio and newspapers immediately demanded retaliation for Grynszpan's crime. Jews in Germany were now considered "hostages."[49] Joseph Goebbels's mouthpiece, *Der Angriff,* called for "the sharpest measures against Jews," urging other nations to unite "for ruthless war against the international Jewish menace and against Jewish murder and Jewish crime."[50] While vom Rath's life hung in the balance, sporadic anti-Jewish rioting broke out in various German cities. In Kassel a synagogue was wrecked in a "spontaneous" display of outrage. The Berlin police chief, Count Helldorf, announced that Jews in the capital had been effectively disarmed over the past few weeks with the confiscation of several thousand handguns and ammunition. The *Jüdische Rundschau* and other Jewish newspapers were shut down (making it impossible to print a statement from the Reichsvertretung expressing the dismay of Germany's Jews at this shooting).[51] On the night of November 8, Hitler spoke to the Nazi "old guard" at its annual Munich beer-hall reunion, but he gave no hint of what he might do to settle accounts with the Jews.[52] (The Führer unleashed his anger instead at the supposed role of the Jews in bringing on Germany's economic collapse after World War I.)[53] However, speaking before the same assemblage of putsch participants, Goebbels bluntly called for "revenge." The word immediately went out to SA groups around the Reich to launch an unprecedented assault against the Jews—a "spontaneous" pogrom that the Nazis had, in fact, been planning for some time.[54] The party and Hitler himself were to remain aloof from the violence. At 4:30 P.M. on November 9, Ernst vom Rath died of his wounds, and the retaliation began.

With lights ablaze in its headquarters all night, the Gestapo watched over a loosely coordinated orgy of violence in Berlin, starting at 2 A.M. on November 10, after police had blocked off Jewish-owned businesses and cut their telephone lines. Police were instructed not to interfere with what was to ensue. Starting in Munich, some five hundred synagogues throughout Germany were set on fire in the early morning hours, and many of them, including Berlin's famed Fasanenstrasse synagogue, burned to the ground in front of jeering SA throngs. Windows of hundreds of Jewish shops on Berlin's Kurfürstendamm, Unter den Linden, and Tauenzienstrasse were shattered, their wares hurled onto the streets; looters hauled away what jewelry, fur, furniture, and other items they could carry.[55] Offices of Jewish organizations and apartments owned by

Jews were ransacked. The Zionist headquarters on the Meineckestrasse was reduced to "splintered wood and mounds of torn records."[56] A total of seven thousand Jewish businesses were destroyed. In Berlin suburbs Jewish mansions were invaded, the men inside arrested and the women raped. Ninety Jews were killed, and some thirty thousand men were imprisoned in concentration camps for "protective custody"[57] in what was accurately described as "the worst pogrom in modern German history."[58] By late afternoon on November 10, a radio announcement by Goebbels declared that the anti-Jewish action—to be later known as *Kristallnacht*, or the Night of the Broken Glass—was over after having accomplished its "desired and expected purpose."

But once out of the bottle, violence was not so easily stopped. Not until dawn on the November 11 did the rioting and looting in most locales cease, and even then the arrest of Jews continued. (In Munich Hitler had called off the pogrom earlier, after the public response to it had been "disappointing.")[59] Among those picked up was Otto Hirsch, Leo Baeck's closest associate in the Reichsvertretung, who was sent to Oranienburg. Baeck was spared incarceration because of his age but was subjected to further degradation by being made to stand facing a wall for three hours while waiting to see a low-ranking Nazi official.[60] He was then told by the Gestapo to stay in his apartment. Other Jewish leaders had to flee their homes at night, to avoid arrest, and for the next several days moved from apartment to apartment to meet secretly and sleep, while during the day, they tried to carry out their official duties. Baeck and his remaining colleagues at the Reichsvertretung frantically attempted to ameliorate the Nazi rampage by seeking to reach officials at the foreign and interior ministries, including state secretary Otto Meissner, chief of Hitler's chancellery.[61] The Jewish spokesmen used the argument that word of Kristallnacht would bring Germany bad publicity abroad. Largely thwarted in these efforts by Himmler and his underlings, they gained some small success when Goebbels agreed to cancel a planned SS parade of arrested Jewish men through the streets of Berlin.[62]

Heads of Jewish newspapers were summoned to the Alexanderplatz headquarters of the Gestapo. Fearing imprisonment, they were released after having been told they would have to cease publication permanently. Thousands of other Jews were let out of concentration camps at Dachau, Buchenwald, Sachsenhausen, and elsewhere after they received a strong dose of Nazi bullying and brutality. They were released only on the condition they would not reveal what had been done to them, but some ignored this warning and went to Baeck's apartment in western Berlin, to fill him in. The rabbi was so moved by these stories of what reminded him of medieval barbarism that he was reduced to tears.[63]

As it turned out, the arrests, looting, and burning of Jewish buildings were only the beginning of this bid to oust Germany's Jews. At a conference on November 12, Goering laid out a series of measures that were designed to reduce the Jewish community to poverty and force its dissolution. It was now high time, he said, to resolve the Jewish question in a well-organized manner. To this end, it was proposed that Jews be prohibited, as of January 1, 1939, from owning retail stores or delivery businesses, as well as from working as independent craftsmen. Jews working for "Aryans" were to be fired. Jews were also to be barred from going to concerts, the cinema, or other forms of public entertainment. They could no longer drive cars or receive public assistance.[64] In effect, what had been left of their cultural and economic life was destroyed. (Paradoxically, the Propaganda Ministry simultaneously ordered the Jewish Cultural Organization—the Kulturbund—to mount a repeat performance of the light comedy it had just staged. After much debate, the Kulturbund agreed to do so, despite the fact that thousands of Jews now languished in Nazi prisons.)[65] But the most ironic and most devastating blow came when it was revealed on the radio, following Goering's instructions, that the German insurance companies that were liable to pay for the damage done to Jewish property were being released from this obligation: The Jews themselves would have to pay for the losses they had suffered at the hands of Nazi mobs. The total bill was put at 1 billion reichsmarks, or $400 million, roughly 3,000 marks for every Jewish man, woman, and child living in the Reich—a sum equal to 20 percent of the community's wealth.

In their zeal to make life in Germany utterly unbearable for the Jews, the Nazis had fallen into the same paradox as in the past: The more they impoverished the Jews and disrupted their lives, the more difficult it became to emigrate. Now, for example, the fact that many leaders of the Reichsvertretung and the Hilfsverein were sitting in prison cells or concentration camps hampered these organizations' ability to handle requests related to emigration.[66] Leo Baeck, for one, told the Gestapo he could not—indeed, would not—resume the Reichsvertretung's efforts (after it had been briefly closed by the authorities) to help Jews leave Germany as long as Otto Hirsch remained imprisoned. "Why, is Hirsch your right-hand man?" Baeck was asked. "No," he replied, "I am Hirsch's left-hand man."[67] However, under Nazi threats and seeing no other realistic alternative, the Reichsvertretung released a statement three days after the Kristallnacht havoc, urging an accelerated exodus of Jews, but it took pains to point out that Jews still needed to find countries that would take them in. This task lay outside the Reichsvertretung's sphere of influence. The best the organization could do was to implore British authorities not to bar the gates to Palestine. To panicked German Jews, the Reichsvertretung could only offer the threadbare advice to "be patient" and meet their "increased obligations" with some residue of self-respect and the will to survive.[68] The next day another restriction was announced: Jews were to be banned from all elementary and secondary schools, as well as from universities in the Reich. Soon all community and youth organizations were similarly prohibited, including the patriotic Reichsbund jüdischer Frontsoldaten (although its members were shown preferential treatment by being released from prison on November 28, ahead of other Jews, who were kept as "hostages" to spur other Jews to leave).[69]

The threats and the street barbarity worked. In the ten months that followed Kristallnacht between 100,000 and 150,000 German Jews departed, roughly as many as had left the Reich during the first six years of Nazi rule.

In its ferocity, Kristallnacht was totally demoralizing to Jews who still clung to frail hopes of persevering under Hitler's yoke, as other Jews had survived earlier periods of oppression and ostracism. It was especially devastating to a man like Leo Baeck who, although he realized that the future of his people lay in Palestine, could not emotionally uproot his Germanic ties and outlook or sincerely ask others of his generation to do so. Somehow, he had thought, older Jews—increasingly the largest group left in the community (by the end of 1938, 73.7 percent of the remaining Jews were aged forty or older)[70]—would be allowed to live out their days in peace, since they posed no threat to the Nazi state.

But now the rampant violence, the arrests, the wanton destruction, had convinced him otherwise. Leo Baeck was a broken man, his optimism finally depleted. When a younger Jewish acquaintance came to visit him on the sunny Thursday after the synagogues had been set on fire, he found the rabbi more despondent than he had ever seen him before, his face contorted with anguish.[71] Another visitor, the newspaper editor Ernst Lowenthal, was startled to find the normally fastidious Baeck in shirtsleeves, looking "bewildered" and "undone."[72] His initial shock at what was happening to Jews all over Germany was compounded by his inability to put a stop to it. To those Nazis he went to see and reason with, Baeck was just another old, groveling Jew taking up their valuable time, deserving only more abuse, another butt for their jokes. Baeck had become just another living manifestation of the caricatured enemy, der Jude. In his heart Baeck had to realize there would be no coming to terms with these thugs, no place in the Nazi realm for any Jews. The only thing to do now was to get out.

But Baeck still bore heavy responsibilities for his fellow Jews—responsibilities he could not, in good conscience, simply walk away from. He was too much of a spiritual leader to do so. Even if the end was now in sight—and the Jews' historical resilience at an end—the chief rabbi vowed to go on serving his people as long as they still needed him. Not long after Kristallnacht, Baeck affirmed to his fellow Berliner, the department store head Wilfrid Israel, that he had no intention of quitting Germany. "I will go when I am the last Jew alive in Germany," he said.[73]

Instead, he tried to pick up whatever fragments of organized Jewish life were still to be found and piece them together. Until other Reichsvertretung leaders were freed, on November 28, Baeck's apartment became the meeting place for his colleagues—a kind of command center for a community driven underground, in disarray, trying to collect information on persons who had been arrested and distribute this news to representatives of the foreign press.[74] Baeck and this inner circle also sought to pass along new policy guidelines on visas, which were relayed to them by various embassies in Berlin.

There was much more to do now, with thousands of Jews making a headlong rush to escape the Gestapo's wrath and with the United States and Great Britain having shown some greater willingness to take in refugees. (From July 1 to November 30, 1938, the United States had issued only 7,701 visas to German citizens.) As Myron Taylor had announced at Évian, the U.S. government was prepared to let refugees from Germany and Austria fill all the available quota slots for those countries. In the wake of Kristallnacht, the State Department still adamantly refused to enlarge this quota, but the demand for the available openings was tremendous. The British, at least for the time being, agreed to take in a greater number of Jews than in the past, and this raised some hopes.

The civilized nations of the world condemned Kristallnacht with resounding moral outrage. President Franklin D. Roosevelt voiced the indignation of the American people by saying "I myself could scarcely believe that such things could occur in a twentieth-century civilization."[75] As a slap in the face to the Nazi regime, he ordered his ambassador, Hugh Wilson, home for "consultation." But beyond these steps, the president was loathe to go—the American people remained opposed to opening their shores to a new wave of European Jews. Roosevelt stuck to the line laid down at Évian that Jews would have to look for a haven elsewhere in the world. (To that end, he instructed Under Secretary of State Sumner Welles, on November 26, to investigate suitable locales for "Jewish colonization.")[76]

In the meantime Baeck and other Jewish leaders had to scramble as best they could to make use of the openings that did exist for would-be émigrés. The specifics of the location no longer mattered. All that mattered was that it be outside Germany. As Max Warburg's associate at the Hilfsverein wrote to the Council for German Jewry, Germany's Jews were now willing to accept "any conditions." The opening of new destinations was now "of vital importance," and any country's offer would be gladly accepted, even from such an unlikely place as British Guyana.[77]

Just how bleak their prospects inside Germany were was spelled out in an article in the SS publication *Das Schwarze Korps.* "Because no power on earth can stop us, we are going to carry out the final solution of the Jewish question," the newspaper boasted. The methods were to be straightforward: Jews would be excluded from the economy and other spheres of German life and enclosed in a ghetto, after all their wealth had been confiscated. Then the Jews were to be destroyed with "fire and the sword." The only hope for them lay in escaping first to Palestine.[78]

Like so many others, Richard Willstätter could no longer deceive himself about his fate inside Germany. He had experienced the Nazi monster firsthand. On the eve of Kristallnacht, his successor at the University of Munich, Heinrich Wieland, had come to his home, bearing a bouquet of flowers and some reassuring words: "No one will dare

touch you." Looking very tired, Willstätter replied grimly that his staying in Germany no longer depended on any "good faith or good
will"—his time had come.[79] He was right. On the following night,
Gestapo officials came looking for him, intending, it appeared, to take
him to Dachau, his age and international renown notwithstanding. As it
happened, Willstätter was waiting outside in his garden, beside his
already-frozen roses, to meet a friend for tea. The Gestapo searched his
house, looking under the bed of Germany's most famous chemist, but
left without finding him. For the next three mornings, Willstätter hid
out in the icy garden, expecting the Gestapo to return. But they did not.
Having escaped a concentration camp "by a hair," he was now, like
Baeck, reduced to despair. He dashed off a "pathetic" letter to the
British Royal Society, declining its invitation for him to give a lecture,
pointing out he had neither the requisite passport nor money to go
abroad. Willstätter conceded that his career, at least in Germany, was
now over; he could not "represent science any longer."[80] The "German
Jews are lost," he acknowledged in another letter. Because he owned a
large, beautiful home, stocked with valuable paintings, furniture, and
other belongings, Willstätter was especially vulnerable to governmental
confiscation, his lawyer advised him. Realizing he could not stay where
he was much longer, the reclusive scientist now ventured forth in search
of the papers he would need to enter Switzerland, where his good friend
Stoll had once again offered him asylum.

But the way out was not easy. Like Baeck and other prominent Jews,
Willstätter was treated as a tottering nuisance, forced to endure long
hours in bare hallways to see low-ranking bureaucrats, who humiliated
him further with their gruff, rude manner. "There can be no question
of right in your case," an official at the foreign exchange office told a
supplicant Willstätter.[81] The local Nazi Blockwart (block leader)
reported to the Gestapo that the chemist had not contributed to the
German winter relief effort (even though, as a Jew, he was not allowed
to do so), whereupon the Gestapo demanded money from him. Someone in the foreign exchange office promised to help Willstätter, but that
person never showed up to see him. Willstätter was further frustrated by
the requirement that he obtain proof, in the form of a copy of his
brother's will, that he actually had financial assets abroad.[82]

The obstacles to getting out of Germany were nearly unsurmount-
able at this late date, and the sixty-six-year-old Willstätter feared he

would never get past them. Impulsively, he set out for the Swiss border without a passport, visa, or money, in his "madness" to flee across Lake Constance and end his ordeal. This was how he described the ensuing adventure in his memoirs:

> Waiting for the American documents and doubting whether they would come at all used up my patience. That was how I, an old man, committed a fateful piece of folly. I drove to the Bodensee, to a town near the border, in order to see whether it was possible to leave the country without a passport and without baggage. It was rainy and stormy, and I tramped about, alone, for hours, in the end thoroughly soaked and tired. Then I wanted to find a tavern or an inn where I could spend the night. But everywhere I came upon the sign, "Entrance to Jews is strictly forbidden." Thereupon I attempted to cross the border in a rowboat. But it miscarried. Then there were examinations that went on for many hours. Although dead tired, I held out until it ended at midnight. The official who was summoned from the secret police was just, and more than that, understanding, humane, and well-meaning. He listened and he understood. I was detained but not arrested. After two days, as my statements were confirmed, I could leave the prison and return as a free man to Munich.[83]

A distressed Stoll now stepped up his efforts to acquire a Swiss visa for Willstätter. The chemist turned down other offers of help from the United States. Despite the presence of his daughter and her family, the country was too remote for him to contemplate living out his days there. He was too old to undertake such a trek, such a huge new beginning.[84] Instead, Willstätter envisioned himself sequestered in some picturesque Swiss village, in another kind of secluded retreat.[85] In the weeks that he had left in Germany, Willstätter had to sort through his treasured possessions and compile a list of what he wanted to take with him. However, the Gestapo simply crossed off many of the sentimental and costly items, so he had no choice but to abandon them. These items included his immense, seven-room library; the Florentine table around which members of the Munich faculty had once held their meetings; and a doge's chair, on which his mother and Fritz Haber had sat on Willstätter's fiftieth birthday many years before.

Hoping to salvage some mementos of his illustrious career, he wrote to the Economics Ministry for permission to take his gold and silver scientific medals with him, but he never received a reply.[86] After having to surrender his home and most of its contents, Willstätter was still kept in Munich until early March, when he finally obtained his exit and entry visas. At that time, he was informed by the foreign exchange office that there was no longer any need for him to emigrate—he was going to be granted the rights of an honorary "Aryan" and have his villa returned to him.[87] But Willstätter did not believe the Nazis' promises any more.

On March 4, 1939, six years, one month, and four days after Adolf Hitler had first waved at the crowd that was delirious at his having just become German chancellor, Richard Willstätter boarded a train at the Munich central station. The train took him westward through the valleys and bare farmland of Bavaria, skirting the snow-draped Alps, to the frontier opposite Basel. With help from a high-ranking German diplomat, he was able to pass through the border station without any repercussions stemming from his previous attempt to flee the country he had loved so much. On the Swiss side, Stoll and several other friends embraced him. Willstätter was close to tears. He did not feel joyful or relieved as Bella Fromm had felt. His first words were: "I have heard that many, who, after managing to overcome many fears and dangers, were able to leave Germany, stood on this side of the border and waved their hats out of joy. I would like to cry."[88] Stoll took him to the home of a friend outside Basel for a brief sojourn. In the guest book Willstätter scribbled: "Homeless I arrived. Due to Stoll's hospitality and friendship I gratefully received a piece of a new home."[89]

Blocked from obtaining a visa for any country in Europe, Hans-Joachim Schoeps kept himself busy in late 1938 by serving as Leo Baeck's liaison to the Confessional Church. While his parents had been forced to leave their apartment on the Hasenheide on November 1, to escape from a Nazi who had been spying on them,[90] Schoeps avoided any personal harm during the Kristallnacht mayhem in Berlin—but not by much. At 6:30 A.M. on November 9, a former neighbor tipped him off that the Gestapo was looking for him. Fleeing on a bicycle, he rode through the Berlin streets, witnessing the horror of Kristallnacht unfold before his eyes.[91] Fear now spurred him to more desperate actions to escape Germany. Schoeps tried to buy an exit visa with 3,000 reichsmarks ($1,200), but the Gestapo apparently foiled his attempt.[92] At the foreign office he discovered he was on a list of two hundred German Jews who were not allowed to leave the country.[93]

Around this time Schoeps gave a lecture in the Dahlem section of Berlin in which—as he later claimed—he advocated greater unity between anti-Nazi Germans and Jews against the Hitler regime. Afterward he was warned that the speech might have been recorded. Panicked, Schoeps decided to flee. Returning to the foreign office, he appealed to his friend Werner Otto von Hentig, head of the Oriental bureau, who was horrified by Kristallnacht and thus agreed to intervene on Schoeps's behalf as he had already done for imprisoned leaders of the Reichsvertretung.[94] Hentig then called the chancellery and explained that the foreign office badly needed a Jew to send on a "secret mission" to Sweden.[95] Under this ruse, Schoeps managed to book a seat on a flight leaving for Stockholm on Christmas eve, just evading the Gestapo.[96] On his exit papers he indicated he would be returning to Germany at the end of five months, when his "mission" was accomplished.[97]

While millions of Germans were gathered around candlelit Christmas trees in their cozy homes, toasting each other with champagne on this, the last such peacetime celebration they would mark for many years, Schoeps's plane soared northward, leaving the twinkling lights of Berlin behind for the blackness of the Baltic and an uncertain future in Scandinavia. On board he carried the manuscript of Kafka's short story "The Village School Teacher," presented to him by Max Brod. It was a fitting talisman.

In Berlin Schoeps left his deeply patriotic father and his doting mother, who had supported him through all his publishing and scholarly endeavors and who would now be cut off from their only surviving child.[98] It was a separation they hoped would be short. Hans-Joachim, or "Hase" as they called him, promised to arrange for visas for his parents to follow him to Sweden. But, in fact, for the elder Schoepses, as for many other older Jews still inside the Third Reich, the chance to escape had come and gone. The separation from their son would be permanent.

For Leo Baeck there would be no flight out. There really could not be one for a man of his deep religious convictions and sense of duty. Baeck saw Judaism as a religion that emphasizes deeds over words. The challenge Judaism poses to believers, he thought, is to reaffirm their faith and the Jews' special destiny on this earth through individual actions. Faith offers sustenance as one passes through the most grueling trials.

However, if Jews lose their faith in Judaism and in God, he believed, then they are hopelessly adrift, and life holds no meaning for them. This was the credo that kept Baeck in Germany. As he wrote to his good and longtime friend, Baron von Veltheim during the war, two years after Hans-Joachim Schoeps flew to Sweden: "We are in a time of crisis, not the least of the mind and of religion. If religion fails, then our tie to a higher world is lost."[99]

For consolation in his prolonged ordeal, Baeck often turned to an unlikely, but apt source. He identified with the agony and bloody divisiveness that had nearly torn a far-off country apart during the nineteenth century, finding in the words of that nation's leader a message that all was not lost, even in the darkest hour. Rather, this was a time for greater determination and renewed dedication to a better future. The words he quoted were those of Abraham Lincoln, uttered on a cannon-rent battlefield in Pennsylvania, in the midst of another kind of civil war, another struggle for survival with a dubious outcome:

> It is for us the living, rather, to be dedicated here to the unfinished work which they who fought here have thus far so nobly advanced. It is rather for us to be here dedicated to the great task remaining before us—that from these honored dead we take increased devotion to that cause for which they gave the last full measure of devotion; that we here highly resolve that these dead shall not have died in vain; that this nation, under God, shall have a new birth of freedom; and that government of the people, by the people, for the people, shall not perish from the earth.

Epilogue

All the German Jewish leaders who have been traced through these pages outlived Adolf Hitler and his Final Solution. Their suffering under the Third Reich had finite limits. All, including Leo Baeck, ultimately got out of Germany. All but one chose not to return to live there ever again. In this fate and choice—survival and a total break from the country they had loved so dearly—they mirrored the lives of the majority of their fellow German Jews. What is often overlooked when one thinks of the Holocaust is that the Jews who were directly under Hitler's thumb were not, compared to Jews elsewhere in Europe, victims of its wholesale slaughter.

Of the 525,000 Jews who were living in Germany when Hitler came to power in 1933, roughly a third left the country before Kristallnacht and another third left during the following ten months, up to the outbreak of World War II. Of the estimated 164,000 who were still within the Third Reich in the fall of 1941, 123,000—or less than a quarter of the original community in the early 1930s—perished in the camps. This number pales beside the staggering number of Polish, Russian, and other European Jews—some 6 million all told—who met this barbaric end. Numerically speaking, the German Jews were fortunate, if there is any comfort in such cold statistical evidence. Poland's 3 million Jews (in 1939) were nearly all murdered, except for a few hundred thousand. Over 700,000 Jews in the Soviet Union were killed after Operation Barbarossa was launched in the late spring of 1941. Some 400,000 of Hungary's 725,000 Jews were exterminated, in spite of the valiant efforts of a Raoul Wallenberg. In Austria, approximately half the Jewish population of 200,000 perished.

Either by deportation or death or by escape into exile, the Jewish communities of Europe dwindled almost to the point of extinction. Nowhere was this more logically so then in Germany, the seedbed of annihilation. A quarter century after Hitler's death and the collapse of his Thousand-Year Reich, only about thirty thousand Jews were living in what was then East and West Germany, and many of them had migrated there from eastern European countries. Few German Jews or their descendants could bring themselves to set foot again on the land they had once loved so dearly, as native sons and daughters, but that had turned so viciously and bestially upon them. In this sense, Hitler won a victory in spite of his military defeat: He made Germany and the rest of the continent free of Jews. This racial "cleansing" remains his enduring legacy; in Germany today the Jew is no longer at home, no longer a citizen among other citizens, to the extent that he once was.

These six people, who lived through the Nazi era of persecution, violence, and, ultimately, mass murder and whose lives were forever shaped by their words and deeds during it, had few experiences in common once the Third Reich collapsed. Strewn about the world, they picked up different threads of existence and stitched together dissimilar lives in their remaining years—testimony to the individual differences in temperament, values, and aspirations that had set them apart before they had been crudely labeled and thrown together as *Jews*. In many ways, their release from that stifling, dehumanizing Nazi environment freed them to become themselves more than might have been the case if Nazism and the Holocaust had never befallen them. Whether this was a liberation they would have just as soon foregone is another matter:

None of these Jews had really ever desired to be anything more than a German Jew. But exile and Auschwitz meant that this once satisfying identity could be only a memory. For better or worse, they were thrust into other worlds, to forge new souls.

The first to succumb in exile was, fittingly enough, the one who had found the thought of abandoning Germany the most distasteful—Richard Willstätter. In poor health during his final years, Willstätter did not benefit physically from his flight to peaceful Switzerland. Joined there by his loyal housekeeper, Elise Schnauffer, the Nobel laureate moved into a villa, appropriately named L'Eremitaggio, in Locarno-Muralto, overlooking Laggo Maggiore, on the Italian border. There, surrounded by his remaining works of art and beds of roses reminiscent of his cherished Munich garden, he resumed the lonely, withdrawn life that was his wont. "I wish nothing more for myself than a little peace and quiet and leisure," he wrote to his fellow scientist, Kasimir Fajans.[1] Willstätter delighted in the plethora of flowers, fruits, and vegetables that flourished in the warm Swiss climate outside his villa.[2]

Even in exile his scientific work continued. He completed his "swan song"—a study of the enzyme system in muscles—during the remainder of 1939. But the prospect of doing more work, for American chemical concerns, was not enticing enough to lure him across the Atlantic, even if it would have meant being closer to his daughter, Margarete. The birth of a grandson in Illinois prompted Willstätter to resume writing his long-neglected memoirs.[3] He did so, at least in part, to tell the story of how he had stubbornly fought during his life against anti-Semitism. This book was, in a sense, his only communication link with the outside world as he was now even further removed from the wild roar of impending European catastrophe.[4] Lacking a radio, Willstätter could not keep abreast of unfolding events as the Wehrmacht stormed across one country after another. News of the war reached him only slowly and, one suspects, without arousing his interest.[5] Willstätter broke off writing his memoirs at the point in his life where he had left Germany, so as to preserve the privacy of his last years from posthumous scrutiny.[6]

In November 1941 he experienced irregularities with his heart and was diagnosed as suffering from arrthymia. Throughout the following year, as the war turned against Germany, he grew weaker, discovering he had a coronary thrombosis. He was treated for this ailment by a former student, a German heart specialist who traveled all the way from Hamburg to help the aging Jewish chemist while, in the east, thousands of nameless, frightened Jews were being driven into the forests and shot by German Einsatz units. Willstätter studied his own malady as if it were another intriguing scientific puzzle, much as he had analyzed the nutritional needs of his children decades before. "I do not notice that my illness requires patience," he wrote to Arthur Stoll. "It only demands some attention, perhaps also initiative. Regrettably, I lack the medical knowledge, and the literature, to study it more deeply."[7]

In the summer of 1942, with battles raging across the Russian steppes and on the burning sands of north Africa, Willstätter's condition worsened. On Monday, August 3, ten days before his seventieth birthday, he died in his sleep, of cardiac failure. The funeral was held in Switzerland. Willstätter's remains were cremated and the ashes entrusted to Frau Schnauffer, with the hope that, one day, they would be returned to Germany. When Frau Schnauffer died in the 1960s, however, Willstätter's ashes were buried near her grave in Switzerland—a final acknowledgment that, in the end, he could not go home again.

Max Warburg remained in New York for the duration of the war, his plan to return to Germany derailed by Kristallnacht. (On hearing the news, he told his son Eric: "Now it's finished.")[8] He lived with his wife Alice in an ample apartment on Park Avenue, in that unhappy limbo known to so many Germans—Jews and Gentiles alike—whose politics or race had hurled them overnight into new and strange lands. No longer part of the old world, they could not bring themselves to enter the new one; instead—whether rich or poor, patriot or anti-Nazi zealot—they passed each day in a kind of existential fog, unsure who they really were anymore. As an emblem of his unfulfilled hopes, Warburg hung in his New York office the portrait of Moses contemplating the Promised Land that he had commissioned in Germany.[9]

Like Willstätter, the eminent Hamburg banker turned his hand to writing his life's story, but he, too, was plagued by failing health and managed to publish only a small excerpt in the time still allotted to him. (Together with his son, Warburg also founded a new branch of the family bank in 1938, giving it new life in the New World.) Warburg did not, however, lose interest in the plight of the Jews who were still trapped in Germany. He continued to advocate a transfer agreement with the Nazi government that would allow Jews to take some of their assets with them when they emigrated. In December 1938 Hjalmar Schacht presented a plan similar to Warburg's that would enable Jews to deposit up to 25 percent of their total wealth—estimated at 6 billion marks—in a trust fund, with the money to be used to purchase German goods, in their new homelands. Hitler even gave this plan his blessing.[10] (Some Jews condemned it as a form of "ransom.") Negotiations with the Reichsbank over the issuance of "emigration marks," or vouchers, to facilitate this transfer of funds went on into 1941. (All told, some $32.4 million exited the Reich via this route.)[11] Working through a refugee assistance organization, Warburg pursued this venture in the same low-key, behind-the-scenes way that had characterized his work in Germany—a "Jewish Quaker" way of avoiding "fuss" and concentrating on getting the job done.[12]

In the United States, Warburg's constitutional modesty was reinforced by the criticism that had been previously directed at him for failing to take a firmer stand against the Nazi regime. Many American Jewish leaders were appalled by what they saw as Warburg's cozy relationship with the Nazi bigwigs and by his refusal to face up to their evil nature—a refusal that had cost the German Jews dearly. These charges gained greater credence after the war ended and the full criminality of Hitler and his henchmen was revealed. From his sanctuary in New York, Warburg read about the horrors discovered at Dachau, Auschwitz, Buchenwald, and Treblinka with disbelief: This terrible inhumanity had little connection in his mind to the Germany he still loved so deeply.

During his final years in exile, Warburg kept up his philanthropic activities, serving on the board of the American Joint Distribution Committee and the American Jewish Committee. He also founded and headed a group that supported refugee children in the United States and grew interested in promoting world peace through greater international cooperation. His financial situation, however, worsened, and by 1942 Warburg was reduced to appealing to relatives for money.[13] He became an American citizen in 1944. Two years later he died after suffering a heart attack in New York. It was the day after Christmas—six months shy of his eightieth birthday.

Leo Baeck had many more harrowing years to face in Germany. As the Final Solution was carried out, he had to survive it as best he could. Even though he found out about the death camps by the summer of

1941, Baeck still declined to escape. To spare his people what he thought would be unnecessary mental anguish, he kept this damning information to himself and devoted his energies not to spiriting Jews out of the Nazis' clutches, but to offering comfort and guidance to those who sought his counsel. When the Gestapo organized the first massive deportation of Berlin's Jews in October 1941, Baeck, chair of the Nazi-controlled Reichsvereinigung der Juden in Deutschland, successor to the Reichsvertretung, agreed to help make this grim operation as humane as possible. Although he was not personally involved in this roundup, it weighed heavily on his conscience, especially in light of his knowledge of the deportees' destiny.[14] Baeck was not among those chosen for transport to the east in 1941, and he was not among the Reichsvereinigung officials picked up for deportation the following June. It was not until January 27, 1943, when the tide of war had already turned against Germany in Africa and Russia, that the Gestapo finally came for him, to take him to Theresienstadt.

Baeck was placed alone, in a compartment of a train bound for the former military outpost in eastern Czechoslovakia, which had served the Nazis as a "show" camp for privileged Jews, but was now merely a way station en route to the gas chambers at Auschwitz. Inside this camp housing some fifty thousand Jews, Baeck refused to surrender his dignity and self-respect. After he was spared physical labor when he turned seventy that spring, he assumed responsibility for overseeing the ghetto's welfare assistance, ministering personally to the elderly, the sick, and the disheartened. In August 1943 he obtained convincing evidence that Jews were being gassed at Auschwitz, yet he decided, again, not to let this news be widely known in the camp. "Living in the expectation of death by gassing would only be harder," he explained after the war.[15] And so the ultimate fate of those taken away on the transport trains heading to Poland was not revealed.

In time, as Theresienstadt shrunk in size, Baeck was asked to serve on its Council of Elders and then to head it. He did what he could to hold the dwindling population together, to keep up everyone's spirits. Because of his prominence, Baeck was eventually singled out by the Nazis for elimination. Toward the end of the war, a high party official—probably Adolf Eichmann—visited Theresienstadt and discovered, to his utter dismay, that Baeck was still alive. He immediately ordered the rabbi shot. But somehow there was a mixup, and the SS executioners murdered a Jew named Beck in his place. Believing that the spiritual leader of German Jewry was dead, the Nazis thereafter left him alone.[16] When the Russians finally liberated Theresienstadt early in May 1945, roughly 30,000 Jews were still alive within its fences, but only 4,000 of them eventually overcame the ravages of disease. Baeck was one of them—one of only three from his Berlin transport of 2,000 to survive the Holocaust.[17]

After the war, Baeck lived in London and regained the moral leadership of a new, widely dispersed and numerically depleted German Jewry. As the head of what became the Council of Jews from Germany, he participated in that organization's quest for reparations for the Nazi crimes committed against the Jewish people. In 1948 Baeck took a post as visiting professor at the Hebrew Union College in Cincinnati, returning annually to teach there. He also became president of the World Union for Progressive Jewry, of which he had been a member in Germany, and occupied himself with other efforts on behalf of Germany's displaced Jews.

At first, Baeck discouraged his fellow survivors from returning to Germany, saying that life there would be "impossible" for them.[18] Later, in his desire to rebuild ties between his people and their homeland, he finally went back to Germany on several occasions to lecture. In 1947 he traveled to Palestine and later issued, along with Albert Einstein, a plea for Arabs and Jews to reject terrorism and to develop that country "on a peaceful and democratic basis."[19] A year later Jews around the world rejoiced at the creation of the state of Israel. On November 2, 1956, Leo Baeck died, in London, at the age of eighty-three.

Bella Fromm arrived in New York with vases, easy chairs, wastebaskets, bookshelves, lamps, a desk, cocktail glasses, a household pharmacy, coffee and tea services, a mirror, pictures, and other belongings, all safely and neatly sealed inside a large shipping container,[20] but with no prospects for making a new life in the United States. She also brought with her a letter, addressed to Cecilia Razovsky of the National Refugee Service, penned by Leo Baeck, praising her work on behalf of Germany's Jews,[21] but this recommendation did not easily translate into a job. The first position the onetime darling of Berlin's diplomatic corps could find was in a factory, making gloves. Later she cooked for a well-to-do family on Manhattan's Upper East Side.[22] Then she was employed as a waitress and as a typist. Shortly after Germany invaded Poland,

Fromm was warned that agents of the Gestapo had been dispatched to New York to kill her, and for the next year she went about her daily business under police protection.

During the war, Fromm had several articles on her experiences under the Nazi regime published in *True Detective* and other magazines. In addition, the publication of a volume of excerpts from her diary, entitled *Blood and Banquets,* brought her considerable renown in England and the United States. Fromm also toured the country and gave talks on the evils of Nazism for a group known as the Joint Defense Appeal. In the aftermath of the 1944 plot against Hitler, her closest friend and lover, Herbert Mumm von Schwarzenstein, was implicated, tried, and executed. Her long-estranged husband, Karl Friedrich Steuermann, had preceded her to the United States, but Fromm had little to do with him. Her chief ties were to her daughter Gonny (who married and had a son in 1948) and to Peter Welles, a physician to whom she was briefly married. (He died before the end of the war.) Fromm remained in New York, at 65 West 95th Street, for the greater part of the next twenty-five years, writing for *Harper's,* the *New York Post,* and other publications. In 1961 she published a novel, *Die Engel weinen* (The Angels Cry). She died on February 11, 1972, at the age of seventy-one.

Finally fulfilling his Zionist dream, Robert Weltsch began a new life as a political journalist in Palestine. For a time he was caught up in the excitement of the unfolding dream, but Europe tugged at him, too. In 1946 Weltsch returned to Germany, to cover the Nuremberg trials of Nazi war criminals. From there, he moved to England, where he settled for the next thirty-two years, working as a correspondent for the Jewish newspaper *Ha'aretz.* While the state of Israel was being born, he was thousands of miles away, in cold, dreary London. Weltsch remarried in 1951 and became active in the Leo Baeck Institute—an archive of records pertaining to the nearly defunct German Jewish community. From 1956 to 1978 he was the founding editor of the institute's yearbook. He also wrote a history of modern Zionism. Finally, for the last three years of his life, Weltsch returned, like an errant son, to the Jewish nation he had always called home. He died in Jerusalem on December 22, 1982, at the age of ninety-one.

In Swedish exile, Hans-Joachim Schoeps carried on his studies of Jewish theology, receiving some financial help from his parents in Berlin (who worried constantly about his health and implored him to write—

which Schoeps seldom did),[23] along with several academic grants. Affiliated with universities in Stockholm and Uppsala, he established contact with other German Jewish émigrés in the country, such as Hans Schäffer. Any professed desire he might have had to return to the Reich was quietly laid to rest: Earlier "political mistakes," Schoeps told his friend Ernst Rosenthal, now made it impossible for him to go back.[24] (His efforts to obtain exit visas for his parents to join him in Sweden were unsuccessful.) After years of having been warned, in his horoscopes, against marriage and having experienced the great love of his life in a 1935 affair with a fellow member of the Deutscher Vortrupp, Schoeps met and decided to marry a German student of art history named Dorothee Busch. (An indirect descendant of the composer Felix Mendelssohn-Bartholdy, she had fled to Sweden in 1938.) It was important, he felt, to fulfill his Jewish obligations to father children and sustain the family. Despite her knowledge of his homosexuality and realization that life with Schoeps could never be wholly satisfying,[25] Dorothee agreed to marry him. They were wed in Stockholm in 1941. The marriage duly produced two sons, Julius (born in 1942) and Manfred (born in 1944). The couple was divorced in 1946.

Meanwhile, in Germany, Schoeps's father, who had once declared of Adolf Hitler "He does not like us Jews, but he is head of state,"[26] was rounded up, along with a thousand other Berlin Jews, in retaliation for Reinhard Heydrich's assassination by Czech partisans in the spring of 1942. One of the "lucky" ones, he was not shot on the spot, but put on a train for Theresienstadt. Unwilling to be separated from him, Schoeps's mother, "Kätchen," voluntarily went along. Conditions in the camp were too much of a strain for the seventy-eight-year-old Julius Schoeps, and two days after his grandson and namesake was born in Sweden, he succumbed to uremia. Schoeps's mother survived, sending off a flurry of postcards and letters to her sole surviving son, full of worry about his welfare, not once mentioning her own dire circumstances. (At Theresienstadt she also met Leo Baeck, who told her he had been receiving copies of Schoeps's scholarly writings.) Her last request to "Hase," as she called him, was that he never set foot on German soil again.[27] Shipped to Auschwitz, Käthe Schoeps died there in 1944.

Her son did not honor his mother's request. Warned by friends in 1945 to stay away from Germany, he ignored that advice, too. He told the Protestant theologian Karl Barth he had "no more burning desire" than to return to his native land, despite what he had once vowed and "all that had happened" there, including the deaths of his parents in concentration camps.[28] As he had told his former comrades in the Deutscher Vortrupp after he went into exile, it was important to keep in mind that "Hitler is not Germany" and that once the Nazi era had passed, German Jews should extend forgiveness to their fellow countrymen.[29] Schoeps was also tired of sitting on the sidelines in Sweden and was eager to resume his academic career.

With Barth's help, he found a teaching post at the University of Erlangen, in the U.S. zone of occupation, in 1946. He became a professor in the history of ideas four years later and remained on the faculty, publishing works on the relationship between Christianity and Judaism, on Prussia, and on his earlier years in the German youth movement. During those years Schoeps could not escape controversy for his staunchly conservative views, as well as his sexual predilection. In 1957 he was expelled from the Freideutsche Konvent, a conservative group, for having had an affair some years before with a seventeen-year-old male sculptor. In West Germany's young democracy, Schoeps stubbornly fought for the rights of homosexuals, comparing their oppression to the Nazis' treatment of the Jews. He died, in Erlangen, on July 11, 1980, at the age of seventy-one, and was buried, as he had always wished, on German soil.

Abbreviations

The following abbreviations are used for major sources of materials cited in the notes:

AJA   American Jewish Archives, Cincinnati

AJC   Blaustein Library, American Jewish Committee, New York

AJHS   American Jewish Historical Society, Waltham, Massachusetts

BOD   Board of Deputies of British Jews, London

BU   Mugar Memorial Library, Boston University

CZA   Central Zionist Archives, Jerusalem

JDC   American Jewish Joint Distribution Archives, New York

JNUL   The Jewish National and University Library, Jerusalem

JTA   Jewish Telegraph Agency, cable dispatches, 1935–38

LBINY Leo Baeck Institute, New York

MPG   Max Planck Gesellschaft zur Förderung der Wissenschaften, Berlin

NA   National Archives, Washington, D.C.
NRC   National Records Center, Suitland, Maryland
SBB   Staatsbibliothek, Berlin
UD   University of Delaware Library
YIVO YIVO Institute for Jewish Research, New York

Notes

Introduction

Epigraphs are quoted from Achim von Borries, ed., *Selbstzeugnise des deutschen Judentums, 1861–1945* (Frankfurt-am-Main: Fischer Taschenbach Verlag, 1988), 17, 41.

1. Leo Baeck, "A People Stands Before Its God," in *We Survived: Fourteen Histories of the Hidden and the Hunted in Nazi Germany*, ed. Eric H. Boehm (Santa Barbara, Calif: Clio Press, 1966), 290.
2. Raul Hilberg, *The Destruction of the European Jews*, rev. ed., vol. 3 (New York: Holmes and Meier, 1985), 1220.
3. Baeck, "A People Stands," 290.
4. Richard Willstätter, *Aus meinem Leben: Von Arbeit, Musse und Freunden*, ed. Arthur Stoll (Weinheim, Germany: Verlag Chemie, 1949), 207.
5. Bella Fromm, "Flight to Freedom," *True Detective* (November 1942): 68.
6. Bella Fromm to Eva Schroeder, 4 August 1938, Folder 1, Box 14, Fromm Papers, BU.
7. Folder 8, Box 10, Fromm Papers, BU.
8. Hans-Joachim Schoeps to Martin Rade, 7 August 1938, in Wilhelm Kantzenbach, "Das wissenschaftliche Werden von Hans-Joachim Schoeps und seine Vertreibung aus Deutschland 1938," *Zeitschrift für Religions-und Geistesgeschichte* 32 (1980): 334.
9. Hans-Joachim Schoeps, *Die letzten dreissig Jahre: Rückblicke* (Stuttgart: Klett, 1956), 112.

10. Max M. Warburg, *Aus meinen Aufzeichungen* (New York: privately printed, 1952), 153–54.
11. Max M. Warburg, "Ansprache gehalten anlässlich der Umwandlung von M. M. Warburg und Co.," 30 May 1938 (microfilm), Max Warburg Papers, LBINY. Here and throughout the text, unless otherwise indicated, translations from the German are the author's.
12. Robert Weltsch to Hugo Bergmann, 1 February 1938. Folder 1, Box 2, Weltsch Papers, LBINY.
13. Weltsch to Bergmann, 19 August 1938. Folder 1, Box 2, Weltsch Papers, LBINY.
14. Weltsch to Bergmann, 17 July 1938. Folder 1, Box 2, Weltsch Papers, LBINY.
15. Weltsch, untitled, undated (1938?) ms. Folder 2, Box 7A, Weltsch Papers, LBINY.
16. Estimates of the German Jewish population in 1933 range from 500,000 to 565,000. The figure 525,000 represents the consensus of opinion.
17. Herbert A. Strauss, "Jewish Emigration from Germany: Nazi Policies and Jewish Responses—I," *Leo Baeck Year Book* 25 (1980): 323.
18. Werner Rosenstock, "Exodus, 1933–1939: A Survey of Jewish Emigration from Germany," *Leo Baeck Year Book* 1 (1956): 373.
19. Michael R. Marrus, *The Holocaust in History* (New York: New American Library, 1987), 104.
20. The number of German Jews who perished in the camps has been put at 123,000. See, for example, Raul Hilberg, *The Destruction of the European Jews*, student ed. (New York: Holmes and Meier, 1985), 339.
21. Leni Yahil, *The Holocaust: The Fate of European Jewry*, trans. by Ina Friedman and Haya Galai (New York: Oxford University Press, 1991), 16.
22. Quoted in David Nachmansohn, *German-Jewish Pioneers in Science, 1900–1913: Highlights in Atomic Physics, Chemistry, and Biochemistry* (New York: Springer Verlag, 1979), 230.
23. Bruno Bettelheim, *The Informed Heart: Autonomy in a Mass Age* (London: Thames and Hudson, 1960), 259.
24. Otto Dov Kulka, "The Reactions of German Jewry to the National Socialist Regime," in *Living with Antisemitism: Modern Jewish Responses*, ed. Jehuda Reinharz (Hanover, N.H.: University Press of New England, 1987), 370.
25. Prior to the fall of the Berlin Wall in 1989, the Jewish population was roughly 40,000. Since then, another 20,000 Jews have come to live in the reunited Germany. See John Tagliabue, "The New German Jews: Living in a Haunted Land," *New York Times*, 23 March 1992, p. A6.
26. Marrus, *Holocaust*, 157.
27. Arno Herzberg, "The Jewish Press under the Nazi Regime: Its Mission, Suppression, and Defiance," *Leo Baeck Year Book* 36 (1991): 367.

Herzberg, manager of the Berlin office of the Jewish Telegraphic Agency from 1934 to 1937, pointed out that for a newspaper suspension meant the loss of jobs and income for its staff, so the journalists learned to practice a form of self-censorship. Herzberg stated that the Jewish press also tended not to print "shocking stories" about the treatment of Jews because doing so might discourage those who hoped for a return to normalcy.

28. Christian Morgenstern, "Die unmögliche Tatsache," in *Gesammelte Werke in einem Band*, ed. Margarete Morgenstern (Munich: Piper, 1965), 34–35.

29. Lucy S. Dawidowicz, *The War Against the Jews, 1933–1945* (New York: Holt, Rinehart and Winston, 1975), xiii.

Chapter I: Antecedents

1. Cited in Karl A. Schleunes, *The Twisted Road to Auschwitz: Nazi Policy Toward German Jews, 1933–1939* (Urbana: University of Illinois Press, 1970), 35.

2. Richard Willstätter, *Aus meinem Leben: Von Arbeit, Musse und Freunden*, ed. Arthur Stoll (Weinheim, Germany: Verlag Chemie, 1949), 17.

3. David Nachmansohn, *German-Jewish Pioneers in Science, 1900–1913: Highlights in Atomic Physics, Chemistry, and Biochemistry* (New York: Springer Verlag, 1979), 199.

4. Willstätter, *Leben*, 394.

5. David Farrer, *The Warburgs: The Story of a Family* (Briarcliff Manor, N.Y.: Stein and Day, 1975), 47.

6. Between 1880 and 1910, some 12,000 German Jews converted to Protestantism. It was estimated that by 1930, one of every four Jews was married to a non-Jew. See Ruth Gay, *The Jews of Germany: A Historical Portrait* (New Haven, Conn.: Yale University Press, 1992), 202, 254.

7. Fritz Stern, *Dreams and Delusions: The Drama of German History* (New York: Vintage Books, 1989), 106.

8. Paul Massing, *Rehearsal for Destruction: A Study of Political Anti-Semitism in Imperial Germany*, 1st ed. (New York: Harper and Bros., 1949), 55.

9. Ibid., 91.

10. Jehuda Reinharz, *Fatherland or Promised Land: The Dilemma of the German Jews, 1893–1914* (Ann Arbor: University of Michigan Press, 1975), 23.

11. Leonard Baker, *Days of Sorrow and Pain: Leo Baeck and the Berlin Jews* (Oxford, Eng.: Oxford University Press, 1980), 16.

12. Nachmansohn, *German-Jewish Pioneers*, 198.

13. Bernhard Kahn, "Tribute to Max M. Warburg by Bernhard Kahn at the Annual Meeting of the Joint Distribution Committee, 1947."

ME 344, LBINY. It is not clear to what extent the younger Warburg experienced this anti-Semitic reaction.

14. Stephen Magill, "Defense and Introspection: The First World War as a Pivotal Crisis in the German-Jewish Experience," (Ph.D. diss., UCLA, 1977), 58.

15. Sanford Ragins, *Jewish Response to Anti-Semitism in Germany, 1870–1914: A Study in the History of Ideas* (Cincinnati: Hebrew Union College Press, 1980), 49–50.

16. By 1916, the Centralverein claimed to have 70,000 members, plus another 200,000 in affiliated organizations. See R. Gay, *The Jews of Germany*, 206.

17. Baker, *Days of Sorrow and Pain*, 11.

18. Nachmansohn, *German-Jewish Pioneers*, 196.

19. Bella Fromm, "I Am Introduced to Murder," *True Detective* (February 1942): 10.

20. Hans-Joachim Schoeps, *Die letzten dreissig Jahre: Rückblicke* (Stuttgart: Klett, 1956), 11.

21. Jehuda Reinharz, *Chaim Weizmann: The Making of a Zionist Leader* (New York: Oxford University Press, 1985), 15.

22. See, for example, Robert Weltsch, "Das deutsche Judentum im Krieg und Revolution," in Weltsch, *Deutsche Judenfrage: Ein kritischer Rückblick* (Königstein/Taunus, Germany: Jüdische Verlag, 1981), 37. Cf. Peter Gay, *Freud, Jews and Other Germans: Masters and Victims in Modernist Culture* (New York: Oxford University Press, 1978), 170.

23. Ragins, *Jewish Response*, 81.

24. Cf. Ernst Pawel, *The Nightmare of Reason: A Life of Franz Kafka* (New York: Farrar, Straus, Giroux, 1984), 24.

25. Interview with Robert Weltsch, April 1970, Weltsch File, Leo Baeck Institute, Jerusalem.

26. Martin Buber, *Briefwechsel aus sieben Jahrzehnten*, 1st ed., vol. 1 (Heidelberg: L. Schneider, 1972), 125.

27. Interview with Robert Weltsch, 1970, Weltsch File, Leo Baeck Institute, Jerusalem.

28. Robert Weltsch, *Bericht über die Tätigkeit im Sommersemester 1912* (Prague: privately printed, 1912), 9. Folder 8, Box 1, Weltsch Papers, LBINY.

29. Eduard Rosenbaum, "M. M. Warburg & Co.: Merchant Bankers of Hamburg," *Leo Baeck Year Book* 7 (1962): 134.

30. Eduard Rosenbaum and Ari J. Sherman, *Das Bankhaus M. M. Warburg & Co., 1798–1938*, 2nd ed. (Hamburg: H. Christians, 1978), 116.

31. Warburg was rudely awakened to this reality when he was blackballed by his fellow officers after a secret vote. See Ron Chernow, *The Warburgs: The Twentieth Century Odyssey of a Remarkable Jewish Family* (New York: Random House, 1993), 38.

32. Rosenbaum, "M. M. Warburg & Co.," 133.

33. Eric Warburg, *Times and Tides* (New York: privately printed, 1956), 11.
34. In 1913 the firm moved into a new, much larger, building in Hamburg that could house three hundred employees—three times as many as the former bank headquarters. See Chernow, *The Warburgs*, 149.
35. Ibid., 25.
36. Kahn, "Tribute to Max Warburg," Kahn Papers, LBINY.
37. Ibid.
38. Willstätter, *Leben*, 26.
39. Ibid., 41.
40. Ibid.
41. Richard Willstätter, "A Chemist's Retrospects and Perspectives: Remarks of Richard Willstätter, Munich, Germany, upon the Presentation to Him of the Willard Gibbs Medal," *Industrial and Engineering Chemistry* 11 (20 September 1933): 275.
42. Willstätter, *Leben*, 396.
43. Ibid., 395.
44. Vladimir Ipat'ev, *The Life of a Chemist: Memoirs of Vladimir N. Ipatieff*, trans. Helen Dwight Fischer and Harold H. Fischer (Stanford, Calif.: Stanford University Press, 1946), 89.
45. Willstätter, *Leben*, 275.
46. Ipat'ev, *Life*, 81.
47. Willstätter, *Leben*, 149.
48. Ibid., 193.
49. Ibid., 157.
50. Ibid., 205.
51. Bella Fromm, *Blood and Banquets: A Berlin Social Diary* (New York: Carol Publishing Group, 1990), 3.
52. Fromm, "I Am Introduced to Murder," 11.
53. Fromm, *Blood and Banquets*, 4.
54. Ibid., 4.
55. Fromm, "I Am Introduced to Murder," 11.
56. Ismar Schorsch, *Jewish Reactions to German Anti-Semitism, 1870–1914* (New York: Columbia University Press, 1972), 14.
57. Herbert Seelinger, "Origin and Growth of the Berlin Community," *Leo Baeck Year Book* 3 (1958): 164.
58. Baker, *Days of Sorrow and Pain*, 39.
59. Ibid., 44.
60. See P. Gay, *Freud, Jews and Other Germans*, 167. Cf. Magill, "Defense and Introspection," viii.
61. Baker, *Days of Sorrow and Pain*, 74.
62. Ernst Halle, "Kriegserinnerungen mit Auszügen aus meinem Tagebuch, 1914–1916," unpublished memoir, ME 250, LBINY, 12.
63. Robert Weltsch to Martin Buber, 17 July 1917. Folder 6, Box 6, Weltsch Papers, LBINY.

64. Robert Weltsch to Theodor and Frieda Weltsch, 2 December 1915. Addenda, Folder 3, Box 2, Weltsch Papers, LBINY.

65. Robert Weltsch to Theodor and Frieda Weltsch, 1 December 1915. Addenda, Folder 3, Box 2, Weltsch Papers, LBINY.

66. Max M. Warburg, *Aus meinen Aufzeichnungen* (New York: privately printed, 1952), 37.

67. Willstätter, *Leben*, 228.

68. Quoted in Tina Levitan, *The Laureates: Jewish Winners of the Nobel Prize* (New York: Twayne Publishers, 1960), 235.

69. Nachmansohn, *German-Jewish Pioneers*, 206.

70. The family lived at Hasenheide 64. The name of the street means literally "rabbit heath."

71. Schoeps, *Rückblicke*, 23.

72. Hans-Joachim Schoeps, "Memories of My First Years," undated ms., Folder 2, Box 5, Schoeps Papers, SBB.

73. Ibid., 14.

74. Fromm, *Blood and Banquets*, entry for 18 August 1917, 8.

75. Ernst Toller, *I Was a German: An Autobiography*, trans. Edward Crankshaw (London: J. Lane, Bodley Head, 1934), 284.

Chapter 2: Setting the Trap

1. Cf. Ernst Hamburger and Peter Pulzer, "Jews As Voters in the Weimar Republic," *Leo Baeck Year Book* 39 (1985): 33.

2. Max M. Warburg, *Aus meinen Aufzeichnungen* (New York: privately printed, 1952), 61.

3. Max Warburg to Alice M. Warburg, 13 May 1919, quoted in ibid., 81.

4. Cf. Eduard Rosenbaum and Ari J. Sherman, *Das Bankhaus M. M. Warburg & Co, 1798–1938*, 2nd ed. (Hamburg: H. Christians, 1978), 155.

5. Ibid., 145.

6. His accuser, Theodor Fritsch, was initially sentenced to three months in prison, but this punishment was later reduced to payment of a fine. See Ron Chernow, *The Warburgs: The Twentieth Century Odyssey of a Remarkable Jewish Family* (New York: Random House, 1993), 272.

7. Ina Lorenz, *Die Juden im Hamburg zur Zeit der Weimarer Republik: Eine Dokumentation*, vol. 2 (Hamburg: H. Christians, 1987), 1019.

8. Carl Duisberg to Richard Willstätter, 10 July 1924, Willstätter Personnel File, Files of the General Administration, MPG.

9. David Farrer, *The Warburgs: The Story of a Family* (Briarcliff Manor, N.Y.: Stein and Day, 1975) , 77.

10. Richard Willstätter, *Aus meinem Leben: Von Arbeit, Musse und Freunden*, ed. Arthur Stoll (Weinheim, Germany: Verlag Chemie, 1949), 301.

11. Richard Willstätter, "Die Geschichte meines Rücktritts," in *Vergangene Tagen: Jüdische Kultur in München*, ed. Hans Lamm (Munich: Langen, 1982), 412–413.
12. Willstätter, *Leben*, 304.
13. Willstätter, "Geschichte," 412.
14. Ibid., 413.
15. Ibid., 413.
16. Willstätter to Willy Wien, 24 June 1924, Willstätter File (MK 18064), Bayerisches Hauptstaatsarchiv, Munich.
17. Quoted in Tina Levitan, *The Laureates: Jewish Winners of the Nobel Prize* (New York: Twayne Publishers, 1960), 38.
18. Kasimir Fajans to Carl Neuberg, undated ms.(July 1924), Willstätter File, Box 5, Fajans Papers, Bentley Historical Library, University of Michigan, Ann Arbor.
19. Felix Haurowitz to Bernhard Witkop, 16 December 1978, quoted in Witkop, "Stepping Stones: Some Biographical Notes," unpublished memoir (ME 176), LBINY, 28.
20. Heinrich Wieland to Richard Willstätter, 30 June 1924, quoted in Willstätter, "Geschichte," 418.
21. See "Der Fall Willstätter," *Allgemeine Zeitung*, 31 July 1924.
22. Richard Willstätter to Karl Scharnagl, 24 January 1927, Manuscript Department, Stadtbibliothek, Munich.
23. Willstätter, *Leben*, 352.
24. Witkop, "Stepping Stones," 26.
25. See, for example, Rockefeller Foundation to Willstätter, 17 July 1933, Series 717D, "Univ. of Munich: Chemistry," Folder 145–46, Box 15, RG I.I, Rockefeller Foundation Papers, Rockefeller Archive Center, North Tarrytown, N.Y.
26. Willstätter, "Geschichte," 419.
27. See, for example, Robert Weltsch's 1913 "Herzl and We" (English trans.), Folder 1, Box 12, Weltsch Papers, LBINY.
28. See Robert Weltsch's 1913 essay, "Über das Wesen des jüdischen Nationalismus," Folder 1, Box 12, Weltsch Papers, LBINY.
29. Weltsch to Buber, 17 November 1918, Folder 6, Box 2, Weltsch Papers, LBINY.
30. Cf. Arthur Ruppin, *Briefe, Tagebücher, Erinnerungen* (Königstein/Taunus, Germany: Jüdische Verlag Athenaeum, 1985), 446.
31. Jehuda Reinharz, *Fatherland or Promised Land: The Dilemma of the German Jews, 1893–1914* (Ann Arbor: University of Michigan Press, 1975), 54.
32. Robert Weltsch, "Die jüdische Presse vor dreissig Jahre," in *Vom Schicksal geprägt: Freundesgabe zum 60. Geburtstag von Karl Marx*, eds. Hans Lamm, E. G. Lowenthal, and Marcel Gärtner (Düsseldorf: privately printed, 1957), 107.

33. Herbert Seelinger, "Origin and Growth of the Berlin Community," *Leo Baeck Year Book* 3 (1958): 167. This was the case in 1925.
34. Quoted in Otto Friedrich, *Before the Deluge: A Portrait of Berlin in the 1920s* (New York: Fromm International, 1986), 112.
35. Cf. Peter Gay, *Freud, Jews and Other Germans: Masters and Victims in Modernist Culture* (New York: Oxford University Press, 1978), 183.
36. Cf. Walter Tausk, *Breslauer Tagebuch, 1933–1940* (Berlin: Rutten and Löning, 1975), 60.
37. Reinharz, *Promised Land,* 155–56.
38. Arnold Paucker, Sylvia Gilchrist, and Barbara Suchy, eds., *The Jews in National Socialist Germany, 1933–1943* (Tübingen, Germany: J. C. B. Mohr, 1986), 22.
39. See Leo Baeck to Martin Buber, 24 September 1918, in Buber, *Briefwechsel aus sieben Jahrzehnten,* 1st ed., vol. I (Heidelberg: L. Schneider, 1972), 538.
40. Gershom Scholem, "On the Social Psychology of the Jews in Germany, 1900–1933," in David Bronsen, ed., *Jews and Germans from 1860 to 1933: The Problematic Symbiosis* (Heidelburg: C. Winter, 1979), 10. In *The Twisted Road to Auschwitz: Nazi Policy Toward German Jews, 1933–1939* (Urbana: University of Illinois Press, 1970), 38, Karl A. Schleunes says the rate was 23 percent by 1929.
41. Only 22,000 Jews converted to Christianity during the entire nineteenth century. See Gay, *Freud, Jews and Other Germans,* 95.
42. Scholem, "Social Psychology," 12.
43. Bella Fromm, *Blood and Banquets: A Berlin Social Diary* (New York: Carol Publishing Group, 1990), 8.
44. Ibid., entry for 20 May 1923, 12.
45. Ibid.
46. Ibid., 19.
47. Ibid.
48. Ibid., entry for 1 October 1928, 18–19.
49. Ibid., 20.
50. Ibid., entry for 16 November 1931, 38.
51. Ibid., entry for 20 March 1920, 11.
52. See, for example, Hans-Joachim Schoeps's undated ms. (1940?), "Erinnerungen aus meinen ersten Lebensjahren," Folder 2, Box 5, Schoeps Papers, SBB.
53. Hans-Joachim Schoeps, *Die letzten dreissig Jahre: Rückblicke* (Stuttgart: Klett, 1956), 23.
54. Walter Laqueur, *Young Germany: A History of the German Youth Movement* (London: Routledge and Kegan Paul, 1962), 95.
55. Schoeps, *Rückblicke,* 28.
56. Ibid., 28, 32.
57. Laqueur, *Young Germany,* 63.

58. Laqueur claimed that one-third of the postwar youth movement was right-wing. See ibid., 105.

59. See, for example, Hans-Joachim Schoeps's "Zur freideutscher Fahne," *Wegwarte* (October 1926), Binder 43, Schoeps Papers, SBB.

60. For a discussion of the Reichsbund's goals, see Ulrich Dunker, *Der Reichsbund jüdischer Frontsoldaten: Geschichte eines jüdischen Abwehrvereins* (Düsseldorf: Droste, 1977), 42–50, passim.

61. Dunker said that the RjF opposed only the Nazis' anti-Semitism, not the movement per se. See ibid., 111.

62. Leonard Baker, *Days of Sorrow and Pain: Leo Baeck and the Berlin Jews* (Oxford, Eng.: Oxford University Press, 1980), 105.

63. Quoted in Carl Rheins, "The Verband nationaldeutscher Juden, 1921–1933," *Leo Baeck Year Book* 25 (1980): 245.

64. Klaus Herrmann, *Das dritte Reich und die deutsch-jüdische Organisationen 1933–1934* (Cologne: Heymann, 1969), 23.

65. Jacob Boas, "The Jews of Germany: Self-Perceptions in the Nazi Era as Reflected in the German Jewish Press, 1933–1938," (Ph.D. diss., University of California, Riverside, 1977), 97. This was in 1933. Klaus Herrmann put the highest number at 10,000. See *Das dritte Reich*, 23.

66. Rheins, "Verband," 248.

67. Max Naumann, "Ganz Deutsche oder Halb-Deutsche?" *Vier Aufsätze* (Berlin: Deutsche Verlagsgesellschaft für Politik und Geschichte, 1922), 8.

68. Abraham Margaliot, "The Dispute over the Leadership of German Jewry (1933–1938)," *Yad Vashem Studies* 10 (1974): 132.

69. Schoeps, *Rückblicke*, 53.

70. Hans-Joachim Schoeps to Ernst Caselmann (undated), "Deutscher Vortrupp" Folder, Box 40, Schoeps Papers, SBB.

71. Schoeps, *Rückblicke*, 74.

72. Schoeps, "Vom geistigen Schicksal der Jugendbewegung," undated typescript, "Youth Movement" Folder, Box 40, Schoeps Papers, SBB.

Chapter 3: The Gathering Storm

1. Arnold Paucker, "The Jewish Defense Against Antisemitism in Germany, 1893–1933," in *Living with Antisemitism: Modern Jewish Responses*, ed. Jehuda Reinharz (Hanover, N.H.: University Press of New England, 1987), 119.

2. Richard Willstätter to Heinrich Berl, 20 September 1929 (K 3075), Berl Papers, Badische Landesbibliothek, Karlsruhe, Germany.

3. Kurt Blumenfeld, *Erlebte Judenfrage: Ein Vierteljahrhundert deutscher Zionismus*, ed. Hans Tramer (Stuttgart: Deutsche Verlags-Anstalt, 1962), 167.

4. Ibid., 169.

5. Carl Duisberg to Richard Willstätter, 2 October 1926, Willstätter Personnel File, Files of the General Administration, MPG.
6. Richard Willstätter to Carl Duisberg, 26 September 1926, Willstätter Personnel File, MPG.
7. For details of Willstätter's arrangement with the Rockefeller Foundation, see Series 717D, "Univ. of Munich: Chemistry," Folder 145-46, Box 15, RG 1.1, Rockefeller Foundation Papers, Rockefeller Archive Center, North Tarrytown, N.Y.
8. Richard Willstätter to Fritz Haber, end of July 1931, quoted in Willstätter, *Aus meinem Leben: Von Arbeit, Musse und Freunden*, ed. Arthur Stoll (Weinheim, Germany: Verlag Chemie, 1949), 384.
9. Cf. Margaret T. Edelheim-Mühsam, "Reactions of the Jewish Press to the Nazi Challenge," *Leo Baeck Year Book* 5 (1960): 313–14.
10. Cf. Hans-Helmuth Knütter, *Die Juden und die deutsche Linke in der Weimarer Republik, 1918–1933* (Düsseldorf: Droste, 1971), 90.
11. Cf. Richard Lichtheim, *Die Geschichte des deutschen Zionismus* (Jerusalem: R. Mass, 1954), 260.
12. Bella Fromm, *Blood and Banquets: A Berlin Social Diary* (New York: Carol Publishing Group, 1990), entry for 14 October 1930, 27.
13. See, for example, Cyrus Adler to Mortimer Schiff, 3 November 1930, "Germany" Folder, Box 13, Adler Correspondence, 1929–39, AJC.
14. Stephen Wise to Julian Mack, 13 September 1932, "Germany, 1923–1933" Folder, Box 82 ("World Affairs: Germany"), Wise Papers, AJHS.
15. Cf. Arthur Ruppin, *Briefe, Tagebücher, Erinnerungen*, ed. Schlomo Krolik (Königstein/Taunus: Germany: Jüdischer Verlag Athenaeum, 1985), entry for 20 April 1929, 412. Chaim Weizmann tried to win Warburg over to the Zionist cause in 1928 but failed. See Ron Chernow, *The Warburgs: The Twentieth Century Odyssey of a Remarkable Jewish Family* (New York: Random House, 1993), 297.
16. David Farrer, *The Warburgs: The Story of a Family* (New York: Stein and Day, 1975), 84.
17. Ibid., 109.
18. Chernow, *The Warburgs*, 330.
19. "Memorandum on Conference on the German Situation, January 28, 1933," "Germany" Folder, Box 13, Adler Correspondence, 1929–39, AJC.
20. Fromm, *Blood and Banquets*, entry for 1 April 1930, 26.
21. Ibid., entry for 20 November 1930, 28–29. Cf. entry for 29 January 1932, 42.
22. Ibid., entry for 28 June 1932, 54. She made special mention of the Krupps.
23. Ibid., entry for 13 July 1932, 55.
24. Ibid., entry for 12 August 1932, 55.
25. Quoted in Edelheim-Mühsam, "Reactions of the Jewish Press," 312.

26. Robert Weltsch to G. Pauli, 15 February 1932, Folder 5, Box 3, Weltsch Papers, LBINY.

27. Robert Weltsch to Chaim Weizmann, 23 February 1932, Weltsch-Weizmann Correspondence, Weizmann Archives, Rehovot, Israel.

28. Paucker, "Jewish Defense," 119.

29. Ibid., 125–27.

30. Benno Cohn, conversation with Kurt Ball-Kaduri, 9 October 1944, "Soziologische Betrachtungen über die Führung des deutschen Judentums vor und nach dem Jahre 1933," 01/24, RG 41, Ball-Kaduri Collection of Testimonies, Yad Vashem, Israel.

31. *Centralverein Zeitung*, 28 November 1930.

32. *Jüdische Rundschau*, 7 November 1930.

33. *Jüdische Rundschau*, 30 November 1930.

34. *Centralverein Zeitung*, 2 January 1931.

35. Cf. speech of Gustav Kronacker, quoted in *Jüdische Rundschau*, 27 January 1931.

36. *Jüdische Rundschau*, 23 March 1931.

37. See, for example, "Wieder ein anti-semitischer Mord," *Jüdische Rundschau*, 20 March 1931.

38. *Der Orden Bne Briss: Mitteilungen der Grossloge für Deutschland*, September 1931.

39. See *Gemeindeblatt der deutsch-israelitischen Gemeinde zum Hamburg*, 10 June 1927.

40. Cf. Adler to Schiff, 3 Nov. 1930, "Germany" Folder, Box 13, Adler correspondence, AJC. Warburg tended to take the view that the Nazi threat would pass. See Chernow, *The Warburgs*, 324.

41. Herbert A. Strauss, "Jewish Emigration from Germany: Nazi Policies and Jewish Response—II," *Leo Baeck Year Book* 25 (1981): 358.

42. The number of foreign aliens allowed into the United States fell from 97,139 in 1931 to 35,576 in 1932. After 1933 the number rose gradually over the next three years, but increased significantly only starting in 1937, when it reached 50,244.

43. See Warburg's "Remarks at the 27th Annual Meeting of the Hilfsverein," 24 March 1928 (Berlin: Scholem, 1929), microfilm, LBINY.

44. Cf. Warburg to Weizmann, 11 February 1930, Warburg-Weizmann Correspondence, Weizmann Archives. See also Warburg to Einstein, 24 April 1930, 47-834, Box 68, Albert Einstein Duplicate Archives, Seeley G. Mudd Manuscript Library, Princeton, N.J.

45. Schoeps to Buber, 26 June 1933, quoted in Martin Buber, *Briefwechsel aus sieben Jahrzehnten*, 1st ed., vol. 2 (Heidelberg: L. Schneider, 1972), 495–96.

46. Hans-Joachim Schoeps to Max Brod, 5 August 1932, quoted in *Im Streit um Kafka und das Judentum, Briefwechsel: Max Brod—Hans-Joachim Schoeps*, ed. Julius H. Schoeps (Königstein/Taunus: Jüdischer Verlag bei Athenaeum, 1985), 15.

47. Cf. George L. Mosse, *Germans and Jews: The Right, the Left, and the Search for a "Third Force" in Pre-Nazi Germany* (New York: Howard Fertig, 1970), 109.

48. See comments on Hans-Joachim Schoeps's "Der Sieg des preussischen Konservatismus über die Hitler Bewegung," *Centralverein Zeitung,* 11 November 1932.

49. Quoted in Fritz Friedländer, "Der deutsche Raum als jüdisches Schicksal," *Centralverein Zeitung,* 25 March 1932.

50. Felix Warburg to Cyrus Adler, 18 February 1932, "Germany" Folder, Box 13, Adler correspondence, 1929–39, AJC.

51. Quoted in Joachim C. Fest, *Hitler,* trans. Richard and Clara Winston (New York: Harcourt Brace Jovanovich, 1974), 311.

52. See "Was enthüllt uns Boxheim?" *Centralverein Zeitung,* 4 December 1931.

53. Blumenfeld, *Erlebte Judenfrage,* 165.

54. *Centralverein Zeitung,* 4 December 1931.

55. *Centralverein Zeitung,* 11 December 1931.

56. *Centralverein Zeitung,* 1 January 1932.

57. Cyrus Adler to Harry Schneidermann, 1 February 1932, "Germany" Folder, Box 13, Adler correspondence, AJC.

58. *Jüdische Rundschau,* 8 December 1931.

59. *Jewish Daily Bulletin,* 29 February 1932

60. Fromm, *Blood and Banquets,* entry for 1 February 1932, 43.

61. Ibid., entry for 6 June 1932, 51.

62. Ibid., entry for 19 November 1932, 61.

63. See *Bayerische-israelitische Gemeindezeitung,* 15 February 1932.

64. Robert Weltsch to G. Pauli, 15 February 1932, Folder 5, Box 3, Weltsch Papers, LBINY.

65. *Jüdische Rundschau,* 11 March 1932.

66. Leni Yahil, *The Holocaust: The Fate of European Jewry, 1932–1945,* trans. Ina Friedman and Haya Galai (New York: Oxford University Press, 1991), 30.

67. *Jewish Daily Bulletin,* 23 June 1932.

68. *Centralverein Zeitung,* 24 June 1932.

69. Ibid.

70. "Politik und Terrorakte," *Jüdische Rundschau,* 5 August 1932.

71. "Kurt Blumenfeld zur Lage," *Jüdische Rundschau,* 24 May 1932.

72. *Jüdische Rundschau,* 12 August 1932.

73. See *Bne Briss,* May 1932, and *Jewish Daily Bulletin,* 23 May 1932.

74. *Jewish Daily Bulletin,* 7 September 1932.

75. Willstätter's only public acknowledgment of this milestone was his consenting to having a bust of him made, to stand beside those of his predecessors at the entrance to his laboratory.

76. Richard Willstätter to Kasimir Fajans, 2 October 1932, Box 5, Fajans Papers, Bentley Historical Library, University of Michigan, Ann Arbor.

77. Quoted in Max Kalter, "Hundert Jahre Ostjuden in München, 1880–1980," in *Vergangene Tagen: Jüdische Kultur in München*, ed. Hans Lamm (Munich: Langen, 1982), 396.

78. Hans-Joachim Schoeps to Buber, 4 October 1931. Quoted in Julius Schoeps, ed., *Im Streit um Kafka*, 66.

79. See review of *Jüdische Glaube in dieser Zeit* in *Bayerische-israelitische Gemeindezeitung*, 1 June 1932.

80. Hans-Joachim Schoeps to Brod, 5 August 1932. Quoted in Julius Schoeps, ed., *Im Streit um Kafka*, 74.

81. Hans-Joachim Schoeps, *Die letzten dreissig Jahre: Rückblicke* (Stuttgart: Klett, 1956), 84, 86.

82. Ibid., 86. Cf. Hans-Joachim Schoeps, *Rufmord/1970* (Erlangen, Germany: Selbstverlag des Verfassers, 1970), 15.

83. *Jewish Daily Bulletin*, 19 October 1932.

84. "Was Nun?" *Jüdische Rundschau*, 8 November 1932.

85. *Centralverein Zeitung*, 16 December 1932.

86. Larry E. Jones, *German Liberalism and the Dissolution of the Weimar Party System* (Chapel Hill: University of North Carolina Press, 1988), 244.

87. Fromm, *Blood and Banquets*, entry for 22 December 1932, 67.

88. Ibid., entry for 28 December 1932, 68.

89. *Jewish Daily Bulletin*, 3 January 1933.

90. *Centralverein Zeitung*, 19 January 1933.

91. Fromm, *Blood and Banquets*, entry for 19 January 1933, 73.

92. Ibid., entry for 23 January 1933, 74–75.

93. Fromm, diary ms., entry for 17 January 1933, Box 1, Fromm Papers, BU.

94. Schoeps to Brod, 15 January 1933. Quoted in *Im Streit um Kafka*, 77.

95. Warburg saw both good and bad in the Nazi movement. But its anti-Semitism kept him from being comfortable with the thought of Hitler coming to power. Cf. Chernow, *The Warburgs*, 371.

96. *Centralverein Zeitung*, 26 January 1933.

97. Fromm, *Blood and Banquets*, entry for 28 January 1933, 75.

98. Ibid., entry for 29 January 1933, 75.

99. Ibid., entry for 31 January 1933, 76.

100. Fromm, diary ms., entry for 31 January 1933, Box 1, Fromm Papers, BU.

Chapter 4: Facing the Unthinkable

1. For Schoeps's 1933 horoscope, see Box 281, Schoeps Papers, SBB.

2. See Leni Yahil, *The Holocaust: The Fate of European Jewry, 1932–1945*, trans. Ina Friedman and Haya Galai (New York: Oxford University Press, 1991), 32.

3. *Jüdische Rundschau*, 31 January 1933.

4. *Centralverein Zeitung*, 2 February 1933.

5. See memoir of Conrad Rosenstein, in *Jewish Life in Germany: Memoirs from Three Centuries*, ed. Monika Richarz, trans. Stella P. Rosenfeld and Sidney Rosenfeld (Bloomington: Indiana University Press, 1991), 168.

6. *Bne Briss*, February–March 1933, 15, 20.

7. The "likely to become a public charge" (LPC) clause of the Immigration Act of 1917 was reactivated by President Herbert Hoover on 8 September 1930. Its intent was to block an anticipated wave of immigration into the United States at a time when large numbers of Americans were jobless. Determination of whether an applicant was likely to need public assistance was made at the consular level, and many officials acted zealously to keep down the number of both applicants and visas granted. Unofficially, some consuls in Europe tried to keep the number at 10 percent of the national quota. Because many would-be émigrés to the United States were discouraged from applying, it is impossible to ascertain the level of demand for visas in countries like Germany. However, it is estimated that between 1930 and 1933, some 500,000 persons worldwide were prevented from applying for U.S. visas because of a strict interpretation of the LPC clause. It should also be noted that in 1933, the United States did not have an immigration policy of extending preferential treatment to victims of religious or political persecution.

8. See, for example, A. Dana Hodgson (chief, Visa Division) to Wilbur Carr, 17 May 1933, 150.01/2114, Box 13, RG 59, NA.

9. See Moacyr Scliar, *Max and the Cats* (New York: Ballantine Books, 1990).

10. Quoted in *Jewish Daily Bulletin*, 9 February 1933.

11. Robert Weltsch to Chaim Weizmann, 12 October 1930, Folder 5, Box 3, Weltsch Papers, LBINY.

12. Robert Weltsch to Martin Buber, 30 December 1931, Folder 6, Box 2, Weltsch Papers, LBINY. Cf. Buber, *Briefwechsel aus sieben Jahrzehnten*, 1st ed., vol. 2 (Heidelberg: L. Schneider, 1972), 422.

13. Alfred Hirschberg, "Vom 30. Januar zum 5. Marz," *Der Schild*, 9 February 1933.

14. Alfred Hirschberg, quoted in Klaus J. Herrmann, *Das dritte Reich und die deutsch-jüdischen Organisationen, 1933–1934* (Cologne: Heymann, 1969), 1.

15. Cf. *Jewish Daily Bulletin*, 19 February 1933.

16. See Arnold Paucker, "The Jewish Defense Against Antisemitism in Germany: 1893–1933," in *Living with Antisemitism: Modern Jewish Responses*, ed. Jehuda Reinharz (Hanover, N.H.: University Press of New England, 1987), 105.

17. Cf. *Jewish Daily Bulletin*, 3 March 1933.

18. See Hilfsverein to Leo Baeck, 10 March 1933, supplement 2, Box E IV, Baker Papers, LBINY.

19. "Recht und Pflicht," *Centralverein Zeitung*, 2 March 1933.
20. Walter Laqueur, *Young Germany: A History of the German Youth Movement* (London: Routledge and Kegan Paul, 1962), 44–45.
21. Cf. Hans-Joachim Schoeps, "Der deutsche Vortrupp: Der Ort geschichtlichen Besinnung" in *Wille und Wege des deutschen Judentums* (Berlin: Vortrupp Verlag, 1935), 46–56.
22. Quoted in Ian Kershaw, *The "Hitler Myth": Image and Reality in the Third Reich* (Oxford, Eng.: Oxford University Press, 1989), 20–21.
23. Philip Metcalfe, *1933* (Sag Harbor, N.Y.: Permanent Press, 1988), 206.
24. Karl A. Schleunes, *The Twisted Road to Auschwitz: Nazi Policy Toward German Jews, 1933–1939* (Urbana: University of Illinois Press, 1970), 57–58.
25. This fact was revealed after Duesterberg ran for president of Germany in 1932 as the candidate of the Deutschnationale Volkspartei (German National Party). See *Jewish Daily Bulletin*, 7 September 1932.
26. Carl J. Rheins, "The Verband nationaldeutscher Juden, 1921–1933," *Leo Baeck Year Book* 25 (1980): 252–53.
27. Hans-Joachim Schoeps, "Das neue Gesicht der Politik—1933," Schoeps Papers, LBINY. Cf. Binder 44, Schoeps Papers, SBB.
28. Ibid.
29. Hans-Joachim Schoeps to Heinz Merländer, 21 May 1937, Binder 94, Schoeps Papers, SBB.
30. Sholom Shafir, "American Jewish Leaders and the Emerging Nazi Threat (1928–January 1933)," *American Jewish Archives* 31 (November 1979), 180–81.
31. Naomi Shepherd, *A Refuge from Darkness: Wilfrid Israel and the Rescue of the Jews* (New York: Pantheon, 1984), 83.
32. Max Warburg, *Aus meinen Aufzeichnungen* (New York: privately printed, 1952), 147.
33. Max Warburg to Kurt Blumenfeld, 3 March 1933, Warburg-Weizmann Correspondence, Weizmann Archives, Rehovot, Israel.
34. Eduard Rosenbaum and Ari Joshua Sherman, *Das Bankhaus M. M. Warburg & Co., 1798–1938*, 2nd ed. (Hamburg: H. Christians, 1978), 198.
35. Ibid., 198.
36. Warburg, *Aufzeichnungen*, 147.
37. Eduard Rosenbaum, "M. M. Warburg & Co., Merchant Bankers of Hamburg" *Leo Baeck Year Book* 7 (1962): 149.
38. Warburg had been a member of the Deutsche Volkspartei (German People's Party) until 1932. See Ron Chernow, *The Warburgs: The Twentieth Century Odyssey of a Remarkable Jewish Family* (New York: Random House, 1993), 366.
39. Michael Wolffsohn, "Banken, Bankiers und Arbeitsbeschaffung im Übergang von der Weimarer Zeit zum dritten Reich," *Bankhistorisches Archiv: Zeitschrift zur Bankengeschichte* 1, no. 3 (May 1977), 56.

40. Warburg, *Aufzeichnungen*, 129. Cf. Bernard Kahn, "Tribute to Max Warburg by Bernard Kahn at the Annual Meeting of the Joint Distribution Committee (1947)," Folder 3, Box I, Kahn Papers, LBINY.
41. Cf. Max Warburg to Felix Warburg, 19 February 1930, Warburg-Weizmann Correspondence, Weizmann Archives, Rehovot, Israel.
42. Eric Warburg, Introduction to Max Warburg, *Aufzeichnungen*, ix.
43. Max Warburg to Kurt Blumenfeld, 5 March 1933, Warburg-Weizmann Correspondence, Weizmann Archives, Rehovot, Israel.
44. Helmut Genschel, *Die Verdrängung der Juden aus der Wirtschaft im dritten Reich* (Göttingen: Musterschmidt, 1966), 26, note 51.
45. Bella Fromm, *Blood and Banquets: A Berlin Social Diary* (New York: Carol Publishing Group, 1990), entry for 25 December 1930, 29.
46. Ibid., entry for 8 March 1933, 81.
47. Item 1977, unpublished memoirs of George S. Messersmith, Messersmith Papers, UD, 2.
48. Fromm, diary ms., entry for 14 March 1933, Box I, Fromm Papers, BU.
49. Fromm, *Blood and Banquets*, entry for 7 March 1933, 80.
50. Ibid., entry for 3 May 1932, 49.
51. Ibid., entry for 10 March 1933, 82–88. Shortly thereafter, the government issued a decree banning the abuse of foreigners and their automobiles, dubbed the "Fromm Act." See Metcalfe, *1933*, 95.
52. Fromm, *Blood and Banquets*, entry for 23 March 1933, 93–94. Cf. diary ms., entry for 23 March 1933, Box I, Fromm Papers, BU.
53. Fromm, *Blood and Banquets*, entry for 23 March 1933, 94.
54. Ibid., entry for 30 March 1933, 96–100.
55. Ibid., entry for 29 March 1933, 96.
56. Ibid., entry for 30 March 1933, 100.
57. Richard Willstätter, *Aus meinem Leben: Von Arbeit, Musse und Freunden*, ed. Arthur Stoll (Weinheim, Germany: Verlag Chemie, 1949), 353, 367.
58. For details of his application, see Richard Willstätter to Rockefeller Foundation, 26 March 1933, Series 717D, "Univ. of Munich: Chemistry," File 145-46, Box 15, RG I.1, Rockefeller Foundation Papers, Rockefeller Archive Center, North Tarrytown, N.Y.
59. Cf. Werner E. Mosse, "German Jews: Citizens of the Republic," in Arnold Paucker, *The Jews in Nazi Germany, 1933–1943: Proceedings of the Leo Baeck Institute's 1985 Berlin International Historical Conference, "Self-Assertion in Adversity"* (Tübingen, Germany: J. C. B. Mohr, 1986), 53.
60. In Lion Feuchtwanger's novel, *The Oppermanns*, the German factory owner Rudolph Weinberg says, in Swiss exile: "If you give the Nationalists a chance to settle down, things will adjust themselves." Lion Feuchtwanger, *The Oppermanns* (New York: Viking Press, 1934), 292.
61. Cf. Hermann Goering's speech of 5 March 1933, following the Reichstag elections. *Jewish Daily Bulletin*, 12 March 1933.

62. See *Jewish Daily Bulletin*, 14 March 1933.

63. William E. Dodd to Harry Ostrow, 14 March 1933, "Germany: Mar.–May 1933" Folder, Box 82, Wise Papers, AJHS.

64. Ibid.

65. Margaret T. Edelheim-Mühsam, "Reactions of the Jewish Press to the Nazi Challenge," *Leo Baeck Year Book* 5 (1960): 318.

66. Cf. Arno J. Mayer, *Why Did the Heavens Not Darken? The "Final Solution" in History* (New York: Pantheon, 1988), 130.

67. Herrmann, *Das dritte Reich*, 68; Fromm, *Blood and Banquets*, entry for 24 March 1933, 95.

68. See, for example, cable of JDC (Paris) to AJJDC, 19 March 1933, File 626, "Germany—General, 1933 (Mar.–July)" JDC: "Unanimous opinion [of German Jewish leaders] Jewish mass meeting presently senseless and may be harmful."

69. Quoted in Martin Rosenbluth, *Go Forth and Serve: Early Years and Public Life* (New York: Herzl Press, 1961), 253.

70. Ibid., 256.

71. Remarks of Stephen S. Wise, 26 February 1933, "Germany, 1923–1933" Folder, Box 82, Wise Papers, AJHS. Cf. cable of Jacob Landau (JTA) to Judge Horace Stern, 5 April 1933, "Germany" Folder, Box 13, Cyrus Adler Correspondence, 1929–1939, AJC. Here the manager of the JTA's Berlin office was quoted as saying that "the appeal of German Jewish organizations to American Jews to cease protests [was] definitely made under intimidation."

72. Cf. cable of the Zionist Bureau to Stephen S. Wise, 27 March 1933, "Germany: Mar.–May, 1933" Folder, Box 82, Wise Papers, AJHS. Cf. also the Centralverein's denial of foreign press stories as "pure inventions," *Jewish Daily Bulletin*, 27 March 1933.

73. Quoted in Fromm, *Blood and Banquets*, entry for 27 March 1933, 95.

74. "Gegen Greuelpropaganda," *Jüdische Rundschau*, 28 March 1933.

75. "Nach dem 5. März," *Jüdische Rundschau*, 7 March 1933.

76. Statement of 29 March 1933, quoted in Herrmann, *Das dritte Reich*, 61.

Chapter 5: "Now We Are All Jews"

1. For one summary of anti-Jewish measures in March, see Messersmith to Hull, 21 March 1933, 862.4016/315, Box 6783, RG 59, NA.

2. Ernst Herzfeld, "Meine letzten Jahre in Deutschland, 1933–1938," 01/8, Ball-Kaduri Collection of Testimonies, RG 41, Yad Vashem Archives, Jerusalem, 4.

3. Undated, untitled typescript, Folder 4, Box 11 (Addendum: "Hilfsverein"), RG 116, YIVO.

4. Bella Fromm, *Blood and Banquets: A Berlin Social Diary* (New York: Carol Publishing Group, 1990), entry for 31 March 1933, 101–02.
5. See, for example, *Jewish Daily Bulletin*, 31 March 1933; and Curt Joseph, "NS-Betriebszellen in Aktion," in *Sie dürften nicht mehr Deutsche sein: Jüdischer Alltag in Selbstzeugnissen 1933–1938*, eds. Margarete Limberg and Hubert Rübsaat (Frankfurt-am-Main: Campus, 1990), 95.
6. See Robert Weltsch, "Die jüdische Presse," 110, and his 3 February 1965 untitled ms., Folder 2, Box 2, Addenda, Weltsch Papers, LBINY.
7. Fromm, *Blood and Banquets*, entry for 1 April 1933, 102–03.
8. Klaus J. Herrmann, *Das dritte Reich und die deutsch-jüdischen Organisationen, 1933–1934* (Cologne: Heymann, 1969), 14.
9. Herbert A. Strauss, "Jewish Emigration from Germany: Nazi Policies and Jewish Responses—I," *Leo Baeck Year Book* 25 (1980): 354.
10. Peter Hanke, *Zur Geschichte der Juden in München zwischen 1933 und 1945* (Munich: Stadtarchiv, 1967), 86.
11. Haber to Willstätter, 1 April 1933, Haber-Willstätter Correspondence, LBINY.
12. Haber to Vorstand of the German Chemical Society, 27 April 1933, Haber-Willstätter Correspondence, LBINY.
13. Richard Willstätter, *Aus meinem Leben: Von Arbeit, Musse und Freunden*, Arthur Stoll, ed. (Weinheim, Germany: Verlag Chemie, 1949), 401.
14. John E. Kehl (U.S. consul general, Hamburg), to George A. Gordon (chargé d'affaires ad interim, Berlin), 4 April 1933, 862.4016/635 GC, Box 6784, RG 59, NA.
15. Ibid.
16. Max Warburg, *Aus meinen Aufzeichnungen* (New York: privately printed, 1952), 150.
17. David Farrer, *The Warburgs: The Story of a Family* (Briarcliff Manor, N.Y.: Stein and Day, 1975), 114.
18. Hans-Joachim Schoeps, *Bereit für Deutschland: Der Patriotismus deutscher Juden und der Nationalsozialismus. Frühe Schriften 1930 bis 1939. Eine historische Dokumentation* (Berlin: Haude and Spener, 1970), 21.
19. Schoeps to Deutscher Vortrupp members, 5 April 1933, "Deutscher Vortrupp" Folder, Box 40, Schoeps Papers, SBB.
20. Ibid.
21. Karl A. Schleunes, *The Twisted Road to Auschwitz: Nazi Policy Toward German Jews, 1933–1939* (Urbana: University of Illinois Press, 1970), 188.
22. Ibid., 189.
23. Reichsbund to Hitler, 4 April 1933, quoted in Herrmann, *Das dritte Reich*, 66–67.
24. Reichsbund (Leo Löwenstein) to Paul von Hindenburg, 3 April 1933, Folder 1, Box 10, Kreutzberger Papers, LBINY.
25. Ulrich Dunker, *Der Reichsbund jüdischer Frontsoldaten: Geschichte eines jüdischen Abwehrvereins* (Düsseldorf: Droste, 1977), 9.

26. *Centralverein Zeitung,* 6 April 1933.
27. Fromm, *Blood and Banquets,* entry for 1 April 1933, 103.
28. Memorandum of William E. Beitz (U.S. Consulate, Berlin), No. 134, 3 April 1933, Messersmith Papers, UD.
29. Schleunes, *Twisted Road,* 85.
30. Cf. Ian Kershaw, *The "Hitler Myth": Image and Reality in the Third Reich* (New York: Oxford University Press, 1989), 234.
31. See Schleunes, *Twisted Road,* 87.
32. Weltsch, "Tragt ihn mit Stolz, den gelben Fleck!" *Jüdische Rundschau,* 4 April 1933.
33. Ibid.
34. Ibid. The yellow badge was the way Jews were distinguished and ostracized in medieval Germany.
35. Weltsch, "Die jüdische Presse," 109–10.
36. The *Jüdische Rundschau* first advertised for subscriptions in its issue of April 1.
37. Weltsch to Buber, 22 April 1933, Ms. Var. 350/880, Robert Weltsch File, Martin Buber Archive, JNUL.
38. Ismar Elbogen, "Haltung!" *Centralverein Zeitung,* 6 April 1933.
39. "Jüdische Zwischenbilanz," *Jüdische Rundschau,* 13 April 1933.
40. Ibid.
41. See, for example, Messersmith to Hull, No. 151, 19 April 1933, Messersmith Papers, UD.
42. See JDC, London (unsigned) to AJJDC, 28 April 1933, 5. File 626, "Germany—General 1933 (Mar.–July)," JDC.
43. Kurt J. Ball-Kaduri, *Das Leben der Juden im Deutschland im Jahre 1933: Ein Zeitbericht* (Frankfurt-am-Main: Europäische Verlaganstalt, 1963), 114.
44. *Jewish Daily Bulletin,* 26 April 1933.
45. "Memorandum With Annexes Concerning Visit to Germany," undated (April? 1933), Folder 11 ("Germany"), Box 288, Felix Warburg Papers, AJA.
46. Strauss, "Jewish Emigration—I," 340.
47. Warburg to Weizmann, 19 April 1933, Warburg-Weizmann correspondence, Weizmann Archives, Rehovot, Israel.
48. *Bne Briss,* February–March 1933.
49. This statement has been cited in a number of secondary sources, including Leonard Baker, *Days of Sorrow and Pain: Leo Baeck and the Berlin Jews* (New York: Oxford University Press, 1980), 145; Kurt J. Ball-Kaduri, *Vor der Katastrophe: Juden in Deutschland 1934–1939* (Tel Aviv: Olamenu, 1967), 12; and Robert Weltsch, "Twenty-Five Years After," *AJR Information,* November 1963, 1. However, it does not appear in any contemporary sources, such as the Jewish press. It is also not clear whether Baeck uttered these words in public.

50. See Hans-Joachim Schoeps, "Die deutsche Juden und das Jahr 1933," undated typescript, Box 60, Schoeps Papers, SBB.

51. Cf. Abraham Margaliot, "The Dispute over the Leadership of German Jewry (1933–1938)," *Yad Vashem Studies* 10 (1974): 141.

52. Cf. Lucie Brent, "The Architects of Jewish Self-Assertion During the Nazi Era" (Master's thesis, Hunter College, New York, 1985), 17.

53. See, for example, Jonah B. Wise, "Report on Conference With Leaders of German District, Grand Lodge, B'nai B'rith, Cologne, July 2, 1933," 49, in "General Summary—German Situation," File 626, JDC.

54. Max Naumann, head of the Verband, wrote to Hitler on 2 May 1933; the National Council on 3 May 1933; and Leo Löwenthal, of the RjF, on 6 May 1933.

55. Quoted in *Jewish Daily Bulletin,* 28 June 1933.

56. Robert Weltsch, "Fanal und Besinnung," *Jüdische Rundschau,* 12 May 1933.

57. W. van Dyck to members of the Mathematics–Natural Science Division, Bavarian Academy of Sciences, 17 May 1933, Willstätter File, Fajans Papers, University of Michigan, Ann Arbor.

58. Haber to Willstätter, undated (early May 1933?), quoted in Fritz Stern, *Dreams and Delusions: National Socialism in the Drama of the German Past* (New York: Vintage Books, 1989), 73.

59. Chaim Weizmann, *Trial and Error: The Autobiography of Chaim Weizmann* (New York: Schocken Books, 1966), 351.

60. Quoted in David Nachmansohn, *German-Jewish Pioneers in Science, 1900–1933: Highlights in Atomic Physics, Chemistry, and Biochemistry* (New York: Springer Verlag, 1979), 228.

61. Richard Willstätter, "A Chemist's Retrospects and Perspectives," *Chemical & Engineering News* 11 (20 September 1933), 275.

62. Ibid.

63. Fromm, *Blood and Banquets,* entry for 6 May 1933, 109.

64. Ibid., entry for 6 May 1933, 110.

65. Ibid., entry for 21 May 1933, 113.

66. Ibid., entry for 15 August 1933, 126.

67. Fromm, diary ms., entry for 22 May 1933, Box 1, Fromm Papers, BU.

68. Warburg to Weizmann, undated (May 1933), Warburg-Weizmann correspondence, Weizmann Archives, Rehovot, Israel.

69. Ibid.

70. See "Joint Foreign Committee, Minutes, June 28, 1933," Folder 1 ("Laski, Neville"), Box 293, Felix Warburg Papers, AJA.

71. Messersmith to Hull, No. 1369, 17 June 1933, 862.4016/1181, Box 6786, RG 59, NA, 11. Messersmith thought it was "not unlikely" that the German banking system would be placed under governmental control, and if it was, "all private banks will be dissolved."

72. Ibid., 2.

73. Ibid., 2–3.

74. Israel Cohen, "The Jewish Situation in Germany," 29 June 1933, File S25/9703, CZA.

75. Warburg, *Aufzeichnungen,* 150. Cf. Warburg to Weizmann, 8–9 June 1933, Warburg-Weizmann correspondence, Weizmann Archives, Rehovot, Israel.

76. Warburg, *Aufzeichnungen,* 150.

77. Schoeps, "Deutsch-jüdische Besinnung," undated ms. (1933), "Deutscher Vortrupp/Youth Movement" Folder, Box 40, Schoeps Papers, SBB.

78. Schoeps to Brod, 25 June 1933, quoted in Julius Schoeps, ed., *Im Streit um Kafka und das Judentum, Briefwechsel: Max Brod–Hans-Joachim Schoeps* (Königstein/Taunus: Jüdischer Verlag bei Athenaeum, 1985), 78.

79. Schoeps to Brod, 25 June 1933, quoted in Schoeps, ed., *Im Streit um Kafka.*

80. Schoeps to Buber, 26 June 1933, in Martin Buber, *Briefwechsel aus sieben Jahrzehnten,* 1st ed., vol. 2 (Heidelberg: L. Schneider, 1972), 495–96.

81. For example, in a memorandum of 21 June 1933, the ZVfD drew a close parallel between the Nazi movement and the Zionist one: "Zionism believes that a rebirth of national life, such as is occurring in German life through adhesion to Christian and national values, must also take place in the Jewish national group. For the Jew, too, origin, religion, community of fate and group consciousness must be of decisive significance in the shaping of his life." Quoted in *A Holocaust Reader,* ed. Lucy S. Dawidowicz (New York: Behrman House, 1976), 151.

82. Hans-Joachim Schoeps, *Rufmord/1970* (Erlangen, Germany: Selbstverlag des Verfassers, 1970), 15. Cf. Hans-Joachim Schoeps, *Die letzten dreissig Jahre: Rückblicke* (Stuttgart: Klett, 1956), 84.

83. Schoeps to Martin Rade, 20 June 1933, quoted in Wilhelm Kantzenbach, "Das wissenschaftliche Werden von Hans-Joachim Schoeps und seine Vertreibung aus Deutschland 1938," *Zeitschrift für Religions-und Geistesgeschichte* 32 (1980): 340.

84. Ernst Simon, "Jewish Adult Education in Nazi Germany as Spiritual Resistance," *Leo Baeck Year Book* 1 (1956): 68.

85. Cf. Ismar Schorsch, *Jewish Reactions to German Anti-Semitism, 1870–1914* (New York: Columbia University Press, 1972), 193.

86. Schoeps to Buber, 26 June 1933, Ms. Var. 350/706, Schoeps File, Buber Archive, JNUL.

87. Schoeps to Buber, 28 September 1933, Ms. Var. 350/706, Schoeps File, Buber Archive, JNUL.

88. See Schoeps's undated typescript, "Die deutsche Juden und das Jahr 1933," Box 60, Schoeps Papers, SBB.

89. Schoeps to Fritz Hellendall, 9 August 1978, Box 37, Schoeps Papers, SBB.

90. Weltsch to Buber, 22 April 1933, Folder 6, Box 2, Weltsch Papers, LBINY.

91. Robert Weltsch, "Ja Sagen zum Judentum," *Jüdische Rundschau*, 16 May 1933.

Chapter 6: Suffering the Slings and Arrows

1. Quoted in William L. Shirer, *The Rise and Fall of the Third Reich: A History of Nazi Germany* (New York: Simon and Schuster, 1960), 205.

2. Ibid., 205.

3. Gustav Warburg, *Six Years of Hitler: The Jews Under the Nazi Regime* (London: George Allen and Unwin, 1939), 102.

4. Karl A. Schleunes, *The Twisted Road to Auschwitz: Nazi Policy Toward German Jews, 1933–1939* (Urbana: University of Illinois Press, 1970), 109. Cf. G. Warburg, *Six Years*, 53, and Siegfried Neumann, *Nacht über Deutschland: Vom Leben und Sterben einer Republik. Ein Tatsachenbericht* (Munich: List, 1972), 88.

5. Cf. Arno J. Mayer, *Why Did the Heavens Not Darken? The "Final Solution" in History* (New York: Pantheon, 1988), 136. Measures taken against the Jews were thought to be "halfhearted and temporary."

6. See, for example, Raymond Geist (U.S. consul general, Berlin), to Hull, 10 September 1934, 150.062 PC/705, Box 38, RG 59, NA.

7. State Department to U.S. consulates, 5 August 1933, quoted in Cyrus Adler and Aaron M. Margolith, *With Firmness in the Right: American Diplomatic Action Affecting Jews* (New York: American Jewish Committee, 1946), 367.

8. See Col. MacCormack to Hull, 26 January 1934, 150.062 PC/677 1/2, RG 59, NA.

9. Werner Rosenstock, "Exodus, 1933–1939: A Survey of Jewish Emigration from Germany," *Leo Baeck Year Book* I (1956): 380.

10. Mayer, *Why Did the Heavens*, 136.

11. For an account of the opening ceremonies, see *Bayerische-israelitische Gemeindezeitung*, 15 April 1934.

12. David Nachmansohn, *German-Jewish Pioneers in Science, 1900–1933: Highlights in Atomic Physics, Chemistry, and Biochemistry* (New York: Springer Verlag, 1979), 194.

13. Chaim Weizmann, *Trial and Error: The Autobiography of Chaim Weizmann* (New York: Schocken Books, 1966), 341.

14. Richard M. Willstätter, *Aus meinem Leben: Von Arbeit, Musse und Freunden*, ed. Arthur Stoll (Weinheim, Germany: Verlag Chemie, 1949), 384.

15. Quoted in Weizmann, *Trial*, 351.

16. Cf. Weltsch, "Bar Kochba," typescript, 17 October 1943, Folder 9, Box I, Weltsch Papers, LBINY.

17. Weltsch to R. Pacovsky, 7 January 1954, 12 November 1967, and 28 April 1972, Folder 9, Box I, Weltsch Papers, LBINY.

18. Cf. Weltsch's comments in *Der Schild*, 2 March 1934.

19. Rosenstock, "Exodus," 381.

20. "Der Weg ins Freie," *Jüdische Rundschau*, 28 March 1934.

21. "Wiedersehen mit Palestine," *Jüdische Rundschau*, 10 April 1934.

22. See "Dr. L." (ZVfD, Berlin) to Weltsch, 24 March 1924, Folder I, Box 3, Weltsch Papers, LBINY.

23. Warburg to Weizmann, undated (May 1933), Warburg-Weizmann correspondence, Weizmann Archives, Rehovot, Israel.

24. Warburg to Buber, I October 1933, Warburg-Weizmann correspondence, Weizmann Archives, Rehovot, Israel.

25. Ibid.

26. Cf. Morris Troper to Paul Baerwald, 3 August 1933, File 627, "Germany-General 1933 (Aug.–Dec.)," JDC.

27. Bernard Kahn to AJJDC, 14 August 1933, File 627, JDC.

28. Cf. Georg Herlitz, "Sammlung!" *Bne Briss*, August 1933.

29. Messersmith to William Phillips, No. 255, 14 August 1933, Messersmith Papers, UD. Cf. William E. Dodd, *Ambassador Dodd's Diary*, eds. William E. Dodd, Jr., and Martha Dodd (New York: Harcourt, Brace and World, 1941), entry for 3 August 1933, 34.

30. Werner Senator, "Observations. . . ." *Centralverein Zeitung*, 15 August 1933.

31. Ludwig Marx, Robert Salomon, and Max Samuel to Warburg, 22 August 1933. Reichsvertretung der deutschen Juden Papers, LBINY.

32. Ron Chernow, *The Warburgs: The Twentieth Century Odyssey of a Remarkable Jewish Family* (New York: Random House, 1993), 403.

33. Ernst Herzfeld, "Meine letzten Jahre in Deutschland, 1933–1938," 01/8, Ball-Kaduri Collection of Testimonies, RG 41, Yad Vashem Archives, Jerusalem, 13, 15.

34. Ibid., 15. Cf. Kurt J. Ball-Kaduri, "The National Representation of Jews in Germany: Obstacles and Accomplishments of its Establishment," *Yad Vashem Studies* 2 (1958): 163–65.

35. This was a view that Baeck frequently espoused, for example, in conversations with a Berlin correspondent for the *New York Times*. Interview with C. Brooks Peters, 3 March 1990.

36. Forty percent of German Jews were aged forty-five or older in 1933.

37. Cf. Jonah B. Wise, "Report on Conference with Leaders," 20 July 1933, "General Summary-German Situation," File 626, JDC, 49. Wise found German Jewish leaders in agreement that Jews were "through" in Germany.

38. Arthur Ruppin, *Briefe, Tagebücher, Erinnerungen*, ed. Schlomo Krolik

(Königstein/Taunus: Jüdischer Verlag bei Athenaeum, 1985), entry for 16 August 1933, 446.

39. Bella Fromm, *Blood and Banquets: A Berlin Social Diary* (New York: Carol Publishing Group, 1990), entry for 10 July 1933, 119.

40. See *Centralverein Zeitung*, 13 July 1933, for details of Hitler's speech on this topic.

41. *Jewish Daily Bulletin*, 3 August 1933.

42. Messersmith to Hull, No. 1537, 24 August 1933, Messersmith Papers, UD.

43. For a report on this 22 July 1933 article, see *Jewish Daily Bulletin*, 24 July 1933.

44. Jonah Wise, "Report on Conference With Leaders," in "General Summary—German Situation," 20 July 1933, File 626, JDC, 49.

45. "Directive of the Reich Economics Ministry With Regard to Jewish Emigration," 28 August 1933, File 657, "Emigration—General, 1933–1937," JDC.

46. Cf. Herzfeld, "Meine letzten Jahre," 24.

47. Quoted in Klaus J. Herrmann, *Das dritte Reich und die deutsch-jüdischen Organisationen, 1933–1934* (Cologne: Heymann, 1969), 15–17.

48. "Die Sonderstellung der Juden," *Jüdische Rundschau*, 27 June 1933.

49. Zentral Ausschuss to Central British Fund for German Jewry, 20 July 1933, File 645, "Zentral Ausschuss, 1933–1934 (June)," JDC.

50. Jonah Wise, "Report on Conference" in "General Summary," File 626, JDC, 49.

51. *Bayerische-israelitische Gemeindezeitung*, 15 April 1934.

52. Quoted in Lucie Brent, "The Architects of Jewish Self-Assertion During the Nazi Era" (Master's thesis, Hunter College, New York, 1985), 32.

53. Weltsch to Buber, 30 June 1933, Ms. Var. 350/880, Weltsch File, Buber Archive, JNUL.

54. For a discussion of the Zionist critique of the Reichsvertretung, see Herrmann, *Das dritte Reich*, 11–12.

55. *Jewish Daily Bulletin*, 1 September 1933.

56. Max Gruenewald, "Education and Culture of the German Jews under Nazi Rule," *Jewish Review* 5 (1948), 57–58.

57. Ernst Simon, "Jewish Adult Education in Nazi Germany as Spiritual Resistance," *Leo Baeck Year Book* 1 (1956): 84–85.

58. Quoted in Leni Yahil, *The Holocaust: The Fate of European Jewry, 1932–1945*, trans. Ina Friedman and Haya Galai (New York: Oxford University Press, 1991), 77.

59. Ibid., 77–78.

60. *Centralverein Zeitung*, 28 September 1933.

61. See Baeck to Buber, 27 August 1933 and 19 September 1933, Ms. Var. 350/856, Baeck File, Buber Archive, JNUL.

62. Warburg's portrait was made the object of mockery at the Dachau concentration camp, along with those of Walther Rathenau and Gustav Stresemann. See address of James McDonald, 6 September 1933, Folder C 11/12/18, Box C 11/12/15 to 22, BOD.

63. Chernow, *The Warburgs*, 417.

64. Warburg to Buber, 1 October 1933, Ms. Var. 350/856, Warburg File, Buber Archive, JNUL.

65. Warburg to Hirschland, 14 September 1933, Reichsvertretung der deutschen Juden Papers, LBINY.

66. Warburg to Buber, 1 October 1933, Ms. Var. 350/856, Warburg File, Buber Archive, JNUL.

67. The Kulturbund provided artistic employment to some twenty thousand Jews. Beginning in Berlin, the group spread to some seventy-five other locales. The Nazis allowed the organization to continue operating until 1940.

68. Margaret Edelheim-Mühsam, "Reactions of the Jewish Press to the Nazi Challenge," *Leo Baeck Year Book* 5 (1960): 318.

69. Cf. Richard Lichtheim, *Die Geschichte des deutschen Zionismus* (Jerusalem: B. Mass, 1954), 250. See also Herzfeld, "Meine letzten Jahre," 22.

70. Weltsch, *Die deutsche Judenfrage: Ein kritischer Rückblick* (Königstein/Taunus: Jüdischer Verlag, 1981), 89. Cf. Edelheim-Mühsam, "Reactions," 318.

71. Herbert Freeden, *Die jüdische Presse im Dritten Reich* (Frankfurt am Main: Jüdischer Verlag bei Athenaeum, 1987), 20.

72. Robert Weltsch, "Die jüdische Presse vor 30 Jahre," in *Vom Schicksal geprägt: Freundesgabe zum 60. Geburtstag von Karl Marx*, ed. Hans Lamm, E. G. Lowenthal, and Marcel W. Gärtner. Düsseldorf: privately printed, 1957), 109–110.

73. *Jüdische Rundschau*, 29 September 1933.

74. Weltsch to Buber, 5 December 1933, Ms. Var. 350/880, Weltsch File, Buber Archive, JNUL.

75. Cf. Freeden, *Die jüdische Presse*, 82, note 95, citing Strauss, "Jewish Emigration—I."

76. Cf. Weltsch to Buber, 3 May 1933, Ms. Var. 350/880, Weltsch File, Buber Archive, JNUL. See also Weltsch to Buber, 22 March 1933, Ms. Var. 350/880. In the latter Weltsch wrote: "We will have to muster a lot of energy to prevent German Jewry from giving up on itself."

77. "On the New Emancipation," *Jüdische Rundschau*, 16 June 1933.

78. Weltsch to Buber, 5 December 1933, Ms. Var. 350/880, Weltsch File, Buber Archive, JNUL.

79. "Gegen die ewig Gestrigen," *Jüdische Rundschau*, 21 July 1933.

80. Cf. "Nürnberg und die Juden," *Jüdische Rundschau*, 8 September 1933.

81. Weltsch to Buber, 5 December 1933, Ms. Var. 350/880, Weltsch File, Buber Archive, JNUL.

82. "Juden und die Volksabstimmung," *Jüdische Rundschau,* 3 November 1933.

83. *Centralverein Zeitung,* 2 November 1933.

84. *Jewish Daily Bulletin,* 1 November 1933.

85. Shirer, *Rise and Fall,* 212. Out of 2,242 votes cast by Dachau prisoners, 2,154 were in favor of the government.

86. Weltsch to Berlin Landesverband, 12 December 1933, quoted in Freeden, *Die jüdische Presse,* 26.

87. Reichsverband to Weltsch, 5 October 1934, quoted in Freeden, *Die jüdische Presse,* 26.

88. Fromm said that "salon spies" were used to gain information from her. See Bella Fromm, "I Fight the Himmler Terror," *True Detective* (18 September 1942): 54–55. Cf. Fromm, *Blood and Banquets,* entry for 24 January 1934, 150.

89. Fromm, diary ms., entry for 29 March 1933, Box 1, Fromm Papers, BU.

90. Ibid., entry for 12 May 1933.

91. Fromm, *Blood and Banquets,* entry for 10 May 1933, 111.

92. Ibid., entry for 10 April 1933, 107.

93. Ibid., entry for 27 May 1933, 113.

94. Ibid., entry for 17 September 1933, 129–31.

95. Undated (December 1933?) comment of Eva von Schroeder, Box 1, Fromm Papers, BU.

96. Fromm, *Blood and Banquets,* entry for 29 November 1933. Cf. diary ms., entry for 1 December 1933, Box 1, Fromm Papers, BU.

97. Diary ms., entry for 13 December. 1933.

98. Ibid., entry for 25 Nov. 1933.

99. Ibid., entry for 1 Dec. 1933.

100. Fromm, *Blood and Banquets,* entry for 25 Jan. 1934, 152.

101. Diary ms., entry for 13 December 1933, Box 1, Fromm Papers, BU.

102. Ibid., entry for 3 January 1934, Box 2, Fromm Papers, BU.

103. Fromm to Dr. Elemer Szego, 24 January 1934, Box 13; Reichsverband to Fromm, 22 February 1934, Box 13, Fromm Papers, BU.

104. Fromm, diary ms., entry for 3 January 1934, Folder 1, Box 2, Fromm Papers, BU.

105. Diary ms., entry for 22 February 1934, Folder 1, Box 2, Fromm Papers, BU.

106. Fromm, *Blood and Banquets,* entry for 16 April 1934, 161. In her diary ms., Fromm put the date for Gonny's departure as 13 April 1934, but in *Blood and Banquets,* she gives it as 6 May 1934.

107. Diary ms., entry for 13 April 1934, Box 2, Fromm Papers, BU.

108. Ibid., entry for 24 August 1934, Box 2, Fromm Papers, BU. See also *Blood and Banquets,* entry for 25 August 1934, 128.

109. *Blood and Banquets,* entry for 7 March 1933, 80.

110. Ibid., entry for 12 September 1933, 129.
111. Hans-Joachim Schoeps, *Die letzten dreissig Jahre: Rückblicke* (Stuttgart: Klett, 1956), 97–98. Cf. Schleunes, *Twisted Road*, 189.
112. Hans-Joachim Schoeps, "Gleiches Los—Ungleiche Lösung," *Der Schild*, 13 April 1934, cited in Herrmann, *Das dritte Reich*, 46. See also Schoeps "Wandlungen im deutschen Menschenbild," *Kölnische Zeitung*, 4 October 1933, Binder 44, Schoeps Papers, SBB. Cf. Schoeps to Frick, 29 September 1933, Schoeps Papers, LBINY.
113. See *Der Vortrupp*, January 1934, Binder 44, Schoeps Papers, SBB.
114. Schoeps, "Nachbemerkung," in *Jugend und Gemeinde*, August 1933, Box 60, Schoeps Papers, SBB.
115. Schoeps, "Wir gehen einen deutschen Weg," *Centralverein Zeitung*, 13 July 1933.
116. He finally rejected this title in September 1934.
117. See, for example, Herbert Loewe to Schoeps, 2 January 1934, Ms. Var. 350/706, Schoeps File, Buber Archive, JNUL.
118. Schoeps to Dr. Herbert Loewe, 15 January 1934, Ms. Var. 350/706, Schoeps File, Buber Archive, JNUL. Schoeps's resentment of "outside" interference recalls the reaction of German Jewish leaders to the efforts of American Jewish figures, such as Stephen Wise, in mounting an anti-German boycott in March 1933.
119. Interior Ministry to Schoeps, 3 October 1933, Schoeps File, LBINY.
120. Schoeps, "Das neue Gesicht der Politik—1933," Binder 44, Schoeps Papers, SBB. See also Schoeps, *Rückblicke*, 89.
121. See Schoeps, "Die deutsche Juden und das Jahr 1933," undated typescript, Box 60, Schoeps Papers, SBB. Cf. Schoeps, *Rückblicke*, 21; and Schoeps to Kreutzberger (May 1966?), Schoeps File, LBINY.
122. See, for example, Schoeps to Buber, 28 September 1933, Ms. Var. 350/706, Schoeps File, Buber Archive, JNUL.
123. Schoeps to Buber, 16 October 1933, Ms. Var. 350/706, Schoeps File, Buber Archive, JNUL.
124. Leo Baeck, "Tage und Leben," *Centralverein Zeitung*, 30 November 1933.

Chapter 7: Testing the "New Jews"

1. Haber to Willstätter, undated (early May 1933?), quoted in Fritz Stern, *Dreams and Delusions: National Socialism in the Drama of the German Past* (New York: Vintage Books, 1989), 73.
2. Haber to Einstein, 7 or 8 August 1933, quoted in Stern, *Dreams and Delusions*, 74.
3. Willstätter to Weizmann, 4 February 1934, Willstätter File, Wiener Library, Tel Aviv.
4. Willstätter to Fajans, 24 October 1935, Willstätter File, Box 5, Fajans Papers, University of Michigan, Ann Arbor.

5. Quoted in Johannes Friedrichs, *Eine Lösung der Judenfrage? Kritische Betrachtungen* (Detmold, Germany: Meyersche Hofbuchhandlung, 1922), 17–18.

6. Cf. Kurt J. Ball-Kaduri, *Das Leben der Juden in Deutschland im Jahre 1933: Ein Zeitbericht* (Frankfurt-am-Main: Europäische Verlagsantalt, 1963), 68.

7. Karl A. Schleunes, *The Twisted Road to Auschwitz: Nazi Policy Toward German Jews, 1933–1939* (Urbana: University of Illinois Press, 1970), 145.

8. Herbert A. Strauss, "Jewish Emigration from Germany: Nazi Policies and Jewish Responses—II," *Leo Baeck Year Book* 26 (1981): 378, note 11.

9. Schleunes, *Twisted Road*, 155.

10. Bernard Kahn, "Report of Activities for the Months of April to October 1934," 14 November 1934, File 628, "Germany—General, 1934," JDC.

11. See, for example, *Der Schild*, 23 February 1934.

12. Leo Löwenstein, "Ich bin ein Deutscher, Ich bin ein Jude," *Der Schild*, 26 January 1934.

13. *Der Schild*, 23 February 1934.

14. Ibid.

15. See, for example, Hans Wollenberg, "Wir hüten das Fronterlebnis," *Der Schild*, 27 April 1934.

16. "Heldengendenktag," *Centralverein Zeitung*, 22 February 1934.

17. See *Der Angriff*, 1 June 1934.

18. Löwenstein to Hindenburg, 23 March 1934, quoted in Klaus J. Herrmann, *Das dritte Reich und die deutsch-jüdischen Organisationen, 1933–1934* (Cologne: Heymann, 1969), 139–40.

19. *Der Schild*, 12 April 1934.

20. *Der Schild*, 12 January 1934.

21. Schoeps to Brod, 23 July 1933, quoted in Julius Schoeps, ed., *Im Streit um Kafka und das Judentum. Briefwechsel: Max Brod—Hans-Joachim Schoeps* (Königstein/Taunus: Jüdischer Verlag bei Athenaeum, 1985), 80.

22. Hans-Joachim Schoeps, "Gleiches Los—Ungleiche Lösung," *Der Schild*, 13 April 1934.

23. Quoted in Hans-Joachim Schoeps, *Rufmord/1970* (Erlangen, Germany: Selbstverlag des Verfassers, 1970), 8.

24. Ibid., 16.

25. *Hamburger Familienblatt*, 26 April 1934, Box 60, Schoeps Papers, SBB.

26. W. Ware Adams, "Current Immigration to the United States from the Consular District of Berlin, Germany," 27 October 1934, 811.111 Quota 62/468, Box 165, RG 59, NRC.

27. See Philip Metcalfe, *1933* (Sag Harbor, N.Y.: Permanent Press, 1988), 179.

28. Between April 1933 and August 1934, the RjF sent twenty-eight let-

ters to the government, arguing that it should be granted special status in the Reich. See Ulrich Dunker, *Der Reichsbund jüdischer Frontsoldaten: Geschichte eines jüdischen Abwehrvereins* (Düsseldorf: Droste, 1977), 133.

29. See Gestapo decree of 12 February 1935, Folder 8, Box 19, Kreutzberger Papers, LBINY.

30. Bella Fromm, *Blood and Banquets: A Berlin Social Diary* (New York: Carol Publishing Group, 1990), entry for 2 August 1934, 177.

31. Schleunes, *Twisted Road*, 179–80.

32. For details of this event, I am indebted to Prof. Gary Lease, University of California, Santa Cruz, who heard this story from Frank Shurman, one of Schoeps's fellow members of the Deutscher Vanguard.

33. Herbert Freeden, *Die jüdische Presse im Dritten Reich* (Frankfurt-am-Main: Jüdischer Verlag bei Athenaeum, 1987) , 39.

34. See Schoeps to "Comrades," undated (1934), "Deutscher Vortrupp" Folder, Box 40, Schoeps Papers, SBB.

35. "Protocol of National Meeting [Bundestag] 1934/35," 29 December 1934, "Deutscher Vortrupp" Folder, Box 40, Schoeps Papers, SBB.

36. Schoeps to his "fellow students," undated typescript (1942?), "Deutscher Vortrupp" Folder, Box 40, Schoeps Papers, SBB.

37. Deutscher Vortrupp, declaration of 22 March 1935, "Deutscher Vortrupp" Folder, Box 40, Schoeps Papers, SBB.

38. Schoeps, *Bereit für Deutschland: Der Patriotismus deutscher Juden und der Nationalsozialismus: Frühe Schriften, 1930 bis 1939: Eine historische Dokumentation* (Berlin: Haude and Spener, 1970), 25, 27. Some 1,000 RjF members, out of a total membership of 50,000–55,000, also pledged their willingness to serve. See Dunker, *Reichsbund*, 9, 173. Cf. Herrmann, *Das dritte Reich*, 49.

39. Dunker, *Reichsbund*, 175.

40. Schoeps, *Bereit für Deutschland*, 54, 57.

41. *Der Schild*, 16 February 1934.

42. *Centralverein Zeitung*, 1 February 1934.

43. Reported in Neville Laski to Adler, 21 March 1934, "1934" Folder, Cyrus Adler correspondence, 1929–35, AJC.

44. Wilfrid Israel, "General Situation," "1934" Folder, Cyrus Adler correspondence, 1929–35, AJC.

45. Remarks of Otto Hirsch, *Der Morgen*, February 1934. Quoted in Fritz Friedlander, "Trials and Tribulations of Education in Nazi Germany," *Leo Baeck Year Book* 3 (1958): 190.

46. Leo Baeck, "Unsre Gemeinde," *Gemeindeblatt der jüdischen Gemeinde zu Berlin*, 2 February 1934.

47. *Bayerische-israelitische Gemeindezeitung*, 1 March 1934.

48. *Jüdische Rundschau* 7 September 1934.

49. *Gemeindeblatt* (Berlin), 14 April 1935.

50. *Bayerische-israelitische Gemeindezeitung,* I November 1934.

51. *Der Schild,* 19 October 1934.

52. For a more complete account of this memorandum, see Leonard Baker, *Days of Sorrow and Pain: Leo Baeck and the Berlin Jews* (New York: Oxford University Press, 1980), 171–74.

53. For a copy of Baeck's remarks of 5 August 1934, see Hindenburg File, LBINY.

54. Baker, *Days of Sorrow and Pain,* 197.

55. Fromm, *Blood and Banquets,* entry for 2 August 1934, 177–79.

56. In late June Max Warburg met with Papen to protest the mistreatment of the Jews, but did not receive any promise of help. See Ron Chernow, *The Warburgs: The Twentieth Century Odyssey of a Remarkable Jewish Family* (New York: Random House, 1993), 429.

57. Fromm, *Blood and Banquets,* xii.

58. Fromm, diary ms., entry for 25 June 1934, Box 2, Fromm Papers, BU.

59. Fromm, *Blood and Banquets,* entry for I July 1934, 170.

60. Ibid., 170–71.

61. *Bayerische-israelitische Gemeindezeitung,* I July 1934.

62. *Jüdische Rundschau,* 3 July 1934.

63. *Gemeindeblatt* (Berlin), 7 July 1934.

64. Arthur Ruppin to Martin Rosenbluth, 11 July 1934, in Ruppin, *Briefe, Tagebücher, Erinnerungen,* ed. Schlomo Krolik (Königstein/Taunus: Jüdischer Verlag bei Athenaeum, 1985), 451.

65. Lazaron to Felix Warburg, 15 July 1934, File 12, Box 382, Felix Warburg Papers, AJA. In private, Max Warburg still maintained that the Nazis would not hold on to power for long. In May he criticized one of his relatives, Siegmund Warburg, for fleeing the country. See Chernow, *The Warburgs,* 413.

66. *Der Schild,* 18 July 1934.

67. *Jüdische Rundschau,* 31 July 1934.

68. Walter Laqueur, *Young Germany: A History of the German Youth Movement* (London: Routledge and Kegan Paul, 1962), 63.

69. Schoeps to Ernst Caselmann, I October 1930, "Deutscher Vortrupp" Folder, Box 40, Schoeps Papers, SBB.

70. Schoeps referred to Abraham as his "tragic love." See Gary Lease, "Deutscher Vortrupp membership," undated typescript, Santa Cruz, Calif.

71. William E. Dodd, *Ambassador Dodd's Diary, 1933–1938,* ed. William E. Dodd, Jr. and Martha Dodd (New York: Harcourt, Brace, 1941), entry for 9 August 1934, 145.

72. Warburg to Hirschland, 15 October 1934, Reichsvertretung der deutschen Juden Papers, LBINY.

73. Felix Warburg to Siegmund Warburg, I June 1936, Folder 10, Box 332, Felix Warburg Papers, AJA.

74. Lazaron to Felix Warburg and Paul Baerwald, 11 April 1935, Folder 10, Box 315, Felix Warburg Papers, AJA.

75. Messersmith to Lazaron, 29 August 1934, Folder 10, Box 315, Felix Warburg Papers, AJA. But by March 1935, Messersmith had changed his mind. See his memorandum of 22 March 1935, No. 495, Messersmith Papers, UD.

76. Dodd, *Diary*, entry for 28 July 1934, 135.

77. Warburg to Weltsch, 7 December 1933, Ms. Var. 350/880, Weltsch File, Buber Archive, JNUL.

78. See Ernst Kahn's report on his visit to the United States, *Jüdische Rundschau*, 20 November 1934.

79. Lazaron to Warburg, 6 December 1934, Folder 10, Box 315, Felix Warburg Papers, AJA.

80. Selig Brodetsky, "Confidential Note of a Brief Visit to Berlin by Dr. Selig Brodetsky, August 29–September 2, 1934," "1934" Folder, Cyrus Adler correspondence, AJC, 192.

81. Geist to Hull, No. 2125, 28 July 1934, 862.4016/410, Box 6787, RG 59, NA.

82. Fromm, *Blood and Banquets*, entry for 1 October 1934, 183.

83. Cf. Reichsverband to Weltsch, 5 October 1934, saying that Goebbels would allow him to continue working. Folder 6, Box 4, Weltsch Papers, LBINY.

84. *Jüdische Rundschau*, 6 June 1935.

85. "The Jew Is a Human Being, Too," *Jüdische Rundschau*, 9 July 1935.

86. Freeden, *Die jüdische Presse*, 22.

87. Lazaron to Felix Warburg and Paul Baerwald, 18 May 1935, Folder 10, Box 315, Felix Warburg Papers. At about the same time, Felix Warburg was receiving reports in New York that his brother was "slipping into despair," seeing no hope for German Jewry other than emigration. Chernow, *The Warburgs*, 432.

88. Willstätter to W. E. Tisdale and H. M. Miller, 2 June 1935, Series 717D, "Univ. of Munich: Chemistry," File 145-46, Box 15, RG I.I, Rockefeller Foundation Papers, Rockefeller Archive Center, North Tarrytown, N.Y.

89. Willstätter to W. E. Tisdale, 11 October 1935, File 717D ("Univ. of Munich: Chemistry"), File 145-46, Box 15, RG I.I, Rockefeller Foundation Papers, Rockefeller Archive Center, North Tarrytown, N.Y.

90. Chaim Weizmann, *Trial and Error: The Autobiography of Chaim Weizmann* (New York: Schocken Books, 1966), 351.

91. See *Bayerische-israelitische Gemeindezeitung*, 15 March 1935, for a preview of Schoeps's lecture on 1 April 1935.

92. Hans-Joachim Schoeps, "Franz Kafka: Der Dichter der tragischen Position," *Der Schild*, 10 May 1935.

93. See Schoeps's account of his trip to Rome in *Centralverein Zeitung,* 17 October 1935.
94. See *Centralverein Zeitung,,* 21 February 1935.
95. See Warburg's speech to the Hilfsverein, 18 June 1935, *Jüdische Rundschau,* 21 June 1935.
96. *Centralverein Zeitung,* 2 September 1934.
97. See *Centralverein Zeitung,* 6 June 1935; and *Gemeindeblatt* (Berlin), 16 June 1935.
98. See editorial in the *Centralverein Zeitung,* 20 December 1934.
99. Ernst Herzfeld, "Meine letzten Jahre in Deutschland, 1933–1938," 01/8, Ball-Kaduri Collection of Testimonies, RG 41,Yad Vashem Archives, Jerusalem, 19.
100. *Centralverein Zeitung,* 17 January 1935.
101. Leni Yahil, *The Holocaust: The Fate of European Jewry, 1932–1945,* trans. Ina Friedman and Haya Galai (New York: Oxford University Press, 1991), 69. Cf. *Gemeindeblatt* (Berlin), 3 March 1935.
102. See Alfred Hirschberg, "Chronik," *Centralverein Zeitung,* 7 March 1935; and *Gemeindeblatt* (Berlin), 10 March 1935.
103. Dodd, *Diary,* entry for 8 March 1935, 219.
104. In April Warburg was more pessimistic about the economic situation facing the Jews. See Lazaron to Felix Warburg and Paul Baerwald, 11 April 1935, Folder 10, Box 315, Felix Warburg Papers, AJA.
105. The fact his bank was still making a profit by doing business with firms, such as Krupp, was one Warburg sought to conceal. See Chernow, *The Warburgs,* 443.
106. As of 2 October 1934, persons emigrating from the Reich could take with them no more than 10 reichsmarks, or $4, without special permission of the Foreign Exchange Bureau. This amount represented a sharp decline from the 25,000 marks, or nearly $6,000, permitted a year before. See W. Ware Adams, "Current Immigration to the United States from the Consular District of Berlin, Germany," 27 October 1934, 811.111 Quota 62/468, RG 59, NRC, 19.
107. By late 1933 German Jews who could offer proof that relatives in the United States would support them or who had firm prospects of employment were no longer being denied visas as a general practice. A July 1933 change in the visa provisions had made it easier for Jews with relatives to qualify for entry into the United States. And, as the consular official W. Ware Adams reported, in October 1934, "the 'public charge' and 'contract labor' provisions of the Act of February 5, 1917, are not operating to hinder the migration to the United States of aliens who will take employment there at the present time as they did during a period beginning at the end of 1929." See his "Current Immigration to the United States," 13.

Still, by September 1934 over 82,000 Jews were on the waiting list for U.S. visas, either because they had been judged "temporarily inadmissible" under the "public charge" clause or because employment conditions during the depression had previously warranted a delay in the processing of their application. See Raymond Geist to Hull, 10 September 1934, 811.111 Quota 62/65, RG 59, NRC.

Chapter 8: Second-Class Citizens

1. Werner Rosenstock, "Exodus, 1933–1939: A Survey of Jewish Emigration from Germany," *Leo Baeck Year Book* 1 (1956): 376.
2. Ron Chernow, *The Warburgs: The Twentieth Century Odyssey of a Remarkable Jewish Family* (New York: Random House, 1993), 402.
3. Rosenstock, "Exodus," 376, 381.
4. Arno Mayer, *Why Did the Heavens Not Darken? The "Final Solution" in History* (New York: Pantheon, 1988), 195.
5. Zionist fund-raising trebled during the years 1933–35 over the 1931–32 level. See Hannah Arendt, *Eichmann in Jerusalem: A Report on the Banality of Evil* (New York: Viking Press, 1963), 54.
6. Quoted in Max Gruenewald, "The Beginning of the Reichsvertretung," *Leo Baeck Year Book* 1 (1956): 59.
7. *Jüdische Rundschau,* 7 May 1935.
8. Martin Rosenbluth, *Go Forth and Serve: Early Years and Public Life* (New York: Herzl Press, 1961), 265.
9. Arendt, *Eichmann,* 36. Eichmann also studied Hebrew in 1937.
10. Leni Yahil, *The Holocaust: The Fate of European Jewry, 1932–1945,* trans. Ina Friedman and Haya Galai (New York: Oxford University Press, 1991), 69, put the date as 1935.
11. *Centralverein Zeitung,* 9 May 1935.
12. See Gruenewald, "Beginning," 58–61.
13. See Margaret T. Edelheim-Mühsam, "Reactions of the Jewish Press to the Nazi Challenge," *Leo Baeck Year Book* 5 (1960): 323. Cf. Gruenewald, "Beginning," 61.
14. See *Jüdische Rundschau,* 11 August 1935, for the compromise solution reached in the Berlin Gemeinde.
15. Ruth Gay, *The Jews of Germany: A Historical Portrait* (New Haven, Conn.: Yale University Press, 1992), 260.
16. *Jüdische Rundschau,* 12 March 1935 and 22 March 1935.
17. Yahil, *Holocaust,* 65.
18. Charles M. Hathaway, Jr. (U.S. consul general, Munich) to William E. Dodd, 13 May 1935, 862.4016/1460, Box 6787, RG 59, NA.
19. Shlomo Shafir, "American Diplomats in Berlin (1933–1939) and their Attitude to the Nazi Persecution of the Jews," *Yad Vashem Studies* 9 (1973): 88.
20. JTA, cable dispatches, 5 August 1935.

21. JTA, 8 August 1935 and 9 August 1935.

22. *Jüdische Rundschau,* 5 August 1935.

23. Quoted in Jeremy Noakes and Geoffrey Pridham, eds., *Nazism: A History in Documents and Eyewitness Accounts, 1919–1945* (New York: Schocken Books, 1984), 531.

24. Yahil, *Holocaust,* 61.

25. Ibid., 70.

26. See Ian Kershaw, *The "Hitler Myth": Image and Reality in the Third Reich* (New York: Oxford University Press, 1989), 235–36. Cf. Gustav Otto Warburg, *Six Years of Hitler: The Jews Under the Nazi Regime* (London: George Allen and Unwin, 1939), 20.

27. *Jüdische Rundschau,* 30 August 1935 and 19 August 1935.

28. J. C. Hyman to Paul Baerwald, 3 October 1935, File 629, "Germany–General, 1935," JDC.

29. Frick's remarks were quoted in *Centralverein Zeitung,* 3 May 1935.

30. *Jüdische Rundschau,* 10 and 11 September 1935. In fact, as late as 1938, one-fourth of Jewish schoolchildren were still attending German schools.

31. "Jewish Schools," *Jüdische Rundschau,* 13 September 1935.

32. JTA, 19 September 1935.

33. See *Jüdische Rundschau,* 24 September 1935, for the entire Reichsvertretung statement.

34. *Centralverein Zeitung,* 26 September 1935.

35. Esriel E. Hildesheimer, "The Central Organization of the German Jews in the Years 1933–1945: Its Legal and Political Status and Its Position in the Jewish Community" (Master's thesis, Hebrew University of Jerusalem, 1982), 54.

36. "Lift Up Your Hearts," *Gemeindeblatt* (Berlin), 22 September 1935.

37. *Der Schild,* 20 September 1935.

38. *Jüdische Rundschau,* 24 September 1935.

39. *Der Schild,* 27 September 1935.

40. *Centralverein Zeitung,* 26 September 1935.

41. Cf. Karl A. Schleunes, *The Twisted Road to Auschwitz: Nazi Policy Toward German Jews, 1933–1939* (Urbana: University of Illinois Press, 1970), 63.

42. Bella Fromm, *Blood and Banquets: A Berlin Social Diary* (New York: Carol Publishing Group, 1990), entry for 15 September 1935, 205.

43. Ibid., entry for 12 October 1935, 206.

44. *Centralverein Zeitung,* 17 October 1935.

45. Fromm, *Blood and Banquets,* entry for 28 October 1935, 209.

46. JTA, 23 September 1935.

47. Geist to Hull, 5 February 1936, 811.III Quota 62/494, RG 59, NRC.

48. Quoted in David S. Wyman, *Paper Walls: America and the Refugee Crisis,*

1938–1941 (Amherst: University of Massachusetts Press, 1968), 4–5.

49. JTA, 6 October 1935.
50. Cf. Leonard Baker, *Days of Sorrow and Pain: Leo Baeck and the Berlin Jews* (New York: Oxford University Press, 1980), 203.
51. See undated typescript, Folder C 11/12/37, Box C 11/12/33 to 40, BOD.
52. Baeck, "Verbatim Text of the Prayer for Kol Nidre 1935, Written by Rabbi Leo Baeck," Folder 2, Box 3, Leo Baeck Institute (London) Papers, LBINY.
53. Quoted in Baker, *Days of Sorrow and Pain*, 206.
54. Ibid., 207–08.
55. Hildesheimer, "Central Organization," 68.
56. Herbert Freeden, *Die jüdische Presse im Dritten Reich* (Frankfurt-am-Main: Jüdischer Verlag bei Athenaeum, 1987), 24. Cf. Messersmith to James Dunn, No. 573, 13 Sept. 1935, Messersmith Papers, UD.
57. *Jüdische Rundschau*, 10 October 1935.
58. *Neues Wiener Tageblatt*, 24 October 1935.
59. JTA, 24 October 1935. Cf. Ernst Herzfeld, "Meine letzten Jahre in Deutschland, 1933–1938," 01/8, Ball-Kaduri Collection of Testimonies, RG 41, Yad Vashem Archives, Jerusalem, 22.
60. *Jüdische Rundschau*, 14 October 1935.
61. "Tröstet, tröstet mein Volk," *Jüdische Rundschau*, 20 September 1935.
62. *Jüdische Rundschau*, 20 September 1935.
63. *Jüdische Rundschau*, 12 November 1935.
64. Die Judenfrage für die Juden," *Jüdische Rundschau*, 22 November 1935.
65. *Der Schild*, 22 November 1935.
66. See "Die Wirtschaftsbetätigung der Juden," *Jüdische Rundschau*, 15 October 1935, for comments on Frick's address.
67. "Klare Scheidung auf legalem Wege," *Jüdische Rundschau*, 5 November 1935.
68. Cf. JTA, 5 November 1935; and Messersmith to Dunn, No. 601, 21 October 1935, Messersmith Papers, UD.
69. JTA, 25 November 1935
70. *Centralverein Zeitung*, 24 December 1935.
71. "Öffnet die Tore!" *Jüdische Rundschau*, 26 November 1935.
72. JTA, 27 November 1935.
73. Quoted, in English trans., in JTA, 27 November 1935.
74. Chernow, *The Warburgs*, 441. In a 1936 speech before members of B'nai B'rith in Berlin, Warburg urged his audience to leave the country, but then retracted his words once the Gestapo officials who were keeping tabs on him left the hall.
75. David Farrer, *The Warburgs: The Story of a Family* (Briarcliff Manor, N.Y.: Stein and Day, 1975), 114. Schacht informed Warburg that the

Nuremberg laws were aimed at restoring "tranquility" to German economic life. See Chernow, *The Warburgs*, 435.

76. William E. Dodd, *Ambassador Dodd's Diary, 1933–1938,* ed. William E. Dodd, Jr. and Martha Dodd (New York: Harcourt, Brace, 1941), entry for 27 November 1935, 280.

77. Avraham Barkai, "German Interests in the Haavara Transfer Agreement, 1933–1939," *Leo Baeck Year Book* 35 (1990): 257.

78. Ernst Marcus, "The German Foreign Office and the Palestine Question in the Period 1933–1939," *Yad Vashem Studies* 2 (1958): 260.

79. Cf. Siegmund Warburg to Felix Warburg, 1 January 1936, and Felix Warburg to Siegmund Warburg, 1 January 1936, Folder 10, Box 332, Felix Warburg Papers, AJA. The Nazis kept these negotiations secret, to avoid the embarrassment of being seen as dealing with Jews as equals. Chernow, *The Warburgs*, 437.

80. See Barkai, "German Interests," 259. This position hardened in February 1936 when the Gestapo took an active role in dealing with Jewish leaders, supplanting governmental officials.

81. Wise to Julian Mack, 28 February 1936, Box 115 ("Corr.-Mack, Julian W., 1934–1936"), Wise Papers, AJHS.

82. Felix Warburg to Siegmund Warburg, 16 March 1936, Folder 10, Box 332, Felix Warburg Papers, AJA.

83. Naomi Shepherd, *Refuge from Darkness:Wilfrid Israel and the Rescue of the Jews* (New York: Pantheon, 1984), 109.

84. Messersmith to William Phillips, No. 550, 20 July 1935, Messersmith Papers, UD.

85. Warburg to Schäffer, 22 November 1935, Box 1B (Corr., 1934–1935), Schäffer Papers, LBINY. Coincidentally, this was the same phrase that Bella Fromm used to describe her efforts on behalf of her fellow Jews.

   Warburg's modest assessment of what his plan could accomplish reflected a deeper pessimism about the Jews' plight in the Third Reich. In January 1936 Stephen Wise met with President Roosevelt, who quoted a letter from Warburg, saying that "nothing can be done" to help Germany's Jews. Wise and Louis Brandeis thought this letter of Warburg dissuaded the American president from taking any steps to help the Jews. (In October Roosevelt told Wise that Warburg was advising him not to make any public comment on the Nazis' treatment of the Jews.) See Richard Breitman and Alan M. Kraut, *American Refuge Policy and European Jewry, 1933–1945* (Bloomington: Indiana University Press, 1987), 98, 100.

86. JTA, 26 April 1936.

87. *Centralverein Zeitung,* 23 January 1936.

88. Siegmund Warburg to Felix Warburg, 1 March 1936, Folder 10, Box 332, Felix Warburg Papers, AJA. This occurred nearly three months

after an article in the Nazi press predicted that Jewish banks would be "slowly but firmly liquidated." JTA, 6 December 1935.

89. Siegmund Warburg to Felix Warburg, 23 June 1936, Folder 10, Box 332, Felix Warburg Papers, AJA.

90. "An die Juden in Deutschland," *Centralverein Zeitung*, 27 May 1936.

91. *Bayerische-israelitische Gemeindezeitung*, 1 June 1936.

92. Rosenstock, "Exodus," 378.

93. Ibid., 377.

94. Cf. the comments that Bruno Bettelheim heard in 1938, when he was imprisoned in Buchenwald. See Bettelheim, *The Informed Heart*, 258.

95. See Richard Lichtheim, *Die Geschichte des deutschen Zionismus* (Jerusalem: R. Mass, 1954), 264.

96. Herbert A. Strauss, "Jewish Emigration from Germany: Nazi Policies and Jewish Responses—I," 344.

97. For a fictional presentation of the view of older German Jews, see Lion Feuchtwanger, *The Oppermanns* (New York: Viking Press, 1934), 311.

98. For a detailed analysis of emigration patterns, see Malcolm C. Burke (U.S. consul general, Hamburg), "Statistics Regarding Groups of Immigrants Receiving Visas at Hamburg During the First Half of 1934," 1 March 1935, 811.111 Quota 62/476, RG 59, NRC.

99. Strauss, "Emigration—I," 317.

100. JTA, 4 March 1936. Cf. Felix Warburg to Siegmund Warburg, 9 March 1936, Folder 10, Box 332, Felix Warburg Papers, AJA.

101. See Warburg's speech on emigration, *Jüdische Rundschau*, 8 May 1936.

102. "Auf die Fahrt nach USA," *Jüdische Rundschau*, 26 May 1936.

103. "Erste Eindrücke in USA," *Jüdische Rundschau*, 19 June 1936.

104. *Jüdische Rundschau*, 18 August 1936.

105. *Centralverein Zeitung*, 6 August 1936.

106. *Der Schild*, 21 August 1936.

107. Hans-Joachim Schoeps, "Die deutsche Juden und das Jahr 1933," Box 60, Schoeps Papers, SBB.

108. Hans-Joachim Schoeps to members of the Deutscher Vortrupp, undated holograph (1939), "Deutscher Vortrupp" Folder, Box 40, Schoeps Papers, SBB.

109. Hans-Joachim Schoeps, *Die letzten dreissig Jahre: Rückblicke* (Stuttgart: Klett, 1956), 102.

110. Ibid., 103. Cf. Bernhard Kahn to J. C. Hyman, "The Situation of German Jewry as of January 1936," File 630, "Germany—General, 1936–37," JDC, referring to the arrest of a Rabbi Maybaum after he attended a meeting with Schoeps, his publisher.

111. Hans-Joachim Schoeps, "Memorandum Regarding the German Vanguard: Rights and Constitution of the German Jews," undated typescript, Box 38, Schoeps Papers, SBB.

112. See Julius H. Schoeps, ed., *Im Streit um Kafka und das Judentum, Briefwechsel: Max Brod–Hans-Joachim Schoeps* (Königstein/Taunus: Jüdischer Verlag bei Athenaeum, 1985), 22.
113. Schoeps to Rade, 22 August 1936, in Wilhelm Kantzenbach, "Das wissenschaftliche Werden von Hans-Joachim Schoeps und seine Vertreibung aus Deutschland 1938," *Zeitschrift für Religions-und Geistesgeschichte* 32 (1980): 343.
114. Barth to Schoeps, 31 August 1936, in Gary Lease, "Der Briefwechsel zwischen Karl Barth und Hans-Joachim Schoeps (1926–1946)," *Menora: Jahrbuch für deutsch-jüdische Geschichte* (Munich: Piper Verlag, 1991), 124–25.
115. Schoeps to Barth, 4 August 1936, in Lease, "Briefwechsel," 123–24; and Schoeps to Barth, 27 December 1936, in ibid., 126.
116. Schoeps, *Rückblicke,* 101.
117. Richard Willstätter to W. E. Tisdale, 27 April 1936, Series 717D: "Univ. of Munich: Chemistry," File 145-46, Box 15, RG 1.1, Rockefeller Foundation Papers, Rockefeller Archive Center, North Tarrytown, N.Y.
118. See, for example, Richard Willstätter to Felix Haurowitz, 17 January 1936, Haurowitz Papers, Manuscripts Department, Lilly Library, Indiana University, Bloomington.
119. In 1936 Willstätter received honorary membership in the India Academy of Science, the Physiological Society (Great Britain), and the Society of Biological Chemistry (India).
120. Richard Willstätter to Kasimir Fajans, 27 October 1935, Willstätter File, Fajans Papers, University of Michigan, Ann Arbor.
121. Fromm, *Blood and Banquets,* entry for 16 July 1936, 222.
122. Ibid., entry for 15 August 1936, 225.
123. Ibid., entry for 15 August 1936, 225.
124. Ibid., entry for 18 August 1936, 227. In her diary ms. (Folder 2, Box 2), Fromm put the period of Gonny's visit as May to July 1936.
125. *Blood and Banquets,* entry for 28 August 1936, 278. Cf. diary ms., entries for 27 and 28 August 1936, Folder 2, Box 2, Fromm Papers, BU.

Chapter 9: Tightening the Noose

1. See, for example, JTA, 8 September 1936.
2. JTA, 9 September. 1936.
3. Quoted in Leni Yahil, *The Holocaust: The Fate of European Jewry, 1932–1945,* trans. Ina Friedman and Haya Galai (New York: Oxford University Press, 1991), 70.
4. Ibid., 90.
5. For an indication of Jewish premonitions, see JTA, 21 October 1936.

6. JTA, 11 September 1936.
7. JTA, 30 September 1936.
8. JTA, 16 October 1936.
9. JTA, 25 October 1936.
10. JTA, 30 October 1936.
11. JTA, 27 November 1936.
12. JTA, 4 December 1936.
13. JTA, 9 and 10 December 1936
14. JTA, 7 February 1937.
15. See January 1937 report of Section II-112 on the "Jewish problem," Folder 4, Box 9, Kreutzberger Papers, LBINY. Cf. "Report on the Stand of Section II-112 in the Fight Against Jewry," 18 December 1936, No. 2934950, Roll 410, "Captured German Records: Records of the Reich Leader SS and Chief of the German Police," Part III, NA.
16. JTA, 11 October 1936.
17. Gestapo decree of 7 October 1936, Folder 8, Box 19, Kreutzberger Papers, LBINY.
18. See Gestapo directive (Hildesheim), 25 November 1935, Folder 52 ("Germany—Göttingen"), Box 8, RG 116, YIVO.
19. Gestapo directive, "Ban of Jewish Meetings and Events," 21 December 1936, Folder 8, Box 19, Kreutzberger Papers, LBINY. Cf. Gestapo directive (Hildesheim), 4 January 1937, Folder 52 ("Germany—Göttingen"), Box 8, RG 116, YIVO.
20. JTA, 22 January 1937.
21. *Jüdische Rundschau*, 27 January 1937. In the period July–September 1936, 3,268 Jews left Germany and 439 moved to Berlin. *Centralverein Zeitung*, 1 January 1937.
22. "The Emigration Question," *Centralverein Zeitung*, 4 March 1937.
23. Werner Rosenstock, "Exodus, 1933–1939: A Survey of Jewish Emigration from Germany," *Leo Baeck Year Book 1* (1956): 376.
24. *Centralverein Zeitung*, 4 February 1937. The South African government also ruled that immigrants could not work in fields currently employing native citizens.
25. JTA, 15 February 1937.
26. The Stuttgart consulate, for example, reported it was overwhelmed by the number of visa seekers, starting in August 1936: the number of applicants had doubled over the previous year.
27. See, for example, John Farr Simmons, (chief, Visa Division) to Benjamin R. Riggs (U.S. consul, Helsinki), 14 May 1937, 150.062 Public Charge/915 1/2, Box 38, RG 59, NRC.
28. See, for example, Samuel W. Honaker (U.S. consul general, Stuttgart) to Hull, "Status of Visa Work at the American Consulate, Stuttgart, Germany, With a Summary of the Work for September 1936," 5

October 1936, 811.111 Quota 62/511, RG 59, NRC. In September 1936, for example, of the 865 visa applicants who were screened in Stuttgart, 75 percent were Jews; 696 received approval for immigration to the United States. Nearly all successful applicants had proof of adequate financial support from relatives or friends in the United States.

29. See J. C. Hyman to Adolph Ginsberg, 1 February 1937, File 657, "Emigration—General, 1933–1937," JDC.

30. See Honaker to Hull, "Comment Regarding Charges of Improper Conduct of Immigration Work at Stuttgart," 24 June 1937, 811.111 Quota 62/550, RG 59, NRC. The Stuttgart consular district encompassed some 30 million German citizens and, along with Montreal, had the largest visa-issuing office in the world. It approved 5,244 Jewish visa applications in 1936 and 2,928 in 1937.

31. JTA, 29 October 1936.

32. *Centralverein Zeitung*, 16 September 1936.

33. *Jüdische Rundschau*, 20 October 1936.

34. "Kundgebungen in Berlin," *Centralverein Zeitung*, 19 November 1936.

35. *Centralverein Zeitung*, 14 January 1937.

36. Robert Weltsch to F. Rosenblüth, 15 March 1930, Hans Kohn correspondence, Box 14, Weltsch Papers, LBINY.

37. Robert Weltsch to Arthur Ruppin, 28 April 1936, A 107/399, CZA.

38. Robert Weltsch to Hugo Bergmann, 18 August 1936, Folder 1, Box 2, Weltsch Papers, LBINY.

39. Robert Weltsch to Martin Buber, 28 April 1936, Ms. Var. 350/880, Buber Archive, JNUL.

40. "Kundgebungen in Berlin."

41. Weltsch to Buber, 28 July 1936, Ms. Var, 350/880, Buber Archive, JNUL.

42. JTA, 11 August 1937.

43. See, for example, Robert Weltsch to Chaim Weizmann, 14 January 1938, Weltsch File, Weizmann Archives. Here Weltsch called the Peel report a "way out" for the Jews.

44. Cf. comments of Alfred Mond, Lord Melchett, at the Zionist Congress: "To my astonishment several speeches dealt with the Jewish Problem, as though the question of the Jews exists in a vacuum." quoted in Anita Shapira, "Did the Zionist Leadership Foresee the Holocaust?" in *Living With Antisemitism: Modern Jewish Responses*, ed. Jehuda Reinharz (Hanover, N.H.: University Press of New England, 1987), 403.

45. Robert Weltsch, "Four Years Ago and Today," *Jüdische Rundschau*, 27 January 1937.

46. "On the First of April," *Jüdische Rundschau*, 1 April 1937.

47. Ernst Herzfeld, "Meine letzten Jahre in Deutschland, 1933–1935," 01/8, Ball-Kaduri Collection of Testimonies, RG 41, Yad Vashem Archives, Jerusalem, 30.
48. "Spirit and Form of Jewish Work," *Centralverein Zeitung*, 11 March 1937. Cf. ibid., 32.
49. See Ruth Berlak to Baron Hans-Hasso von Veltheim, 15 April 1937, Box 3, Baker Papers, LBINY.
50. JTA, 19 March 1937.
51. For details of the Gestapo raid, see Grete Baer, "The Closing of the Berlin Lodge of B'nai B'rith in April 1937," 01/234, Ball-Kaduri Collection of Testimonies, RG 41, Yad Vashem Archives, Jerusalem.
52. JTA, 21 May 1937.
53. JTA, 21 May 1937. One B'nai B'rith member supposedly was a former Communist member of the Prussian Landstag.
54. In its May–June 1934 report, Section II-112 described B'nai B'rith as the strongest Jewish organization for executing the Jewish "line" of policy. See *SS Lagebericht*, May–June 1934, Folder 1, Box 9, Kreutzberger Papers, LBINY.
55. Kahn to Hyman, 11 May 1937, Folder 630, "Germany—General, 1936–1937," JDC.
56. Carl J. Rheins, "The Verband nationaldeutscher Juden, 1921–1933," *Leo Baeck Year Book* 25 (1980): 260.
57. Richard Lichtheim, *Die Geschichte des deutschen Zionismus* (Jerusalem: R. Mass, 1954), 258.
58. See Kareski's article in *Der Staatszionist*, 31 March 1935, and his interview in *Der Angriff*, 23 December 1935.
59. Herbert S. Levine, "A Jewish Collaborator in Nazi Germany: The Strange Career of Georg Kareski (1933–37)," *Central European History* 8 (September 1975): 266.
60. Ibid., 237.
61. Herbert A. Strauss, "Jewish Emigration from Germany: Nazi Policies and Jewish Responses—II," *Leo Baeck Year Book* 26 (1981): 353.
62. Herzfeld, "Meine letzten Jahre," 34. See also "Report on the Difficulties of the Reichsvertretung," 6 July 1937, Box EI, Baker Papers, LBINY.
63. Quoted in Lucy S. Dawidowicz, *The War Against the Jews, 1933–1945* (New York: Holt, Rinehart and Winston, 1975), 195.
64. Samuel Goldsmid to Felix Warburg, 10 June 1937, File 643, "Reichsvertretung der deutschen Juden—General, 1935–1943," JDC.
65. "Protocol of the Session of the Presiding Committee and Council of the Reichsvertretung of Jews in Germany," 15 June 1937, Folder 1, Box 18, Kreutzberger Papers, LBINY.
66. Herzfeld, "Meine letzten Jahre," 36.

67. See "Report on the Difficulties of the Reichsvertretung," 6 July 1937, Box EI, Baker Papers, LBINY.
68. Leonard Baker, *Days of Sorrow and Pain: Leo Baeck and the Berlin Jews* (New York: Oxford University Press, 1980), 202. Cf. Baeck to von Veltheim, 8 February 1935, Box 3, Baker Papers, LBINY.
69. Arthur Prinz called Baeck one of a dozen "honest, capable, and upstanding Jews" left in the country. See Prinz to Anita Warburg, 30 May 1937, Folder 2, Box 7, Prinz Papers, LBINY.
70. Weltsch, introduction to *Leo Baeck Year Book* I (1956), x.
71. Quoted in Baker, *Days of Sorrow and Pain*, 203.
72. Ibid., xiii.
73. Ernst Simon, "Jewish Adult Education in Nazi Germany as Spiritual Resistance," *Leo Baeck Year Book* I (1956): 89.
74. Arthur Ruppin, *Briefe, Tagebücher, Erinnerungen*, ed. Schlomo Krolik (Königstein/Taunus: Jüdischer Verlag bei Athenaeum, 1985), entry for 23 August 1937, 489.
75. Cf. Schoeps to Rade, 22 August 1936, in Wilhelm Kantzenbach, "Das wissenschaftliche Werden von Hans-Joachim Schoeps und seine Vertreibung aus Deutschland 1938," *Zeitschrift für Religious-und Geistes-geschichte* 32 (1980): 343.
76. Schoeps to Rade, 8 June 1937, in Kantzenbach, "Das wissenschaftliche Werden," 345.
77. See, for example, Dr. Leonard Goldschmidt to Schoeps, 25 April 1937, Binder 94, Schoeps Papers, SBB.
78. Schoeps to Barth, 8 April 1946, in Gary Lease, "Briefwechsel zwischen Karl Barth und Hans-Joachim Schoeps (1929–1946)," *Menora: Jahrbuch für deutsch-jüdische Geschichte* 2 (1991): 130.
79. See Schoeps to Gestapo, 20 December 1937, Binder 94, Schoeps Papers, SBB.
80. Ibid.
81. Society for the Advancement of Economic Interests to Schoeps, 3 November 1937, Binder 94, Schoeps Papers, SBB.
82. Schoeps to Buber, 30 October 1937, Ms. Var. 350/706, Schoeps File, Buber Archive, JNUL.
83. See B. Melamede to directors of HICEM, 12 March 1937, Records of the Council of Administration, Jewish Colonization Association (ICA), London.
84. See Yahil, *Holocaust*, 254.
85. JTA, 24 January 1937.
86. Arthur Prinz to Max Warburg, 25 June 1937, Folder 7, Box 2, Prinz Papers, LBINY.
87. "Protocol of the Meeting of the Governing Board and Steering Committee of the Reichsvertretung, 7 July 1937," File 602, Wiener Library, London.

88. Max Warburg to Sir Osmond Goldsmid, 28 August 1937, File 657, "Emigration—General, 1933–1937," JDC.

89. *Centralverein Zeitung,* 21 October 1937.

90. See, for example, *Bayerische-israelitische Gemeindezeitung,* 1 June 1937; and *Centralverein Zeitung,* 6 June 1937.

91. Warburg to Prinz, 10 April 1937, Folder 7, Box 2, Prinz Papers. Here, as elsewhere, Warburg cited the need for a vade mecum for emigrating Jews, which would emphasize the themes of "Judaism and Fatherland."

92. Warburg to Schäffer, 17 July 1937, Box 2 ("Corr.-1937"), Schäffer Papers, LBINY.

93. Karl A. Schleunes, *The Twisted Road to Auschwitz: Nazi Policy Toward German Jews, 1933–1939* (Urbana: University of Illinois Press, 1970), 222.

94. "The New Wave of Terror," *Jüdische Rundschau* 3 September 1937.

95. In July 1937 the government strengthened this barrier by denying the Jewish press the right to quote from non-Jewish papers in Germany. See JTA, 27 July 1937. In November the Berlin office of the JTA was closed, cutting off news from the outside world.

96. Schocken to Weltsch, 20 December 1934, Addenda, Folder 11, Box 6, Weltsch Papers, LBINY.

97. See "The Problem of Emigration," *Centralverein Zeitung,* 23 September 1937; *Jüdische Rundschau,* 17 December 1937; and *Der Schild,* 3 December 1937.

98. *Centralverein Zeitung,* 28 October 1937.

99. See, for example, Willstätter to Fajans, 3 October 1937, Willstätter File, Fajans Papers, University of Michigan, Ann Arbor.

100. Ibid.

101. Willstätter to Fajans, 13 November 1939, Fajans Papers, University of Michigan, Ann Arbor.

102. Arthur Stoll, epilogue to *Aus meinem Leben: Von Arbeit, Musse und Freunden,* ed. Arthur Stoll (Weinheim, Germany: Verlag Chemie, 1949), 422.

103. Bella Fromm, *Blood and Banquets: Berlin Social Diary* (New York: Carol Publishing Group, entry for 2 February 1937, 239.

104. Ibid., entry for 17 December 1936, 234–35.

105. Ibid., entry for 12 February 1937, 241.

106. Ibid., entry for 8 September 1937, 253; diary ms., entries for 10 May 1937 and 15 December 1937, Folder 2, Box 2, Fromm Papers, BU.

107. Fromm, *Blood and Banquets,* entry for 5 February 1937, 240–41.

108. Fromm, diary ms., entry for 28 August 1936, Folder 2, Box 2, Fromm Papers, BU. Schacht did not understand the difficulties Fromm was facing in her journalistic profession.

109. Ibid., entry for 26 April 1936.

110. Fromm, *Blood and Banquets,* entry for 30 June 1937, 245. In her diary ms., however, Fromm said that this meeting occurred during a Fourth of July celebration at the Hotel Esplanade. See entry for 4 July 1937, Folder 2, Box 2, Fromm Papers, BU.
111. Fromm, *Blood and Banquets,* entry for 20 August 1937, 249.
112. Ibid., entry for 13 September 1937, 254.
113. Ibid., entry for 1 January 1938, 263.
114. Diary ms., entry for 22 December 1937, Folder 2, Box 2, Fromm Papers, BU.
115. Ibid.
116. Joachim Fest, *Hitler,* trans. Richard and Clara Winston (New York: Harcourt Brace Jovanovich, 1974), 539.
117. Fromm, diary ms., entry for 25 December 1937, Fromm Papers, BU.
118. Fromm, *Blood and Banquets,* entry for 1 January 1938, 263.
119. Ibid., entry for 15 January 1938, 264. But Fromm filed an application for emigration on 8 January 1938. See diary ms., entry for 8 January 1938, Folder 1, Box 3, Fromm Papers, BU.

Chapter 10: Rushing for the Exits

1. Werner, Rosenstock, "Exodus, 1933–1939: A Survey of Jewish Emigration from Germany," *Leo Baeck Year Book* 1 (1956): 376.
2. Ernst Herzfeld, "Meine letzten Jahre in Deutschland, 1933–1938," 01/8, Ball-Kaduri Collection of Testimonies, RG 41, Yad Vashem Archives, Jerusalem, 39.
3. Quoted in Herbert A. Strauss, "Jewish Emigration from Germany: Nazi Policies and Jewish Responses—II," *Leo Baeck Year Book* 26 (1981): 356.
4. Ernst Marcus, "The German Foreign Office and the Palestine Question in the Period 1933–1939," *Yad Vashem Studies* 2 (1958): 200.
5. Quoted in Karl A. Schleunes, *The Twisted Road to Auschwitz: Nazi Policy Toward German Jews, 1933–1939* (Urbana: University of Illinois Press, 1970), 66.
6. Until the fall of 1937, half the Jewish-owned firms were still in Jewish hands. See Strauss, "Emigration—I," 332.
7. Schleunes, *Twisted Road,* 66.
8. See Leni Yahil, *The Holocaust: The Fate of European Jewry, 1932–1945,* trans. Ina Friedman and Haya Galai (New York: Oxford University Press, 1991), 107, and Strauss, "Emigration—I," 343.
9. Cf. Schleunes, *Twisted Road,* 65.
10. William L. Shirer, *The Rise and Fall of the Third Reich: A History of Nazi Germany* (New York: Simon and Schuster, 1960), 351.
11. JTA, 13 March 1938 and 20 April 1938.
12. Cf. Shirer, *Rise and Fall,* 351; Yahil, *Holocaust,* 105.

13. Gardiner Richardson to State Department, No. 971, 27 March 1938, Messersmith Papers, UD.

14. Yahil, *Holocaust*, 105.

15. JTA, 26 April 1938, citing the *Völkischer Beobachter.* The Nazi goal was to have thirty thousand Jews emigrate from Austria during the remainder of 1938.

16. The JTA reported that 2,800 German and Austrian Jews left for Palestine in March.

17. The JTA reported in its issue of 5 July 1938 that as many as five thousand Jews from Austria and Germany were eager to emigrate there.

18. Bella Fromm, *Blood and Banquets: A Berlin Social Diary* (New York: Carol Publishing Group, 1990) entry for 19 March 1938, 267.

19. JTA, 4 April 1938.

20. Circular of Propaganda Ministry to Jewish press representatives, 1 April 1938, Folder G62.2, Box 3, RG 215 ("Berlin Collection"), YIVO.

21. JTA, 21 April 1938.

22. Cf. JTA, 27 April 1938.

23. Leo Baeck to Council for German Jewry (Stephany?), 14 March 1938, File 606, Wiener Library, London.

24. *Jüdische Rundschau*, 5 April 1938. Cf. JTA, 10 April 1938.

25. "Awakened Strengths," *Jüdische Rundschau*, 4 March 1938.

26. "The Way in the World," *Jüdische Rundschau*, 29 March 1938.

27. "New Order Is Needed," *Jüdische Rundschau*, 13 March 1938.

28. Weltsch to Hugo Bergmann, 28 January 1938, Folder 1, Box 2, Weltsch Papers, LBINY.

29. Weltsch to Bergmann, 1 February 1938, Folder 1, Box 2, Weltsch Papers, LBINY.

30. Cf. Weltsch to Weizmann, 14 January 1938, Weltsch File, Weizmann Archives, Rehovot, Israel.

31. Ibid.

32. Weltsch to Bergmann, 17 July 1938, Folder 1, Box 2, Weltsch Papers, LBINY.

33. Weltsch, "Recollections—1938," 24 August 1963, Addenda, Folder 2, Box 2, Weltsch Papers, LBINY.

34. Max Warburg, *Aus meinen Aufzeichnungen* (New York: privately printed, 1952), 154. Cf. Helmut Genschel, *Die Verdrängung der Juden aus der Wirtschaft im dritten Reich* (Göttingen, Germany: Musterschmidt Verlag 1966), 238.

35. Siegmund Warburg to Hans Schäffer, 27 January 1938, Box 5 ("1938: M-Z"), Schäffer Papers, LBINY. The bank benefited from the acquisition of funds from many financially desperate Jews. See Ron Chernow, *The Warburgs: The Twentieth Century Odyssey of a Remarkable Jewish Family* (New York: Random House, 1993), 467.

36. Frieda S. Warburg, *Reminiscences of A Long Life* (New York: Thistle Press, 1956), 31.
37. D. Wischnitzer (Hilfsverein) to Jewish Colonization Association (ICA), 10 December 1937, Records of the Council of Administration, ICA, London.
38. The government also needed the Warburg bank to maintain foreign-exchange credits. See Chernow, *The Warburgs*, 466.
39. Genschel, *Verdrängung*, 239.
40. See Bernhard Kahn, "Tribute to Max Warburg by Bernhard Kahn at the Annual Meeting of the Joint Distribution Committee (1947)," ME 344, Leo Baeck Institute, New York. Cf. Naomi Shepherd, *Refuge from Darkness: Wilfred Israel and the Rescue of the Jews* (New York: Pantheon, 1984), 92, put the total number of German Jews who reached Palestine through the transfer agreement at fifty thousand.
41. Shepherd, *Refuge*, 116.
42. JTA, 3 January 1938.
43. Ibid.
44. Margarete Limberg and Hubert Rübsaat, *Sie dürften nicht mehr Deutsche sein: Jüdischer Alltag in Selbstzeugnissen, 1933–1938* (Frankfurt-am-Main: Campus, 1990), 82.
45. Max Warburg, "Words of Greeting at the Dedication of the Jewish Community House," 9 January 1938, Max Warburg Papers, LBINY. Other sources put the 1933 Jewish population in Hamburg at twenty thousand.
46. Max Warburg to Arthur Prinz, 21 April 1938, Folder 7, Box 2, Prinz Papers, LBINY.
47. Max Warburg, "Address Held on the Occasion of the Conversion of M. M. Warburg & Co.," 30 May 1938, LBINY (microfilm).
48. *Der Schild*, 3 June 1938.
49. Brauer to Wise, 10 June 1938, Box 82, "Germany: Dec. 1936–1940," Wise Papers, AJHS.
50. JTA, 9 June 1938.
51. JTA, 13 June 1938.
52. JTA, 16 June 1938.
53. JTA, 19 June 1938.
54. JTA, 22 June 1938.
55. Bella Fromm, "Flight to Freedom," *True Detective* (November 1942): 68.
56. Fromm, *Blood and Banquets*, entry for 18 June 1938, 273.
57. Ibid., entry for 28 June 1938, 273–75.
58. Ibid., entry for 4 July 1938, 276.
59. Diary ms., entry for 10 February 1938, Folder 2, Box 2, Fromm Papers, BU.
60. Ibid., entry for 7 March 1938.
61. Ibid., entry for 15 March 1938.

62. Ibid., undated entry, May 1938.

63. *Blood and Banquets,* entry for 10 August 1938, 277.

64. For Schoeps's horoscopes, see Box 281, Schoeps Papers, SBB.

65. Hans-Joachim Schoeps to Ministry for Science, Education, and Popular Culture, 26 March 1938, Binder 95, Schoeps Papers, SBB.

66. Hans-Joachim Schoeps, *Die letzten dreissig Jahre: Rückblicke* (Stuttgart: Klett, 1956), 107. Schoeps was teaching twelve-year-old boys.

67. Circular of Propaganda Ministry (Hinkel), 24 September 1937, Folder G-60, Box 3, RG 215, YIVO.

68. See Vortrupp Verlag (Schoeps) to Jewish Private School, Grunewald, 16 December 1937, Binder 94, Schoeps Papers, SBB.

69. Hans-Joachim Schoeps to B. Gobits (Rotterdam), 7 January 1938, Binder 95, Schoeps Papers, SBB.

70. Selfridge (Booksellers) to Schoeps, 18 January 1938, Binder 95, Schoeps Papers, SBB.

71. Dr. S. Hoffmann to Schoeps, 22 February 1938, Binder 95, Schoeps Papers, SBB.

72. Richard Fuchs (Lehranstalt) to Schoeps, 8 February 1938, Binder 95, Schoeps Papers, SBB.

73. Schoeps to Ismar Elbogen, 7 October 1937, Binder 94, Schoeps Papers, SBB.

74. So reported the JTA on 23 January 1938.

75. *Der Schild,* 18 February 1938.

76. JTA, 30 January 1938.

77. Quoted in Prentiss Gilbert to Hull, 25 February 1938, Confidential File: "Germany—12 July 1937–8 Sept. 1938," Box 26, President's Secretary's File, Franklin D. Roosevelt Library, Hyde Park, N.Y.

78. Richard M. Willstätter, *Aus meinem Leben: Von Arbeit, Musse und Freunden,* ed. Arthur Stoll (Weinheim, Germany: Verlag Chemie, 1949), 401.

79. Cf. Richard Willstätter to Kasimir Fajans, 13 November 1939, Willstätter File, Box 5, Fajans Papers, University of Michigan, Ann Arbor.

80. Richard Willstätter to Arthur Stoll, 22 August 1940, quoted in Stoll, afterword to Willstätter, *Leben,* 427–28.

81. David Nachmansohn, *German-Jewish Pioneers in Science, 1900–1933: Highlights in Atomic Physics, Chemistry, and Biochemistry* (New York: Springer Verlag, 1979), 213.

82. Between 1 March 1933 and 16 March 1938, 3,574 Jews left Munich and its surrounding communities. See Peter Hanke, *Zur Geschichte der Juden im München zwischen 1933 und 1945* (Munich: Stadtarchiv, 1967), 171.

83. "Leitheft des Rasse—und Siedlungshauptamtes," 15 July 1937, No. 2934830, Roll 410, Captured German Records: Records of the Reich Leader SS and the Chief of German Police, III, NA.

84. Quoted in Yahil, *Holocaust*, 105.
85. This quota for April–September 1938 was set at three thousand.
86. Honaker to Hull, "Expanding Activities and Increase of Official and Clerical Personnel at Stuttgart," 12 January 1938, 811.III Quota 62/564, RG 59, NRC.
87. For the text of Hull's letter outlining the conference, see Solomon Adler-Rudel, "The Évian Conference on the Refugee Question," *Leo Baeck Year Book* 13 (1968): 237.
88. *Centralverein Zeitung*, 31 March 1938.
89. Alfred Hirschberg, "Thoughts for Évian," *Centralverein Zeitung*, 9 June 1938.
90. JTA, 10 June 1938.
91. Leonard Baker, *Days of Sorrow and Pain: Leo Baeck and the Berlin Jews* (New York: Oxford University Press, 1980), 226.
92. *Centralverein Zeitung*, 23 June 1938.
93. See, for example, issue of 24 June 1938.
94. *Jüdische Rundschau*, 28 June 1938.
95. Yahil, *Holocaust*, 117.
96. "Open the Gates!" *Jüdische Rundschau*, 5 July 1938.
97. Robert Weltsch to Chaim Weizmann, 14 January 1938, Weltsch File, Weizmann Archives, Rehovot, Israel.
98. Herbert Freeden, *Die jüdische Presse im Dritten Reich* (Frankfurt-am-Main: Jüdischer Verlag bei Athenaeum, 1987), 27.
99. Conversation of Warburg with Earl Winterton, 29 August 1938, W 11759/104/98, Public Record Office, Kew, England.
100. Warburg to Prinz, 26 May 1937, Folder 7, Box 2, Prinz Papers, LBINY.
101. H. Pineas, "Meine Erinnerungen an Dr. Leo Baeck," unpublished memoir, ME 502, LBINY, 4. See also Baker, *Days of Sorrow and Pain*, 202.
102. Quoted in Baker, *Days of Sorrow and Pain*, 227.
103. Fromm, "Flight to Freedom," 69.
104. For Fromm's application to emigrate, with letters of recommendation, see Folder 1, Box 14, Fromm Papers, BU.
105. See George Messersmith to Bella Fromm, 6 July 1936, Folder 8, Box 10, Fromm Papers, BU.
106. Fromm, diary ms., 17 June 1938, Folder 2, Box 2, Fromm Papers, BU.
107. Fromm, *Blood and Banquets*, entry for 4 July 1938, 276.
108. For mention of Schoeps's application, see Schoeps to Arnold Herrmann, 19 July 1938, Binder 95, Schoeps Papers, SBB.
109. F. M. Heidel to Schoeps, 11 August 1938, Binder 95, Schoeps Papers, SBB.
110. See Käthe Schoeps to Schoeps, 28 June 1938, Box 280, Schoeps Papers, SBB.

111. Schoeps to Bishop Berggrav, 9 August 1938, Binder 94, Schoeps Papers, SBB.
112. Hans-Joachim Schoeps, *Rufmord/1970* (Erlangen, Germany: Selbstverlag des Verfassers, 1970), 28.
113. Schoeps, *Rückblicke*, 107.
114. Quoted in *Jüdische Rundschau*, 1 July 1938.
115. Adler-Rudel, "Évian Conference," 237.
116. Ibid., 245, 251.
117. Monty N. Penkower, *The Jews Were Expendable: Free World Diplomacy and the Holocaust* (Urbana: University of Illinois Press, 1983), 105.
118. David S. Wyman, *Paper Walls: America and the Refugee Crisis, 1938–1941* (Amherst: University of Massachusetts Press, 1968), 47.
119. "Today Évian Comes to a Close," *Jüdische Rundschau*, 15 July 1938.
120. Reichsvertretung statement of 20 July 1938, quoted in JTA, 20 July 1938.
121. "Pause for Inspiration?" *Centralverein Zeitung*, 28 July 1938.

Chapter 11: The Night of Broken Glass

1. Quoted in Karl A. Schleunes, *The Twisted Road to Auschwitz: Nazi Policy Toward German Jews, 1933–1939* (Urbana: University of Illinois Press, 1970), 65.
2. From March 1938 to March 1939 100,000 Austrian Jews emigrated, despite visa restrictions abroad. See David S. Wyman, *Paper Walls: America and the Refugee Crisis, 1938–1941* (Amherst: University of Massachusetts Press, 1968), 28.
3. JTA, 24 July 1938.
4. By October 1938 only 709 Jewish doctors were allowed to treat Jewish patients. See Herbert A. Strauss, "Jewish Emigration from Germany: Nazi Policies and Jewish Responses—I," *Leo Baeck Year Book* 26 1981), 339.
5. JTA, 3 August 1938.
6. *Jüdische Rundschau*, 29 July 1938.
7. *Centralverein Zeitung*, 24 August 1938.
8. *Bayerische-israelitische Gemeindezeitung*, 15 August 1938.
9. *Centralverein Zeitung*, 4 August 1938.
10. Schoeps to Rade, 7 August 1938, in Wilhelm Kantzenbach, "Das wissenschaftliche Werden von Hans-Joachim Schoeps und seine Vertreibung aus Deutschland 1938," *Zeitschrift für Religions-und Geistesgeschichte* 32 (1980): 346. In June Baeck had told Schoeps there was no money in the Reichsvertretung to finance study abroad. Baeck to Schoeps, 30 June 1938, Binder 95, Schoeps Papers, SBB.
11. Schoeps to Rade, 7 August 1938, 346. Cf. Schoeps to Paul Goodman, 20 August 1938, Binder 95, Schoeps Papers, SBB.

12. Schoeps to Prof. Schmalenbach, 20 August 1938, Binder 95, Schoeps Papers, SBB.

13. Schoeps to Rade, 10 September 1938, in Kantzenbach, "Das wissenschaftliche Werden," 348; F. M. Heidel to Schoeps, 11 August 1938, Binder 95, Schoeps Papers; and Schoeps to Pastor Birger Pernow (Stockholm), 20 August 1938, Binder 95, SBB.

14. For a more critical appraisal of the political position of the Confessional Church under Hitler, see Jack Forstman, *Christian Faith in Dark Times: Theological Conflicts in the Shadow of Hitler* (Westminster, Eng.: John Knox, 1993); and Victoria Barnett, *For the Soul of the People: Protestant Protest Against Hitler* (New York: Oxford University Press, 1993).

15. Hans-Joachim Schoeps, "Die deutsche Juden und das Jahr 1933," Box 60, Schoeps Papers, SBB. Schoeps claimed that he showed Baeck all his writings between 1933 and 1938. See Schoeps to Fritz Hellendall, 19 August 1978, Box 37, Schoeps Papers, SBB.

16. Bella Fromm, *Blood and Banquets: A Berlin Social Diary* (New York: Carol Publishing Group, 1990), entry for 10 August 1938, 277.

17. Ibid., entry for 10 August 1938, 278. Cf. Fromm to Schacht, 20 August 1938, Folder 5, Box 58, Fromm Papers, BU.

18. Fromm, diary ms., entry for 12 August 1938, Folder 2, Box 2, Fromm Papers, SBB.

19. Fromm, *Blood and Banquets,* entry for 18 August 1938, 278.

20. Max Warburg to Martin Goldschmidt, 16 August 1938, Max Warburg Papers, LBINY.

21. Max Warburg, *Aus meinen Aufzeichnungen* (New York: privately printed, 1952), 157–58.

22. Max Warburg to Earl Winterton, 29 August 1938, FO 371/22533 (W 11759/104/98), Public Record Office, Kew, England.

23. *Centralverein Zeitung,* 18 August 1938.

24. Weltsch to Hugo Bergmann, 19 August 1938, Folder 1, Box 2, Weltsch Papers, LBINY.

25. William L. Shirer, *The Rise and Fall of the Third Reich: A History of Nazi Germany* (New York: Simon and Schuster, 1960), 377.

26. JTA, 29 August 1938.

27. *Centralverein Zeitung,* 1 September 1938. This meant a total of 4,772 from Germany.

28. See, for example, "Waiting," *Centralverein Zeitung,* 1 September 1938.

29. Fromm, *Blood and Banquets,* entry for 2 September 1938, 280.

30. Ibid., entry for 4 July 1938, 281.

31. Ibid., entry for 4 September 1938, 283.

32. Ibid., 281.

33. Ibid., entry for 9 September 1938, 284.

34. "The Reichsvertretung and the Jews in Germany," *Centralverein Zeitung,* 22 September 1938.

35. It is not clear how Weltsch obtained the required exit papers and visa for Palestine in such a short time.

36. Weltsch, untitled, undated typescript (1938 or 1939), Folder I, Box 7A, Weltsch Papers, LBINY.

37. Weltsch's criticism of the Jewish response in this unpublished manuscript is at odds with his published writings during the postwar years that continued to hail the rebirth of Judaism under Hitler.

38. Richard M. Willstätter, *Aus meinem Leben: Von Arbeit, Musse und Freunden,* ed. Arthur Stoll (Weinheim, Germany: Verlag Chemie, 1949), 401.

39. Leni Yahil, *The Holocaust: The Fate of European Jewry, 1932–1945,* trans. Ina Friedman and Haya Galai (New York: Oxford University Press, 1991), 109.

40. JTA, 16 October 1938.

41. Quoted in Shaul Esh, "Between Discrimination and Extermination," *Yad Vashem Studies* 2 (1958): 92.

42. *Das schwarze Korps,* 26 October 1938.

43. Schoeps to Rade, 25 October 1938, in Kantzenbach, "Das wissenschaftliche Werden," 348.

44. *Jüdische Rundschau,* 26 October 1938.

45. So says Yahil, *Holocaust,* 109. Other sources put the number somewhat lower.

46. JTA, 28 October 1938.

47. Cited in JTA, 2 November 1938.

48. For this account of the vom Rath shooting, see Anthony Read and David Fisher, *Kristallnacht: The Nazi Night of Terror* (New York: Random House, 1989), 6–7.

49. JTA, 7 November 1938.

50. Quoted in Otto Tolischus, "Nazis Ask Reprisal in Attack on Envoy," *New York Times,* 9 November 1938.

51. *New York Times,* 10 November 1938.

52. Yahil, *Holocaust,* 102.

53. *New York Times,* 9 November 1938.

54. For discussion of Nazi preparations, see Yahil, *Holocaust,* 112.

55. *New York Times,* 10 November 1938.

56. JTA, 11 November 1938.

57. Richard Breitman and Alan M. Kraut, *American Refugee Policy and European Jewry, 1933–1945* (Bloomington: Indiana University Press, 1987), 53.

58. JTA, 11 November 1938.

59. Read and Fisher, *Kristallnacht,* 98.

60. "Report on Mr. Troper's Trip to Germany and Poland, Nov. 9 to Nov. 27, 1938," 30 November 1938, File 631, "Germany—General, 1938–1944," JDC.

61. Leo Baeck, "In Memory of Two of Our Dead," *Leo Baeck Yearbook* I (1956): 55.

62. Esriel E. Hildesheimer, "The Central Organization of the German Jews in the Years 1933–1945: Its Legal and Political Status and Its Position in the Jewish Community" (Master's thesis, Hebrew University of Jerusalem, 1982), 145.

63. Ernst Englander to Ralph Wolf, 25 November 1938, File 631, "Germany—General, 1938–1944," JDC.

64. Ari J. Sherman, *Island of Refuge: Britain and Refugees from the Third Reich* (Berkeley: University of California Press, 1973), 168.

65. Ball-Kaduri, ed., "The Central Jewish Organizations in Berlin During the Pogrom of November 1938 ('Kristallnacht')," *Yad Vashem Studies* 3 (1959): 274–75.

66. Arthur Prinz, "The Role of the Gestapo in Obstructing and Promoting Jewish Emigration," *Yad Vashem Studies* 2 (1958): 214. The Nazis had set a goal of four thousand Jewish émigrés a month following Kristallnacht.

67. Ernst Herzfeld, "Meine letzten Jahre in Deutschland, 1933–1935," 01/8, Ball-Kaduri Collection of Testimonies, RG 41, Yad Vashem Archives, Jerusalem, 45.

68. "Resolution of the Reichsvertretung, 13. 11. 1938," File 642, "Reichsvertretung der deutschen Juden," JDC.

69. Ulrich Dunker, *Der Reichsbund jüdischer Frontsoldaten: Geschichte eines jüdischen Abwehrvereins* (Düsseldorf: Droste, 1977), 177. See also Read and Fisher, *Kristallnacht*, 122.

70. Henry L. Feingold, *The Politics of Rescue: The Roosevelt Administration and the Holocaust, 1938–1945* (New Brunswick, N.J.: Rutgers University Press, 1970), 318. In 1933, by comparison, 40 percent of the Jews were over age forty.

71. Igor Paleologue, "Meine Bekanntschaft mit Grossrabbiner Dr. Leo Baeck," unpublished memoir, ME 172, LBINY, 18.

72. Quoted in Leonard Baker, *Days of Sorrow and Pain: Leo Baeck and the Berlin Jews* (New York: Oxford University Press, 1980), 234.

73. Quoted in a letter of Baeck to Ismar Elbogen, 25 January 1939, cited in ibid., 238.

74. Ibid., 235.

75. For the text of Roosevelt's statement, see OF 76c, Box 6, President's Official File, Roosevelt Library, Hyde Park, N.Y.

76. Roosevelt to Welles, 26 November 1938, OF 76c, Box 6, President's Official File, Roosevelt Library, Hyde Park, N.Y.

77. Prinz to Stephany (Council for German Jewry), 24 November 1938, File 607("Hilfsverein"), Wiener Library, London.

78. Quoted in Herzfeld, "Meine letzten Jahre," 45.

79. Bernhard Witkopf, "Stepping Stones: Some Biographical Notes," ME 176, LBINY, 7.

80. Log of W. E. Tisdale (Rockefeller Foundation), entry for 23 Novem-

ber 1938, Series 717D: "Univ. of Munich: Chemistry," File 145-46, Box 15, RG I.I, Rockefeller Foundation Papers, Rockefeller Archive Center, North Tarrytown, N.Y.

81. Willstätter, *Leben*, 403.

82. Ibid., 407.

83. Ibid, 407.

84. Willstätter to Hiram Halle, 19 November 1938, 53 318, Box 77, Einstein Duplicate Archives, Seeley G. Mudd Manuscript Library, Princeton, N.J.

85. Cf. log of W. E. Tisdale, entry for 25 January 1939, 717D: "Univ. of Munich: Chemistry," RG I.I, Rockefeller Foundation Papers.

86. Richard Willstätter, "Die Geschichte meines Rücktritts," in *Vergangene Tagen: Jüdische Kultur in München*, ed. Hans Lamm (Munich: Langen, 1982), 412.

87. Willstätter, *Leben*, 406.

88. Stoll, epilogue to ibid., 413.

89. Richard Kuhn, "Richard Willstätter," *Die Naturwissenschaften* I (1949): 4–5.

90. Schoeps, *Rückblicke*, 107.

91. Ibid., 108.

92. So Schoeps claimed after the war. *Rückblicke*, 110.

93. Schoeps, undated 1939 ms. ("Dear comrades"), Folder 2, Box 40, Schoeps Papers, SBB.

94. Cf. Schoeps to (?), 22 December 1941, Box 280, Schoeps Papers, SBB. In this letter Schoeps said he was also helped by Hentig's superior in the foreign ministry. Cf. Ball-Kaduri, "Central Jewish Organizations," 264–65.

95. Schoeps, *Rückblicke*, 112.

96. Schoeps, *Rückblicke*, 113, 115. In an 8 April 1946 letter to Karl Barth, Schoeps said he had to leave Germany as an "anti-Nazi and Jew." See Gary Lease, "Der Briefwechsel zwischen Karl Barth und Hans-Joachim Schoeps (1929–1946)," *Menora: Jahrbuch für deutsch-jüdische Geschichte* 2 (1991): 129.

97. Cited in Ernst Rosenthal to Schoeps, 1 June 1939, Box 85, Schoeps Papers, SBB.

98. Schoeps's older brother, Konrad, died of a heart attack in 1936. He was only in his early twenties.

99. Baeck to Veltheim, 31 December 1940, Box 3, Baker Papers, LBINY.

Epilogue

1. Richard Willstätter to Kasimir Fajans, 18 November 1939, Box 5, Fajans Papers, University of Michigan, Ann Arbor.

2. Willstätter to Sommerfeld, 4 October 1940, Willstätter File, Manuscript Department, Deutsches Museum, Munich.

3. Arthur Stoll, Afterword, in Richard M. Willstätter, *Aus meinem Leben: Von Arbeit, Musse und Freunden,* ed. Arthur Stoll (Weinheim, Germany: Verlag Chemie, 1949), 415.

4. See, for example, Willstätter to Sommerfeld, 4 October 1940, Willstätter File, Manuscript Department, Deutsches Museum, Munich.

5. Richard Kuhn, "Richard Willstätter," *Die Naturwissenschaften* I (1949): 5.

6. Stoll, Afterword to Willstätter, *Leben,* 416.

7. Willstätter to Stoll, 25 January 1942, quoted in ibid., 433.

8. Frieda S. Warburg, *Reminiscences of A Long Life* (New York: Thistle Press, 1956), 31.

9. Ron Chernow, *The Warburgs: The Twentieth Century Odyssey of a Remarkable Jewish Family* (New York: Random House, 1993), 516.

10. Naomi Shepherd, *A Refuge from Darkness: Wilfrid Israel and the Rescue of the Jews* (New York: Pantheon, 1984), 155. Cf. David S. Wyman, *Paper Walls: America and the Refugee Crisis, 1938–1941* (Amherst: University of Massachusetts Press, 1968), 52–53.

11. Leni Yahil, *The Holocaust: The Fate of European Jewry, 1932–1941,* trans. Ina Friedman and Haya Galai (New York: Oxford University Press, 1991), 101.

12. Warburg to Paul Baerwald, 20 February 1941, C15-PB59, Correspondence File: "Max Warburg," Baerwald Papers, Columbia University, New York.

13. Chernow, *The Warburgs,* 516.

14. See Leonard Baker, *Days of Sorrow and Pain: Leo Baeck and the Berlin Jews* (New York: Oxford University Press, 1980), 271–72.

15. Ibid., 311.

16. See Leo Baeck, "A People Stands Before Its God," in *We Survived: Fourteen Histories of the Hidden and Hunted in Nazi Germany,* ed. Eric H. Boehm (Santa Barbara, Calif.: Clio Press, 1966), 295, and Igor Paleologue, "Meine Bekanntschaft mit Grossrabbiner Dr. Leo Baeck," unpublished memoir, ME 172, LBINY, 6. Baker said that Eichmann never carried out the orders to kill Baeck because the war came to an end. See *Days of Sorrow and Pain,* 315–16.

17. Baeck, "A People Stands Before Its God," 299.

18. See Baeck's obituary, *New York Times,* 3 November 1956.

19. Ibid.

20. For a complete list of the items Fromm brought with her, see Folder 8, Box 14, Fromm Papers, BU.

21. For the text of Baeck's letter, see Folder 7, Box 14, Fromm Papers, BU.

22. Bella Fromm, *Blood and Banquets: A Berlin Social Diary* (New York: Carol Publishing Group, 1990), 286–87.

23. See, for example, Ernst Rosenthal to Schoeps, 22 July 1939, Box 85, Schoeps Papers, SBB.

24. Ibid.

25. See Dorothee Busch to Felix Busch, 10 April 1942, Box 280, Schoeps Papers, SBB.

26. Quoted in Hans-Joachim Schoeps, *Die letzten dreissig Jahre: Rückblicke* (Stuttgart: Klett, 1956), 15.

27. Schoeps, undated 1939 ms., Folder 2, Box 40, Schoeps Papers, SBB.

28. Schoeps to Barth, 8 April 1946, quoted in Gary Lease, "Der Briefwechsel zwischen Karl Barth und Hans-Joachim Schoeps (1929–1946)," *Menora: Jahrbuch für deutsch-jüdische Geschichte* 2 (1991): 129.

29. Schoeps, undated 1939 ms., Folder 2, Box 40, Schoeps Papers, SBB.

References

Published Sources

Adler, Cyrus, and Aaron M. Margalith. *With Firmness in the Right: American Diplomatic Action Affecting Jews.* New York: American Jewish Committee, 1946.

Adler-Rudel, Solomon. "The Évian Conference on the Refugee Question." *Leo Baeck Year Book* 13 (1968): 235–73.

Angress, Werner T. *Between Fear and Hope: Jewish Youth in the Third Reich.* Translated by Christine Granger. New York: Columbia University Press, 1988.

Arendt, Hannah. *Eichmann in Jerusalem: A Report on the Banality of Evil.* London: Farber and Farber, 1963.

———. *The Jew As Pariah: Jewish Identity and Politics in the Modern Era.* New York: Grove Press, 1978.

Baeck, Leo. "A People Stands Before Its God." In *We Survived: Fourteen Histories of the Hidden and Hunted in Nazi Germany,* edited by Eric H. Boehm. Santa Barbara, Calif.: Clio Press, 1966.

———. "Excerpts from Leo Baeck's Writings." *Leo Baeck Year Book* 3 (1958): 361–74.

———. "In Memory of Two of Our Dead." *Leo Baeck Year Book* 1 (1956): 51–56.

———. "Plan eines jüdischen Konkordats." *Bulletin des Leo Baeck Instituts* 1–4 (1957–58): 14.

Baker, Leonard. *Days of Sorrow and Pain: Leo Baeck and the Berlin Jews.* New York: Oxford University Press, 1980.

Baldwin, Peter M. "Zionist and Non-Zionist Jews in the Last Years Before the Nazi Regime." *Leo Baeck Year Book* 27 (1982): 87–108.

Ball-Kaduri, Kurt J. "The Central Jewish Organizations in Berlin During the Pogrom of November 1938 ('Kristallnacht')." *Yad Vashem Studies* 3 (1959): 261–81.

———. *Das Leben der Juden in Deutschland im Jahre 1933: Ein Zeitbericht.* Frankfurt-am-Main: Europäische Verlagsanstalt, 1963.

———. "Leo Baeck and Contemporary History." *Yad Vashem Studies* 6 (1967): 121–30.

———. "The National Representation of Jews in Germany: Obstacles and Accomplishments at its Establishment." *Yad Vashem Studies* 2 (1958): 159–78.

———. *Vor der Katastrophe: Juden in Deutschland 1934–1939.* Tel Aviv: Olamenu, 1967.

Barkai, Avraham. *Vom Boykott zur "Entjudung": Der wirtschaftliche Existenzkampf der Juden im dritten Reich, 1933–1943.* Frankfurt-am-Main: Fischer Taschenbuch Verlag, 1988.

———. "German Interests in the Haavara-Transfer Agreement, 1933–1939." *Leo Baeck Year Book* 35 (1990): 245–66.

Bednarz, Dieter, and Michael Lüders, eds. *Blick zurück ohne Hass: Juden aus Israel erinnern sich an Deutschland.* Cologne: Bund-Verlag, 1981.

Behrend-Rosenfeld, Ilse. *Ich stand nicht allein: Erlebnisse einer Jüdin in Deutschland, 1933–1944.* Munich: C. H. Beck, 1988.

Bein, Alex. "The Jewish Parasite: Notes on the Semantics of the Jewish Problem, With Special Reference to Germany." *Leo Baeck Year Book* 9 (1964): 3–40.

Benz, Wolfgang, ed. *Die Juden im Deutschland, 1933–1945: Leben unter nationalsozialistischer Herrschaft.* Munich: C. H. Beck, 1988.

Berghash, Mark W. *Jews and Germans: Aspects of the True Self.* Riverside: University of California Press, 1985.

Berl, E. "Richard Willstätter." *Chemical and Engineering News* 20 (10 August 1942): 954.

Bettelheim, Bruno. *The Informed Heart: Autonomy in a Mass Age.* London: Thames and Hudson, 1960.

Bienenfeld, F. R. *The Germans and the Jews.* London: Secker and Warburg, 1939.

Blumenfeld, Kurt. *Erlebte Judenfrage: Ein Vierteljahrhundert deutscher Zionismus.* Edited and introduced by Hans Tramer. Stuttgart: Deutsche Verlags-Anstalt, 1962.

———. *Im Kampf um den Zionismus: Briefe aus fünf Jahrzehnten.* Edited by Miriam Sambursky and Jochanan Ginat. Stuttgart: Deutsche Verlags-Anstalt, 1976.

————. *Zionistische Betrachtungen: Fünf Aufsätze, anlässlich des zehnjährigen Bestehens der V. J. St. Maccabea, Berlin.* Berlin: [no publisher], 1916.

Boas, Jacob. "German-Jewish Internal Politics Under Hitler, 1933–1938." *Leo Baeck Year Book* 29 (1984): 3–26.

————. "Germany or Diaspora? German Jewry's Shifting Perceptions in the Nazi Era (1933–1938)." *Leo Baeck Year Book* 27 (1982): 109–26.

Borries, Achim von, ed. *Selbstzeugnisse des deutschen Judentums, 1861–1945.* Frankfurt-am-Main: Fischer Taschenbuch Verlag, 1988.

Breitman, Richard, and Alan M. Kraut. *American Refugee Policy and European Jewry, 1933–1945.* Bloomington: Indiana University Press, 1987.

Brenner, Michael. "The Jüdische Volkspartei: National-Jewish Communal Politics during the Weimar Republic." *Leo Baeck Year Book* 35 (1990): 219–44.

Brod, Max. *Gustav Mahler: Beispiel einer deutsch-jüdischen Symbiose.* Frankfurt-am-Main: Ner-Tamid-Verlag, 1961.

Brody, Elaine. "The Jewish Wagnerites." *Opera Quarterly* I (Autumn 1983): 66–80.

Bronsen, David, ed. *Jews and Germans from 1860 to 1933: The Problematic Symbiosis.* Heidelberg: C. Winter, 1979.

Buber, Martin. *Briefwechsel aus sieben Jahrzehnten.* 1st ed. Heidelberg: L. Schneider, 1972–75.

Chernow, Ron. *The Warburgs: The Twentieth Century Odyssey of a Remarkable Jewish Family.* New York: Random House, 1993.

Cochavi, Yehoyakim. "Georg Kareski's Nomination as Head of the Kulturbund: The Gestapo's First Attempt—and Last Failure—to Impose a Jewish Leadership." *Leo Baeck Year Book* 34 (1989): 227–46.

Cohen, Arthur A. *The Natural and Supernatural Jew: An Historical and Theological Introduction.* New York: McGraw-Hill, 1964.

Craig, Gordon A. *Germany: 1866–1945.* New York: Oxford University Press, 1980.

Dawidowicz, Lucy S. *The War Against the Jews, 1933–1945.* New York: Holt, Rinehart and Winston, 1975.

Deutschkron, Inge. *Ich trug den gelben Stern.* Cologne: Verlag Wissenschaft und Politik, 1978.

Dickinson, John K. *German and Jew: The Life of Sigmund Stein.* Chicago: Quadrangle Books, 1967.

Dodd, William E. *Ambassador Dodd's Diary, 1933–1938.* Edited by William E. Dodd, Jr., and Mary Dodd. New York: Harcourt, Brace, 1941.

Dunker, Ulrich. *Der Reichsbund jüdischer Frontsoldaten: Geschichte eines jüdischen Abwehrvereins.* Düsseldorf: Droste, 1977.

Duesterberg, Theodor. *Der Stahlhelm und Hitler.* Wolfenbüttel, Germany: Wolfenbütteler Verlaganstalt, 1949.

Ebert, Wolfgang. *Das Porzellan war so nervös: Memoiren eines verwöhnten Kindes.* Frankfurt-am-Main: Ullstein, 1987.

Edel, Peter. *Wenn es ans Leben geht: Meine Geschichte.* 2nd ed. Berlin: Verlag der Nation, 1979.

Edelheim-Mühsam, Margaret T. "Reactions of the Jewish Press to the Nazi Challenge." *Leo Baeck Year Book* 5 (1960): 308–29.

Engelmann, Bernt. *Deutschland ohne Juden: Eine Bilanz.* Munich: Schneeklüth, 1970.

Esh, Shaul. "Between Discrimination and Extermination." *Yad Vashem Studies* 2 (1958): 79–94.

Farrer, David. *The Warburgs: The Story of a Family.* New York: Stein and Day, 1975.

Feder, Ernst. *Heute sprach ich mit . . . : Tagebücher eines Berliner Publizisten, 1926–1932.* Edited by Cécile Lowenthal-Hensel and Arnold Paucker. Stuttgart: Deutsche Verlags-Anstalt, 1971.

Feinberg, Nathan. "The Activities of Central Jewish Organizations Following Hitler's Rise to Power." *Yad Vashem Studies* 1 (1957): 67–84.

Feingold, Henry L. *The Politics of Rescue: The Roosevelt Administration and the Holocaust.* New Brunswick, N.J.: Rutgers University Press, 1970.

Feuchtwanger, Lion. *The Oppermanns.* New York: Viking Press, 1934.

Fraenkel, Sigmund. *Aufsätze und Reden: Ein Spiegelbild deutsch-jüdischer Geschichte aus dem Beginn des zwanzigsten Jahrhunderts.* Edited by Adolf Fraenkel. Munich: B. Heller, 1930.

Frankel, Jonathan. "Crisis as a Factor in Modern Jewish Politics, 1840 and 1881–82." In *Living With Antisemitism: Modern Jewish Responses,* edited by Jehuda Reinharz. Hanover, N.H.: University Press of New England, 1987.

Freeden, Herbert. *Die jüdische Presse im Dritten Reich.* Frankfurt-am-Main: Jüdischer Verlag bei Athenaeum, 1987.

Friedlander, Albert H. *Leo Baeck: Teacher of Theresienstadt.* New York: Holt, Rinehart and Winston, 1968.

Friedlander, Fritz. "Trials and Tribulations of Education in Nazi Germany." *Leo Baeck Year Book* 3 (1958): 187–201.

Friedrich, Otto. *Before the Deluge: A Portrait of Berlin in the 1920s.* New York: Fromm International, 1986.

Friedrichs, Johannes. *Eine Lösung der Judenfrage? Kritische Betrachtung.* Detmold, Germany: Meyersche Hofbuchhandlung, 1922.

Fromm, Bella. *Blood and Banquets: A Berlin Social Diary.* New York: Carol Publishing Group, 1990.

Frye, Bruce B. "The German Democratic Party and the 'Jewish Problem' in the Weimar Republic." *Leo Baeck Year Book* 21 (1976): 143–72.

Fuchs, Richard. "The 'Hochschule für die Wissenschaft des Judentums' in the Period of Nazi Rule." *Leo Baeck Year Book* 12 (1967): 3–31.

Furet, Francois, ed. *Unanswered Questions: Nazi Germany and the Genocide of the Jews.* New York: Schocken Books, 1989.

Gay, Peter. *Freud, Jews and Other Germans: Masters and Victims in Modernist Culture.* New York: Oxford University Press, 1978.

Gay, Ruth. *The Jews of Germany: A Historical Portrait.* New Haven, Conn.: Yale University Press, 1992.

Genschel, Helmut. *Die Verdrängung der Juden aus der Wirtschaft im dritten Reich.* Göttingen, Germany: Musterschmidt Wissenschaftlicher Verlag, 1966.

Gilman, Sander. *Jewish Self-Hatred: Anti-Semitism and the Hidden Language of the Jews.* Baltimore: Johns Hopkins University Press, 1986.

Ginzel, Günther B. *Jüdischer Alltag in Deutschland, 1933–1945.* Düsseldorf: Droste, 1984.

Glick, David. "Some Were Rescued: Memoirs of a Private Mission." *Harvard Law School Bulletin* 12 (December 1960): 6–9.

Goldschmidt, Fritz. *Meine Arbeit bei der Interessen der jüdischen Ärzte in Deutchland seit dem Juli 1933.* Edited by Stephen Leibfried and Florian Tennstedt. Bremen: University of Bremen, 1979.

Gordon, Sarah. *Hitler, Germans and the "Jewish Question."* Princeton, N.J.: Princeton University Press, 1984.

Gross, Walter. "The Zionist Students' Movement." *Leo Baeck Year Book* 4 (1959): 143–64.

Grossman, Kurt R. "Zionists and Non-Zionists Under Nazi Rule in the 1930s." *Herzl Year Book* 4 (1961–62): 329–44.

Gruenewald, Max. "The Beginning of the 'Reichsvertretung.'" *Leo Baeck Year Book* 1 (1956): 57–67.

———. "Critic of German Jewry: Ludwig Feuchtwanger and his Gemeindezeitung." *Leo Baeck Year Book* 27 (1972): 75–92.

———. "Education and Culture of the German Jews Under Nazi Rule." *Jewish Review* 5 (January–December 1948): 56–83.

Grunfeld, Frederic. *Prophets Without Honor: A Background to Freud, Kafka, and Their World.* 1st ed. New York: Holt, Rinehart and Winston, 1979.

Gumpert, Martin. *Hölle im Paradis: Selbstdarstellung eines Arztes.* Stockholm: Bermann and Fischer, 1939.

Gutman, Israel, and Cynthia J. Haft, eds. *Patterns of Jewish Leadership in Nazi Europe, 1933–1945: Proceedings of the Third Yad Vashem International Historical Conference, Jerusalem, April 4–7, 1977.* Jerusalem: Yad Vashem, 1979.

Hamburger, Ernst, and Peter Pulzer. "Jews As Voters in the Weimar Republic." *Leo Baeck Year Book* 30 (1985): 3–66.

Hamburger, Wolfgang. "Teacher in Berlin and Cincinnati." *Leo Baeck Year Book* 2 (1957): 26–34.

Hanke, Peter. *Zur Geschichte der Juden in München zwischen 1933 und 1945.* Munich: Stadtarchiv, 1967.

Heilers, Margarete. *Lebensration: Tagebuch einer Ehe 1933 bis 1945.* Frankfurt-am-Main: Tende, 1985.

Herrmann, Klaus J. *Das dritte Reich und die deutsch-jüdischen Organisationen, 1933–1934.* Cologne: Heymann, 1969.

Hilberg, Raul. *The Destruction of the European Jews.* rev. ed. New York: Holmes and Meier, 1985.

Hirschberg, Alfred. "Ludwig Hollaender, Director of the C.V." *Leo Baeck Year Book* 7 (1962): 39–74.

Hoffmann, Ruth. *Meine Freunde aus Davids Geschlecht.* Berlin: Chronos, 1947.

Ipat'ev, Vladimir. *The Life of a Chemist: Memoirs of Vladimir N. Ipatieff.* Translated by Helen Dwight Fisher and Harold H. Fischer. Stanford, Calif.: Stanford University Press, 1946.

Jones, Larry E. *German Liberalism and the Dissolution of the Weimar Party System, 1918–1933.* Chapel Hill: University of North Carolina Press, 1988.

Joseph, Artur. *Meines Vaters Haus: Ein Dokument.* Stuttgart: Cotta, 1959.

Juden in Preussen: Ein Kapitel deutscher Geschichte. Bildarchiv preussischer Kulturbesitz. Dortmund, Germany: Harenberg, 1987.

Kafka, Franz. *Brief an den Vater.* Munich: Piper, 1960.

Kahler, Erich. *Deutsche und Juden.* Darmstadt, Germany: Erato-Presse, 1964.

Kantzenbach, Wilhelm. "Das wissenschaftliche Werden von Hans-Joachim Schoeps und seine Vertreibung aus Deutschland 1938." *Zeitschrift für Religions-und Geistesgeschichte* 32 (1980): 319–52.

Kaplan, Marion A. "Der Alltag jüdischen Frauen im NS-Deutschland." Translated by Renate Steinchen. *Journal für Geschichte* I (1986): 50–58.

Kershaw, Ian. *The "Hitler Myth": Image and Reality in the Third Reich.* New York: Oxford University Press, 1989.

Kneppe, Alfred, and Josef Wiesehöfer. *Friedrich Muenzer: Ein Althistoriker zwischen Kaiserreich und Nationalsozialismus.* Bonn: R. Habelt, 1983.

Knütter, Hans-Helmuth. *Die Juden und die deutsche Linke in der Weimarer Republik, 1918–1933.* Düsseldorf: Droste, 1971.

Kuhn, Richard. "Richard Willstätter." *Die Naturwissenschaften* I (1949): I–5.

Kwiet, Konrad, and Helmut Eschwege. *Selbstbehauptung und Widerstand: Deutsche Juden im Kamp um Existenz und Menschenwürde, 1933–1945.* Hamburg: H. Christians, 1984.

Lamm, Hans, ed. *Vergangene Tagne: Jüdische Kultur in München.* Munich: Langen, 1982.

Landsberger, Edgar. *Meine Erlebnisse als Jude in Deutschland unter dem Naziregime.* Gmunden, Austria: Salzkammergut-Druckerei, 1945.

Laqueur, Walter. "The German Youth Movement and the 'Jewish Question.'" *Leo Baeck Year Book* 6 (1961): 193–205.

————. *A History of Zionism.* New York: Schocken Books, 1978.

————. *Young Germany: A History of the German Youth Movement.* London: Routledge and Paul, 1962.

Lease, Gary. "Der Briefwechsel zwischen Karl Barth und Hans-Joachim Schoeps (1929–1946)." *Menora: Jahrbuch für deutsch-jüdische Geschichte* 2 (1991): 105–37.

Leschnitzer, Adolf. *Saul und David: Die Problematik der deutsch-jüdischen Lebensgemeinschaft.* Heidelberg: L. Schneider, 1954.

Levine, Herbert S. "A Jewish Collaborator in Nazi Germany: The Strange Career of Georg Kareski, 1933–37." *Central European History* 8 (September 1975): 251–81.

Levitan, Tina. *The Laureates: Jewish Winners of the Nobel Prize.* New York: Twayne Publishers, 1960.

Liebeschutz, Hans. "Judaism and the History of Religion in Leo Baeck's Work." *Leo Baeck Year Book* 2 (1957): 8–20.

Lichtheim, Richard. *Die Geschichte des deutschen Zionismus.* Jerusalem: R. Mass, 1954.

Limberg, Margarete, and Hubert Rübsaat. *Sie dürften nicht mehr Deutsche sein: Jüdischer Alltag in Selbstzeugnissen, 1933–1938.* Frankfurt-am-Main: Campus, 1990.

Loerke, Oskar. *Tagebücher, 1903–1939.* Edited by Hermann Kasack. Heidelberg: L. Schneider, 1955.

Lorenz, Ina. *Die Juden im Hamburg zur Zeit der Weimarer Republik: Eine Dokumentation.* Hamburg: H. Christians, 1987.

Lowenthal, Marvin. *The Jews of Germany: A History of Sixteen Centuries.* Philadelphia: Jewish Publication Society, 1939.

Maier, Charles S. *The Unmasterable Past: History, Holocaust, and German National Identity.* Cambridge, Mass.: Harvard University Press, 1988.

Marcus, Ernst. "The German Foreign Office and the Palestine Question in the Period 1933–1939." *Yad Vashem Studies* 2 (1958): 179–204.

Margaliot, Abraham. "The Dispute over the Leadership of German Jewry (1933–1938)." *Yad Vashem Studies* 10 (1974): 129–48.

Marrus, Michael R. *The Holocaust in History.* New York: Meridian, 1989.

Mayer, Arno J. *Why Did the Heavens Not Darken? The "Final Solution" in History.* New York: Pantheon, 1988.

Metcalfe, Philip. *1933.* Sag Harbor, N.Y.: Permanent Press, 1988.

Morgenstern, Christian. *Gesammelte Werke in einem Band.* Edited by Margareta Morgenstern. Munich: Piper, 1965.

Moses, Siegfried. "The Impact of Leo Baeck's Personality on His Contemporaries." *Leo Baeck Year Book* 2 (1957): 3–7.

Mosse, George L. *Germans and Jews: The Right, the Left, and the Search for a "Third Force" in Pre-Nazi Germany.* New York: H. Fertig, 1970.

Mosse, Werner E. *Jews in the German Economy: The German-Jewish Economic Elite, 1820–1935.* Oxford, England: Clarendon Press, 1987.

Nachmansohn, David. *German-Jewish Pioneers in Science, 1900–1933: Highlights in Atomic Physics, Chemistry, and Biochemistry.* New York: Springer Verlag, 1979.

Naumann, Max. *Ganz-Deutsche oder Halb-Deutsche? Vier Aufsätze.* Berlin: Deutsche Verlagsgesellschaft für Politik und Geschichte, 1922[?].

———. "Die nationaldeutschen Juden nach dem 19. August 1934." Berlin: Verband nationaldeutscher Juden, 1934.

———. "Sozialismus, Nationalismus und national-deutsches Judentum." Berlin: 1932.

Neebe, Reinhard. *Grossindustrie, Staat und NSDAP 1930–1933: Paul Silverberg und der Reichsverband der deutschen Industrie in der Krise der Weimarer Republik.* Göttingen, Germany: Vandenhoeck and Ruprecht, 1981.

Neumann, Siegfried. *Nacht über Deutschland: Vom Leben und Sterben einer Republik: Ein Tatsachenbericht.* Munich: List, 1978.

Nicosia, Francis R. J. "Weimar Germany and the Palestine Question." *Leo Baeck Year Book* 24 (1979): 321–48.

Niewyk, Donald L. *The Jews in Weimar Germany.* Baton Rouge: Louisiana State University Press, 1980.

Noakes, Jeremy, and Geoffrey Pridham, eds. *Nazism, 1919–1945: A History in Documents and Eyewitness Accounts.* Vol. I. New York: Schocken Books, 1984.

Paucker, Arnold. "Gerechtigkeit!" The Fate of a Pamphlet on the Jewish Question." *Leo Baeck Year Book* 8 (1963): 238–51.

———, ed. *The Jews in Nazi Germany, 1933–1943: Proceedings of the Leo Baeck Institute's 1985 Berlin International Historical Conference, "Self-Assertion in Adversity."* Tübingen, Germany: J. C. B. Mohr, 1986.

Pawel, Ernst. *The Nightmare of Reason: A Life of Franz Kafka.* New York: Farrar, Straus, Giroux, 1984.

Penkower, Monty N. *The Jews Were Expendable: Free World Diplomacy and the Holocaust.* Urbana: University of Illinois Press, 1983.

Peukert, Detlev. *Inside Nazi Germany: Conformity, Opposition, and Racism in Everyday Life.* London: B. T. Batsford, 1987.

Prinz, Arthur. "The Role of the Gestapo in Obstructing and Promoting Jewish Emigration." *Yad Vashem Studies* 2 (1958): 205–18.

Prinz, Joachim. . . . *Wir Juden.* Berlin: Erich Reiss, 1934.

Pulzer, Peter. *The Rise of Political Anti-Semitism in Germany and Austria.* New York: John Wiley and Sons, 1964.

Ragins, Sanford. *Jewish Responses to Anti-Semitism in Germany, 1870–1914: A Study in the History of Ideas.* Cincinnati: Hebrew Union College Press, 1980.

Rathenau, Walther. *Eine Streitschaft vom Glauben.* Berlin: Fischer, 1917.

Read, Anthony, and David Fisher. *Kristallnacht: The Nazi Night of Terror.* New York: Random House, 1989.

Reichmann, Eva G. *Hostages of Civilization: The Social Sources of National Socialist Anti-Semitism.* London: V. Gollancz, 1950.

———. "Leo Baeck Centennary: A Personal Tribute." *Leo Baeck Year Book* 18 (1973): vii–x.

———. "Symbol of German Jewry." *Leo Baeck Year Book* 2 (1957): 21–26.

Reinharz, Jehuda. *Chaim Weizmann: The Making of a Zionist Leader.* New York: Oxford University Press, 1985.

———. *Fatherland or Promised Land: The Dilemma of the German Jew, 1893–1914.* Ann Arbor: University of Michigan Press, 1975.

———, ed. *Living With Antisemitism: Modern Jewish Responses.* Hanover, N.H.: University Press of New England, 1987.

Reinharz, Jehuda, and Walter Schatzberg, eds. *The Jewish Response to German Culture: From the Enlightenment to the Second World War.* Hanover, N.H.: University Press of New England, 1985.

Reitlinger, Gerald. *The Final Solution: The Attempt to Exterminate the Jews of Europe, 1939–1945.* London: Vallentine, 1953.

Rheins, Carl J. "Deutscher Vortrupp, Gefolgschaft deutscher Juden, 1933–1935." *Leo Baeck Year Book* 26 (1981): 207–29.

———. "The Schwarzes Fähnlein, Jungenschaft, 1932–1934." *Leo Baeck Year Book* 23 (1978): 173–97.

———. "The Verband nationaldeutscher Juden, 1921–1933." *Leo Baeck Year Book* 25 (1980): 243–68.

Richarz, Monika, ed. *Jewish Life in Germany: Memoirs from Three Centuries.* Translated by Stella P. Rosenfeld and Sidney Rosenfeld. Bloomington: Indiana University Press, 1991.

Rosenbaum, Eduard. "M. M. Warburg & Co., Merchant Bankers of Hamburg." *Leo Baeck Year Book* 7 (1962): 121–49.

Rosenbaum, Eduard, and Ari Joshua Sherman. *Das Bankhaus M. M. Warburg & Co., 1798–1938.* 2nd ed. Hamburg: H. Christians, 1978.

Rosenbluth, Martin. *Go Forth and Serve: Early Years and Public Life.* New York: Herzl Press, 1961.

Rosenstock, Werner. "Exodus, 1933–1939: A Survey of Jewish Emigration from Germany." *Leo Baeck Year Book* 1 (1956): 373–92.

Ruppin, Arthur. *Briefe, Tagebücher, Erinnerungen.* Edited by Schlomo Krolik. Königstein/Taunus: Jüdischer Verlag bei Athenaeum, 1985.

Scheffler, Wolfgang. "Die nationalsozialistische Judenpolitik." *Zur Politik und Zeitgeschichte,* Vol. 4–5. Berlin: Otto Suhr Institut an der Freien Universität, 1960.

Schacht, Hjalmar. *My First Seventy-Six Years.* Translated by Diana Pyke. London: Wingate, 1955.

Schleunes, Karl A. *The Twisted Road to Auschwitz: Nazi Policy Toward German Jews, 1933–1939.* Urbana: University of Illinois Press, 1970.

Schoeps, Hans-Joachim. *Bereit für Deutschland: Der Patriotismus deutscher Juden und der Nationalsozialismus: Frühe Schriften, 1930 bis 1939: Eine historische Dokumentation.* Berlin: Haude and Spener, 1970.

———. *Gestalten an der Zeitenwende: Burckhardt, Nietzsche, Kafka.* Berlin: Vortrupp Verlag, 1936.

———. *Ja, Nein und Trotzdem: Erinnerungen, Begegnungen, Erfahrungen.* Mainz: Von Hase and Köhler, 1974.

———. *Jüdische Glaube in dieser Zeit: Prolegomena zur Grundlegung einer systematischen Theologie des Judentums.* Berlin: Vortrupp Verlag, 1934.

———. *Jüdische Identität und jüdisches Bewusstsein in Zeiten der Bedrängnis und Verfolgung: Ein im Jahre 1943.* Cologne: E. J. Brill-Verlag, 1984.

———. *Jüdisch-christliches Religions-Gespräch in 19te Jahrhundert: Geschichte einer theologischen Ausseinandersetzung.* Berlin: Vortrupp Verlag, 1937.

———. *Die letzten dreissig Jahre: Rückblicke.* Stuttgart: Klett, 1956.

———. *Rufmord/1970.* Erlangen, Germany: Selbstverlag des Verfassers, 1970.

———. *Wir deutschen Juden.* Berlin: Vortrupp Verlag, 1934.

Schoeps, Julius H., ed. *Im Streit um Kafka und das Judentum, Briefwechsel: Max Brod–Hans-Joachim Schoeps.* Königstein/Taunus: Jüdischer Verlag bei Athenaeum, 1985.

Scholem, Gershom. "Juden und Deutschen." In *Deutsche und Juden: Beiträge von Nahum Goldmann, Gershom Scholem, Golo Mann, Salo w. Baron, Eugen Gerstenmaier und Karl Jaspers.* Frankfurt-am-Main: Suhrkamp, 1967.

Schorsch, Ismar. *Jewish Reactions to German Anti-Semitism, 1870–1914.* New York: Columbia University Press, 1972.

Schwab, Hermann. *1933: Ein Tagebuch.* Zurich: Jüdischer Volksschriftenverlag, 1953.

Seeliger, Herbert. "Origin and Growth of the Berlin Community." *Leo Baeck Year Book* 3 (1958): 159–68.

Shacker, Henry J. (with Lucie Schacker). *Our Years With the Nazis, 1935–1943.* Columbia, S.C.: R. L. Bryan, 1976.

Shepherd, Naomi. *A Refuge from Darkness: Wilfrid Israel and the Rescue of the Jews.* New York: Pantheon, 1984.

Sherman, Ari J. *Island Refuge: Britain and Refugees from the Third Reich, 1933–1939.* Berkeley: University of California Press, 1973.

Shirer, William L. *Berlin Diary: The Journal of a Foreign Correspondent, 1934–1941.* New York: Alfred A. Knopf, 1943.

———. *The Rise and Fall of the Third Reich: A History of Nazi Germany.* New York: Simon and Schuster, 1960.

Sholom, Shafir. "American Jewish Leaders and the Emerging Nazi Threat (1928–Jan. 1933)." *American Jewish Archives* 31 (November 1979): 150–83.

Simon, Ernst. "Jewish Adult Education in Nazi Germany as Spiritual Resistance." *Leo Baeck Year Book* I (1956): 68–104.

Stachura Peter D. *The German Youth Movement, 1900–1945: An Interpretative and Documentary History.* London: Macmillan, 1981.

Stern, Fritz. *Dreams and Delusions: National Socialism in the Drama of the German Past.* New York: Vintage Books, 1989.

Stern-Taubler, Selma. "The German Jew in a Changing World." *Leo Baeck Year Book* 7 (1962): 3–10.

Strauss, Herbert A. "The Immigration and Acculturation of the German Jew in the United States of America." *Leo Baeck Year Book* 16 (1971): 63–96.

———. "Jewish Emigration From Germany: Nazi Policies and Jewish Responses—I." *Leo Baeck Year Book* 25 (1980): 313–62.

———. "Jewish Emigration From Germany: Nazi Policies and Jewish Responses—II. *Leo Baeck Year Book* 26 (1981): 343–409.

Strauss, Herbert A., and Norbert Kampe, eds. *Antisemitismus: Von der Judenfeindschaft zum Holocaust.* Bonn: Bundeszentrale für politische Bildung, 1984.

Suchy, Barbara. "The Verein zur Abwehr des Antisemitismus (I): From Its Beginnings to the First World War." *Leo Baeck Year Book* 28 (1983): 205–39.

Szanto, Alexander. "Economic Aid in the Nazi Era." *Leo Baeck Year Book* 4 (1959): 208–19.

Tal, Uriel. *Christians and Jews in Germany: Religion, Politics, and Ideology in the Second Reich, 1870–1914.* Translated by Noah Jonathan Jacobs. Ithaca, N.Y.: Cornell University Press, 1975.

Tausk, Walter. *Breslauer Tagebuch, 1933–1940.* Berlin: Rütten-Löning, 1975.

"Theodor Herzl and Walther Rathenau: Exchange of Letters." Introduced by Alex Bein. *Zion* 2, (1951): 62–74.

Toller, Ernst. *I Was A German: An Autobiography.* Translated by Edward Crankshaw. London: J. Lane the Bodley Head, 1934.

Walter, Hermann. *Der gelbe Fleck: Ein Bericht von Frühjahr 1933.* Prague: Selbstverlag des Verfassers, 1933.

Wandel, Eckhard. *Hans Schäffer: Steuermann in wirtschaftlichen und politischen Krisen, 1886–1967.* Stuttgart: Deutsche Verlags-Anstalt, 1974.

Warburg, Eric. *Times and Tides.* New York: privately printed, 1956.

Warburg, Frieda S. *Reminiscences of A Long Life.* New York: Thistle Press, 1956.

Warburg, Gustav Otto. *Six Years of Hitler: The Jews Under the Nazi Regime.* London: George Allen and Unwin, 1939.

Warburg, James P. *The Long Road Home: The Autobiography of a Maverick.* Garden City, N.Y.: Doubleday, 1964.

Warburg, Max M. "Ansprache in der Jahresversammlung des Hilfsvereins der deutschen Juden, Berlin, 24 März 1929." Berlin: Scholem, 1929. Microfilm.

———. *Aus meinen Aufzeichnungen.* New York: privately printed, 1952.

Wassermann, Jakob. *Mein Weg als Deutscher und Jude.* Berlin: S. Fischer, 1921.

Weinberg, Werner. "Why I did Not Leave Nazi Germany in Time." *Christian Century* 99 (21 April 1982): 478–81.

Weizmann, Chaim. *Trial and Error: The Autobiography of Chaim Weizmann.* New York: Schocken Books, 1966.

Weltsch, Robert. *An der Wende des modernen Judentums: Betrachtungen aus fünf Jahrzehnten.* Tübingen, Germany: J. C. B. Mohr, 1972.

———. *Die deutsche Judenfrage: Ein kritischer Rückblick.* Königstein/Taunus, Germany: Jüdischer Verlag, 1981.

———. Introduction to *Leo Baeck Year Book* I (1956): xix–xxxi.

———. "Judenfrage und Zionismus." In *Klärung: 12 Autoren, Politiker über die Judenfrage.* Berlin: Verlag Tradition Wilhelm Kolk, 1932.

———. "Die jüdische Presse vor 30 Jahre." In *Vom Schicksal geprägt: Freundesgabe zum 60. Geburtstag von Karl Marx.* Edited by Hans Lamm, E. G. Lowenthal, and Marcel W. Gärtner. Düsseldorf: privately printed, 1957.

———. "Looking Back Over Thirty Years." *Leo Baeck Year Book* 27 (1982): 379–90.

———. *Tragt ihn mit Stolz, den gelben Fleck: Eine Aufssatzreihe der "Jüdischen Rundschau" zur Lage der Juden in Deutschland 1933.* Nördlingen, Germany: Greno Verlagsgesellschaft, 1988.

Westheimer, Ruth K. *All in a Lifetime: An Autobiography.* New York: Warner Books, 1987.

Wilk, Curt. *Leo Baeck: Rabbiner, Geschichtsphilosoph, Humanist und Representant der Judenheit Deutschlands in ihrer Schlussepoche.* Buenos Aires: Ani T. de Walz, 1970.

Wille und Wege des deutschen Judentums. Berlin: Vortrupp Verlag, 1935.

Willstätter, Richard M. *Aus meinem Leben: Von Arbeit, Musse und Freunden.* Edited by Arthur Stoll. Weinheim, Germany: Verlag Chemie, 1949.

———. "A Chemist's Retrospects and Perspectives: Remarks of Richard Willstätter, Munich, Germany, upon the Presentation to Him of the Willard Gibbs Medal." *Chemical and Engineering News* 11 (20 September 1933): 275–76.

Wise, Stephen. *The Challenging Years: The Autobiography of Stephen Wise.* New York: G. P. Putnam's Sons, 1949.

Wolffsohn, Michel. "Banken, Bankiers und Arbeitsbeschaffung im Übergang von der Weimarer Zeit zum dritten Reich." *Bankhistorisches Archiv: Zeitschrift zur Bankengeschichte* 1 (May 1977): 54–70.

Wyman, David S. *The Abandonment of the Jews: America and the Holocaust, 1941–1945.* New York: Pantheon, 1984.

———. *Paper Walls: America and the Refugee Crisis, 1938–1941.* Amherst: University of Massachusetts Press, 1968.

Yahil, Leni. *The Holocaust: The Fate of European Jewry, 1932–1945.* Translated by Ina Friedman and Haya Galai. New York: Oxford University Press, 1991.

Zuckmayer, Carl. *A Part of Myself.* 1st American ed. New York: Harcourt, Brace, Jovanovich, 1970.

Zweig, Arnold. . . . *Insulted and Exiled: The Truth About the German Jews.* London: J. Miles, 1937.

Zweig, Stefan. *The World of Yesterday.* London: Cassell, 1953.

Unpublished Sources

Adler, Cyrus. Papers. Blaustein Library, American Jewish Committee, New York.

Adler-Rudel, Solomon. Papers. Leo Baeck Institute, Jerusalem.

Baeck, Leo. File. Martin Buber Archive. Jewish National and University Library, Jerusalem.

Baeck, Leo. Papers. Leo Baeck Institute, New York.

Baeck, Leo. "Rechtsstellung der Juden in Europa." Vols. 1, 5. Leo Baeck Institute, New York.

Baerwald, Paul. Papers. Lehman Suite, Columbia University, New York.

Baker, Leonard (Leo Baeck). Papers. Leo Baeck Institute, New York.

Ball-Kaduri, Kurt J. Collection of Oral Testimonies. Yad Vashem Archives, Jerusalem.

Berl, Heinrich. Papers. Badische Landesbibliothek, Karlsruhe, Germany.

Berlin Collection. YIVO Institute for Jewish Research, New York.

Board of Deputies of British Jews. Papers. Woburn House, London.

Boas, Jacob. "The Jews of Germany: Self-Perceptions in the Nazi Era as Reflected in the German Jewish Press, 1933–1938." Ph.D. diss., University of California, Riverside, 1977.

Boehm, Erich. Papers. Leo Baeck Institute, New York.

Brent, Lucie. "The Architects of Jewish Self-Assertion During the Nazi Era." Master's thesis, Hunter College, 1985.

Breslauer, Walter. Papers. Leo Baeck Institute, New York.

Cahnmann, Werner. "The Nazi Threat and the Centralverein: A Recollection." Paper presented at the American Federation of Jews From Central Europe Conference on Anti-Semitism, 23 March 1969. Central Verein/Vertical File. Blaustein Library, American Jewish Committee, New York.

Cohn, Emil B. Papers. Leo Baeck Institute, New York.

Decimal File 150.62/Public Charge. General Records of the Department of State. Record Group 59. National Archives, Washington, D.C.

Decimal File 811.111/Quota. General Records of the Department of State. Record Group 59. National Archives, Washington, D.C.

Decimal File 862.4016. General Records of the Department of State. Record Group 59. National Archives, Washington, D.C.

Einstein, Albert. Duplicate Archives. Seeley G. Mudd Manuscript Library, Princeton University, Princeton, N.J.

Fajans, Kasimir. Papers. Bentley Historical Library, University of Michigan, Ann Arbor.

Fajans, Kasimir. Papers. Staatsbibliothek preussischer Kulturbesitz, Berlin.

Feuchtwanger, Ludwig. Papers. Leo Baeck Institute, New York.

Foreign Office. Papers. Public Record Office, Kew, Richmond, England.

Frank, James. Papers. University of Chicago Library, Chicago.

Frisch, Max. "Juden in deutschen Bankwesen." ME 50. Leo Baeck Institute, New York.

Fromm, Bella. Papers. Mugar Memorial Library, Boston University.

Germany. Files. American Jewish Joint Distribution Committee, New York.

Germany. Files. YIVO Institute for Jewish Research, New York.

Glick, David. Papers. Leo Baeck Institute, New York.

Goldschmidt, Fritz. "Mein Leben im Deutschland vor und nach dem 30. Januar 1933." ME 193. Leo Baeck Institute, New York.

Gruenewald, Max. Papers. Leo Baeck Institute, New York.

Haber, Ernst, and Richard Willstätter. Correspondence File. Leo Baeck Institute, New York.

Halle, Edwin. "Kriegserinnerungen mit Auszügen aus meinem Tagebuch, 1914–1916." ME 502, Leo Baeck Institute, New York.

Haurowitz, Felix. Papers. Lilly Library, Indiana University, Bloomington.

Herzfeld, Ernst. "Meine letzten Jahre in Deutschland, 1933–1938." Yad Vashem Archives, Jerusalem.

Hildesheimer, Esriel E. "The Central Organisation of the German Jews in the Years 1933–1945: Its Legal and Political Status and Its Position in the Jewish Community." Ph.D. diss., Hebrew University, Jerusalem, 1982.

Hilfsverein der Juden in Deutschland. File. Wiener Library, London.

Hindenburg, Paul von. File. Leo Baeck Institute, New York.

Hinkel, Hans. File. Gestapo Records, Berlin Document Center, Berlin.

Jacobson, Jacob. "Bruchstücke, 1939–1945." ME 329. Leo Baeck Institute, New York.

Jewish Colonization Association. Files. London.

"Jüdische Gemeinde in Hamburg." W224, microfilm. Leo Baeck Institute, New York.

Kahn, Bernhard. Papers. Leo Baeck Institute, New York.

Kahn, Bernhard. "Tribute to Max Warburg by Bernhard Kahn at the Annual Meeting of the Joint Distribution Committee, (1947)." ME 344. Leo Baeck Institute, New York.

Kreutzberger, Max. Papers. Leo Baeck Institute, New York.

Lamm, Hans. "Über die innere und äussere Entwicklung des deutschen Judentums im dritten Reich." Ph.D. diss., University of Erlangen, Germany, 1951.

Landauer, Georg. Papers. Leo Baeck Institute, New York.

Lehman, Herbert. Papers. Lehman Suite, Columbia University, New York.

Leo Baeck Institute, London. Papers. Leo Baeck Institute, New York.

Levi, Leopold. Papers. Leo Baeck Institute, New York.

Lichthelm, Richard. "Ein Rest ist zurückgekehrt." ME 391, Leo Baeck Institute, New York.

Lochner, Louis. Papers. State Historical Society of Wisconsin, Madison.

Magill, Stephen. "Defense and Introspection: The First World War as a Pivotal Crisis in the German-Jewish Experience." Ph.D. diss. University of California, Los Angeles, 1977.

McDonald, James. Papers. Lehman Suite, Columbia University, New York.

Messersmith, George S. Papers. University Library, University of Delaware, Newark.

Meyer-Gerstein, Senta. "So wie es war: Ich erinnere . . . " ME 313, Leo Baeck Institute, New York.

Miller, Douglas G. "The Lives of Some Jewish Germans Who Lived in Nazi Germany." Master's thesis, Wesleyan University, Middletown, Conn., 1976.

Morgenstern, Julian. Papers. American Jewish Archives, Cincinnati.

Mumm von Schwanzenstein, Herbert. File. Nazi Party Records. Berlin Document Center, Berlin.

Nazi Party Archive. (NSDAP Hauptarchiv) Hoover Institution on War, Revolution and Peace, Stanford University, Stanford, Calif.

Official File. Franklin D. Roosevelt Library, Hyde Park, N.Y.

Oral Histories. Oral History Project. Pollack Library, Yeshiva University, New York.

Paleologue, Igor. "Meine Bekanntschaft mit Grossrabbiner Dr. Leo Baeck." ME 172. Leo Baeck Institute, New York.

Pineas, Hermann. "Meine Erinnerungen an Dr. Leo Baeck." ME 502, Leo Baeck Institute, New York.

Plaut Family. Papers. Staatsarchiv, Hamburg.

President's Secretary's File, Franklin D. Roosevelt Library, Hyde Park, N.Y.

Prinz, Arthur. Papers. Leo Baeck Institute, New York.

Records of the Reich Leader SS and Chief of the German Police (Parts 3–4). Captured German Records, National Archives, Washington, D.C.

Reichsbund jüdischer Frontsoldaten. File. Wiener Library, London.

Reichsvertretung der deutschen Juden. Papers. Leo Baeck Institute, New York.

Reichsvertretung der deutschen Juden. File. American Jewish Joint Distribution Committee, New York.

Reichsvertretung der deutschen Juden. Files. Wiener Library, London.

Rockefeller Foundation. Papers. Rockefeller Archive Center, North Tarrytown, N.Y.

Schäffer, Hans. Papers. Leo Baeck Institute, New York.

Schiff, Jacob H. Papers. American Jewish Archives, Cincinnati.

Schoeps, Hans-Joachim. File. Leo Baeck Institute, New York.

Schoeps, Hans-Joachim. File. Martin Buber Archive. Jewish National and University Library, Jerusalem.

Schoeps, Hans-Joachim. Papers. Staatsbibliothek preussischer Kulturbesitz, Berlin.

Schultz, Sigrid. Papers. State Historical Society of Wisconsin, Madison.

Seligmann, Caesar. "Mein Leben: Erinnerungen eines Grossvaters." ME 595. Leo Baeck Institute, New York.

Simonis, Rudolf J. Papers. Leo Baeck Institute, New York.

Stahl, Heinrich. Papers. Leo Baeck Institute, New York.

Sulzbach, Walter. Untitled ms. on German-Jewish bankers. ME 154, Leo Baeck Institute, New York.

Waldmann, Morris D. Papers. American Jewish Archives, Cincinnati.

Waldman, Morris D. Papers. YIVO Insitute for Jewish Research, New York.

Warburg, Felix M. Papers. American Jewish Archives, Cincinnati.

Warburg, Max M. File. Martin Buber Archive. Jewish National and University Library, Jerusalem.

Warburg, Max M. Papers. Leo Baeck Institute, New York.

Weizmann, Chaim. Papers. Weizmann Archives, Rehovot, Israel.

Weltsch, Robert. File. Martin Buber Archive. Jewish National and University Library, Jerusalem.

Weltsch, Robert. File. Leo Baeck Institute, Jerusalem.

Weltsch, Robert. Papers. Central Zionist Archives, Jerusalem.

Weltsch, Robert. Papers. Leo Baeck Institute, New York.

Willstätter, Richard M. File. Bayerisches Hauptstaatsarchiv, Munich.

Willstätter, Richard M. File. Deutsches Museum, Munich.

Willstätter, Richard M. Personnel File. Files of the General Administration. Archives of the Max Planck Gesellschaft für die Förderung der Wissenschaften, Berlin.

Willstätter, Richard M. File. Rockefeller Foundation Papers. Rockefeller Archive Center, North Tarrytown, N.Y.

Willstätter, Richard M. File. Stadtbibliothek, Munich.

Willstätter, Richard M. File. Stadtbibliothek, Nuremberg.

Willstätter, Richard M. Papers. Staatsbibliothek preussischer Kulturbesitz, Berlin.

Willstätter, Richard M. File. Wiener Library, Tel Aviv University, Tel Aviv.

Wilson, Hugh R. Papers. Herbert Hoover Library, West Branch, Ia.

Wise, Stephen S. Papers. American Jewish Historical Society, Waltham, Mass.

Witkop, Bernhard. "Stepping Stones: Some Biographical Notes." ME 176. Leo Baeck Institute, New York.

World Union for Progressive Judaism. Papers. American Jewish Archives, Cincinnati.

Zentral Ausschuss der deutschen Juden für Hilfe und Aufbau. File. American Jewish Joint Distribution Committee, New York.

Newspapers

Bayerische-israelitische Gemeindezeitung: Nachrichtenblatt der israelitischen Kultusgemeinde München, Augsburg, Bamberg und des Verbandes bayerischer-israelitischer Gemeinden, Munich, 1932–1938.

Der Orden Bne Briss: Mitteilungen der Grossloge für Deutschland, Berlin, 1928–1937.

Centralverein Zeitung: Blätter für Deutschtum und Judentum, Berlin, 1929–1938.

Gemeindeblatt der jüdischen Gemeinde zu Berlin: Ämtliches Organ des Gemeindevorstandes, Berlin, 1931–1938.

Gemeindeblatt der deutsch-israelitischen Gemeinde zum Hamburg, Hamburg, 1925–1938.

Jewish Daily Bulletin, New York, 1932–1934.

Jewish Telegraphic Agency, New York. Cable dispatches (mimeographs), 1935–1938.

Jüdische Rundschau, Berlin, 1927–1938.

Der Schild: Zeitschrift des Reichsbundes jüdischer Frontsoldaten, Berlin, 1932–1938.

Der Vortrupp: Blätter einer Gefolgschaft deutscher Juden. Berlin: October 1933–April 1935.

Index